JADED TASKS

BRASS PLATES, BLACK OPS & BIG OIL

The Blood Politics of George Bush & Co.

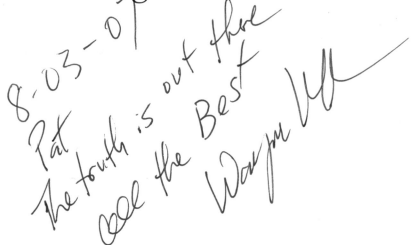

8-03-07
Pat
The touth is out there
all the Best
Wayne Md

WAYNE MADSEN

Jaded Tasks—Brass Plates, Black Ops & Big Oil:
The Blood Politics of Bush & Co.
Copyright © 2006 Wayne Madsen. All rights reserved.

TrineDay
PO Box 577
Walterville, OR 97489

www.TrineDay.com
support@TrineDay.com

Madsen, Wayne
    Jaded Tasks—Brass Plates, Black Ops & Big Oil: The Blood Politics of Bush
& Co. / Wayne Madsen ; with forward by Len Bracken — 1st ed.
    p. cm.
    ISBN 0-9752906-9-X (acid-free paper)
    1. Political Corruption—United States. 2. United States—Politics and Gov-
ernment—1992- . 1. Title
    364.

First Edition
10 9 8 7 6 5 4 3 2 1

Printed in the USA

Distribution to the Trade By:
    Independent Publishers Group (IPG)
    814 North Franklin Street
    Chicago, Illinois 60610
    312.337.0747
    www.ipgbook.com

For my mother, a bright light in a dark world.

For all the victims of the criminal wars of the Bush crime family and their associates: Americans, Iraqis, Africans, Afghans, and the rest of the innocents, who have been sacrificed for the most evil of purposes... greed.

ACKNOWLEDGEMENTS

There are a number of people I wish to thank for their support, words of infinite wisdom, friendship, time, and advice over the years. Without them, I would have been writing this book in a void. Many expanded my knowledge of international politics and the world of covert intelligence. From professors to bartenders, to current and former intelligence agents, diplomats and statesmen, and old friends and new acquaintances, they and many others were there with much-needed advice, information, and consultation. I am eternally grateful to all of them.

I also thank those who recognized that I had, at least a little bit of "the right stuff," to begin an exploratory campaign for the U.S. House of Representatives in 2003 to try to eject one of the many scandal-tainted so-called "representatives of the people" and bring some of the issues discussed in these pages to the floor of the "House of the People."

My thanks go to all my family, friends, colleagues, associates, and contacts over the recent and distant years who provided encouragement, "over the transom" documents of the "official use only" and "classified" variety, background information, or just time from their busy schedules. Because of the nature of this book, I obviously do not wish to provide their full names but I hope they all know to whom I am referring.

Thanks also go to Kris Millegan and the people at TrineDay for helping to get around the corporate "Big Publishers" and the Bush administration strong-armers to get this book to print.

War is just a racket. A racket is best described, I believe, as something that is not what it seems to the majority of people. Only a small inside group knows what it is about. It is conducted for the benefit of the very few at the expense of the masses.

—Major General Smedley Butler, USMC

The real menace of our Republic is the invisible government, which like a giant octopus sprawls its slimy legs over our cities states and nation. At the head is a small group of banking houses generally referred to as "international bankers." This little coterie... run our government for their own selfish ends. It operates under cover of a self-created screen... [and] seizes... our executive officers... legislative bodies... schools... courts... newspapers and every agency created for the public protection.

—New York City Mayor John F. Hylan

Behind the ostensible government sits enthroned an invisible government owing no allegiance and acknowledging no responsibility to the people. To destroy this invisible government, to befoul the unholy alliance between corrupt business and corrupt politics is the first task of the statesmanship of today.

—Theodore Roosevelt

The real rulers in Washington are invisible and exercise power from behind the scene.

—Justice Felix Frankfurter

We have come to be one of the worst ruled, one of the most completely controlled and dominated Governments in the world.

—Woodrow Wilson

[The war in Iraq is] a rare opportunity to move toward a historic period of cooperation. Out of these troubled times... a new world order can emerge.

—George Herbert Walker Bush (1990)

Let us never tolerate outrageous conspiracy theories concerning the attacks of September the 11th; malicious lies that attempt to shift the blame away from the terrorists, themselves, away from the guilty.

—George Walker Bush

When you have no basis for argument, abuse the plaintiff.

—Marcus Tullius Cicero

Remember, no one can make you feel inferior without your consent.

—Eleanor Roosevelt

Contents

Introduction

Online with Wayne Madsen

By Len Bracken

Since its inception in May 2005, *Wayne Madsen Report* has broken new ground in the blogosphere. Madsen's blog attracts over 50,000 visits per day, including many by the prominent journalists who seek access to his sources.

The transformation of this former Navy officer, once assigned to the National Security Agency, was slow coming, but it is now bearing fruit for the fifty-one-year-old who has made investigative journalism his calling. His byline has been seen in major papers across the country, notably on his periodic columns in such papers as the *Miami Herald* and *Kansas City Star*, and he has appeared as an expert on innumerable news shows on CBS, ABC, Fox, Al Jazeera, etc. Nonetheless, his scoops on *Wayne Madsen Report* have been truly exceptional.

In a story that has gone unreported in the mainstream media, for example, Madsen posted Truth and Reconciliation Commission documents that were supplied from high-level African National Congress politicians to support his claims concerning the Jack Abramoff affiliation with South African Intelligence under apartheid, and the Reagan administration's collusion in the affair.[1]

Madsen's anecdote about the events at a Pentagon party on the night of the unsuccessful April 2002 Venezuelan coup against

---

[1] <http://www.waynemadsenreport.com/tonyleonthreat.htm> <http://www.wayne-madsenreport.com/jan21-2606.htm>

President Hugo Chavez, picked up by the *Guardian* and *Boston Globe*, were read with equal pleasure and displeasure in Caracas and Washington.

The domestic eavesdropping scandal finally erupted long after Madsen reported on it more comprehensively than the mainstream press. For example, Madsen's sources conveyed in May 2005 that a major spying operation, codenamed FIRSTFRUITS, extended to an "enemies list" comprising journalists who were writing about the NSA. It soon grew to include their sources and friends and family members.[2]

When the news of secret CIA flights with stopovers in Europe first leaked to the press, Wayne became the whistleblowers' voice, and soon posted the tail numbers of some of the planes involved and exposed their registration charades. Later he stepped out of a bar in Arlington, VA on a snowy December night, and confirmed the news for Finnish media by cell phone.

His "anonymous activists," as whistleblowers are sometimes called, also alerted him to the fact that the National Security Agency had heard Italian intelligence officer Nicola Calipari's phone conversations in Iraq, and certainly knew that he was with recovered hostage Giuliana Sgrena on the way to the Baghdad airport when they were shot at by U.S. troops. Calipari, the deputy head of Italian intelligence, was killed. Transmitting this information on the possible "premeditated" quality of the event has made Madsen a frequent guest on Italian television, and a potential witness for the investigation.

Madsen has appeared on an antiwar panel with America's Gold Star mom of conscience, Cindy Sheehan, and covered her September 2005 anti-war protest with a vest emblazoned PRESS in black electric tape letters and an early Sony Mavica in hand.

The same digital camera was used when Madsen covered Africa for his book *Genocide and Covert Operations in Africa 1993-1999* (Edwin Mellen Press, 1999), because he could pop a floppy disk from the camera into an Internet café computer and send off the image without any wires. Nowadays when he heads over to the National Press Club and updates *Wayne Madsen Report*, say with scenes of the media circus at the courthouse awaiting Pat-

---

[2] <http://www.onlinejournal.org/Special_Reports/042505Madsen/042505madsen.html> < http://www.altpr.org/modules.php?op=modload&name=News&file=article&sid=562&mode=thread&order=0&thold=0>

rick Fitzgerald's indictments of Scooter Libby, he uses the USB memory stick on his key chain.

This former computer security expert with RCA and Computer Sciences Corporation (CSC), who tangled with the Clinton administration over the proposed "Clipper Chip" electronic eavesdropping program and other issues, has taken the personal reporting blog to new heights. Operating in the tradition of Jack Anderson and his *Washington Merry Go Round*, Madsen posts insider stories based on leaks from anonymous sources in intelligence and law enforcement agencies worldwide.

In one alarming report, Argentine sources let on to Madsen that Muslim terrorists now operating in Paraguay had cut deals with the drug lords in Northern Mexico to use their sophisticated tunneling under the U.S. border. According to other sources, no testing for nuclear residues in the tunnel was conducted by the Department of Homeland Security, nor would one be.

On other fronts, Madsen skirmishes with neocons and the Christian right everywhere he can—from the 2005 false-flag violence in Europe perpetrated by right-wing elements in the name of Muslims in places such as Brittany and Normandy, to the influential Christian Fellowship in his Arlington neighborhood, which he covered for *Hustler*.[3]

His writings concerning the Bushes have been particularly revealing. On George the Elder's eightieth birthday, when all of his friends had gathered in Houston, they were treated to Madsen's editorial in the *Houston Chronicle*, which stated that Ronald Reagan's legacy, still much the talk of the nation two days after his funeral, was irreparably tarnished because his vice president had enmeshed him in the Iran-Contra affair.

Madsen has also probed the suspicious death of Bertha Champagne, "maid" to W.'s brother Marvin Bush (Bertha was somehow run over by her own car), going so far as to post the incriminating police report on his Web site.[4] Madsen's revelations concerning 9-11, money laundering with the bin Ladens to finance election fraud, and White House interest in torture videos should have citizens questioning the loyalty and sanity of George the Younger.

3 <http://www.larryflynt.com/notebook.php?id=134>
4 < http://www.waynemadsenreport.com/marvinbush.htm?

As for his own family history, Madsen was born in Ridley Park, Pennsylvania to a warm Philadelphia gal who had grown up in a south Philadelphia family and a Danish merchant mariner who fought with the International Brigades in the Spanish Civil War and stayed in the United States after World War II, first installing radios on ships for Philco, then driving a city bus. Wayne likes to recall that his father is the son of Victoria Madsen, a wartime resistance leader in Copenhagen who, after the war, was deported by J. Edgar Hoover's FBI when she tried to organize hospital workers in America.

Madsen showed signs of that radical spirit in the first column he wrote for his high school newspaper, in which he said that the investigation of the My Lai massacre in the court-martial of Lt. William Calley should go right to the top. Then the future blogger attended the University of Mississippi, where he was enrolled in Navy ROTC.

At his first posting, Surface Warfare Officer's School in Newport, Rhode Island, Ensign Madsen would meet the disgruntled "oldest lieutenant in the Navy." The way the story went, this oldest lieutenant, after being told by the notorious Admiral Rickover, in an interview for the nuclear submarine program, "You have 15 seconds to piss me off," had picked up a model Nautilus submarine from the admiral's desk and smashed it.

The lieutehant was told to go out and wait. And he waited and waited until told by the secretary there was no need to stay. He would never be in the nuclear submarine program. Later on, Madsen himself would be passed over for promotion to lieutenant commander because, as strange as this sounds, he busted his commanding officer for pedophilia.

* * * *

Madsen's early career had seemed promising. During his stints in Delaware, Barbados and Iceland, Madsen picked up a Navy Unit Commendation, for being part of the team in Iceland that found the first acoustic signature of a Soviet Alpha-class titanium-hull submarine. He earned the nickname "Mad Dog"—for "telling people to get fucked and drinking with the [Navy] chiefs," as well as fraternizing with Navy women in Icelandic hot pools—in short, for what Madsen called "going back to my Viking roots."

But when he was stationed in Coos Bay, Oregon, still engaged in sound surveillance anti-submarine warfare operations, his commanding officer was Larry William Frawley, a Naval Academy grad whose uncle played Fred Mertz on *I Love Lucy*. There were security concerns that Frawley may have been compromised by the Soviet Union during an unauthorized trip he took in 1974, which had been uncovered through a later examination of the visas on his passport. Frawley wasn't a drinker, gambler or womanizer, Madsen explains, but he was "a serial predatory pedophile" (and a member of the Officer Christian Fellowship). Madsen knows this because he received a Navy Achievement Medal for his central role in a successful sting operation.

In that event, one of Madsen's enlisted subordinates—Madsen was the operations officer and third in command—gave Frawley a magazine that he said was "found" in Madsen's quarters. The commanding officer invited Madsen to dinner.

Madsen was set to wear a wire for the FBI and Naval Investigative Service. But right before the operation, he received a call from Pacific Fleet Command at Pearl Harbor and was told not to proceed. Madsen ignored the order, and heard Frawley imply how powerful the pedophile association was: "If you're on the level, you'll make commander and probably captain; if you're not on the level, you could have me arrested," which is what happened.

Madsen was, for the sting, appointed to serve as a temporary special agent for the FBI, and while in the field office he couldn't resist quipping at the J. Edgar Hoover portrait: "I see you've got a picture of America's most famous closet queen." The G-men apparently didn't find this funny.

They uncovered the considerable evidence in Frawley's home, including videos of Frawley engaged in lewd sex acts with children, and another of a woman holding a chicken while some lothario engaged it in intercourse. Even the cops were reportedly disgusted. When one asked if there was anywhere to get something to eat, Madsen again ventured a joke the agents wouldn't like: "There's a KFC across the street."

Frawley would receive a four-year sentence in Leavenworth.

Madsen was in turn branded with a bad fitness report from his executive officer, who resented not being in on the sting. The next commanding officer, Jim Onorato, who would later emerge as an ex-shipmate of John Kerry, sent a Mayflower moving van to wake Madsen up unannounced ... and cart his possessions off to his next duty station, Washington, DC. During his early days in the nation's capital, without pay records transferred, Madsen was forced to sleep in shared officers' quarters or in his car parked outside the Officers' Club at Andrews Air Force Base.

He would become established in Maryland, and then try to get his fitness report corrected, and also to expose the pedophile investigation that had been limited to one person and only one base ... all to no avail. When he resigned in 1985, Madsen had the same status as the disgruntled officer he had met in Newport: the most senior lieutenant in the U.S. Navy.

* * * *

Stories about Frawley slated for several papers were spiked; most editors simply ignored the information Madsen sent them. In 1984, Madsen received a threat regarding talking about what happened in Oregon: "Something will happen to you or to someone you love." Madsen points out that a few years later, senior Republican officials, including George H.W. Bush, were beginning to be implicated in a pedophile scandal perhaps best remembered now by a front-page story in the *Washington Times*.[5]

On the professional front, Madsen benefited from the 1983 bombing of the Computer Area at the Washington Navy Yard, and a 1984 White House screening of the film *War Games* that prompted President Reagan to put money into computer security. This was Madsen's field, having initiated the security program for the Navy Telecommunications Command and then being assigned to the National Security Agency after a "by name" transfer request came to the Navy from the Fort Meade, Maryland-based spy agency.

5 "Homosexual prostitution inquiry ensnares VIPs with Reagan, Bush" *Washington Times*, June 29, 1989

After his resignation from the Navy, Madsen would go on to work for RCA, doing NSA work, for the Navy as a civilian, for his own information security firm, for the National Bureau of Standards, and for the State Department. In 1991, he wrote a book on computer security, *Handbook of Personal Data Protection* (Macmillan/ Stockton Press), and attended the first joint U.S.-Soviet conference on the topic in Russia, which drew the attention of the FBI and CIA.

While in Moscow, Madsen witnessed the decimated Warsaw Pact Headquarters building, noting, "They didn't even keep up appearances." He also made contact with the student underground—in a smoke-filled tea room in Leningrad—during what would prove to be Gorbachev's slide from power. Madsen saw the writing on the wall, and allowed as much in an informal debriefing with the U.S. government.

He would eventually settle in at Computer Sciences Corporation, from the end of 1990 to 1997, under the protection of an anti-Clipper Chip executive, until a pro-NSA crowd took over. EPIC (Electronic Privacy Information Center) hired Madsen in 1997 to be its first Senior Fellow, handling ECHELON, law enforcement and intelligence portfolios.

* * * *

The Republican purge of Washington insiders was not limited to Tom DeLay's notorious K Street Project for lobbyists. Think tanks were similarly leaned on to eliminate those seen as too aligned with the Democrats and liberal causes. Wayne sees all this as the "new McCarthyism."

Madsen likes to tell the story that his editorial endorsing John Edwards for vice president appeared in the *Charlotte Observer*. Later, the former senator thanked him for it when they met, having remembered because it was in his hometown paper. "I made a mistake," Madsen told Edwards, "when I wrote that editorial. *You* should have picked Kerry as *your* running mate."

While at CSC and EPIC, Madsen's travels spanned the globe—Australia, Austria, Sarawak, Brunei, Finland, Hong Kong, Israel,

Cyprus, Switzerland, Ireland, Denmark, Liechtenstein, the Isle of Man, Estonia, Lithuania, Costa Rica, Rwanda and Uganda. At conferences and seminars in far-flung locales, he developed contacts that led him to many eye-opening conclusions. We can imagine a younger Madsen at an outdoor café, perhaps in Brunei, with his white cane hat and cotton linen jacket, peering over the top of the *South China Morning Post*, and looking for his next tip.

But unfortunately the neocon ideology has been imposed from above, wreaking havoc, increasing vulnerabilities and creating an army of dissidents out of those who witness its destructive power on a daily basis. The "good spooks," as they sometimes refer to themselves, express their frustrations to Madsen, who in turn transmits them to the world on his blog, way ahead of even Seymour Hersh. Madsen had the scoop on plans to nuke Iran, to mention one example, over a year before the revelations in the April 17, 2006 issue of the *New Yorker*.

The ideologues therefore hound Madsen in his Washington haunts, an Irish pub and a watering hole just two blocks from the White House, taking his photo and leaving quickly, making threats and generally suffering his shrewd wit, which recalls a remark he made on the Stephanie Miller radio show: "The Bushes make the Sopranos look like Ozzie and Harriet."

Wayne is not alone in the sense that he is transmitting—and to a vast audience—important messages from his friends behind shifting and obscure lines. With his mix of humor and activism, however, his superb memory and sharp wit, his innumerable contacts and exemplary courage, Madsen stands in a class of his own. On Web sites such as *Online Journal*, and now his own *Wayne Madsen Report*, Madsen divulges more about those running the world to ruin than a dozen prizewinning journalists combined.

His *Jaded Tasks* is a mirror where the diabolical ones will see themselves, and their acts of destruction, without the distortions of the mainstream press.

—§—

Len Bracken is the editor of *Extraphile*, described by the *New Yorker* as fusion conspiracy theory. Len is the author of *The Shadow Government*

(Adventures Unlimited, 2002) and *The Arch Conspirator* (Adventures Unlimited, 1999). He is also the author of the underground novels *Freeplay* (Writers Club Press 2001) and *Snitch Jacket* (iUniverse 2005), and a frequent radio talk show guest. His work has appeared in *Paranoia, Steamshovel Press* and the *Village Voice*. He lives in Washington, DC.

Carlyle Group's Washington headquarters located at 1001 Pennsylvania Avenue in Washington between the White House and the U.S. Congress.

The main participants of International Strategic & Tactical Organization (ISTO)—KBR Halliburton and Armitage & Associates LC (AALC) —occupy a building at 1550 Wilson Boulevard in Rosslyn, Virginia, only a few miles from the Pentagon.

Foreword

The murky world of big multinational oil companies, covert operations teams ("black operations" or, simply, "black ops"), and nebulous brass plates firms (otherwise known as carve outs, cuts outs, and pass through companies) is one which, by its very nature, intends to remain below the radar screens of public attention and governmental oversight and supervision. There we find a subterranean labyrinth of multinational oil companies, international lobbyists, greedy politicians, private military contractors, offshore companies, and various ne'er-do-wells, some of whom sharpened their teeth in the infamous Iran-Contra and Bank of Credit and Commerce International (BCCI) scandals.

The title of this book, *Jaded Tasks*, is courtesy of the U.S. Special Operations Command, which came up with the cover term OPERATION JADED TASK for the Bush administration's March 2004 coup d'état against the democratically elected President of Haiti, Jean Bertrand Aristide. The American Heritage Dictionary defines "jaded" as "cynically or pretentiously callous." The Special Operations Command could not have come up with a better term to describe its Haitian black op, which like so many others became a hallmark of the Bush administration's foreign policy. The policy was an outgrowth of a basic neoconservative principle known as "creative destruction," the upending of governments and national traditions to achieve American dominance and extend American cultural "values" throughout the world. The cynicism and callous-ness of a foreign policy that closely marries the interests of oil com-panies (and other powerful corporate players) with the military and intelligence complex will be a touchstone for future historians when they describe the Bush foreign policy.

Also ominous is the expanding use of mercenary forces as an in-strument of U.S. foreign policy. By their very nature, private military companies hide behind interconnecting relationships, interlocking directorships, and offshore front operations. The involvement of such companies in U.S. torture centers in Abu Ghraib prison in Iraq, various detention camps in Afghanistan, and Guantanamo Bay Naval Station in Cuba are cases in point. The lack of jurisdic-tion of U.S. military law and the Geneva Conventions over private contractors resulted in a number of these privateers escaping pros-ecution for war crimes.

In many respects, the blending of U.S. corporations and the mili-tary into one entity is not a new phenomenon. U.S. Marine Corps General Smedley Butler, who had commanded U.S. Marines in overthrowing governments in Latin America to make their coun-tries safe for U.S. corporations, later turned on his old corporate and military masters to tell the truth about their misdeeds:

> There isn't a trick in the racketeering bag that the military gang is blind to. It has its "finger men" to point out enemies, its "muscle men" to destroy enemies, its "brain men" to plan war preparations.... In many ways, it may seem odd for me, a military man to adopt such a comparison. Truthfulness compels me to. I spent thirty-three years and four months in active military service as a member of this country's most agile military force, the Marine Corps. I served in all commissioned ranks from Second Lieutenant to Major General. And during that period, I spent most of my time being a high-class muscle-man for Big Business, for Wall Street and for the Bankers. In short, I was a racketeer, a gangster for capitalism.
>
> I suspected I was just part of a racket at the time. Now I am sure of it. Like all the members of the military profession, I never had a thought of my own until I left the service. My mental faculties re-mained in suspended animation while I obeyed the orders of higher-ups. This is typical with everyone in the military service.
>
> I helped make Mexico, especially Tampico, safe for American oil

interests in 1914. I helped make Haiti and Cuba a decent place for the National City Bank boys to collect revenues in. I helped in the raping of half a dozen Central American republics for the benefits of Wall Street. The record of racketeering is long. I helped purify Nicaragua for the international banking house of Brown Brothers in 1909-1912. I brought light to the Dominican Republic for American sugar interests in 1916. In China I helped to see to it that Standard Oil went its way unmolested.

During those years, I had, as the boys in the back room would say, a swell racket. Looking back on it, I feel that I could have given Al Capone a few hints. The best he could do was to operate his racket in three districts. I operated on three continents.[1]

General Butler's successors continue to make sure that U.S. oil companies remain "unmolested," from Iraq to Colombia and from Azerbaijan to Angola.

The cynicism that I attach to the Bush foreign policy (and, to a lesser extent, that of the Clinton administration) derives from some ten years of investigating various misdeeds by multinational companies, mercenary firms, and shady businessmen. In some ways, much of this book represents a personal memoir. I have had meetings with former UN Secretary General Boutros Boutros-Ghali, given testimony before a French special anti-terrorism judge, been given invitations (abruptly withdrawn twice) to appear before the International Criminal Tribunal for Rwanda as an expert witness, and had numerous conversations with a number of Washington "insiders." I want to share with you some of my conclusions, many of which must remain of necessity speculative, as well as various sensitive documents that either "came over the transom" or were the product of Freedom of Information Act requests.

The first Bush presidency, the Clinton interregnum, and the George W. Bush administration have all contributed to making the world a safer place for those who sneak around in the shadows, launder billions of dollars, and formulate their aggressive agenda for global domination by powerful elites. There was never a full accounting of where all the billions of dollars from the BCCI and Savings and Loans scandals, as well as the Enron Ponzi scheme, eventually landed. Offered as possibilities for your consideration:

[1] Speech by General Smedley Butler delivered in 1933.

the financing of wars; coups; election campaigns; the de facto re-colonization of Africa, Asia, the Pacific, and Latin America; and professional hits on "troublemakers."

The Clinton administration opened the door for non-state private military contractors and other private players to exercise undue influence over U.S. foreign policy—a *public* policy arena. The Bush administration sealed the deal and closed the door to all but those corporate and murky private contractors, many of whom cut their teeth in the Reagan-Bush administration, to virtually dictate U.S. foreign policy objectives.

The story of the Bush foreign policy is one of oil and back room deals. The influence of UNOCAL, Halliburton, Enron, and others in restoring negotiations with the Taliban over the Central Asian Gas (CentGas) pipeline deal in Afghanistan, after the Clinton administration shut those negotiations down following Al Qaeda's attack on the *USS Cole* in Aden harbor, shows what happens when a country makes its foreign policy subservient to the narrow interests of corporations seeking to maximize their profits. The Bush administration's flirtation with the Taliban indirectly contributed to those thousands of people losing their lives on September 11, 2001. This was perhaps the most shameful and traitorous act ever committed by an American President and members of his administration.

As with the influence of Big Oil over U.S. policy vis-à-vis the Taliban and its "guests," Al Qaeda, Big Oil and multinational mining interests have held sway over U.S. policy in Africa with devastating results, including a cross-border genocide that has seen the loss of over 4 million human lives. Africa needs a closer look, because the continent has afforded the covert operators and their big business paymasters the most lucrative opportunities for exploitation and black ops since events of the early 1990s plunged Africa into untold chaos.

Also in need of a closer look is the role of the media and how it abets a willful and well-financed Bush administration policy to sow disinformation around the world with the help of the world-wide neoconservative media network. Washington's media elite appeared to be anesthetized to Bush's drive to turn the United States into some domestic mirror image of East Germany or Pinochet's Chile, and an international version of the Roman Empire or the Third Reich.

The media elite, in some perverted and confused quest to show its loyalty to the Bush family, decided that journalists who linked Bush policies in Afghanistan and Iraq to its past oil dealings, were somehow "off the mark," "out there," or otherwise unworthy of consideration. Journalists allowed themselves to be misled and "embedded" by a Pentagon intent on carrying out its well-planned policy of "information operations," "information warfare," psychological operations or "psyops," "information superiority," "information containment," and "strategic influence operations." In the end, the public's right to know has suffered, and the media shills for the Bush administration and their powerful corporate friends have continued to violate the traditional and professional canons of journalism.

Not only conservatives and neoconservatives, but reconstructed liberal and progressive journalists threw around the "C word" (i.e., "conspiracy") to disparage those who wrote about the massive evidence that pointed to the Bushes having traded the nation's economic well-being and national security for personal profit. Prescott Bush certainly engaged in this activity during World War II, when his investments included stakes in companies that supported Nazi Germany's war effort. Sons and grandsons continued the family tradition.

More disturbing is a series of deaths of individuals who either crossed swords with the Bush administration or may have posed a problem for it. I have never been a subscriber to the Internet "Death Lists" that circulated during both the Bush and Clinton administrations; however, considering the character assassinations that the Bush administration has engaged in against its enemies, its consistent failure to fully investigate its own conduct, as well as the influence of a number of unsavory covert operators in the Bush administration, one cannot remain sanguine in light of the unexplained deaths of a number of key people.

One remembers the so-called suicide in August 1991 of journalist Danny Casolaro in a hotel in Martinsburg, West Virginia.

Casolaro had been conducting research for a book tying together BCCI, the first Bush administration, theft and re-engineering by the U.S. Justice Department and Israel of a powerful database program called the Prosecutor's Management Information System (PROMIS), drug smuggling, covert operators, the activities of a company called Hadron (which later became Analex and hired former Soviet anthrax expert Ken Alibek as its chief bio-weapons executive), and the world of mercenaries and weapons smugglers. He referred to this subterranean network as "The Octopus."

Casolaro was on to something big, and his investigations and suspicions have provided me with a firm baseline to understand how this network has morphed itself into the Bush II administration. Casolaro's multiple wrist-slash "suicide" death, the theft of his notes, a botched autopsy, and police incompetence were eerily similar to the 2003 "suicide" of British Ministry of Defense weapons of mass destruction expert Dr. David Kelly. Kelly supposedly committed suicide with over-the-counter painkillers and a dull pocketknife two days after testifying before the British Parliament's Foreign Affairs Committee about the "sexing up" of an intelligence report on Iraq's weapons program. Casolaro and Kelly were threats to governments with scandalous and dark agendas, and their alleged "suicides" were too convenient to be considered as anything other than professional hits. Political assassinations have been common through history. However, if these and other mysterious deaths are linked, it may be that we are seeing a new "Assassination Bureau" at work.

Around the world individuals have split into two major factions: a minority who support the agenda of the powerful "free trade and exploitation" elites, and a majority who stand against it. In their articles and media appearances the neoconservatives have relied on a simple pre-school phrase, "bad guys," to describe those who oppose their sordid global imperial agenda. And we proceed further into the uncertain and potentially disastrous abyss known as the second George W. Bush administration.

In the neocon vernacular, "bad guy" may also be applied to anyone who simply reports an inconvenient truth. But as Daniel Moynihan once said, "Everyone's entitled to their own opinion; no one's entitled to their own facts." If we wish to stop the transformation of our cherished democratic institutions into mere ritual drama, it is essential that official misconduct be exposed, and "rewarded" appropriately.

Some of ISTO's handiwork? The wreckage of the Rwanda One airplane; the missile attack on it killed two African presidents, their staff, and the French crew and triggered a genocide, counter-genocide, and a civil war in the Congo that killed up to 6 million people. (Photo courtesy of Keith Harmon Snow.)

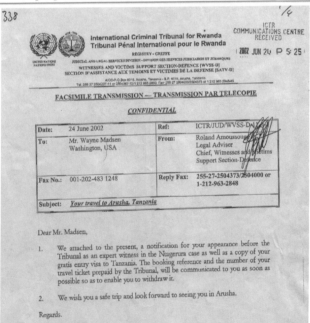

Invitation issued for the author to testify on the Rwanda aircraft terrorist attack. One of two invitations withdrawn due to pressure from the State Department.

Chapter One

Shining Light on a Dark Continent

Not All War Criminals Are Berated Equal

Once upon a time, former Yugoslav President Slobodon Milosevic sat in a Dutch prison awaiting trial for alleged war crimes in Kosovo while former Chilean strongman General Augusto Pinochet enjoyed a convalescent retirement in Chile, after a failed attempt to extradite him to Spain to stand trial for the murder of Spanish nationals during his 1973 coup against Chile's President Salvador Allende. In all likelihood, Pinochet ordered the murder of more innocent people than did Milosevic, but such is the hypocrisy of the international judicial system. Milosevic incurred the wrath of Czech-born former Secretary of State Madeleine Albright while Pinochet enjoyed the protection of Albright's State Department bureaucracy in withholding critical evidence that might have led to his extradition and ultimate conviction. After her service in the Clinton administration Albright was lauded with the title of Distinguished Professor in the Practice of Diplomacy at Georgetown University.

In the Spring of 1994, Albright and her co-conspirator UN Secretary General Kofi Annan, chose to promote international thuggery over diplomacy. They ignored warning signs in central Africa that led to a genocide and counter-genocide in Rwanda, Burundi, and Congo that claimed the lives of some three million people—that's right, 3,000,000. If willful negligence were criminalized by the tainted UN criminal justice system, Albright and Annan would certainly be sitting in prison in the Netherlands awaiting trial.

While Milosevic and Pinochet committed crimes against humanity by commission, the acts of omission by Albright and Annan in 1994 resulted in death and mayhem in what could only have been dreamt of by the Serb and Chilean dictators. Albright, then America's ambassador to the UN, and Annan, the head of UN peacekeeping operations, conveniently chose to ignore evidence that a U.S.-trained and supplied guerrilla force—the Tutsi-led Rwandan Patriotic Front (RPF)—was responsible for the fateful April 6, 1994 terrorist missile attack on the aircraft carrying the Hutu presidents of Rwanda and Burundi home from a peace summit in Tanzania.

Instead, the two diplomats decided to ignore pleas for additional UN peacekeepers to be deployed to Rwanda to forestall the predictable mass murder of Tutsis by revenge-seeking Hutus. Rwanda at that time was a dangerous tinderbox, with Rwanda's President Juvenal Habyarimana negotiating a power-sharing agreement with the RPF. Although Hutus make up 90 per cent of Rwanda's population, Tutsi refugees based in neighboring Uganda had launched a guerrilla war against Rwanda in 1990, an event that had the military backing of the first Bush administration, including Secretary of Defense Dick Cheney. The RPF sought to overthrow Habyarimana, whom they claimed to be a dictator backed by French military and economic assistance. The plane's destruction made this a *fait accompli*.

When the RPF launched its invasion of Rwanda in 1990, U.S. military specialists at the US Army Command and General Staff College in Fort Leavenworth, Kansas, were training its deputy leader, Paul Kagame. Kagame, freshly armed with knowledge of U.S. military and intelligence tactics, arrived in Uganda to take up arms against Rwanda. After the leader of the RPF was killed in combat, Kagame became the head of the guerrilla army, and his ties with the Pentagon, CIA, and State Department became closer.

In 1994, Albright and her senior advisers at the UN were well aware of the assistance that had been granted by the U.S. to Kagame and his mentor, Uganda's President Yoweri Museveni. In fact, Albright argued that Kagame and Museveni represented a new breed of African leader—each was a "beacon of hope" for the future of Africa, in her estimation.

However, two classified UN documents clearly indicate that the RPF planned and committed the terrorist attack on the Rwandan presidential aircraft. The documents, one Secret and the other Confidential, were prepared in 1997 by the National Team for the UN's Independent Oversight Office (a sort of Inspector General for the UN). The documents state that an "Intelligence Network" of the RPF used three rocket sites to shoot down President Habyarimana's aircraft.

The documents also state that "hard evidence" existed that could have be supplied to Judge Louise Arbour, at the time the head of the International Criminal Tribunal for Rwanda and now a member of Canada's Supreme Court. Arbour, a friend of Albright, chose to ignore the evidence against the American-backed guerrillas. In addition, the UN oversight team obtained intelligence that the same RPF hit squad also killed three members of the "Doctors Without Borders" group and five staffers with the UN Human Rights Commission. No wonder at the UN Senior Investigator, former Royal Canadian Mounted Police officer Al Breau, in the report refers to the findings of his UN team as "sensitive" and "explosive."

The United States, which trained and supplied the RPF, certainly would have known about the plans of its surrogates. The American ambassador to Rwanda, David Rawson, was a virtual proconsul for the RPF leadership. According to a French National Assembly inquiry and former RPF officials, the U.S. even supplied the RPF with the Soviet-made surface-to-air missiles that were used to shoot down the Rwandan presidential aircraft. Members of the UN investigation team received intelligence that a company linked to the CIA leased the warehouse used to assemble the missile launchers. The team could never complete the investigation because Arbour—reportedly at the urging of Albright—quickly shut down the investigation when the American connection became clear.

Albright, who constantly shared U.S. intelligence with then-UN Undersecretary General for Peacekeeping Operations Annan, but not with Secretary General Boutros Boutros-Ghali, did everything she could to block a capable UN peacekeeping force from being dispatched to Rwanda. Instead, according to people close to Boutros-Ghali, Albright consistently referred to the Secretary General as "Frenchie," and conspired with Annan to keep him out the loop. During an interview with me in 1998 in Paris, where he served as the Secretary General for the Francophone Agency, the French-speaking commonwealth of nations, Boutros-Ghali said he was aware that certain U.S. intelligence reports that were shared with his deputies never reached him. On Albright's remarks, the urbane Egyptian diplomat, who cut short a prior meeting with a delegation from Kazakhstan in order to meet with me, said, "I'm a gentleman, and gentlemen don't comment about a lady."

However, the "lady" opposed every attempt by General Romeo Dallaire, the Canadian head of the UN Assistance Mission to Rwanda (UNAMIR), to prevent the impending Hutu-Tutsi conflagration. That charge was made by both Boutros-Ghali and former Rwandan President Faustin Twagiramungu, a Hutu who had agreed to become the first Prime Minister in the post-genocide RPF-led government, and was later living in exile in Belgium. Twagiramungu returned to Rwanda to run in the 2003 elections, which, due to voter intimidation and government-sponsored violence against the opposition, Kagame won handily with 95 percent of the vote to Twagiramungu's 3.6 percent. Twagiramungu was even warned by his supporters that Kagame might have attempted a Benigno Aquino-style reception at Kigali airport, a reference to the murder of the Philippine opposition leader by President Ferdinand Marcos's assassins upon his return to Manila from exile in the United States.

In the event, Twagiramungu received no encouragement from the Bush administration. His visit to the State Department in Washington in February 2003 resulted in his being told that Washington did not look with favor upon a race against its ally Kagame. Dr. Cindy Courville, of the Central and Southern Africa desk at the National Security Council (who later became the "Africa Team Chief" at the Pentagon) was polite and gave Twagiramungu her card, but she was totally noncommittal on his electoral campaign.

Ironically, Twagiramungu's visit to Washington occurred while there was a Special Operations/Low Intensity Conflict seminar and exhibition at the Wardman Park Marriott in Washington's fashionable Woodley Park neighborhood. He and I walked through the rows and rows of the sophisticated special operations military equipment that Kagame had at his disposal. The former prime minister seemed truly bewildered at the military machine he was up against. America was no longer the land of the free, but the land of military contractors who sold killing machines to ruthless dictators.

By contrasting Albright's attitude toward black-populated Rwanda with her hasty willingness to commit NATO troops to war in white-populated Kosovo, we might add racism to Albright's list of atrocities. The UN justice system seems to reward the victors of battles, regardless of the facts. Currently in Arusha, Tanzania, some 50 Rwandan Hutus are imprisoned at a UN Detention Facility for war crimes in Rwanda. Although the evidence against many of them is substantial, for others it appears their only crime was to take on the current Kagame dictatorship. President Kagame, backed by the United States, has purged all Hutus from his government, including the former Hutu figurehead president. Anyone who disagree with Kagame is branded as a genocidal murderer of Tutsis back in 1994—a *genocidaire*—and at the snap of Kagame's finger the UN law enforcement mechanism, backed by the FBI and Interpol, issues international arrest warrants.

Meanwhile, those who virtually got away with murder sit at Georgetown University and at UN Headquarters in New York, where Annan was re-elected Secretary General for another five-year term. For his part, Kagame, who enriches himself with stolen minerals from neighboring Congo, and who was accused in a Congolese report of being behind the January 2004 assassination of Congo's President Laurent Kabila, uses the "genocide" card to justify his brutal dictatorship.

French magistrate Jean-Louis Bruguière, who successfully prosecuted Carlos the Jackal and Libyan and Corsican terrorists, had every intention of bringing charges against Kagame for the terrorist attack on the French-crewed Rwandan aircraft. Kagame temporarily continued to enjoy the protection of Arbour's successor, Carla del Ponte, but when she began to investigate the role of Kagame and the RPF in the aircraft attack and other human rights abuses, Kagame succeeded in having her removed as UN prosecutor for Rwanda in August 2003. Even the UN's General Dallaire voiced his concerns about Kagame's duplicity and involvement in the attack, stating, "The RPF rebel movement, now in power, did not have the well-being of the people as its first priority, but a long-time hatched plan that would allow the Tutsis to return from exile and control power. I could see that the RPF wanted to take control of the whole country, and was not necessarily ready to establish an ethnically balanced government."[1]

There was more than enough evidence to bring Kagame to trial but Rwanda and the United States signed a mutual treaty granting each other's leaders immunity from any prosecutions by the International Criminal Court. Any apprehension of Kagame would bring France face-to-face with the Rwandan terrorist's main protector, the United States.

* * * *

In early 2004, French anti-terrorism Judge Jean-Louis Bruguière completed his five year investigation of the terrorist missile attack on the airplane that carried the Presidents. The families of the plane's three-man French crew, who were killed in the attack, had requested the investigation. Bruguière's final report, which was sent to French President Jacques Chirac, concluded that the plane was shot down by the guerrilla forces of the current Rwandan President, Paul Kagame, a client and ally of the United States.

Investigators close to the case reported they uncovered a link between the terrorist attack and a previously unknown and shadowy organization said to be a "front" for powerful interests comprising influential members of the Republican Party and major U.S. oil companies. Their investigation of the American group, simply known as the "International Strategic and Tactical Organization,"

---

[1] Antoine Roger Lokongo, "The 1994 Genocide In Rwanda: 10 Years On… Why Did This Killing Happen?" Congo Panorama, March 19, 2004. <http://www.indymedia.org.uk/en/2004/03/287358.html>

or "ISTO," was prompted by the uncovering of evidence primarily in Africa and Canada. From the evidence, ISTO was tied to the attack.

In addition to the French crew and the two heads of state, many cabinet ministers and other important officials were killed in the crash. The missile attack, termed an "act of international terrorism" by UN police investigators, was blamed on militant Hutus but, in fact, was carried out by mercenaries and troops loyal to the Kagame's Rwandan Patriotic Army (RPA).

Initial reports of CIA involvement in the shoot-down now appear to have been a false flag to deter investigators from the ISTO link to its own U.S. corporate interlocutors. By 1994, the CIA had closed a number of stations in Africa and did not maintain a heavy presence on the continent. Therefore, European law enforcement investigators began looking at the covert world of brass plate companies and mercenaries. ISTO was subsequently identified as a main culprit behind the 1994 aerial assassination.

The attack on the plane triggered a massive wave of genocide of Tutsis and moderate Hutus in Rwanda, which was used by Kagame as a reason to seize power, and then later to attack neighboring Zaire, since renamed the Democratic Republic of the Congo (DRC). Since Rwanda's and Uganda's two invasions of the DRC, in 1996 and 1998, respectively, the country has been divided into fiefdoms controlled by warlords who act on behalf of Western mining and oil companies.

* * * *

According to European law enforcement officials, ISTO was connected to the consulting firm Armitage and Associates LC, which is now known as "AALC." AALC was founded by Richard Armitage, George W. Bush's first Deputy Secretary of State, who stepped down early in 2005. Armitage had turned over the operation of the company to his partners when he assumed the post at State in 2001. Other AALC principals included other top level State Department officials, including Heather A. Conley, who was a Senior Associate of AALC and is now the Deputy Assistant Secretary of

State for European and Eurasian Affairs, and Lincoln P. Bloom-field, a former Partner of AALC and now the Assistant Secretary of State for Political Military Affairs. Conley is a particular focus of the European law enforcement probe.

Another AALC principal is Dr. Paul A. Jureidini, an Associate of AALC and an active participant in the anti-Syrian Lebanon Study Program. Jureidini, according to a long-time U.S. Middle East specialist, is a veteran Maronite activist who has opposed Syrian influence in Lebanon. Through his work with the Lebanon Study Group, Jureidini is close to such neoconservatives as Donald Rumsfeld's Undersecretary of Defense for Policy Douglas Feith, Center for Security Police head and former Reagan administration official Frank Gaffney, and Daniel Pipes, a Director of the U.S. Institute of Peace. In addition, there are close ties between the Lebanon Study Group and the U.S. Committee for a Free Lebanon (USCFL). The latter, headed by Ziad K. Abdelnour, consists of a "Golden Circle" of top neoconservatives, including David Wurmser, the former assistant to Counter Proliferation Assistant Secretary of State and now-UN ambassador John Bolton; Richard Perle; Michael Ledeen; and Douglas Feith.[2] Former Lebanese Army Commander and Prime Minister Michael Aoun, a harsh critic of assassinated Lebanese leaders Elie Hobeika and Rafik Hariri, was also a top mover and shaker inside the USCFL.

According to CIA sources, another link in the ISTO ring is F. Michael Maloof, a Lebanese-American who has been tied to both Imad el Hage, a Lebanese-American businessman who was arrested at Dulles International Airport in early 2003 for suspicion of arms smuggling, and to Douglas Feith, the main force behind the creation of a CIA-rivaling intelligence operation within the Pentagon. El Hage carries a Liberian diplomatic passport and was close to former Liberian dictator Charles Taylor. In what would become yet an additional nexus of activity between the neoconservatives and Al Qaeda, the UN Special prosecutor for war crimes in Sierra Leone, David Crane, charged in May 2005 that Taylor was harboring Al Qaeda members and training rebels throughout West Africa in exchange for blood diamonds.[3] Taylor was also a

[2] <http://www.freelebanon.org/gc-f.htm>
[3] "Al Qaeda "working with Taylor," News24 (South Africa), May 25, 2005,

business partner of Christian televangelist Pat Robertson, who was also a strong supporter of Israel's Likud government and Prime Minister Ariel Sharon.

Maloof, who worked for the Office of Special Plans under Feith, had twice lost his security clearance for suspicious activities involving foreign intelligence agents and people connected to terrorists. Maloof was eventually put on paid leave after Pentagon security officials trumped an intervention by Feith on Maloof's behalf. Maloof and David Wurmser, a neoconservative staffer first under the State Department's Counter-Proliferation chief John Bolton and later under Vice President Dick Cheney, ran a parallel intelligence disinformation shop in the Pentagon, the Policy Counterterrorism Evaluation Group, which challenged CIA and Defense Intelligence Agency (DIA) analyses of the situation in Iraq. Armitage reportedly ordered U.S. troops into Monrovia, the Liberian capital, before the fall of Taylor in order to capture incriminating documents linking Taylor to El Hage, Maloof, and AALC. Armitage had often been described as a close Colin Powell ally and at loggerheads with the neoconservatives within the Pentagon. As a result of the Rwanda terrorism investigation, it was discovered that Armitage's business activities had probably been part of the neoconservative agenda for quite some time.

Maloof eventually had his security clearance yanked by the DIA after it was discovered the Pentagon official failed to disclose an intimate relationship he had with a Georgian woman he met while working in the Republic of Georgia. Maloof later married the woman in question. The DIA took its action after Maloof authored intelligence reports showing questionable links between Sunni and Shia terrorists in Iraq and links between Al Qaeda and Saddam Hussein's government. Maloof later stated that the CIA and DIA disagreed with his assessment, with one DIA official telling him, "We don't like people like you looking over our shoulders."[4] Maloof maintained a secret, off-the-books, intelligence gathering operation inside Feith's office code named the "Bat Cave," which siphoned off classified material from various government agencies. The Bat Cave also involved Wurmser, who later became an assis-

< http://www.news24.com/News24/Africa/News/0,,2-11-1447_1710397,00.html>
[4] "Spy agencies broke rules: agents," UPI News Track, February 20, 2005.

tant to Vice President Dick Cheney after he left Bolton's office at the State Department.[5]

* * * *

But someone was looking over the shoulders of Maloof, Feith, and other neoconservative hawks in the Pentagon and its affiliated think tanks and groups like the American Israel Public Affairs Committee (AIPAC). In 2004, the FBI and Justice Department began a criminal investigation of a possible Israeli-run espionage ring in the Pentagon involving Deputy Defense Secretary Paul Wolfowitz, Feith, analyst Lawrence A. (Larry) Franklin, and others. The FBI conducted two raids of AIPAC's Washington headquarters, seizing computer hard drives and files. Maloof defended the targeted cell in the Pentagon, stating, "I know that this is part of a campaign against us."[6]

Franklin, a colonel in the U.S. Army Reserve and a Defense Intelligence Agency official, was indicted for passing classified information to two operatives of AIPAC in June 2003. Two officials of AIPAC—Steve Rosen and Keith Weissman—were fired over the affair and were subjects of the overall FBI probe. A number of Israeli intelligence officers were also investigated by the FBI, including Naor Gilon, political officer of the Israeli embassy in Washington and Uzi Arad, a former Mossad senior officer.[7]

The FBI discovered that Franklin had 83 classified documents, 38 of which were TOP SECRET, illegally stored in his West Virginia home. Nine of the documents, including three TOP SECRET SPECIAL COMPARTMENTED INFORMATION (SCI) documents, were of concern to the FBI and were described in the government's criminal complaint against Franklin:

- Terrorist Threat Integration Center, terrorism situation report— TOP SECRET/SENSITIVE COMPARTMENTED INFORMATION (SCI), dated June 8, 2004.

---

[5] Confidential Department of Defense sources.

[6] James Risen and David Johnston, "Spy Case Renews Debate Over Pro-Israel Lobby's Ties to Conservatives at Pentagon," *New York Times*, September 6, 2004, p. 10.

[7] Associated Press, "FBI questions ex-Mossad official in AIPAC probe," May 2, 2005; Jerry Seper, "Analyst Abused job, say charges," The *Washington Times*, June 14, 2005.

- Central Intelligence Agency document concerning Al-Qaida—top secret/SCI, dated June 9, 2004.
- CIA document concerning Osama Bin Laden and Al-Qaida—secret/SCI, dated Oct. 7, 2003.
- CIA document concerning Al-Qaida—secret, dated May 12, 2004.
- CIA memorandum on Iraq—secret, dated June 4, 2004.
- CIA defense executive intelligence view concerning terrorists—secret, dated June 10, 2004.[8]

Maloof's involvement in questionable activities did not stop with the Pentagon espionage scandal. In February 2004, U.S. District court for Manhattan, Judge Loretta Preska, was stunned to hear the defendant's attorney, Samuel Abady, request more time to file court papers in a cocaine trafficking case. Abady handed Judge Preska an affidavit supporting a delay in the trial. The affidavit stated, "Mr. Abady is currently involved in a highly sensitive matter which is vital to U.S. national security and potentially affects the lives of our military personnel in the Middle East. I am not free to discuss the nature of his work. I can say generically it involves matters which bear directly on U.S. national security interests, and in particular, the worldwide war on terrorism." The affidavit was signed, "Michael Maloof." It was later revealed that Abady, a Lebanese-American, was the attorney who represented former Reagan Pentagon Deputy Defense Secretary and arch neoconservative war-hawk Richard Perle in matters stemming from his perceived conflict of interests between his job as Chairman of Donald Rumsfeld's Defense Policy Board and his personal business involving contracts in Iraq and elsewhere in the Middle East. There was also evidence that Abady was tied to Lebanese politician, and Maloof friend el Hage.[9]

* * * *

---

[8] Juliet A. Terry, "Ex-Analyst Faces New Government Charges; An Eastern Panhandle Man is Accused of Keeping Classified Documents in His Home," WTRF-TV (Wheeling), May 26, 2005 <http://www.wtrf.com/story.cfm?func=viewstory&storyid=3014>

[9] Robert Gearty, "Lawyer Has Secret Job As Terror Foe," *New York Daily News*, May 2, 2004, p. 22.

Another company linked closely to AALC and ISTO was Kellogg, Brown & Root (KBR), a subsidiary of Halliburton, which was once headed by Vice President Dick Cheney, who continued to draw a deferred salary from the firm. AALC and KBR/Halliburton share the same office building at 1550 Wilson Boulevard in the Rosslyn subdivision of Arlington County, not far from the Pentagon. AALC is in Suite 701 on the top floor of the office building; KBR/Halliburton is a mere elevator ride away on the fourth floor.

KBR was linked by well-placed sources within the U.S. European Command to human rights abuses in Rwanda and the DRC since Kagame's seizure of power in 1994. KBR was also involved in building training camps for Kagame's forces inside Rwanda. A DRC intelligence official revealed that KBR has built special camps in Ethiopia to train Kagame's forces for military operations in the DRC.

ISTO's involvement in Canada was tied to its work on behalf of oil and mining companies based in Toronto and Vancouver. These companies are heavily involved in mining and oil operations in the DRC and Uganda. In the DRC, these overt and covert forces have continuously sought to fracture the nation into warring parties in order to leave the bulk of the nation's mineral wealth to exploitive Western companies.

KBR/Halliburton reaped tremendous windfall profits from the clandestine influence of ISTO over U.S. foreign policy. After the U.S. occupation of Iraq, Halliburton and KBR landed major contracts to run Iraq's oil industry and provide various services to the U.S. military. In the case of KBR, it received its Pentagon contract through a no-bid process. Bechtel, a major player in ISTO's operations in central Africa, received a Pentagon contract to rebuild Iraq's infrastructure.

Although ISTO, AALC, Halliburton/KBR, senior State Department, and other Bush administration officials may be under criminal investigation in Europe for links to terrorism and other criminal activity, they would have also been subject to U.S. criminal charges involving the Racketeer Influenced and Corrupt Organizations (RICO) statutes and the Foreign Corrupt Practices Act.

However, with John Ashcroft and Alberto Gonzales as U.S. Attorneys General, any prosecution of the culprits was rendered moot given their close ties to some of the suspects, including Cheney.

BLOOD ON THE HANDS OF THE UNITED STATES

When he was a Senior Associate of the Forum for International Policy in 1996, recently departed Assistant Secretary of State for African Affairs, Walter Kansteiner III, advocated the splitting up of the DRC, Rwanda, and Burundi into ethnically-based states through a process of "forced migration." When Kansteiner worked for then-Secretary of Defense Dick Cheney during the first Bush administration, he was in charge of the Strategic Minerals Task Force, a Pentagon unit that was analyzing the mineral resources of Africa and other regions for U.S. defense needs. The Forum for International Policy is headed by George H.W. Bush's National Security Adviser, Brent Scowcroft, and its Board of Trustees once included Colin Powell, Condoleezza Rice, and former Enron Chairman Kenneth L. Lay. Since leaving the State Department, Kansteiner has joined the board of Sierra Holdings, Ltd., a Ghanaian-owned firm that is exploiting the bauxite deposits in war-torn Sierra Leone.

At first, Rwanda and Uganda seemed unlikely places to attract the interests of oil companies. Neither was known to have any large deposits of oil. It was believed that the interest of ISTO-related firms was directed at Zaire/DRC, because of its wealth of gold, diamonds, columbite-tantalite (col-tan, the mineral used in the production of micro-electronics in cell phones and lap top computers), as well as oil. Uganda and Rwanda were considered convenient jumping off points from which to invade Zaire/DRC. That was until large oil/hydrocarbon reserves were discovered in 1998 in the Lake Albert region of Uganda and Congo and the Lake Kivu Region of Rwanda and Congo. An Israeli company, Israeli Electric Company, announced a joint plan with President Kagame to exploit methane gas in Lake Kivu.[10]

Thus, Uganda's President Yoweri Museveni and Kagame became the newest clients of Big Oil. They and Big Oil would kill to pro-

---

[10] Israelis in Kivu Gas Deal?" *Africa Energy Intelligence*, July 24, 2002.

tect their newly found wealth, and kill they did, in their own countries and in the neighboring Congo. By 2003, plans were underway
to construct oil pipelines from Kampala, Uganda to Mombassa,
Kenya and Eldoret, Tanzania. Shell Oil was the prime backer of
the projects.[11]

The only reason ISTO could have been interested in the Great
Lakes region of Central Africa in the early 1990s was to use nations like Uganda and Rwanda as launching pads to gain control
of Zaire/Congo and loot the country of its wealth of natural resources. However, as private military companies and their associated oil prospectors penetrated the region, it became clear that the
Great Lakes region, itself, was sitting on important oil reserves,
mainly concentrated under Lake Albert and Lake Victoria. The
region, like others where oil was recently discovered, would never
be the same.

* * * *

The long-asked question of what type of training was provided
by the U.S. military to the Rwanda Patriotic Front (RPF) before,
during, and after its shooting down of the Rwandan presidential
aircraft on April 6, 1994 continued to be asked as reports surfaced
of RPF assassination teams being deployed around the world to
intimidate opponents of Kagame. There was a belief that Roman
Catholic Archbishop of Bukavu, Emmanuel Kataliko, was assassinated in October 2000 in Rome by members of a Rwandan hit
team acting on orders from Kagame. Other Tutsi and Hutu leaders who opposed Kagame's regime continued to flee Rwanda to
the U.S., Belgium, and France in fear of their lives. Rwanda's figurehead Hutu President Pasteur Bizimungu was forced to resign
in 2000 under pressure from the only real power in Rwanda, his
then-Vice President, Paul Kagame. He was placed under house arrest. Two Hutu Prime Ministers who served under Kagame, Faustin Twagiramungu and Pierre-Celeste Rwigyema, fled the country
rather than go to one of Kagame's prisons. They both have charged
Kagame and his allies within the UN of abusing the Arusha In-

[11] *The East African*, "Tanzania to Establish Second Oil Pipeline," *Africa News*, November 3, 2003.

ternational Criminal Tribunal for Rwanda by threatening to indict any Rwandan who opposes Kagame's aims as a *genocidaire*.

Deus Kagiraneza, a former intelligence officer in Kagame's Military Intelligence Directorate (DMI), interim Prefect of the Ruhengeri province, and member of the Parliament, is now in exile in Belgium. He charged that Kagame's top government and military officials were responsible for torturing and executing political opponents. Kagiraneza maintains that the RPF pursued such policies since the time of the 1990 invasion of Rwanda from Uganda.[12]

* * * *

One troubling aspect of the UN's criminal trials in Arusha, Tanzania was the involvement of the U.S. military and government in the process. The United States, far from being an honest broker in the conflicts in central Africa, showed an intense interest in the criminal process even as it railed against the International Criminal Court and elected to withdraw its signature of the treaty establishing the court. The United States has loaned military Judge Advocate General (JAG) corps attorneys to aid the UN prosecution team in Arusha. Ironically, some of the military attorneys involved in war crimes prosecutions in Africa were associated with U.S. government agencies that were culpable in the chaos in the Great Lakes region.

One such individual was Dr. David Crane, whom the Bush administration nominated as the lead prosecutor for the International Criminal Tribunal for Sierra Leone. Crane was the Assistant General Counsel for the Defense Intelligence Agency from 1996 to 1997—the time frame during which the DIA was involved with the Rwandan and Ugandan invasion of then-Zaire as part of a JCET exercise code-named FALCON GORILLA. During Crane's stint at DIA, the agency hosted a Pentagon symposium of private military contractors (PMCs) and diamond companies. Crane was also the Chair of the U.S. Army's International and Operational

---

[12] Deus Kagiraneza, Testimony, 12 July 2000. <http://www2.minorisa.es/inshuti/kagirana.htm>

Law Department at the JAG School from 1993 to 1996.[13] During that time the E-IMET program provided training to 19 military and civilian officials of the RPF. Of these, 12 served with the RPA.[14] Present at the June 24, 1997 PMC-DIA-corporate meeting were representatives of Executive Outcomes of South Africa; Sandline International of the UK; MPRI of Alexandria, Virginia; Texaco; and Exxon.[15]

Requests by two different defense teams in Arusha for me to testify as an expert and fact witness at the International Criminal Tribunal for Rwanda were rejected at the eleventh hour by nervous prosecutors and judges under intense pressure from Kagame and his patrons in Washington. The testimonies were to focus on the RPF's role in shooting down Habyarimana's plane—clearly an incident of international terrorism, but one that had the fingerprints of the United States all over it. Revelations of the U.S. role in the attack would embarrass a country spearheading a "war" against international terrorism. ICTR prosecutors clearly wanted to shield the court from evidence collected by UN investigators, who combed Rwanda for people knowledgeable about the perpetrators. The evidence was damning against Kagame's government.

Further damaging the reputation of the ICTR process was the Bush administration naming Pierre-Richard Prosper as Ambassador-at-Large for War Crimes Issues. Prosper's conflict of interest in holding such a position was readily apparent: he was a lead war crimes prosecutor for the ICTR from 1996 to 1998. According to tribunal insiders, it was Prosper who was largely responsible for leaning on the judges to reject my testifying about my conclusions regarding the perpetrators of the plane attack. More repugnant, was Bush naming Prosper to head the U.S. delegation at the April 7, 2004 Kigali ceremony marking the tenth anniversary of the Rwandan killings, the tenth anniversary of the implementation of Kansteiner's forced migration plan for the Great Lakes region of Africa—a plan the Hutu exiles dubbed "Plan Evil."

[13] Marguerite Feitlowitz, "UN War Crimes Court Approved for Sierra Leone," 8 January 2000. <www.crimesofwar.org/onnews/news-sierra.html>

[14] Summary–Report to Congress on U.S. Military Activities in Rwanda, 1994-August 1997. <www.defenselink.mil/pubs/rwanda/summary.html>

[15] Attendance list, closed conference: "The Privatization of National Security Functions in Sub-Saharan Africa."

* * * *

In August 1997, the National Team leader of the UN Investigation Section of the Office of Internal Oversight Services (OIOS)
submitted a witness report on the plane attack. Three Tutsi witnesses were given a credibility rating of 2 by the UN team (defined
by the UN as "possibly true, but untested").[16] The three witnesses
claimed they were part of "an elite covert strike team known as
the 'Network' and [which] with the assistance of a foreign government shot down the Presidential aircraft." The informants also
stated "Major General Paul Kagame was the overall operations
commander." The three also provided "accurate descriptions of the
operation together with names, ranks, and roles of each soldier
involved." The UN team also reported that the three witnesses
were able to "produce hard copy documents of the operation." [17]
When two of the witnesses said they would cooperate with the
investigations if their safety could be assured, Judge Arbour of the
International Criminal Tribunal for Rwanda endorsed the development, but quickly reversed herself when she decided the issue
of the attack on the airplane was outside the ICTR's mandate and
"would not be investigated."

A secret internal UN memorandum from 1997 revealed the
names of the RPF's Network responsible for the terrorist attack
on the Rwandan presidential Falcon Mystere aircraft. None of
these individuals was investigated or indicted and brought before
the ICTR. The report described the "Network" as a "cell of elite
soldiers who are activated and deactivated from time to time to
conduct special operations. One such operation was the successful
rocket attack upon President Habyarimana in 1994." The report
continued, "We have also been advised that there is a distinct possibility that the same cell was responsible for the recent murders
of *Medecine Monde* staff (3 persons) in Ruhengeri in January 1997
and UN Human Rights staff (5 persons) in Cyangugu."[18] The use
of elite units that are activated and deactivated according to special

---

[16] Paragraph 17, Report, Investigations Section/OIOS, dated August 1, 1997, classified CONFIDENTIAL.

[17] Ibid.

[18] National Team Inquiry Internal Memorandum, March 1997, classified SECRET.

requirements is a hallmark of CIA and DIA operations around the world.

The report alleged the RPF used three rocket sites: Masaka Hill (SAM) which was used by the attack team; Gasogi Hill (SAM), also used by the attack team; and Camp Kanombe (rocket propelled grenades). Ultimately, Camp Kanombe was not required to be used by the attack team. The RPF informants revealed the assassination was planned from three control posts: Camp Kanombe (operational control), Kigali (field control), and Arusha (initial control regarding the presidential aircraft's schedule). The report also states two [RPF] soldiers fired SAMs from Masaka and Gasogi Hills and that one of them survived and "may be available to the ICTR."[19] Later information received from UN investigators claimed that Kagame silenced this particular source.

Another witness to the attack, former RPF hitman David Kiwanuka, was prepared to give evidence to the UN about the role of the RPF in the aircraft attack. On February 24, 2004, Kiwanuka's body was found in the trunk of a car in Kenya with a single bullet in his head. Other potential witnesses to Kagame's terrorism met with similar fates. Kiwanuka's control officer, Alphonse Mbayire, an RPF officer working out of the Rwandan embassy in Nairobi, was shot in the face. Colonel Theoneste Lizinde died after being thrown from a moving car.

All were members of the Network. Other Network members who were assassinated included Major John Birasa (the member in charge of weapons), Captain H. Kamugisha (an intelligence officer), Wilson Rutayisira (a close aid to Kagame), and Sergeant Peter Sempa (who transported the SAMs, which were concealed as firewood, in a truck to Kigali). Former Kagame government cabinet minister Seth Sendashonga, who was prepared to testify before the UN about the missile attack, was also assassinated after he fled to Nairobi. Another member of the Network, Captain Abdul Ruzibiza, who provided important information to the independent French judicial inquiry into the terrorist attack, fled to Norway for safety.[20]

---

[19] Ibid.

[20] Jon Swain, "Riddle of the Rwandan assassins' trail," *Sunday Times* (London), April 4, 2004, p. 26.

Several other RPF witnesses also stated they could provide the ICTR with hard copy evidence of the attack plan and, to no surprise, the report revealed that the ICTR rejected the evidence. Another RPF intelligence witness, First Lieutenant Aloys Ruyenzi, a Tutsi veteran of Kagame's who was originally from Uganda and who ultimately fled into exile in Norway, testified in writing that Kagame ordered Habyarimana's plane shot down. He said he was at the March 31, 1994 meeting at which the assassination of the president was planned by Kagame and his top henchmen. He also added that Kagame and his lieutenants ordered the massacre of Hutus in Rwanda.[21]

One of the UN investigators was Jim Lyons, a retired FBI agent who spent most of his career investigating terrorism in the New York field office. He told a meeting convened by Georgia Congresswoman McKinney on Capitol Hill in April 2001 that "as the Commander of Investigations, I believed that the investigation of the rocket attack was within the mandate of the ICTR. It was the spark that ignited all of Rwanda into a conflagration, which would ultimately take the lives of 700,000 to 1,000,000 men, women and children." He added, "The UN Security Council had expressed its abhorrence at this terrorist attack and had directed that all information regarding the event be gathered. The ICTR Statute, Article 4, specifically included Acts of Terrorism in its list of offenses. In my view, there was more than ample justification for the ICTR to consider the rocket attack as an international criminal event falling well within its jurisdiction."[22]

However, when the UN investigation team began to investigate the charges by the RPF informants, they began to smell an American connection to the RPF "Network." One UN investigator discovered that the warehouse near Kigali's airport that was used to assemble the SAM-16s was owned by a Swiss front company known to be connected to the CIA.[23] The United States had provided official and unofficial training to the RPF beginning in 1990 when Kagame was training in the United States. The sophistica-

---

[21] Letter signed by Aloys Ruyenzi, dated May 7, 2004.
[22] Seminar: "Covert Action in Africa: A Smoking Gun in Washington, DC," Rayburn House Office Building, April 16, 2001.
[23] Confidential information provided by the UN investigator.

tion of the RPF attack on the aircraft—the use of three attack sites and three control points—is consistent with the type of military training provided by U.S. Special Forces.

The U.S. military attaché to Rwanda, Lt. Col. Richard Orth arrived in Kigali on April 7, 1994,[24] the day after the attack, and he became a virtual proconsul for the Kagame regime, staying on as attaché in Kigali for an amazingly long five-year tour of duty. A former senior RPF government official source claimed Orth was one of Kagame's best friends during his tenure in Kigali.[25]

* * * *

Faustin Twagiramungu, an ethnic Hutu, was Kagame's first Prime Minister. He saw first-hand the control the United States had over the guerrilla leader. While he was Prime Minister, Twagiramungu was invited to the residence of U.S. ambassador David Rawson. The date was August 15, 1995, Twagiramungu's birthday. Present at the residence were Rawson, Assistant Secretary of Defense for International Security Affairs Joseph S. Nye, Jr.; Deputy Assistant Secretary of State for Africa (and DIA officer) Vince Kern; and Orth. Twagiramungu was "informed" that the United States government had decided to cooperate with Rwanda on military issues and assist the Rwandan Army. The Prime Minister insisted that Kagame's RPA was not a national army, but a "personal army of Kagame." He then asked the Americans if the U.S. was planning on setting up a joint national army of Hutus and Tutsis. The U.S. reaction to his question was negative. In two weeks Twagiramungu was out as Prime Minister. Later, Twagiramungu said he had been under great pressure because he let it be known that he "wasn't there just to please the RPF [but] represented all parties."[26]

Diamonds, oil, and other valuable resources continued to be the scourge of Africa. The scramble for these resources fueled violence in the DRC, Angola, and West Africa. Just one week prior to leaving office, President Clinton's National Security Adviser, Sandy

[24] Lt. Col. Orth, African Studies Association Conference, Philadelphia, Session: "The Multiple Dimensions of Conflict in Africa: Rwanda's Hutu Extremist Genocidal Insurgency, An Eyewitness Perspective, November 12, 1999.

[25] Confidential information.

[26] Interview with Faustin Twagiramungu, 25 May 2001.

Berger, convened a White House conference on technologies to identify and certify diamonds. After permitting the diamond companies to influence America's Africa policy, to the detriment of the African people, the Clinton administration, in the eleventh hour, belatedly showed interest in one of the real causes of Africa's problems: diamonds.

A particularly troubling aspect of the accession to power of the Bush administration was that many of the same players who were instrumental in the failed Africa policy of the Clinton administration continued to maintain influence in the foreign policy apparatus of the United States. In a number of ways, given its close ties to multinational companies, right-wing Christian fundamentalist groups, and the intelligence community, the Bush administration would view Africa as a source of not only vast reserves of raw materials, but inexpensive labor, a fount of "faith-based" humanitarian assistance, and questionable covert activities.

The Bush administration brought back most of the same faces involved in George H.W. Bush's Africa policy apparatus. Condoleezza Rice brought Jendayi Frazer to head the Africa desk at the NSC. Frazer studied under Rice at Stanford University. Frazer was on loan to the Pentagon from the Center for Strategic and International Studies (CSIS) during the Clinton administration, and he had established close ties with Richard Orth, the chief of U.S. covert operations in the Great Lakes region, and currently serving as U.S. defense attaché in Ethopia.

After his Kigali service, Orth was appointed the U.S. Defense Attaché in Kampala, Uganda, a stone's throw from Kigali and a center for U.S. covert activities in Sudan, the DRC, and the Horn of Africa. It was highly advantageous for Orth's Sudan game plan, which included militarily shoring up Uganda for a possible U.S. attack on Sudan, that the United States provided logistics aid to airlift a battalion of Rwandan Army troops to Sudan's genocide-plagued Darfur region. In a case of hypocrisy mixed with irony, Rwandan troops, many of whom had been involved with genocide of refugees in the DRC and Rwanda, were placed in a region to defend black African Sudanese, including many refugees, from preying Arab Janjaweed militias.

* * * *

Gearing up for a war with Iraq, Secretary of Defense Donald Rumsfeld visited the Horn of Africa in December 2002. He secured long-term commitments for U.S. basing rights in Djibouti, Eritrea, and Ethiopia. The U.S. previously secured basing rights in Somaliland (a country Washington refused to recognize as independent) and Kenya; and reportedly finally secured rights to the Yemeni island of Socotra for an electronic listening post.[27] In addition, U.S. Special Forces teams operating out of Djibouti made several forays into the Jebel Kurush mountains of northeast Sudan in search of Al Qaeda units.[28]

In 2002, U.S. troops arrived in Kenya to take part in OPERATION EDGED MALLET, another of a series of joint military maneuvers with Kenyan forces that have included, since 2000, OPERATION NATURAL FIRE/NATIVE FURY, OPERATION NOBLE PIPER, and OPERATION GOLDEN SPEAR/NEON SPEAR.

American eavesdroppers also arrived in Kenya and across the border in Somalia. In an effort to step up the monitoring of Islamist groups in the Horn of Africa, the National Security Agency (NSA), according to European intelligence sources who visited the area, established two small Signals Intelligence (SIGINT) stations on Kenya's coast. One was located in the backyard of the Governor's residence on the island of Lamu, an ancient center for Islamic culture in East Africa. Replacing flowers and trees in the yard were omnidirectional and directional SIGINT antennas. In early January 2004, U.S. and Kenyan forces held joint military exercises on Lamu to root out suspected Al Qaeda sympathizers.

Burr Gaabo, a small rocky and depopulated island near the Kenyan border but in Somali territorial waters, hosted a small spy station equipped with surveillance cameras and electronic listening devices. In addition, another small electronic surveillance site was located in the Somali town of Ras Kambooni, reportedly a former base for an Al Qaeda allied group. U.S. surveillance platforms

---

[27] Bill Gertz, "Pentagon Sought Spy Post off Yemen Coast," *Washington Times*, 14 October 2000. Philippe Vasset, *Africa in Washington: The Permanent Guide*, Paris: Indigo Publications, June 2001.

[28] Damien McElroy, "US forces hunt down al-Qa'eda in Sudan," *Daily Telegraph*, August 1, 2004.

and Special Forces troops also concentrated their attention on the Kenyan island of Pate, a remote island north of Lamu populated mostly by fishermen.

Another U.S. listening station was reported in the Kenyan town of Kilifi, south of Lamu on the Kenyan coast. Kilifi is the location of the Israeli-owned Paradise Hotel, which was bombed by Al Qaeda terrorists in November 2002. U.S. intelligence also closely monitored Garissa, a Kenyan town near the Somali border that had been the scene of anti-American demonstrations. These sites complemented the SIGINT site on the island of Socotra, the former site of a Soviet eavesdropping installation strategically located astride the oil tanker routes of the Gulf of Aden.

A major priority for the war-centric Bush administration was to militarize an African continent in order to 1) make it safe for U.S. investments; 2) help stamp out insurgencies that stymied natural resource exploration and exploitation; and 3) increase market share for the U.S. defense industry. U.S. military assistance to Africa reached new heights, especially in the wake of September 11 when the U.S. military established new staging and training areas in Uganda, Djibouti, Somaliland, Kenya, Morocco, Ethiopia, and Eritrea. The latter two countries represented a true double game for Washington, considering that the Pentagon actually backed both sides (with a strong tilt to Ethiopia) during their bloody border war.

* * * *

George W. Bush, whose father helped nurture, arm, and finance UNITA's Savimbi in Angola, decided the old anti-Communist guerrilla leader was too much of a liability. Although the reasoning behind getting rid of Savimbi and his top lieutenants was to safeguard vast U.S. oil interests in Angola, there was also a major Angolan financial scandal with deep ties to the Bush administration.

Known as "Angolagate" in France, the Angolan scandal involved arms-for-oil deals between French businessman Pierre Falcone, the head of a firm called Brenco International; his colleague Jean-

Christophe Mitterand; and a Russian-born Israeli named Arkadi Gaydamak whose Israeli passport identifies him as Arye Barlev.

According to *All the Presidents' Men*, a March 25, 2002 report on Angolagate by Global Witness, Gaydamak funneled billions of dollars in arms and oil-backed loans to Angola's government in return for lucrative oil contracts with Western oil companies. Falcone and Gaydamak, relying on the special access that Mitterand had to the Angolan government, managed to transfer some $633 million in arms to Angola.[29]

The net effect of the Angolan arms buildup was the scrapping of the 1994 Lusaka Peace Agreement between Angolan President Jose Eduardo dos Santos and long-time UNITA rebel leader Jonas Savimbi, a one-time favorite of the CIA, and a person who President Reagan once hailed as the "George Washington of Africa."

The newly armed Angolan Army—supported by MPRI and AirScan—was eventually able to push Savimbi's rebels farther into the jungles in the eastern part of the country. This compelled UNITA to mine and sell more diamonds on the black market to buy arms. The trade in "blood diamonds," in turn, led to a number of human rights abuses by UNITA. Ironically, Savimbi, Reagan's "George Washington of Africa," was gunned down by Angolan Army troops in a remote area of Angola on February 22, 2002, the birthday of George Washington.

According to Global Witness, in addition to the French oil giant Total-Fina-Elf, companies like Chevron, Texaco, Philipps Petroleum, Exxon Mobil, and BP-Amoco—all with close links to Bush and members of his administration like Secretary of State Rice and Vice President Richard Cheney—were heavily involved in propping up dos Santos in return for profitable offshore oil concessions.

After transferring some $770 million in oil revenues to their own private bank accounts, dos Santos and his advisers became convinced that pluralism in their country would be a very dangerous thing for their future business deals. They also quickly abandoned their former Marxist beliefs in favor of the type of capitalist principles embraced by George W. Bush and Jacques Chirac.

---

[29] Global Witness, *All the President's Men*, 2002.

Falcone's wife, Sonia, a former Miss Bolivia and a friend of First Lady Laura Bush, became a big-ticket contributor to Bush's 2000 election campaign. Contributions were made to the campaign through Sonia's Essanté Corporation, a distributor of health, beauty, and sexual pleasure products.[30]

In 2000, Esssanté, which is linked to Falcone's arms trafficking Brenco through the same corporate addresses and shareholding accounts in the United Kingdom and British Virgin Islands, respectively, gave the GOP and Bush campaign over $100,000. Sonia was also an early supporter of Bush. Federal Election Commission records reveal she was on board with a $1000 contribution to Bush's presidential exploratory committee on April 14, 1999. She also rubbed shoulders with George H.W. Bush at an October 6, 2000 fund-raiser—a Bush campaign event that netted $10,000 per person.[31]

Only after *Newsweek* and the *Arizona Republic* published details of Falcone's international arms dealing involving Gaydamak was the money returned by the GOP to Essanté, and then only a few days prior to Bush's inauguration. The money, of course, was available to Bush all during the contested Florida election and the state and federal Supreme Court battles. The Republican National Committee said in a statement that the money was returned to "avoid the appearance of impropriety."[32]

More noteworthy, just before Falcone was arrested in France in December 2000 (along with Jean-Christophe Mitterand), police discovered computer files that included a letter from Falcone inviting then-candidate Bush to meet with dos Santos at Falcone's Arizona Paradise Valley ranch. Although there is no record of such a meeting taking place, Bush did host dos Santos at the White House shortly after the killing of Savimbi. The timing of this meeting raises serious questions about the transfer of money to Bush's campaign coffers and its impact on changing the Republican Party's long-held policy of support for Savimbi.

It is also interesting that one of Bush's top Arizona campaign officials, State Senator Scott Bundgaard, arranged for Sonia Falcone

---

[30] Ibid.
[31] Ibid.
[32] Ibid.

to meet Bush at the Phoenix Airport just after Essanté dropped one down payment of $20,000 into Bush's campaign chest. According to Global Witness, there is good reason to believe the donations to Bush were actually made by Pierre Falcone himself, using "coded accounts" maintained at the UBS Bank in Switzerland, Bank Leumi in Tel Aviv, and Banque Rothschild in Monaco.

The Global Witness report also reveals that French investigators discovered questionable links between the Angolan government and Vice President Cheney's old firm Halliburton and its subsidiary Kellogg, Brown & Root. The investigators believe Halliburton's success in Angola is tied to Falcone's intercessions with Luanda: actions that would have directly benefited Cheney when he headed the firm between 1995 and 2000. According to an Associated Press report on October 26, 2000, the U.S. Embassy in Luanda assisted Halliburton in securing a $68 million U.S. Export-Import Bank loan for Angola in 1998, during the height of much of the arms-running activity between dos Santos, Falcone and Gaydamak. The AP cited a cable from the U.S. Embassy in Luanda to Secretary of State Madeleine Albright that states, "Our commercial officer literally camped out at the offices of the national oil company, petroleum ministry and central bank, unraveling snag after snag to obtain the transfer of funds… The bottom line: thousands of American jobs and a foot in the door for Halliburton to win even bigger contracts."[33]

Cheney, a one-time supporter of UNITA, appears to have switched horses after the former CIA-backed guerrillas were deemed a threat to U.S. oil interests. Savimbi, like Laurent Kabila and Mobutu before him, became just another disposable CIA asset who outlived his usefulness.

National Security Adviser Rice, a former Chevron director and the namesake of a Chevron supertanker, the SS *Condoleezza Rice* (later renamed the SS *Altair Voyager*), also had good reason to see Angola stabilized under the dos Santos regime, thus permanently eliminating the UNITA threat to her old employer.

Perhaps the most ironic link described in the Global Witness report was one involving the "fugitive financier" Marc Rich. He

---

[33] Ibid.

appears as a major player in the arms-for-oil scandal through a Swiss-based oil trading company named Glencore. The firm played a major role in guaranteeing a total of $1 billion in oil-backed loans for Angola in 1998. The first set of oil-backed loans in 1993 involved Glencore, Falcone, and Gaydamak. Soon after, Gaydamak arranged for the sale of Russian helicopters and ammunition through a Slovak company called ZTS-OSOS. The 1998 billion-dollar loan deal included the Export-Import Bank loans being pushed by Halliburton and Cheney.[34] The Republican Party condemned President Clinton's pardon of Rich without describing Cheney's own links to the fugitive financier's vast international money-lending and influence-peddling empire.

There is yet another disturbing element involved in Bush's ties to dos Santos. There was a secret agreement between the French firm Communications et Systémes, the French Defense Ministry, and dos Santos to acquire during 2000 two types of communications monitoring equipment suites to triangulate the location of Savimbi's GSM cell and satellite telephone calls in the Angolan bush country. The two systems—Murene (for GSM calls) and Menta (for satellite calls), were supposed to help dos Santos' forces locate Savimbi's constantly moving jungle headquarters.[35]

Apparently, the multimillion-dollar systems were not all that helpful in locating Savimbi. However, legitimate questions exist about what U.S. official and unofficial intelligence resources were brought to bear on the recalcitrant ex-U.S. ally Savimbi. Under ex-CIA Director George Tenet's expanded authority to eliminate terrorists listed in a "worldwide attack matrix," it was open season on anyone the U.S. branded a terrorist. According to U.S. government sources, Savimbi was tracked by the military forces of U.S. NATO ally Portugal, who were aided by private mercenaries from Israel and South Africa.

Jardo Muekalia, who headed UNITA's Washington office until it was forced to close in 1997, says the military forces that ultimately succeeded in assassinating Savimbi were supported by commercial satellite imagery and other intelligence support provided by Houston-based Kellogg, Brown & Root. Both the State Department

---

[34] Ibid.
[35] Ibid.

and Pentagon vehemently denied any U.S. government role in the killing of Savimbi.

Yet another suspicious death arose from the Falcone affair and the scramble for economic advantage in Angola. Thierry Imbot, a DGSE agent and the son of General Rene Imbot, a former head of the DGSE, died in a fall from his French apartment in October 2000. Imbot's name was listed on one of the seized diskettes as a "consultant for China" for Brenco International, and he was paid $120,000 for his services through Nations Bank of Virginia.[36] No investigation into the mysterious death of a consultant for a company tied to the Bush family just weeks before Bush's tainted presidential election victory ensued in any American media.

The ties of President Chirac's administration to Angolagate were as close as those of other leading French politicians—right and left, Socialist and Gaullist. What is not clear is what Chirac and then-President-elect Bush spoke about on December 18, 2000 in Washington, DC at the French Embassy during an unprecedented meeting between a president-elect and a foreign leader inside a foreign diplomatic mission. Coming just four days after the Supreme Court handed the White House to Bush, the Bush-Chirac meeting took on an even greater aura of mystery.

The Black Box and the Black Op

The most dramatic revelation in the shameful Rwandan episode concerned the whereabouts of the downed Mystere Falcon 50's cockpit voice recorder or "black box." According to officials involved with UN air movements in the region, the black box was secretly transported to UN Headquarters in New York where it remains to this day. Officially, the Rwandan government claims the black box went missing. Actually, according to former UN sources, the black box was spirited away by UN officials from Kigali to New York via Nairobi. The movement of the black box was known to U.S. Government officials. According to the UN sources, data from the black box was withheld by the UN under pressure from the government of the United States. The UN sources were convinced that the missiles that downed the presidential aircraft came

---

[36] Ibid.

from the United States and were delivered to the RPF. According to UN and U.S. government sources, the UN's covert activities in Rwanda on behalf of the United States and Canada were supported by then-UN Peacekeeping Operations Undersecretary Kofi Annan, who acted on the instructions of then-U.S., ambassador to the UN Madeleine Albright and Susan Rice, who was, at that time, posted to the National Security Council. Eventually, Rice became the Assistant Secretary of State for African Affairs and reported to Secretary of State Albright. UN Secretary General Boutros Boutros-Ghali was specifically kept out of the picture by the United States, which succeeded in dumping him from his post in 1996, replacing him with Annan.

Ultimately, the UN was forced to admit it had in its possession a black box cockpit voice recorder since 1994. The revelation came after Judge Bruguière's final report on the aircraft attack was leaked to the French newspaper *Le Monde* almost ten years from the date of the terrorist attack. Bruguière's investigation concluded that Kagame gave direct orders to his RPF forces to fire the missiles at the plane.

Le Monde also reported that the black box was from the presidential Falcon 50 aircraft. UN spokesman Fred Eckhard said that a black box mysteriously turned up in a filing cabinet at the Air Safety Unit at UN headquarters in New York. This admission came after he first said the *Le Monde* story was false, stressing the UN had no such black box.

Denis Beissel, who retired from the UN in 2003, and was the peacekeeping department's acting director of field administration and logistics at the time, said he received the black box three months after the plane was attacked and "thought it was important," but added that he had other duties to attend. "When we tried to get a lot of attention to the issue and tried to get it analyzed, nobody would. I suppose it got put on a shelf," he said.[37] It is important to note that Beissel's ultimate boss was Kofi Annan, the head of peacekeeping operations.

The same Washington spin machine that justified the war in Iraq went into operation on the black box. From Kigali, Washington's

---

[37] Associated Press, "Rwanda black box 'put on shelf,'" March 13, 2004.

ally Kagame said, "What does the black box tell you about what happened? Maybe it will tell you that the plane crashed and it was shot, but it will not tell you the identity of the one who shot it down.... It is as if the black box... explains or gives the excuse as to why genocide took place in Rwanda. Again for me that is nonsense.... The black box, the plane, this is just a red herring and diversionary."[38] After ten years at the helm of Rwanda, America's close ally had become very articulate in the art of disinformation and perception management.

The Bush administration agreed to have the National Transportation Safety Board (NTSB) in Washington, the international center of media spin, examine the black box. The fix was in.

The NTSB said an analysis of the 30-minute tape provided no evidence that the black box was from the Rwandan presidential aircraft. Eckhard, who had been having trouble with the truth, said, "Some conversation in French could be heard on the 30-minute tape but nothing so far links the CVR [cockpit voice recorder] to the crash on 6 April 1994." Sighs of exasperation could be heard throughout Africa, which knew better. Moreover, French intelligence sources reported that there were clear indications that the black box had been tampered with, with critical sections erased.[39]

But the black box story was not over. In April 2004, Francois Pascal, a senior investigator for the UN's Office of Internal Oversight Services, was fired by his boss, Undersecretary General Dileep Nair, for insisting on investigating the shooting down of the Rwandan plane and why the UN had covered up the existence of the black box for ten years.[40] Nair had already been under fire for covering up a multitude of UN scandals, including the skimming of funds from the UN's Iraqi "oil-for-food" program. The involvement of Nair in both the black box cover-up and the Iraqi oil sales program provides yet another nexus between the tragedy of Rwanda and international scandals involving the oil industry.

French law enforcement sources had stressed that any investigation or questions asked by anyone about ISTO would result in

---

[38] Irwin Arieff, "UN scrambles to unlock Rwanda black box secrets," Reuters, March 12, 2004.

[39] Confidential information from French Interior Ministry source, December 5, 2005.

[40] Jonathan Hunt, "U.N. Official Suspended for Probing '94 Crash," Fox News, June 17, 2004. <http://www.foxnews.com/story/0,2933,122878,00.html>

great danger to the questioner. Twice, I had been prepared to testify about who was behind the plane attack at the International Criminal Tribunal for Rwanda in Arusha, Tanzania. Twice, the U.S. State Department intervened with the tribunal to block my testimony. Once, after the tribunal agreed to hear my testimony, I received a very credible death threat: "Your car won't make it from Arusha airport to your hotel." The intimidation having been successful, I struck Arusha from my travel plans.

* * * *

ISTO represents the type of operation that has been a hallmark of U.S. black ops for a number of years. George H.W. Bush, while he headed the CIA, made no secret of his willingness to engage in "wet affairs" to dispose of nettlesome individuals. During Bush's one-year stint as CIA Director, clandestine activities involving "hits" by agents with licenses to kill were carried out in Latin America, Asia, and Africa.

On September 28, 1976, former Chilean Foreign Minister Orlando Letelier and Ronni Karpen Moffitt, his secretary, were killed on Massachusetts Avenue, in the middle of northwest Washington's Embassy Row and in broad daylight, when a bomb destroyed their car. George H.W. Bush and then-Secretary of State Henry Kissinger were suspected by Chilean and Spanish prosecutors of involvement with the assassination, along with agents of Chile's dictator General Augusto Pinochet, but his son, George W. Bush, quashed American cooperation with recent Chilean and Spanish investigations of the Letelier murder.

Bush Jr. is perfectly content with chasing terrorists as long as the trail does not lead to his father and his old CIA colleagues. The right-wingers in the Republican Party have nothing but disdain for any mention of the Letelier case, even though (or perhaps because) it involved state-sponsored terrorism with the possible involvement of the elder Bush and Kissinger. In 1994, for instance, when the Institute for Policy Studies sent out invitations to its annual fundraising dinner honoring Letelier, a Republican staffer for Republican Representative Gerald Solomon of New York returned the invitation with a note: "Don't send us any more of your Communist Bull Crap."[41]

Then there is the case of Orlando Bosch, a member of the terrorist network which planted a bomb on a Cubana airline in 1976. The plane exploded in midair, killing 73 people. Later Mr. Bosch applied for residence in the United States, and the Justice Department and the INS deemed him an undesirable person, pointing to 30 years of terrorist activity including the bombing, and asked that he be barred from entry. But Orlando Bosch had a friend in Florida, a young man who wanted to be governor: his name was Jeb Bush.

He intervened with his father who was then the President of the United States, and George Bush Sr. overruled the Justice Department and the INS, and granted Orlando Bosch residence in the United States. He now walks as a free man in Miami, Florida. In fact, many individuals close to this case report that southern Florida is a virtually independent right-wing republic, acting with its own foreign policy, a foreign policy that is pampered and supported by southern Florida's Cuban GOP congressional delegation, particularly Rep. Ileana Ros-Lehtinen.

It is also noteworthy that when Bosch and his CIA-trained team bombed the Cubana airliner off of Barbados on October 6, 1976, the director of the CIA was none other than George H.W. Bush.

Less than a year after the Cuban exiles bombed the Cubana plane, I arrived for Navy duty in Barbados. The government of Barbados had called for help from the U.S. Naval Facility to assist in rescue operations, which had soon become an operation to recover bodies, including those of women and children. U.S. Navy scuba divers, as well as Navy corpsmen, assisted in the recovery operations. They were traumatized by what they had seen, but even more troubling was what they later discovered—that their own government aided and abetted in the terrorism.

An Intel Corporation activity within the deep-water harbor zone in Bridgetown turned out to be a CIA-front operation aimed at derailing leftist political parties in nearby islands like Grenada, Dominica, Antigua, St. Vincent, Trinidad, and St. Lucia. The

---

[41] Al Kamen, "In the Loop," *The Washington Post*, October 19, 1994, p. A21.

Barbadians were incensed at these activities. In the aftermath of Bush Sr.'s stewardship of the CIA, the spy agency was deeply immersed in all sorts of unsavory activities, from terrorist bombings to dealings with super-weapons designer Gerald Bull. After Jimmy Carter named Admiral Stansfield Turner as Bush's replacement, and Congress shined a light on CIA covert activities, many of the activities promoted by Bush were dismantled.

* * * *

On March 29, 2003, Orlando Bosch called for a march in Miami to support George W. Bush's military attack on Iraq. On March 22, 2004, Florida GOP Rep. Lincoln Diaz Balart called for the assassination of Fidel Castro.

Later that Spring, after Republican Senator John McCain and three other moderate GOP senators, along with moderate Democratic Senator Ben Nelson, managed to block Bush's $2.5 trillion Fiscal Year 2005 budget, much to the chagrin of the Republican leadership and the White House, McCain "joked" about what could change their minds about their continued opposition to the budget: "Some of us could get killed in tragic accidents."[42] Considering the timing and circumstances of a number of "tragic accidents" prior to and since Bush's election, including the airplane crash that killed Minnesota Senator Paul Wellstone, his family, staff, and pilots in October 2002, McCain may have been consciously or subconsciously offering more than some black humor.

In light of the activities of ISTO and other clandestine groups, a number of other suspicious deaths, based on circumstances, timing, and surrounding intelligence activities before and after 9-11, deserve a much closer look.

—§—

---

[42] "GOP leaders retreat, postpone budget vote," *Marin Independent Journal*, May 21, 2004.

A 1960's postcard showing the Breezeway in its prime.

Porter Goss' problems began when his House Permanent Select Committee on Intelligence's Executive Director, John Millis, supposedly committed suicide in this seedy Fairfax, Virginia motel. The Millis "suicide" would be the first of many problems for Goss—who would take over the CIA from George Tenet.

Goss left his post as CIA Director, while a scandal engulfed a number of his former cronies, who came under FBI investigation in a poker party and alleged hooker scandal involving jailed California Republican Congressman Randy "Duke" Cunningham, defense and intelligence contractor Brent Wilkes, Goss' executive Director Kyle "Dusty" Foggo, and former HPSCI staffer Brant "Nine Fingers" Bassett. Goss' first pick as his CIA Executive Director was another HPSCI staffer, Michael Kostiw, who left the CIA in the early 1980s after being arrested for shoplifting a package of bacon from a supermarket near the CIA headquarters. Kostiw's selection was sidelined after this information was revealed by CIA personnel office sources. Nevertheless, Goss found another senior position for Kostiw within the agency. Millis was undoubtedly well aware of Goss and his pals, and possibly was in a position in 2000 to derail Goss' future plans.

RIP: John Millis

John Millis, the late Executive Director of the House Permanent Select Committee on Intelligence (HPSCI) who allegedly committed suicide on June 4, 2000, died a day after he forced the CIA to release a controversial report dealing with cocaine trafficking. Police in Fairfax, Virginia still refuse to reveal the contents of a suicide note allegedly written by Millis. The magazine *Insight*, owned by the right-wing *Washington Times*, reported in August 2000 that its CIA sources reported that Millis killed himself after his wife, Linda, discovered he was involved in a homosexual relationship.

Friends of John and Linda Millis scoffed at this character assassination by the Moonies and confided that Linda had initiated legal proceedings against the magazine. Other CIA sources reported to the *Washington Times* that Millis committed suicide after he was accused of improperly disclosing classified information. *Washington Times* correspondent Bill Gertz, who enjoys a very close relationship with senior U.S. military and intelligence officials, including some leading neoconservatives in the Pentagon, first proffered this theory.[1]

The disinformation campaign against Millis held no water with the Association of Former Intelligence Officers (AFIO), which posted the following on its Web site: "JOHN MILLIS CHILDREN'S EDUCATION FUND—Dr. John Millis was a strong supporter of the Intelligence Community and of AFIO. His death was a tragedy. A contribution to this Education Fund established by the HPSCI staff honors a good man, a good friend and a patriot."[2]

The alleged disclosures of classified information surrounded Millis's very public condemnation of former CIA Director John Deutch. CIA officials contend that by talking publicly about Deutch's use of classified CIA computers at home to surf the Internet, Mil-

---

[1] Jamie Dettmer and Paul M. Rodriguez, "The Strange Death of John Millis," *Insight*, August 14, 2000. http://www.insightmag.com/news/2000/08/14/InvestigativeReport/ The-Strange.Death.Of.John.Millis-210701.shtml>; Bill Gertz, "Spy panel director who killed himself was under a probe," *Washington Times*, June 28, 2000.

[2] < http://www.afio.com/sections/wins/2000/2000-30.html>

lis in some way compromised the investigation of the affair by the CIA's Inspector General. Millis had said that Deutch's activities severely harmed the agency's clandestine operations.

According to well-placed congressional sources, Millis and his then-boss, HPSCI Chairman Rep. Porter Goss of Florida (who like Millis is a former CIA officer), also disagreed on many fundamental intelligence issues.

On May 11, a few weeks prior to his death, Millis authored a report on the CIA's alleged links to cocaine smuggling by Nicaraguan drug rings to gangs in Los Angeles. Although the HPSCI report, like previous reports by the CIA and Justice Department, cleared the CIA of any wrongdoing, some informed observers believe that Millis may have actually written a different version of the report that was more critical of the CIA's involvement in drug trafficking, and that he may have been silenced because he knew too much. Millis was considered by some CIA officials to be constantly wishing to "re-invent the wheel" on CIA intelligence activities.

* * * *

Former White House counsel and Clinton confidant Charles Ruff was reportedly briefed on HPSCI's findings by Millis. Ruff died on November 20, 2000. His body was found by his wife outside a shower in his home. Police ruled the death as resulting from natural causes and not foul play. It was later determined that Ruff suffered an "apparent heart attack."

A few weeks after Ruff's death, HPSCI ranking member Representative Julian Dixon, who was also briefed on the HPSCI cocaine report, died suddenly from an apparent heart attack, on December 8, 2000.

On December 10, 2004, Gary Webb, the Pulitzer Prize-winning former journalist for the *San Jose Mercury News* (and a dogged investigator whose investigation into the crack cocaine-CIA-Los Angeles story received both deserved praise from those suspicious of past CIA involvement in drug dealing and unjustified condemnation and derision from the corporate media) was found dead of an "apparent" suicide in his Sacramento home. He was working on

some hard-hitting investigative stories for the *Sacramento News &
Review*. Police reported that Webb died from a gunshot wound to
the head.

* * * *

There is also some reason to believe that Millis was unhappy with
Goss' reluctance to investigate the CIA's handling or mishandling
of alleged Mossad penetration of the White House communications system, and its failure to investigate the identity of Israel's alleged high-level U.S. government mole, the so-called "Mega." Goss
reportedly said that he was concerned that Israel had penetrated
White House communications, but he did not want to pursue any
investigation of the matter. Goss once remarked to a congressional
colleague that if anyone took a look at his Florida district, his reluctance to criticize Israel would be totally understandable.

Over considerable Democratic grumbling, Porter Goss was confirmed by the Senate as the permanent replacement for George
Tenet at the CIA in September 2004. Sources claim he did not
want any problems associated with the Millis case to derail his
chances.

But there are clearly many unanswered questions involving
Goss and the HPSCI. For example, Goss press secretary Jennifer
Millerwise abruptly resigned her position a few weeks after Millis'
death and was not available for interviews. Fairfax police refused
to release both the contents of Millis' suicide note and the Fairfax County coroner's autopsy report. The Director of Emergency
Services for Fairfax County said that he was never informed that
Millis' body had been transported into his jurisdiction, a violation
of his agency's procedures. Interestingly, Millerwise would later
surface as Vice President Cheney's press spokesperson. Later, she
worked for the Bush-Cheney 2004 re-election campaign and then
rejoined Porter Goss as his press spokesperson at the CIA. Now
married, her name is Jennifer Millerwise Dyck. Her husband, Paul
Dyck, is a former associate political director for Karl Rove who
transferred from the White House to the State Department to
work for Condoleezza Rice after she became Secretary of State.

Porter Goss' tenure as CIA Director came to an abrupt end on May 5, 2006. Amid scandals involving GOP congressmen, prostitutes, San Diego-based CIA contractors, and parties at the Watergate, in addition to difficulties with Director of National Intelligence John Negroponte, Goss resigned. The White House named his replacement—Negroponte's deputy and former National Security Agency director, General Michael Hayden.

Fairfax city detectives told residents of the city's rather seedy Breezeway Motel, where Millis allegedly took his life, not to talk to anyone about the "suicide," including the media. When asked, a female teen resident of the motel (which rents rooms for either a few hours or in periods of several months to welfare families) said that after Millis' death, she saw a few unmarked vans in the parking lot around Millis' room, one with District of Columbia license tags. The teen also told me, "Detective Boone [of the Fairfax Police Department Criminal Investigation Division] told us not to talk to anyone about what happened to that man." Congressional sources revealed that the CIA wanted to secure any copies of the drug report Millis may have had in his possession.

Senior GOP congressional and CIA officials hoped the Millis matter would simply disappear as a news item. They got their wish.

—§—

The American Enterprise Institute, the citadel of neoconservative policy making. Located not far from the White House at 1150 17th Street, Washington. DC

The perception management Rendon Group is located on the fourth floor of 1875 Connecticut Avenue in Washington, DC.

Chapter Two

America's
Disinformation Factory

In a move recalling the Nazi's *Weltanschauungskrieg* ("world view warfare"), the use of the Teutonic term "homeland" to describe the United States of America snuck into our country's lexicon like a thief in the night. The term "homeland" is not a traditional American term, and has an unsavory past usage.

Michael Ratner, vice president of the Center for Constitutional Rights, said "homeland security ... sounds like a name the Nazis would have used, like the fatherland, and it has a slight ring of repression to it."[1] Historically, the term was favored by Germany (Heimat), along with "fatherland" (Vaterland), under the Kaiser and Nazis. The right-wing Likud Party in Israel often uses the term to defend repression of Palestinians, as did former Prime Minister Yitzhak Shamir on June 10, 1990: "It is for all our enemies to know that no one knows better than Israel in the hour of need to roar like a lion and defend its homeland and security."[2]

"Homeland security" was also used by the Soviet Union to describe its own domestic defense. The USSR's Minister of Defense Marshal S. L. Sokolov, referred to homeland security (*Sovetskaia rodina*) in an article he write in 1987 in Pravda.[3] In fact, Chekists

---

[1] Julie Mason, "America Responds; Experts are skeptical of new office's command, the *Houston Chronicle*, September 22, 2001, p. 27.

[2] "Likud Bloc Clears Way For Cabinet," *St. Louis Post-Dispatch*, 11 June 1990, p. A10.

[3] Marshal of the Soviet Union S.L. Sokolov, "'Watching over peace and the homeland's security," *Pravda*, February 23, 1987.

(KGB agents) in the Soviet Union were awarded medals based on their commitment to preserving Soviet homeland security.

On May 12, 1999, the late ethnic cleanser Yugoslav President Slobodon Milosevic, declared, "I wish sincerely to greet and pay tribute to all members of the Interior Ministry and security forces for their contribution to the protection of the homeland's security, in honor of 13th May, Security Day. You have had remarkable success in crushing the separatist movement and routing its terrorist gangs in Kosovo-Metohija—who were supported by the foreign forces who have carried out the criminal aggression against our country."[4]

The National Progressive and Patriotic Front (NPPF), a rump organization of Sadaam Hussein's regime, was also fond of the term: "The NPPF parties lauded the [Iraqi] leadership's call for beginning a lengthy national discussion to adopt an appropriate national stance to protect the people's higher interests and the homeland's security and sovereignty."[5]

Apartheid-era South Africa used the term "homeland security" to describe the measures taken to crack down on opposition within the various ethnic-based "homelands" (Bantustans) that it set up to advance the cause of racial superiority and separatism. Upon majority rule, South Africa scrapped the homeland contrivances along with their security apparatuses, two of which—those of Ciskei and Bophuthatswana—were nurtured by Israeli security personnel.

Until September 11, no major Western democracy used the term "homeland security" in the context now used by the United States to describe the new measures required for public safety and security. However, in the Orwellian "New World Order" of Bush-Cheney, "homeland security" equals huge profits for American companies who have discovered that fear is a great marketing tool. In particular, a number of small companies have reaped huge profits from catering to the fears of the government and the whims of the Bush administration. For example, a num-

---

[4] "Milosevic says many members of security forces have died fighting Kosovo rebels," Radio Belgrade in Serbo-Croat, 12 May 1999, BBC Summary of World Broadcasts, May 14, 1999.

[5] "Iraq: National Progressive and Patriotic Front Discusses Statement on Sanctions," Iraqi TV, Baghdad, 31 July 1998, BBC Worldwide Monitoring, August 1, 1998.

ber of large firms and small firms alike, nestled inside and outside the Washington, DC beltway, came up with all sorts of methods to covertly monitor the personal activities of American citizens.

* * * *

It is inherent in current U.S. military doctrine that virtual "cones of silence" are brought down on information dealing with areas of conflict. Defense "information operations" war games have included interdiction of news from, to, or about particular war zones and settings.[6]

One cone of silence was created by the November 7, 2001 decision by the Bush administration to freeze the assets of two Somali companies: the Somali Internet Company and the financial and telecommunications services company, Al Barakaat. When the companies were forced to cease their operations, all Internet cafes around the country were closed and the major Internet gateway, run jointly by AT&T and British Telecom, was shut down.

The closure adversely affected the Somali government, the United Nations, local and international aid agencies throughout the country, and two autonomous regions in Somalia generally friendly to the West—Somaliland[7] and Puntland[8]—which could have been quite valuable friendly assets. At the same time there were reports that teams of U.S. Special Forces and CIA were combing Somalia in preparation for a U.S. attack against terrorist targets.[9] The cone of silence brought down on Somalia thus seemed to have more to do with U.S. military information operations than actually stemming terrorism.

The idea of the Internet serving as a virtual unlimited source of information irks counter-terrorism planners. They are arguing that

---

[6] "Military Lessons in Twisting the Truth," *Intelligence Newsletter*, No. 376, February 17, 2000.

[7] "Attacks on Somalia openly discussed," Afro News, 29 November 2001. http://www.afrol.com/Categories/terrorism.htm; Karl Vick, "Fighting in Somalia Draws U.S. Attention," *Washington Post*, November 29, 2001, p. A28. http://www.washingtonpost.com/ac2/wp-dyn?pagename=article&node=&contentId=A31119-2001Nov28

[8] Hassan Barise, BBC Correspondent, "US shuts down Somalia internet," BBC Africa Service, 23 November 2001.

[9] Bob Drogin and Paul Watson, "Battlefield Clues Key to Bush's Next Step," *Los Angeles Times*, 9 December 2001. < http://www.latimes.com/news/printedition/asection/la-000097775dec09.story>

what the government deems to be sensitive should be removed from the Web. Decision Support Systems, Inc., in an intelligence study paper, claimed that Al Qaeda directly benefited from the information provided by the Internet. It recommended that the U.S. government take measures to prevent the Internet from providing "open source intelligence" to the adversary. "The U.S. free market and transparency," the report contends, "dramatically reduces Al-Qaida decision cycle costs—capability acquisition (channel, training), data-information acquisition, transaction costs, operational costs, etc."[10]

The scope of the policy of information interdiction was never more evident than on October 10, 2001, when National Security Adviser Condoleezza Rice, in a conference call to the heads of five U.S. networks (ABC, NBC, CBS, CNN, and Fox), persuaded them to "voluntarily comply" with a White House request to limit their broadcasting of speeches by Osama bin Laden that were being carried over the Arab satellite network Al Jazeera. Rice was concerned about the spread of propaganda and the potential for Bin Laden to transmit coded messages to his operatives. Critics pointed out that Bin Laden's Arabic speeches in text and streaming video were available on the Internet; so the idea that he could send coded messages through English translations was far-fetched at best.

On October 3, 2001, Secretary of State Powell urged visiting Emir of Qatar to restrain the broadcasts of Al Jazeera, which is based in the Emirate. Al Jazeera had featured taped interviews with Bin Laden, interviews with anti-American political leaders, and broadcasts favorable to the Palestinians. Ironically, the Emir of Qatar had to press upon Powell the need for a "free and credible media."[11] Eventually, Powell's persuasion succeeded when Al Jazeera also agreed to limit the amount of airtime it gave to Bin Laden's taped statements.

By early 2002, as White House officials back-peddled and waffled on revelations surrounding the Pentagon's short-lived Office

<hr>

[10] Decision Support Systems, Inc., "Hunting the Sleepers: Tracking Al Qaida's Covert Operatives," 31 December 2001. <http://www.metatempo.com/huntingthesleepers.pdf>

[11] Andrea Koppel and Elise Labott, "U.S. pressures Qatar to restrain TV outlet," CNN, 3 October 2001.

of Strategic Influence (OSI), the expansion of psychological warfare operations (psyops) and their inherent influencing of the media had been on military planning drawing boards for some time. Countless Pentagon study commissions and panels have issued public reports and white papers on the need to limit free information flows in time of war. A common theme of Pentagon information operations personnel is that "the press is against us."

When senior White House officials expressed dismay that whoever leaked the story concerning the OSI did a disservice to President Bush while he was conferring with leaders in Asia, they failed to check the daybooks and calendars of senior Pentagon officials. It had been Principle Deputy Assistant Secretary of Defense Robert Andrews who first publicly admitted the existence of the office at a defense industry seminar in Arlington, Virginia on February 7, 2002. Andrews was very clear about the nature of "strategic influence" when he said that it "concentrates on delivering messages to targeted audiences ... and controlling channels of communications."

Appearing on Andrews' panel was Brigadier General Simon ("Pete") Worden, the former head of the defunct OSI. Worden reported to Undersecretary of Defense for Policy and Plans Douglas Feith. Worden had a long history of selling new defense policies to international audiences. While a major, he had worked for then-Vice President George H. W. Bush in explaining "Star Wars" to a worldwide audience. Before assuming his job as head of OSI, he was Deputy Defense Secretary Paul Wolfowitz's communications director. He also awarded a $70,000 per month propaganda contract to the Rendon Group, a public relations firm with longstanding links to the CIA, which worked closely with the U.S. Army's 4th Psychological Operations Group.[12]

Bush II surrounded himself with people who championed disinformation programs. He named as his new counter-terrorism chief, retired Army General Wayne Downing. Downing, in turn, named an old friend, retired Army Colonel Jeffrey Jones, to be the Special Assistant to the President for Strategic Communications and Information. General Worden stated that Jones was charged with integrating "strategic influence" across the U.S. government.

---

[12] "Consultants Preparing for War in Iraq," *Intelligence Online*, December 5, 2002.

Since Jones worked in the National Security Council alongside Bush's National Security Advisor Condoleezza Rice, the President was surely aware of the Pentagon's plans to conduct disinformation campaigns. But if the President was out of the loop when these plans were hatched—perhaps clearing brush at the ranch—such plans must have been known to senior policy makers in the West Wing, including Karen Hughes and Karl Rove, the president's senior counselors.

But Hughes appeared to be unaware of what President Bush's new homeland security advisors were up to. With the Pentagon having other ideas concerning the feeding of disinformation to the international media, Hughes failed to clear with her boss her own stated commitment to provide reporters with "the facts." The information war planners at the Pentagon declared that their goals were to interdict and censor news, something the Pentagon called "influence operations." Worden declared in February 2002 that the Pentagon "can control the Internet, the electromagnetic spectrum, radio, and television."

One of Worden's colleagues, Lieutenant Colonel Brad Ward, the head of the "International Military Information Group," a relatively new group within the State Department's International Information Programs (IIP) Bureau, was even more precise about the Pentagon's activities. Ward revealed that his group worked with the Voice of America on influence operations. From its base within the State Department, he said, the military operated Internet sites in seven languages directed at select foreign media in targeted countries, and ran "secondary radio stations" that broadcast programs through the auspices of Non-Governmental Organizations (NGOs). A more troubling aspect of Ward's operations was found in his statement that his group assisted in the UN War Crimes Tribunals in The Hague and Arusha, Tanzania to "discredit rebel factions." Such a revelation threw into question the fairness of the trials.

Ward also admitted other "successes" of his group:

• It worked on the Serbian presidential election campaign to "ensure Slobodon Milosevic did not get elected."

• It operated Internet sites in seven languages that were password protected, but gave select foreign media access in targeted countries.

• It worked with the UN Security Council in certain "support missions."

• It produced videos illustrating the crimes of Liberian President Charles Taylor in Conakry, Guinea for distribution in Liberia.

• It was involved in "detaining operations" at Camp X Ray and Camp Delta in Guantanamo Bay, Cuba.

More ominously, Ward disclosed that his group would be supplemented by a 20-person Operational Center, which was to draw from CIA and other intelligence personnel. People who live by the maxim "when you screw up, you cover up" thus were able to decide what the U.S. government wrote and broadcast to foreign audiences. And such propaganda did not stop abroad—when false stories were run by foreign news agencies they were frequently picked up by U.S. media outlets.

During the Iraq war, the Pentagon's disinformation factory expanded its role to include the "embedding" of journalists who spun Pentagon propaganda to their broadcast networks, newspapers, and magazines. It was revealed by *The Washington Post* in April 2006 that the exploits Jordanian "Al Qaeda" terrorist Abu Musab al Zarqawi was purposefully hyped by the Pentagon to make him appear more dangerous than he was and convince the American people that the presence of Zarqawi in Iraq linked the 9-11 attacks to the Iraq war. Internal Pentagon documents revealed that one of the targets of the Pentagon disinformation campaign about Zarqawi was the "U.S. Home Audience." The *Post* quoted comments made to an Army meeting in Fort Leavenworth, Kansas by Col. Derek Harvey, a U.S. Army intelligence officer in Iraq: "Our own focus on Zarqawi has enlarged his caricature, if you will -- made him more important than he really is, in some ways ... The long-term threat is not Zarqawi or religious extremists, but these former regime types and their friends." Brig. Gen. Mark Kimmitt, the Pentagon's chief spokesman in Iraq, said, "The Zarqawi PSYOP program is the most successful information campaign to date." [13]

[13] Thomas E. Ricks, "Military Plays Up Role of Zarqawi; Jordanian Painted As Foreign Threat To Iraq's Stability," *The Washington Post*, April 10, 2006, p. A01.

The Pentagon's ruse worked. Many media outlets reported that the acts of violence in Iraq were the work of foreign terrorists linked to Al Qaeda and not nationalists fighting the U.S. occupation. An Army-produced PSYOP videotape on the human rights abuses of Saddam Hussein was actually broadcast on Fox News.[14]

* * * *

The fact that Ward's group represented a military psyops component within a State Department bureau that had once been the independent U.S. Information Agency should have troubled anyone concerned with receiving untainted news from its own government. It should come as no surprise that it was retiring arch-conservative Senator Jesse Helms, wielding the power of Senate Foreign Relations Committee chairman, who had forced the USIA to come under the State Department's bureaucratic umbrella in 1997. That move effectively made the entire U.S. public diplomacy apparatus vulnerable to the professional propagandists and deceivers within the military and intelligence community.

Even America's infamous School of the Americas at Fort Benning, Georgia discovered the public relations and media manipulation business. Renamed the Western Hemisphere Institute for Security Cooperation, the school, which had trained some of Latin America's most brutal dictators and death squads, spent $250,000 to track what the media was reporting about the school, and to respond to negative news reports by sending letters to the editors of newspapers. The tracking system also focused on the activities of Roman Catholic Father Roy Bourgeois, the founder of School of the Americas Watch.[15]

Efforts by the State Department to portray Bush administration policies in a favorable light abroad were shaken by the abrupt resignations of two people brought in to head the State Department Public Affairs Bureau as Undersecretary of State. The first person to handle the job, Charlotte Beers, a New York advertising executive, resigned in March 2003 after an unsuccessful campaign to improve U.S. relations with the Muslim world. Her replace-

---

[14] Ibid.
[15] "Image Problems," *The Progressive*, April 005.

ment, Margaret Tutwiler, the former spokesperson for Secretary of State James Baker III and ambassador to Morocco, announced she would resign on June 30, 2004, the same day the Bush administration planned to transfer sovereignty to an Iraqi transitional government. In March 2005, Bush named former White House communications director Karen Hughes to take over what was largely considered to be a failed propaganda program. With Bush's National Security Adviser Condoleezza Rice taking over as Secretary of State, diplomats in the United States and abroad feared the U.S. foreign policy apparatus would become a surrogate for the neoconservatives—a subservient bureaucracy that would serve the right-wing agenda in the same manner that both the Defense Department under Rumsfeld and his neoconservative cell, and the CIA under Porter Goss, became echo chambers for the Bush-Cheney White House.

The Pentagon disinformation machine was also used to hoodwink people here and abroad about the true nature of U.S. military involvement in certain locations. Ed Frothingham, the chief assistant to the Deputy Assistant Secretary of Defense for Counternarcotics, stated that Special Operations Forces (SOF) counternarcotics personnel were using their presence in certain countries to pave the way for access by other U.S. military forces. He conceded that some countries that "don't want a U.S. military presence get around this by letting in SOF for counter-narcotics and law enforcement." Frothingham emphasized that the presence of such forces in Uzbekistan in the summer of 2001 paved the way for U.S. military forces to enter the country in OPERATION STRONGHOLD FREEDOM, subsequent to the 9-11 terrorist attacks on New York and Washington. His boss, Andrews, re-emphasized that the counter-narcotics role played by U.S. SOF in Uzbekistan "allowed us to go in later." It was the same template that had been used for U.S. special operations missions in Colombia and Peru.

* * * *

When Secretary of Defense Donald Rumsfeld claimed that the OSI and its mission were only embryonic and misunderstood—

including his assertion that the "Pentagon does not lie"—the statements of his own subordinates pointed in another direction. Rumsfeld eventually announced he was scrapping OSI in its entirety, but this was disinformation in itself. The OSI became the Office of Special Plans (OSP), the Pentagon group that concocted the phony reasons why Saddam Hussein was a threat and why a war was absolutely necessary. The professional deceivers had carved out a new protected niche in the Bush administration.

The OSP got to work immediately on hyping the Iraq threat. It used two public relations firms to carry out its disinformation program—The Rendon Group and Benador Associates.

The Rendon Group had some experience in hyping news about Saddam Hussein. It also had close ties to the Bush family. It was Rendon that developed the propaganda used against Panama's Manuel Noriega prior to George H. W. Bush's 1989 military assault against him in Operation Blue Spoon, Plan 90-2, and Operation Just Cause. Former Democratic political operative John W. Rendon founded the firm and runs its Washington, DC operation, while his brother Rick, a senior partner, runs the Boston office. John Rendon's wife, Sandra Libby, also works with him on his various propaganda endeavors. I asked Vice-Presidential press secretary Jennifer Millerwise if Sandra Libby was related to Cheney's Chief of Staff I. Lewis ("Scooter") Libby. She said that she asked Libby, who had responded, "Sandra? Never heard of her!" It was an odd response from someone who was a key person in the efforts of the White House Iraq Group and Rendon to hype the Iraq war.

During the elder Bush's administration, Rendon received a lucrative contract from the Citizens for a Free Kuwait, which in effect, was the exiled Kuwaiti government. Before Operation Desert Storm, it was Rendon that produced a tearful exiled Kuwaiti nurse who told a panel co-chaired by Democratic Representative Tom Lantos and Republican Representative John Porter a story that proved false: that she personally witnessed Iraqi soldiers throwing Kuwaiti babies out of incubators. It was later revealed the "nurse" was the daughter of the Kuwaiti ambassador to the United States.[16] That sort of disinformation ploy would be reused for the

---

[16] Rachel Van Dongen, "US's 'private army' grows," *Christian Science Monitor*, September 3, 2003, p. 6.

invasion of Iraq, namely in hyping weapons of mass destruction and links to Al Qaeda.

The Rendon Group also got involved in other psychological warfare efforts, from Zimbabwe to Kosovo and from Haiti to Colombia. In fact, Rendon told the U.S. Air Force Academy in 1996, "I am an information warrior and a perception manager."[17] Both areas form the core of a new U.S. defense strategy cobbled together by blue-ribbon task forces convened by the Defense Policy and Science Boards throughout the 1990s. This policy put a military imprimatur on Orwell's "Newspeak" and "Ministry of Truth."

Rendon had honed its skills when it received a contract to represent Panamanian opposition leader Guillermo Endara, the U.S. supported candidate against Noriega's candidate in Panama's 1989 presidential election. The first Bush administration contributed $10 million to Endara's campaign, and Endara reported that payments from him to Rendon were made through an account at Miami's Dadeland Bank.[18] In April 1990, the U.S. government froze accounts at Dadeland Bank that were used to launder money for Colombian drug cartels.[19]

Rendon received a contract from the Pentagon to run the Balkan Information Exchange, a propaganda-oriented Web site, and a USAID contract to "promote privatization."[20] In Afghanistan, Rendon, under contract to the Pentagon, set up a similar propaganda center called the Coalition Information Center, with offices in Washington, London, and Islamabad, to counter such charges as that the U.S. committed atrocities in Mazar-i-Sharif. Rendon reportedly earned a "small fortune" from the effort.[21]

During DESERT STORM, Rendon had handed out American flags to newly liberated Kuwaitis to wave at incoming U.S. troops. Afterwards, Rendon landed a five-year contract from the CIA to support the Iraqi National Congress (INC) of Ahmed Chalabi, the close confidant of a neoconservative cabal in the Pentagon, consisting mainly of Richard Perle, Paul Wolfowitz, Abram Shul-

---

[17] Stephen J. Hedges, "U.S. pays PR guru to make its points; Firm's Pentagon work is lucrative, and top secret," *Chicago Tribune*, May 12, 2002, p. 1C.
[18] Ibid.
[19] "U.S. lists banks with cartel's drug money," *USA Today*, April 18, 1990, p. 6A.
[20] Ibid.
[21] Foer, op. cit.

sky, Douglas Feith, and Harold Rhode. In 1995, the CIA launched an audit of Rendon's spending on the INC. It was estimated that Rendon associates in London earned $19,000 per month, more than the salary of the CIA director. It was estimated that Rendon spent $23 million in the first year of the company's work for the INC.[22]

Another Rendon connection to the neocons was its former employee Linda Flohr, a CIA clandestine services officer who went to work for Rendon after she left the agency, and then joined Bush's Office of Homeland Security and National Security Council, where she worked as deputy for Counterterrorism chief retired General Wayne Downing.[23] The National Security Council also housed the leading neoconservatives Stephen Hadley, who succeeded Condoleezza Rice as director, and former Iran-Contra felon Elliot Abrams, who was put in charge of the Middle East and human rights issues.

During OPERATION IRAQI FREEDOM, Rendon suffered a killed-in-action when one of its employees in Iraq, Paul Moran, an Australian cameraman, was killed by a suicide bomber.[24] Moran was working for Rendon as part of a contracted U.S. government propaganda program called OPERATION EMPOWER PEACE. Its purpose was to sway public opinion about Iraq throughout the Arab world.[25]

During the war against the Taliban, one former Rendon employee, Francis Brooke had questioned Rendon's effectiveness. Brooke said that Rendon's London office, located on Catherine Street near Buckingham Palace, had been staffed by a "room full of employees who had difficulty in culturally adapting to London, let alone the Middle East."[26] Brooke and his associate Margaret Bartel later faced the wrath of the politically connected Rendon network, when U.S. Iraq administrator for Iraq Paul Bremer charged them with obstruction of justice during a U.S. military/Dyncorp raid of

---

[22] Ibid.

[23] Greg Hazley, "Rendon brothers 'empower' peace and help with war," *O'Dwyer's PR Services Report*, June 2003, p. 11.

[24] Jack O'Dwyer, "TRG Advises 'Combatant Commanders,'" *Jack O'Dwyer's Newsletter*, June 11, 2003, p. 11.

[25] Hazley, op. cit.

[26] Ken Silverstein, "Selling the Afghan War," *The Nation*, November 7, 2001.

Ahmad Chalabi's Baghdad offices. The two public relations specialists, still working for Chalabi under a DIA contract, claimed that the charges, which were later dropped, were trumped up after Chalabi fell out of favor with the White House.[27]

Prior to the Iraqi invasion, one Arabic translator for Rendon spoke of the preparations by the firm for the psyops efforts: "All I can say is that nothing has changed—the work is still an expensive waste of time, mostly with taxpayer funds."[28]

Rendon's client, the Iraqi National Congress, was the outfit that produced an Iraqi informant code-named "Curveball." An Iraqi exile, who in 1988 claimed to the German intelligence agency, the Bundesnachrichtendienst (BND), that he worked on Saddam Hussein's mobile chemical laboratories, Curveball sold Secretary of State Colin Powell the story about two Iraqi mobile biological weapons laboratories. This became a key factor in Powell's February 5, 2003 briefing to the UN Security Council.

Although Powell told the Security Council, "What we are telling you is based on facts and conclusions drawn from solid intelligence reports," this statement was false. It was later discovered that Curveball was the cousin of a senior aide to Chalabi, and his "story" was a complete fraud: yet another in a long line of disinformation campaigns developed by the INC's American disinformation contractors.

The bogus intelligence from Curveball, known to U.S. intelligence to be a liar and drunkard, came via the DIA's Information Collection Program, a multimillion-dollar program actually run by the INC and designed to produce intelligence from within Iraq. What the DIA program actually provided was phony intelligence cooked up by Chalabi and his associates. The Presidents Bush each used some of these lies to support wars against Iraq.[29]

Rendon may also have provided some advice about beating up on seasoned Scandinavian diplomats over Iraq policy. Prior to the neoconservative attack on UN Swedish chief weapons inspector Hans Blix, Rendon had battered former Finnish President Mar-

---

[27] Richard Leiby," The Reliable Source," *The Washington Post*, March 24, 2005.

[28] Ian Urbina, "Broadcast Ruse," *The Village Voice*, November 19, 2002, p. 32.

[29] Markus Wendler, "Powell's Unsound German Sources," Deutsche Welle, April 6, 2004; Edward Helmore, "US relied on 'drunken liar' to justify war," *The Observer* (London), April 3, 2005.

tti Ahtisaari, who was opposed to the disastrous UN sanctions on Iraq.30 During 2004 and 2005, Rendon continued to hold a major Pentagon contract with the U.S. Strategic Command to conduct "foreign media analysis."

* * * *

Two companies with financial links to Chalabi, Nour USA Ltd., and Erinys Iraq, an associated firm, were awarded more than $400 million in contracts by the U.S. authorities in Iraq to provide security for the Iraqi oil industry and services for the Iraqi army. Erinys's counsel was Salem Chalabi, a nephew of Ahmed Chalabi. Salem Chalabi was later named by the U.S. Coalition Provisional Authority to head up the tribunal that would prosecute Saddam Hussein. Salem's partner in his Baghdad law firm is Marc Zell, the Jerusalem-based former law partner of the Pentagon's Undersecretary for Policy and Plans Douglas Feith. Zell and Feith were also colleagues of Ledeen and Richard Perle, who resigned as a member of the Defense Policy Board amid allegations of wrongdoing with regard to the Hollinger Corporation's stock scandal. Perle headed Hollinger Digital, part of Conrad Black's neoconservative publishing empire that owned the *Jerusalem Post*, *Chicago Sun-Times*, and *Daily Telegraph*. Not as well known was the fact that Perle was once employed by the Israeli weapons manufacturer Soltam, and was a lobbyist for the Israeli defense industry.[31]

While Perle was working his way up the food chain in Senator Scoop Jackson's office and the Reagan Pentagon, his understudy was Paul Wolfowitz, whom a Republican senator once called a dangerously dogmatic "weirdo."[32] Wolfowitz spurred the Bush administration's modern Crusade against Islam as advocated by Harvard Professor Samuel P. Huntington is his book *The Clash of Civilizations*. Following his screeds about the dangers of Muslims, Huntington took up another ideological cause, warning that America has another enemy: Hispanics. Writing in *Foreign Policy*, Huntington posited,

---

[30] Foer, op. cit.
[31] "The Pentagon's Dynamic Duo: Richard Perle and Paul Wolfowitz," op. cit.
[32] Ibid.

The persistent inflow of Hispanic immigrants threatens to divide the United States into two peoples, two cultures, and two languages. Unlike past immigrant groups, Mexicans and other Latinos have not assimilated into mainstream U.S. culture, forming instead their own political and linguistic enclaves—from Los Angeles to Miami—and rejecting the Anglo-Protestant values that built the American dream. The United States ignores this challenge at its peril.[33]

In Iraq U.S. defense contractors were awarded contracts to develop the Iraqi news media along propagandistic and sensationalistic American lines. On January 8, 2004, Florida-based Harris Corporation was awarded a $100 million contract by the Coalition Provisional Authority (CPA) to establish the Iraqi Media Network (IMN). Iraqi Communications Minister Haider Abadi expressed frustration that he was not consulted about the award beforehand, and said he viewed the contract as "giving too much control to the American government and media."[34] Harris inherited the contract from Science Applications International Corporation (SAIC), a defense and intelligence contractor that has done covert work in trouble spots from Indonesia to Rwanda and Bosnia to Kuwait. The CPA said the purpose of IMN was to replace Saddam's Ministry of Information apparatus. But soon, the CPA expelled international networks it could not control, including Dubai-based Al Arabiya and Qatar-based Al Jazeera.

On March 11, 2003, the Pentagon awarded SAIC a sole-source $15 million contract to run the IMN. By September 2003, SAIC had overrun costs to a whopping $82.3 million. Moreover, the SAIC work was an utter failure. Former NBC News correspondent Don North, who consulted on the project, wrote, "IMN has become an irrelevant mouthpiece for Coalition Provisional Authority propaganda, managed news and mediocre programs." The Pentagon's Inspector General found several examples of waste in the IMN project. One SAIC manager bought a Hummer H2 and a Ford C-350 pickup truck for himself, and chartered a DC-10 cargo jet

---

[33] Samuel P. Huntington, "The Hispanic Challenge," *Foreign Policy*, March-April 2004. <http://www.foreignpolicy.com/story/cms.php?story_id=2495>

[34] "U.S. Firm Awarded Contract to Run Iraqi Media Network," News Hour, PBS, January 12, 2004.

to fly the vehicles into Iraq. One SAIC invoice identified as "Office and Vehicle" totaled some $381,000.[35]

Another public relations firm linked to Rendon from at least 2004 was the Lincoln Group, headed by British-born Christian Jozefowicz, who later changed his name to Christian Bailey. Already linked to the Young Republicans, the organization that nurtured Karl Rove and Jack Abramoff, Bailey formed the Lincoln Group in 1999 as a "business intelligence" firm. Just before the Iraq war, Bailey and a former Marine named Page Craig formed a Lincoln Asset Management subsidiary called Lincoln Alliance Corporation. Also formed was an additional subsidiary called Iraqex. Lincoln also shared phone and fax numbers with a firm called Omnicept for which Page was listed as a point of contact. Soon, the thirty-something Bailey and Page landed 20 Pentagon contracts, including one worth $100 million.

The firm was also active in Lebanon, Afghanistan, Colombia, Indonesia and other neocon bridgeheads for global domination around the world. Lincoln planned to move into the same building that housed the defunct Pennsylvania Avenue restaurant "Signatures," the GOP lobbying and campaign contribution laundering business owned by Abramoff.[36] One Lincoln Group contract with the Pentagon was to translate into Arabic and place within Iraqi newspapers U.S. military-generated propaganda disguised as actual news articles. Lincoln group employees and contractors masqueraded as freelance journalists and turned in the fake stories to Iraqi media outlets. The Pentagon's disinformation operation was run out of the Information Operations Task Force—a unit buried deep within the bowels of the Pentagon and the U.S. military command in Baghdad.[37] The unit assumed much of the responsibilities of the defunct Office of Strategic Influence.

* * * *

[35] Bruce Bigelow, "Report rips SAIC over Iraq contracts," *San Diego Union-Tribune*, March 25, 2004.

[36] Justin Fox, "Secret No More: Inside the Pentagon's Iraqi PR Firm," *Fortune*, January 20, 2006; Jason Vest, "The Hazy Story of the Lincoln Group, *Government Executive*, November 30, 2005.

[37] Mark Mazzetti and Borzou Daragahi, "U.S. Military Covertly Pays to Run Stories in Iraqi Press," *Los Angeles Times*, November 30, 2005.

Another company at the forefront of America's disinformation factory is Benador Associates, a firm with offices in New York, London, and Paris that is tied umbilically to the neoconservatives. Founded by the Peruvian-born Swiss-American Eleana Benador, her company, which employs one assistant and one part-timer, acts as a virtual news agency for the neoconservative movement. Benador was described by a *Guardian* columnist as a champion for the "total war and creative destruction crowd."[38]

Benador actually described herself as a "liberal neocon," a term that could also apply to Connecticut's Democratic Senator Joseph Lieberman, an ardent supporter of the war in Iraq and a friend of Benador's.[39] Benador Associates usually fronts for the Foundation for the Defense of Democracies, the Hudson Institute (where Perle served as a Trustee), the Washington Institute for Near East Policy (WINEP) (where Perle serves as an adviser), the Middle East Forum, Freedom House, and the American Enterprise Institute (where Perle was a Senior Fellow).[40]

Benador consistently organized press conferences featuring Richard Perle, including one that rolled out *An End to Evil: How to Win the War on Terror*, Perle's book co-authored with George W. Bush's former speechwriter, David Frum (of "Axis of Evil" fame). Benador also produced a pro-Iraq invasion press conference at the National Press Club that featured Perle and Kanan Makiya, a rather odd Iraqi exile who believes that the Dome of the Rock (or Al Aqsa Mosque) in Jerusalem is the Third Jewish Temple of Israel, and that Mohammed never ascended into heaven from the spot where the mosque now stands.

Makiya also believes that Islam was an offshoot of Judaism and that Muslims and Jews were originally allied against the Christian Byzantine Empire. He outlines his unconventional beliefs in his book, *The Rock: A Tale of Seventh-Century Jerusalem*.[41] This press

---

[38] Brian Whitaker, "Conflict and Catchphrases," *The Guardian*, February 24, 2003.

[39] Holly Yeager, "Power Behind the Throne - Eleana Benador," *Financial Times*, August 9, 2003, p. 10.

[40] According to a Nixon administration top adviser, Lynne Cheney, the wife of Vice President Cheney, also maintained a senior fellowship at the American Enterprise Institute. Her $125,000 chair, according to the former White House official, was funded directly from sources linked to the scandal-plagued Israeli Likud Party.

[41] Nick Cohen, "A question of faith; By challenging religious orthodoxy, Kanan Makiya has offended Left and Right, Jew and Muslim," *The Observer*, May 12, 2002.

conference with Makiya was the venue for Perle's fatuous prognosis that American troops would be welcomed to Iraq by throngs of cheering Iraqis throwing flowers and candy at them.

Makiya also just happened to run Makiya Associates, an Iraqi architectural and building company that hoped to cash in on Iraqi rebuilding efforts, including the construction of a Saddam "atrocities museum" modeled on the Holocaust Memorial Museum in Washington.[42] Makiya's father, Mohammed Makiya, was one of Saddam Hussein's top architects, and helped build the dictator's spacious and opulent palaces.

Benador also publicized the anti-State Department book written by the *National Review*'s muckraking journalist Joel Mowbray. A televised interview of Mowbray by televangelist Pat Robertson, who plugged Mowbray's book, *Dangerous Diplomacy: How the State Department Threatens America's Security*, ended with Robertson calling for someone to carry a nuclear weapon inside the State Department and set it off. (I immediately provided a tip about Robertson's threat to the FBI's counter-terrorism Web site, stressing that I lived some four miles from State's Foggy Bottom headquarters, and was concerned about the threat to detonate a nuclear weapon there. My tip went unanswered by the Bureau.)

Benador also enjoys a close relationship with the leading neoconservative media outlets, including the *New York Sun*, *Jerusalem Post*, *Washington Times*, *Weekly Standard*, *National Review*, *National Post*, *New York Post*, *Daily Telegraph*, *New Republic*, and the *Wall Street Journal*. They, and the "liberal neocon" *Washington Post*, have all run a number of articles written by Benador's neoconservative clients. Benador runs a speaker's bureau for a number of well-known neoconservative pundits, including Richard Perle, Michael Ledeen, the Center for Defense Policy's Frank Gaffney, the *Jerusalem Post*'s editor Tom Rose, former CIA chief James Woolsey, former Secretary of State Alexander Haig, columnist Charles Krauthammer, the anti-Arab polemicist Richard Pipes, WINEP's Patrick Clawson, the Council on Foreign Relations resident neoconservative Max Boot, Hudson's Meyrav Wurmser, the *New York Times*'s former star reporter Judith Miller, Fox News foreign affairs

---

[42] Robert F. Worth, "Museum on Saddam's atrocities to be built, but who will tell the story?" *International Herald Tribune*, September 10, 2003.

analyst Mansoor Ijaz, author Laurie Mylroie, Hillel Fradkin, and Michael Rubin (a supporter of the return of the Shah's son, Reza Pahlavi, to the Peacock Throne of Iran).

Benador also fronted for Khidhir Hamza, the former Iraqi nuclear expert whose claims that Saddam possessed a nuclear capability were later debunked by chief UN weapons inspector Hans Blix, U.S. weapons inspector David Kay, Treasury Secretary Paul O'Neill, U.S. ambassador Joseph Wilson, Bush counter-terrorism coordinator Richard Clarke, and countless other US and foreign government officials. Benador said that Makiya and Hamza are "really my most powerful voices right now," adding that her firm was "more of a mission than a business."[43] In fact, she said that clients like Perle and Woolsey "don't pay her a dime,"[44] though she also credited Woolsey with helping her company get started.[45]

Eleana Benador, who is married to Emmanuel Benador, a Swiss art dealer, became associated with the neoconservative cause in 2000, through her involvement with Richard Pipes' Philadelphia-based Middle East Forum. She established Benador Associates in October 2001, only a month after 9-11. Currently, she divides her time between anti-terrorism and art history. Like Teresa Heinz Kerry, Benador comes from a family of doctors, speaks French, and worked for a while as a UN translator. Her company's disinformation efforts directly aided and abetted the march to war in Iraq.

* * * *

Another small, and equally important, disinformation mill is the Middle East Media Research Institute (MEMRI), which translates the Arab media, publicizing Islamist fundamentalist stories that are rabidly anti-Israeli and anti-American. MEMRI was co-founded by the Hudson Institute's Meyrav Wurmser and Colonel Yigal Carmon, a former Mossad officer. MEMRI is a murky tax-exempt organization, run from a Washington, DC post office box—a classic brass plate operation. Not surprisingly, MEMRI

[43] Jim Lobe, "The Andean Condor Who Deploys The Hawks," IPS-Inter Press Service, August 13, 2003.
[44] Joe Hagan, "She's Richard Perle's Oyster," *New York Observer*, April 7, 2003, p. 1.
[45] Lobe, op. cit.

also maintains offices in Jerusalem and London. MEMRI's "contributions" to the news media have, not surprisingly, been cited in neocon media outlets such as the *New York Sun, Weekly Standard, New York Post,* Fox News, *Wall Street Journal, Sunday Times of London, World Net Daily, Washington Times,* and UPI.[46]

MEMRI widely publicized a story in a new Iraqi newspaper named Al-Mada regarding alleged cash payoffs of Western politicians by Saddam Hussein's government. The list, ostensibly taken from Saddam Hussein's government's archives, was said to contain the names of 270 former government officials, legislators, political activists and journalists from more than forty-six countries, who stood accused of personally profiting from oil money garnered by Saddam Hussein as part of the United Nations food-for-oil deal. Very little was known about Al-Mada, and, considering the fact that propaganda was the modus operandi of Ahmad Chalabi and his Washington promoters, the payola story appeared to be another masterful work by the neoconservative media network both in Iraq and Washington.[47] It was later revealed that Al Mada was one of the favorite targets for the pro-U.S., propaganda "news" stories supplied by the Pentagon through the Lincoln Group.[48]

Neoconservative involvement in the Al-Mada story was clearly indicated by its revelation that it had first showed to the Hollinger-owned *Daily Telegraph* some alleged incriminating documents from the Iraqi Oil Ministry that were later used to create the list. In 2003, the *Daily Telegraph* had been caught disseminating disinformation about documents its Baghdad correspondent "found" in the ruins of the Iraqi Intelligence Ministry. The paper suggested that British Labor Member of Parliament George Galloway had received bribes from Saddam. The documents were later proved to be crude forgeries. In the case of the Al-Mada list, Agence France Presse reported from Baghdad that Al-Mada's management "refused to disclose how the daily procured the documents."[49]

---

[46] "The Pentagon's Dynamic Duo: Richard Perle and Paul Wolfowitz," *Washington Report on Middle East Affairs*, April 1, 2003, p. 14.

[47] Wayne Madsen, "Another outrageous lie from the neocons," *Online Journal*, February 5, 2004. <http://www.onlinejournal.com/Special_Reports/020504Madsen/020504madsen.html>

[48] Mazzetti and Daragahi, *op. cit.*

[49] Wayne Madsen, *Online Journal,* op. cit.

In May 2005, the U.S. Senate Permanent Subcommittee on Investigations, chaired by Minnesota Republican Norm Coleman, known as a large benefactor of AIPAC funding, regurgitated the Saddam oil payment charges against Galloway, in addition to former French Interior Minister Charles Pasqua, former French Foreign Minister Jean-Pierre Chevenement, Russian opposition leader Vladimir Zhironovsky, and other politicians. Galloway, newly elected as the anti-war Respect Party's Member of Parliament for London's Bethnal Green and Bow constituency, flew to Washington and appeared before Coleman's committee to refute the charges and to declare Coleman's evidence forgeries.

Curiously, the Al-Mada list of alleged recipients of Saddam Hussein's cash included Glencore Ltd., of Switzerland, which was headed by American fugitive Marc Rich, later pardoned by Bill Clinton. If the list was authentic, by naming Glencore, Saddam's payoffs implicated Rich's former attorney, who was none other than Lewis "Scooter" Libby, long Vice President Cheney's chief of staff, and an important neoconservative.[50]

* * * *

The disinformation factory in the Pentagon was at the forefront of creating phony "intelligence" to convince the American people that the war with Iraq was an urgent matter of national security. Intelligence officials close to the investigation by the FBI into the creation of bogus Niger government documents regarding attempts by Saddam Hussein to obtain yellowcake uranium from that West African nation focused on the relationship between Bush administration consultant Michael Ledeen and Iranian businessman and former Iran-Contra figure Manucher Ghorbanifar.

The Niger documents first appeared in Rome and were offered to the U.S. Embassy there by Elisabetta Burba, a journalist working for the Silvio Berlusconi-owned *Panorama* magazine. Berlusconi became even more beloved by the xenophobic neoconservatives when he stated in Berlin on September 26, 2001, that the West "should be confident of the superiority of our civilization,"

---

[50] Ibid.

and "Europe should reconstitute itself on the basis of its Christian roots."[51] Berlusconi's right-wing coalition had its own political roots in the Fascist movement of Benito Mussolini.

Ghorbanifar, who owns shady businesses in Rome, attempted, through Ledeen, to pass information to the White House and Pentagon that Iraq secretly shipped its enriched uranium to Iran. CIA officers and U.S. weapons inspectors scoffed at Ghorbanifar's information. In fact, the CIA had long considered Ghorbanifar and Ledeen as agents of influence for Israeli intelligence. Pentagon officials Harold Rhode and Larry Franklin, colleagues of Ledeen, eventually met officially with Ghorbanifar in Rome. Ghorbanifar became a prime suspect of the FBI probe into the Niger document scam. He and Ledeen are old colleagues who met when Ledeen was a correspondent for the *New Republic* magazine in Rome during the 1970s.[52] At the same time, Ledeen was also close to a number of neo-fascist figures in Italian intelligence and politics, some of whom would become involved in Berlusconi's right-wing political movement.[53] "The links between Berlusconi, Ledeen, and Ghorbanifar are developing into a conspiracy," said one source close to the FBI investigation.[54]

Ghorbanifar and Ahmed Chalabi of the Iraq National Congress were also old associates and reportedly both served as agents of influence for the late Shah of Iran's intelligence service, SAVAK. CIA sources claimed they repeatedly warned against doing any business with Ghorbanifar or Ledeen, but were overruled consistently by the Bush White House. The CIA sent former U.S. envoy to Iraq and Gabon, Ambassador Joseph Wilson, to Niger to check on the veracity of the claims of Niger's involvement with Iraq. He came back empty-handed and later said the charge was baseless. Wilson's evidence that Niger had not supplied uranium to Iraq was backed by U.S. ambassador to Niger Barbro Owens-Kirkpatrck and General Carlton Fulford, the Deputy Commander of EUCOM.

---

[51] Allen Nacheman, "Prodi seeks to distance EU from Berlusconi remarks on Islam," Agence France Presse, October 10, 2001.

[52] "Michael Ledeen," Panorama, BBC. <http://news.bbc.co.uk/1/hi/programmes/panorama/3031803.stm>

[53] Solomon Hughes, "Taking the War to Iran," Red Pepper, October 2003. <http://www.redpepper.org.uk/KYE/x-kye-Oct2003.html>

[54] Confidential interview.

The retaliation of the Bushites for such truth telling has blown up into "the Valerie Plame Affair": the outing of Wilson's wife as a covert CIA operative, the apparent resulting murder of some CIA sources, the indictment of VP Cheney's aide Scooter Libby for the "leak," and the promise of more fallout as the crucial midterm Congressional elections approach with the investigation continuing.

* * * *

It appears that the neoconservatives, like their McCarthyite forbearers, curry power by convincing the masses that there are threats lingering everywhere: Arabs, Muslims, Hispanics, Asians, etc. Following on the theme that there are enemies in our midst, Tom Ridge and John Ashcroft constantly used the news media to raise the specter of domestic terrorists driving trucks, wearing scuba gear, sporting beards, and even carrying almanacs and road atlases.

In March and April 2004, the wheels began to come off of the Bush administration's disinformation campaign after the Iraqi uprising in Fallujah. Although the Pentagon ordered a massive retaliation against the uprising in OPERATION VIGILANT RESOLVE, the mutilation of four American private military contractors and the U.S. attack on a mosque during Friday prayers brought raw videos of the carnage into the United States. The Pentagon's propaganda machine was virtually powerless to explain a combined Sunni and Shia uprising against the U.S. occupation force.

The Iraq debacle, combined with revelations about what the Bush administration knew about Al Qaeda's plans to attack the United States prior to 9-11, resulted in a sharp decline in Bush's popularity polling numbers. Some in the corporate media began to demonstrate a degree of independence from the White House and Pentagon not seen since the Bush administration came to power. Even the terminology began to change. The Bush administration was not only obfuscating but also lying, bellowed some Big Media commentators. With a presidential election looming, America's disinformation factory hit a minor temporary snag.

However, in retaliation, right-wing GOP influence peddlers and dirty tricks operators managed to reverse the slight decline of the disinformation machine. Planned by people like White House deputy chief of staff and master manipulator Karl Rove, Karen Hughes, and others, a frontal assault was launched on what remained of the relatively independent media. CBS's *60 Minutes* was largely defanged, after optically-scanned, photocopied, and faxed Bush Texas Air National Guard documents were handed off to the investigative news show as originals. Right-wing operative Kenneth Tomlinson, who later resigned under an ethics cloud, was named chairman of the Corporation for Public Broadcasting. Right-wing shows began to appear on the Public Broadcasting System. There was a real fear that the religious right and the neoconservatives would achieve the much desired cone of silence over what was left of the independent media in the United States and abroad.

* * * *

Yet there continued to be unresolved issues dealing with the nation's domestic security. For example, the FBI was suddenly seized with paralysis when it came to pursuing the culprits who, following 9-11, sent U.S. weapon grade aerosolized anthrax through the U.S. Postal System to the Democratic leadership in Congress during the time when Bush's so-called Patriot Act was being debated. During a time when Congress's normal activities ceased to exist, it hastily passed the Patriot Act, thus negating and nullifying many constitutional guarantees.

The same type of small and large government contractors who cashed in on the war on terrorism had links to the individuals and organizations with the expertise to select the high-speed sorting machines of the U.S. Postal Service as the mechanism to further mill and make deadlier the powdered anthrax. Every time the FBI approached those involved in such research, the case died down and ultimately evaporated. But the companies involved in violating the 1972 US-USSR-UK Biological Warfare treaty, and which continued to pursue research funded by the U.S. government and military into banned areas, continued to escape FBI prosecution.

While being browbeaten to sign off on the USA PATRIOT Act, the U.S. Senate's Democratic leadership received deadly anthrax via the postal system. The major media also was targeted by anthrax mailings in a clever perception-management campaign to stoke the public's fears. Postal employees at Washington DC's Brentwood postal facility died, along with others across the country. The business of the U.S. Congress was derailed. It became clear that the anthrax sent to the Democratic leadership came not from Iraqi, North Korean, or Al Qaeda stocks, but from a strain developed by the U.S. Army's biological warfare laboratory at Fort Detrick, Maryland. The aerosolization of anthrax occurred at the U.S. Army's Dugway Proving Grounds, a fact confirmed by a Utah National Guard source. Furthermore, aerosolized anthrax was tested during 2000 in Nevada in a top secret exercise called PROJECT BACCHUS.

The FBI began an investigation of the anthrax terrorist attack. But when all roads ended up at the front doors of the U.S. Army and some of the Central Intelligence Agency's favorite contractors—Science Applications International Corporation (SAIC), Battelle Memorial Institute, and Hadron, Inc. (since renamed Analex)—the anthrax investigation seemed to suddenly die as fast as the unfortunate victims.

Former CIA Director James Woolsey, true to form, maintained that the anthrax attacks could not have originated from a dangerous right-wing *group* in the United States. Shortly after the bulk of the anthrax attacks, he told the Cato Institute, "One hypothesis that some in the government are following is that this is entirely separate from September 11—that a crazed American Nazi PhD microbiologist with a fully-equipped laboratory somewhere in a Trenton, New Jersey, cave just gets his anthrax ready and mails it." However, Woolsey, who was at the forefront of beating the war drums against Iraq, steered his audience away from the Nazi connection and tried to implicate Saddam Hussein in the anthrax attacks.[55]

In 2004, when Congress took up a possible extension of the USA PATRIOT Act and a follow-on bill dubbed the PATRIOT II Act,

[55] Nina Easton, "The Hawk; James Woolsey Wants Iraq's Saddam Hussein Brought to Justice," the *Washington Post*, December 27, 2001, p. C01.

the office of Senate Republican Majority Leader Bill Frist was said to have tested positive for the deadly ricin toxin. After the Senate went into a temporary period of stasis, it was later discovered that the "ricin" was powdered paper dust from a mail-processing machine.

* * * *

Despite the shadowy nature of much of the disinformation factory, many of its aims can be construed when its actions are properly deconstructed, as we saw clearly in the instance of homeland security. A similar program of "world view warfare" is revealed by observing how many traditional national flags of other countries have been replaced by flags imposed by foreign interests. The flags of Georgia and Adjaria were replaced by neoconservative interests based in Washington.

In November 2002, Rwanda's Tutsi-led government, which had been advised by international Holocaust and genocide consultants in the wake of the 1994 mass deaths, scrapped the traditional Hutu and pan-African red, green, black, and yellow flag, replacing it with a non-traditional flag of green, blue, and two tones of yellow.

In April 2004, Iraq's Governing Council selected a white flag with two blue stripes, a differently blue-hued crescent moon, and a white stripe. The Council scrapped the traditional and historic flag using the pan-Arab red, green, white, and black colors, replacing it with one that resembled the flag of Israel, but the transitional Iraqi government eventually scrapped the Israel "look alike" flag.

In 1998, Bosnian Serbs, Muslims, and Croats had expressed dismay that a dark blue, white, and yellow European Union-style flag was imposed on Bosnia-Herzegovina that failed to represent their traditional colors: red for the Croats, medium blue for the Serbs, and green for the Muslims. And the UN has dictated a new red, yellow, white, and blue Cypriot flag for a yet-to-be re-united Cyprus, even though the white Cypriot flag with the map of the island embraced by olive branches had been selected in a contest held by Cyprus's first President, Archbishop Makarios. A Turkish Cypriot artist had designed the original Cypriot "peace" flag before independence in 1961.

On February 18, 2006, Democratic Republic of the Congo President Joseph Kabila was forced to scrap the post-Mobutu flag adopted by his father, Laurent D. Kabila, after the ouster of that long-time U.S.-supported dictator. That was the flag used after Congo's independence from Belgium in 1960 but soon became associated with the Kabila regime—one that was despised by the United States and its regional clients—Rwanda and Uganda. In a UN-supervised referendum, a new constitution was adopted on February 18, 2006. It stipulated that the post-independence/post-Mobutu flag was to be replaced with essentially the same flag used by Congo from 1963 to 1971, the time of the Mobutu dictatorship. There were also plans afoot to scrap Marxist-era flags in Angola and Mozambique, but these met with stiff opposition from veterans of the nationalist struggle against the Portuguese and South Africans. One of America's favorite clients in Africa, Yoweri Museveni of Uganda, also spoke of scrapping his nation's flag after his fraudulent February 2006 election victory over Kizza Besigye.

The destruction of long-standing national vexillological and heraldic symbols is a major neoconservative precept. American Enterprise Institute Senior Fellow and Reagan National Security Council official Michael Ledeen, an architect of neoconservative policies, subscribed to the notion of "creative destruction," which he defines as the tearing down of the old order in nation states. A senior U.S. State Department source who spoke to me on a non-attributable basis described Ledeen, who became enamored with Italian Fascism while he was assigned as a journalist in Rome in the 1970s, as "the most dangerous man in America."

—§—

UNCOVERING MILOSÉVIC · THE WEIRD ECONOMY · NASCAR WIVES

Newsweek

July 23, 2001 · $3.95

newsweek.msnbc.com

With all the hype and news attenion, little is truly known, and questions abound still.

THE FRENZY OVER CHANDRA LEVY

EXCLUSIVE

GARY CONDIT
His Secret Life

THE PARENTS VS. THE CONGRESSMAN
Inside the Investigation

LOPEZ IN LOVE: Jennifer and her dancer get engaged

People
weekly

GARY CONDIT TALKS

Blunt one moment, ducking tough questions the next, the embattled Congressman, in a PEOPLE interview, goes public about Chandra Levy

RIP: CHANDRA LEVY

The story of the death of 24-year-old Chandra Levy, an intern for the federal Bureau of Prisons, was surrounded by so much news hype concerning her alleged affair with California Representative Gary Condit that the obvious story was sadly missed. Only *The Scotsman* newspaper in the U.K. referred to "mysterious subplots" to the Levy case.[1]

Condit was a senior ranking Democrat on the House Permanent Select Committee on Intelligence (HPSCI). At the time of Levy's disappearance around May 1, 2001, the HPSCI had already been wracked by one unexplained death (HPSCI Executive Director John Millis the previous June). Condit would have been privy to a number of classified intelligence briefings, including, conceivably, warnings about possible terrorist attacks against the United States. The real issue is what information, including classified intelligence, Condit might have passed to Levy, either inadvertently or purposefully.

Washington police were, at first, extremely slow to investigate Condit. Later in their investigation of the Levy disappearance, police searched Condit's Washington apartment and took a DNA sample from him. However, police also kept insisting that Condit was never a suspect in Levy's disappearance.

Washington police conducted a thorough search of the neighborhood and areas where Levy may have been at the time of her disappearance: Adams Mill Park, Rock Creek Park and several buildings in the Adams Morgan neighborhood where she and Condit both resided. Throughout the summer of 2001, police remained essentially clueless. It was not until May 22, 2002 that DC police announced that "quite a bit" of Levy's skeletal remains were found in Rock Creek Park, the same area that the police painstakingly swept the previous summer with sniffer dogs, police cadets, and a number of other personnel. Nearly one year later, it was a man walking his dog and looking for turtles who discovered the remains.

---

[1] Eamonn O'Neill, "Dangerous Liaison Part I," *The Scotsman*, February 23, 2002, p. 9.

Police decided to change Levy's case from a "missing persons" case to a "death investigation" but not necessarily a criminal one. Later, the police began to treat Levy's death as a homicide. Some observers remained skeptical about whether Levy's body had been in the park for a year, reckoning it may have been moved to the park after the police conducted their massive search. The Levy death was later assigned "cold case" status by the Washington, DC Metropolitan Police.

* * * *

According to sources close to the Congress and Washington police, the aversion of the police to investigate Condit at the outset of Levy's disappearance may have had its roots in a 1997 police scandal in which the head of the police Special Investigation Division, Lt. Jeffrey Stowe, was discovered extorting large sums of cash from patrons of homosexual and bondage bars in southeast Washington. It was reported at the time that Stowe identified several patrons of the establishments—primarily the X-rated Follies Theater—as prominent Washington politicians and businessmen and targeted them for blackmail. Many of these officials were more than happy to pay Stowe rather than have their names revealed to their families. DC police call such blackmail "fairy shaking." Stowe's housemate, then-Police Chief Larry Soulsby, was forced to resign his post amid the scandal. In January 1998, Stowe pleaded guilty to extortion and theft charges.

Anne Marie Smith, an airline flight attendant who claimed to have had an affair with Condit, revealed through her attorney, Jim Robinson, the alleged sexual tastes of the congressman on Fox News: "Apparently, Congressman Condit had some peculiar sexual fantasies that a normal heterosexual man does not have. That's her testimony, not mine." Referring to possible sadomasochistic tendencies on the part of Condit, Robinson said, "There were ties, neckties tied together and tied underneath the bed as if someone had been tied up in bed."[2] The mere reference to such matters, alleged or not, would have been enough for new DC Police Chief

---

[2] Fox News, *The Edge with Paula Zahn*, July 9, 2001. < http://www.foxnews.com/story/0,2933,29212,00.html>.

Charles Ramsey to steer clear of the entire Condit-Levy matter. After all, he had been hired to put the Stowe-Soulsby scandal to rest, once and for all.

However, a bewildering question remains about Levy and Condit. Considering that Condit would have been privy to highly-classified information about terrorist threats against the United States, and the fact that Levy disappeared some four months before 9-11, why did she hesitate to make return airplane reservations from Dulles to California (the same route of American Airlines Flight 77 that was turned around and crashed into the Pentagon on 9-11)? Levy's parents, Susan and Robert, expressed bewilderment about their daughter's secretiveness regarding her return airline reservations. Susan Levy told Fox News, "She wouldn't give us a time exactly when she was coming home, as far as airplane time, and that I found kind of bothersome to me, because I would think she would tell me exactly when and what time she was coming home, like what reservation and what plane she's going to come in on."[3]

* * * *

If Condit, either from official intelligence briefings or from unofficial intelligence sources, was told of the possibility that terrorists might soon hijack fully-fueled Boeing 757 and 767 aircraft from the East to the West coasts, might he have passed some of this information on to Levy? There were a number of concrete intelligence reports from abroad that indicated terrorists would hijack airplanes and crash them into targets. Some reports specifically mentioned New York and Washington while others merely stated the target was the East Coast of the United States.

The intelligence on hijackers possibly seizing airplanes in the United States was known by the CIA, FBI, and other U.S. intelligence agencies during the spring and summer of 2001. Sibel Edmonds, who worked as an FBI Turkish, Azerbaijani, and Farsi translator from September 20, 2001 to March 2002, testified before the 9-11 Commission and the Senate Judiciary and Intelli-

---

[3] CNN, "Parents: Chandra never made return plane reservation," July 15, 2001, < http://www.cnn.com/2001/US/07/14/missing.intern/>

gence committees that she saw documents that "clearly showed that the hijackers were in the country and plotting to use airplanes as missiles." She added, "There are many documents out there that would prove what they knew, when they knew and how they knew."[4] That information, most certainly, would have been made available to members and staff of the congressional intelligence oversight committees, including Condit.

In yet another bizarre twist, Edmonds claimed that her FBI supervisor erased her translations from her computer after she left for the day, and told her to go slow on the translations. The supervisor was eventually promoted. The translation sabotage was verified by Senator Charles Grassley of Iowa, who said Edmonds' story was corroborated by other FBI employees. A Justice Department Inspector General report issued in July 2004 also supported Edmonds' contention that she was fired for blowing the whistle on a foreign intelligence operation within the FBI's translation unit.

Edmonds said her colleague, Melek Can (Jan) Dickerson, whom she linked to a Turkish intelligence official who was under investigation by the FBI's counter-intelligence division, constantly deleted from her translations critically important information about Turkish intelligence activities in the United States.

Edmonds maintained that the Turkish intelligence officer, who was attached to the Turkish embassy in Washington, had a network of spies inside the Pentagon and State Department. Informed intelligence sources confirmed that the intelligence operation involved Turkish and Israeli elements, the smuggling of nuclear materials and that the name Douglas Feith turned up in FBI wiretaps of principal members in the smuggling operation. Feith's father, Dalck Feith, is a longtime activist and supporter of the ardently pro-Israel Zionist Organization of America (ZOA).[5]

Edmonds, who said that the FBI seized her home computer and constantly shadowed her, was eventually fired, but her story was buttressed by John Roberts, the chief of the FBI's Internal Affairs Department. Roberts said that he had found cases since Sept. 11

---

[4] Chris Strohm, "Rice: Red tape hindered pre-9-11 efforts," *Government Executive*, April 8, 2004. <http://www.govexec.com/dailyfed/0404/040804c1.htm>

[5] Zionist Organization of America, Press Release, "Dalck Feith and Douglas Feith Will Be the Guests of Honor," October 13, 1997. <http://www.zoa.org/pressrel/19971013a.htm>

where FBI employees were involved in misconduct. They were not reprimanded, but were actually promoted. Edmonds filed a whistleblower suit against the FBI, but the Bush administration argued successfully for its dismissal because it would "compromise national security." Malek Can Dickerson denied the charges against her, and she quit the FBI and moved to Brussels, where her U.S. Air Force husband, who was assigned to the Defense Intelligence Agency, was assigned to NATO.[6]

* * * *

On May 1, 2001, the day she disappeared, inexplicably leaving her wallet, credit cards, and cell phone in her apartment, Chandra Levy was searching the Amtrak Web site, and she did mention to a friend that she might take a train home. Why, after a prolonged stay in Washington, would Levy be interested in a three or four-day train trip home?[7]

Two days before Levy vanished, she had left a telephone message for her aunt, Linda Zamsky: "I really have some big news or something important to tell. Call me ..."[8] The tabloid television shows, echoing an article in the supermarket tabloid *National Enquirer*, salaciously reasoned that the big news or "something important" might have involved pregnancy.

And the so-called "responsible media" missed Condit's role on the scandal-plagued HPSCI and his obvious access to high-level intelligence. Was any classified information conveyed to Levy by Condit during alleged "pillow talk" or other conversations? Was the information sensitive enough to endanger Levy's life if she told others about the "big news"? Why was no grand jury ever convened to get access to the information that could have shed light on who or what may have been behind Levy's tragic murder?

Why did Levy frantically try to contact Condit on his cell phone on April 30, the day before she disappeared? Had she been threatened? Did anything Levy know contribute to the fact that the

---

[6] Ed Bradley, "Lost in Translation," *60 Minutes*, July 13, 2003; Gail Sheehy, "Whistleblower Coming in Cold from the FBI," *New York Observer*, January 21, 2004.
[7] CNN, "How Are the Police Handling the Investigation into Chandra Levy's Disappearance?" *The Point with Greta Van Susteren*, July 19, 2001.
[8] Fox News, "Source: Condit Admits to Affair with Levy," July 8, 2001.

only airline she checked out on the Internet for a flight home to California was Southwest, which does not fly from Dulles? Did her "big news" have anything to do with the airplane hijacking warning likely briefed to Condit by the CIA and other intelligence agencies? Did the Washington police decide, after talking to HPSCI officials, that Condit's only real infraction was that he might have improperly disclosed classified information to a non-cleared person? Indeed, could Chandra Levy have been, in a sense, the first victim of 9-11?

In January 2005, the media was satisfied to wrap up the Levy case: Condit had successfully sued writer Dominick Dunne for slander in suggesting that the now-former congressman was involved in Levy's disappearance. In a sworn deposition on September 29, 2004, Condit denied he ever had a romantic relationship with Levy, emphasizing that they were just "friends." That prompted a response from Levy's aunt, Linda Zamsky: "It's just too, too strange.… She wasn't lying. Maybe you had to be there; you had to see the stars in her eyes. She wasn't lying. And anyway, why would she have his personal number?"[9]

---

[9] Helen Kennedy, "Under Oath, Condit Still Denies Fling With Levy," *New York Daily News*, January 12, 2005, p. 17.

Applied Energy Services (AES) Headquarters, 1001 North 19th Street in Rosslyn, Virginia, a few blocks from the building housing KBR/Halliburton and Armitage Associates.

Center for Strategic and International Studies (CSIS), 1800 K Street, Washington, DC. Funded by major U.S. corporations, CSIS ensures that U.S. foreign policy benefits Corporate America.

CHAPTER THREE

BUSINESS AS USUAL
... AND UNUSUAL

COFFEE ANYONE?

During the massacre of East Timor's civilians in September 1999 by Indonesian armed forces and militias, the conversations at coffee klatches at Starbucks around the country were predictable, considering the trendy clientele. Pointing to front-page stories in the *New York Times*, *USA Today*, and the *Washington Post*, politically-correct Starbucks patrons voiced their *angst du jour*. "Isn't it awful what the Indonesians are doing to those poor people in East Timor?" they groaned, as they sipped their tall latte made from organically-grown coffee beans. Little did they realize that the aromatic East Timorese coffee blend they were savoring may have actually prolonged the long suffering of the same people whose fate they were bemoaning.

It turns out that Starbucks enjoyed a very cozy relationship with the Indonesian military-backed coffee-growing colonists who ran East Timor's large plantations. Protestors highlighted Starbucks' practices in East Timor and other countries during the anti-World Trade Organization protests in Seattle in late November and early December 1999. Starbucks, a company that prided itself as being progressive, had egg on its face. Its trade practices turned out to be no different from those of Shell, British Petroleum, Nike, Chiquita Brands, and other companies that exploit workers in poor developing nations. Starbucks had a public relations nightmare on its hands, and, in the weeks leading up to April's anti-World Bank protests in Washington, DC, it needed a public relations coup.

Timed to coincide with the protests in Washington and, more important, the opening of the trade show of the Specialty Coffee Association of America in San Francisco, Starbucks agreed to place "Fair Trade" labels on its products as proof that it was paying coffee farmers a fair price for some of their coffee. The Fair Trade labels are the brainchild of Trans Fair USA, the American branch of a self-regulatory international industry watchdog group that guarantees coffee, tea, chocolate, and banana growers receive a fair price without the markup of middlemen, and that farm laborers work under safe conditions.

Starbucks, as the first company to adopt the Fair Trade labeling scheme, offered its "fair trade" coffee free to passers-by during Washington's World Bank protests. Although Starbucks wanted to get ahead in the public relations contest, fair trade labels are not found on most of the company's products, including those packaged or brewed and served over the counter. In addition, there is no real way of determining how much of Starbucks' business is actually conducted through "fair trade" entities, or if only a small percentage of its coffee purchases are "greenwashed" for public relations reasons.[1]

In Chiapas, the rebellious Mexican state, such a "greenwashing" effort may be operating. In an attempt to drive independent squatters off of the sensitive rain forest land in Montes Azules, where farmers slash and burn for agricultural land, groups such as Conservation International and the World Wildlife Fund, as well as the always-suspect U.S. Agency for International Development (USAID), began a campaign to protect the land for the 66 surviving Lacandon Mayan families.

Ernesto Ledesma Arronte of the Center for Political Analysis and Social and Economic Research (CAPISE), based in Chiapas, suspected ulterior motives by the environmental groups. He cited their major funders—Starbucks, Pulsar Group, Chiquita, and Exxon—as a reason for caution. He said the companies all had

---

[1] Mark Townsend and Nick Mathiason, "The coffee trade: A bitter aftertaste: Even with 25 million Starbucks customers a week, the world makes too much coffee and the poor are paying the price," *The Observer*, September 14, 2003, p. 21.

their eyes on Montes Azules's rich resources—coffee, fruit, oil, and pharmaceutical products. Conservation International denied that the companies had any plans to exploit the rain forest. The Zapatista National Liberation Front said it would fight any attempt to remove any villagers from Montes Azules, once again pitting Starbucks and its agents of influence against the poorest of the poor.[2] Starbucks' history in East Timor was not a good one. In 1994, the U.S. Agency for International Development (USAID) officially took control of East Timorese coffee plantations from the Indonesian armed forces. One of the Indonesian military bigwigs in on the deal was former Indonesian armed force commander General Benni Murdani, a favorite of the CIA. Although Murdani was forced to resign as commander in 1993, his influence over East Timor's coffee production remained significant. Operating through a local super-cooperative called the Timor Coffee Project, which acted like a modern-day British East India Company, USAID and the U.S. National Cooperative Business Association (NCBA) administered the coffee plantations and arranged for most of the organically-grown reddish-hued Arabica bean crop to be sold to none other than Starbucks.

NCBA has an interesting international background. It has been active in setting up similar agricultural cooperatives in both Nicaragua and El Salvador, two countries among many where USAID and U.S. intelligence agencies have often worked hand in glove.

Chemonics, a firm tied to the Republican Party and covert U.S. operations in Iraq and Afghanistan, became involved in El Salvador's coffee production under a Bush administration contract. In early 2005, Chemonics led a USAID-funded delegation of U.S. and Canadian coffee roasters to visit El Salvadorean coffee growing regions.[3] Chemonics was also active in the Guatemalan coffee sector under a USAID contract.[4]

In East Timor, many of the local officials of the coffee cooperative were not even native Timorese, but migrants from Java and Bali who

---

[2] Matthew MacLean, "Rain forest sits at the center of Chiapas standoff," *Christian Science Monitor*, July 16, 2003, p. 8.

[3] Tracy Ging and Julie Barrett O'Brien, "El Salvador is Back," *Tea & Coffee Trade Journal*, No. 4, Vol. 177, April 20, 2005, p. 38.

[4] Suzanne J. Brown, "It's still quality that makes the difference," *Tea & Coffee Journal*, No. 4, Vol. 177, p. 32.

wanted to turn a quick profit on the backs of underpaid East Timorese farm workers. The East Timorese plantation workers amounted to nothing more than indentured servants of the U.S. government. Although the Timorese received better wages from the Americans than they got from the Indonesians, USAID and its NCBA contractor negotiated prices and did all marketing on their behalf. And according to one businessman who is familiar with the deal, the salaries that the East Timorese plantation workers received from their U.S.-backed Indonesian overseers amounted to nothing more than "slave wages."

Although the 1994 deal between USAID, NCBA, and the local coffee potentates was advertised as advantageous to the native East Timorese, during the summer of 1995 several coffee workers rioted in the towns Baucau, Emera, and Pante Makasar (in the all-but-forgotten East Timorese exclave of Ambeno Ocussi) over the arbitrary decision by Indonesia to lower coffee prices.

The cozy relationship worked out between USAID, Starbucks, and the ever-present Indonesian military seemed like the perfect Third World deal. So when it looked like East Timor might drift toward independence as a result of political changes in Jakarta, the Clinton administration got worried. So did Starbucks. According to *Business Week*, the coffee company received the entire 1998 crop of East Timor's coffee, said to be worth around $20 million. The 1999 yield was estimated to be a record-setting bumper crop, worth some $100 million.

Although the Indonesian military officially got out of the coffee business in East Timor, its top officials still controlled much of the production of raw materials in the country, including coffee. In fact, the Indonesian army intended to claim East Timor's coffee-growing hill country as part of Indonesia.[5] The specter of violence being triggered by a change in East Timor's political status did not auger well with the American, Indonesian, and Timorese coffee barons. In fact, as the Indonesians and their supporters departed East Timor, they actually stole some of the 1999 coffee crop from the fields. According to East Timor Action Network (ETAN) sources, the Indonesians brazenly demanded compensation for the coffee fields they plundered in East Timor.

---

[5] Michael Shari, "Was Timor's Chaos Part of a Plan?" *Business Week*, October 4, 1999, p. 54.

ETAN also reported that in the years prior to the independence plebiscite, officials of the U.S. Institute of Peace, an organization whose Board of Directors are appointed by the President on the advice of Congress, began providing political seminars to East Timorese in which they stressed that integration into Indonesia with some local autonomy was preferable to outright independence. The Institute of Peace counted among its directors many individuals with extensive ties to the U.S. military and intelligence community.

Many of the East Timorese coffee entrepreneurs made no secret of their preference for Indonesian rule. After all, they were making money, and, even better than that, they were under the umbrella of a U.S. government agency that guaranteed a virtual continuous flow of coffee beans to corporations like Starbucks. Along with the Indonesian military occupiers, coffee plantation "quislings" provided support to the pro-autonomy militias. Not all the East Timorese coffee workers bought into the autonomy argument. A number were killed by the militias when they made their pro-independence views known.

Reminiscent of Trans Fair USA and its Fair Trade labels, USAID officials, proclaimed their Timor Coffee Project a success (note that they chose not to use the proper name of the country—East Timor—but the Indonesian name for the entire island "province"). However, many East Timorese were wary of the real goals of Washington toward the hapless former Portuguese colony. In a 1997 interview with the *Los Angeles Times*, East Timorese activist and Nobel Peace Prize winner Jose Ramos-Horta said, "I am skeptical about U.S. good intentions or professed ideals about promoting democracy because U.S. policy is full of complex contradictions."[6] One of those contradictions was the Clinton administration's tendency to put the interests of economics and political expediency ahead of human rights.

Behind every American foreign policy tilt you can usually find a bevy of political contributors. East Timor is no exception. The chief beneficiary of those delectable East Timor organic coffee beans that flow through the U.S. government-sponsored supply

---

[6] Nancy Yoshihara, "Jose Ramos-Horta; Fighting In Exile For Self-Determination In East Timor," *Los Angeles Times*, May 25, 1997, P. M3.

line was Howard Schultz, the Seattle-based Chief Executive Officer of Starbucks. Not surprisingly, Schultz was a major campaign contributor to Bill Clinton. Ironically, Schultz fancied himself as a progressive Democrat (he joined Bill Bradley's presidential fundraising campaign). But while he has championed health care reform, liberal employee benefits, and the environment by banning the doubling of coffee cups in his stores, Schultz was much less concerned about the East Timorese, who have weathered one of the world's most brutal military occupations while providing his corporate brew pots with the much desired East Timor coffee beans. As East Timor descended into chaos in September 1999, Starbucks' public affairs machine assured its customers that its East Timor suppliers were guaranteeing that coffee supplies would not be interrupted, even though the lives of some 800,000 inhabitants of the province were irrevocably thrown into turmoil.

But it was clear that Starbucks would have to re-negotiate the lucrative East Timor coffee deal with the National Council of East Timorese Resistance (CNRT), the organization that formed the post-independence government, since independence threatened to upset the cozy mercantile arrangement worked out between Indonesia, the Timor coffee cooperative, and Starbucks.

The powerful lobbying interests in Washington had quickly gone to work when East Timor began drifting toward independence. Following East Timor's overwhelming vote for independence, every statement issued by Washington concerning the Indonesian genocide against the people of that province was tainted by assertions that any United Nations relief operation would have to be worked out with the authorities in Jakarta. Oddly, no such preconditions concerning Belgrade's acquiescence were ever attached to NATO's invasion of Kosovo.

Washington's preference for the *status quo ante* in East Timor was made clear during a speech Clinton delivered on federalism in Mont Tremblant, Quebec on October 8, 1999. The president opined, "Wouldn't it have been better if they [the East Timorese] could have found their religious, their cultural, their ethnic and their economic footing and genuine self-government in the framework of a larger entity, which would also have supported them economically and reinforced their security instead of undermined it?" Clinton, it will be recalled, owed a debt of gratitude to Indonesia's Riady family for political contributions to his presidential campaign.

And Clinton's predecessor, George H.W. Bush reportedly had a significant financial interest in the Badak natural gas wells in Indonesia. His financial partner in the Badak wells was fellow Houstonian Roy Huffington, the father of former California Republican Representative Michael Huffington. The elder Huffington was Bush's ambassador to Austria.

And Bush the Elder had been as ardent a supporter of the Indonesian military dictatorship as anyone could have been. His Deputy Undersecretary of Defense for Policy under Dick Cheney, Paul Wolfowitz, in 1989, had just finished his stint as the Reagan-Bush administration's ambassador to the Suharto regime. In the end, East Timor achieved independence not because of America but in spite of it. More menacing, the discovery of oil in the Timor Sea, off East Timor's shores, spelled inevitable trouble for the fledgling state. Almost immediately, Australia, backed by its friends in Washington, began making unreasonable claims on East Timor's offshore oil blocks.

* * * *

Starbucks' support for unsavory regimes did not end with the Indonesian military occupiers of East Timor. After Rwandan President Paul Kagame transformed his country into a virtual one-party state, Starbucks announced it was interested in buying Rwandan coffee.[7] In April 2004, Kagame made a pilgrimage to Seattle, the home of Starbucks, with his trade and agriculture ministers in tow. Rwanda's coffee industry received financial support from the Bush administration, anxious to bolster its client in Kigali. The *Assistance a la Dynamisation de l'Agribusiness au Rwanda* (ADAR), a Rwandan enterprise designed to spur entrepreneurship in the coffee industry, received U.S. government funding.[8]

---

[7] Orla Ryan, "Rwanda's Struggle to Rebuild Economy," BBC News, April 1, 2004.

[8] Carter Dougherty, "Rwanda Savors the Rewards of Coffee Production," *New York Times*, July 27, 2004.

In an appearance in Seattle to promote his movie *Hotel Rwanda*, director Terry George, used the occasion to promote Rwandan coffee: "If Starbucks would carry Rwandan coffee—which is extremely good, by the way—that alone could save the country from economic disaster."[9]

East Timor was not the only part of Indonesia where U.S. businesses have benefited from a less-than-forceful American human rights policy. In West Papua, the Indonesian-controlled half of the island of New Guinea, the Louisiana-based mining giant Freeport McMoRan Copper and Gold has cooperated with the Indonesian military to keep at bay native peoples like the Amungme and Kmoro, who are not only opposed to Indonesia's occupation of their country but also to Freeport's environmental despoiling of their native lands.

Not surprisingly, West Papuans fared no better than the East Timorese in getting Washington to raise their plight with the Indonesian authorities. The reason is simple and the scenario is familiar. Freeport McMoRan Copper and Gold had some powerful friends in Washington and Jakarta. Freeport's Chief Executive Officer, James "Jim Bob" Moffett, counted among his closest of friends Louisiana's senior senator John Breaux, a moderate Democrat, who, more often than not, voted with the Republican majority. It also did not hurt that both Henry Kissinger and former Louisiana Democratic Senator J. Bennett Johnston both served on Freeport's Board of Directors. Current President of the World Bank Paul Wolfowitz, a former U.S. ambassador to Indonesia, remained a staunch supporter of resuming U.S. military aid to Jakarta when Clinton suspended all such assistance.

In 1995, the U.S. government-sponsored Overseas Private Investment Corporation had cancelled Freeport's $100 million political risk insurance policy after the agency discovered Freeport's environmental abuses in West Papua. After Freeport's friends in and out of Congress pressured the U.S. government, the company's insurance policy was restored just six months after it was cancelled. U.S. taxpayers continued to underwrite Freeport's malevolence toward the people and lands of West Papua.

---

[9] William Arnold, "Rwandan Hero's Story Had To Fight Its Way To The Screen," *Seattle Post-Intelligencer*, January 6, 2005, p. C1.

Coffee may also determine West Papua's fate. In the highlands of West Papua grows some of the same type of Arabica coffee that Starbucks shipped from East Timor. According to Washington businessman Jim Hope, who spent a considerable amount of time in West Papua, the West Papuan coffee crop is just waiting for someone to process it. Based on the East Timor example, however, the coffee in all likelihood will be harvested at the expense of the indigenous population.

Indonesian President Abdurrahman "Gus Dur" Wahid, who oversaw Indonesia's withdrawal from East Timor and had begun making overtures to pro-independence groups in West Papua and Acheh, was too much for Western multinational corporations and the Pentagon operatives that favored a united Indonesia. When Wolfowitz, the Indonesian military's best friend, took over as the number two man in Washington, Wahid began to be pressured.

In August 2001, he was ousted in a dubious political coup d'etat. Wahid's foreign policy adviser Alwi Shihab said that Wolfowitz had called him after Wahid decided to stand up to the National Assembly and refused to resign from office. Alwi said Wolfowitz asked "why Gus Dur refused to compromise with the Assembly, why he threatened a state of emergency?" When Alwi told Wahid about Wolfowitz's comments, the blind and sickly leader remained silent.[10]

Bullying Wahid out of office would not be Wolfowitz's only outrageous behavior directed against a democratically elected leader. Wolfowitz's machinations in Indonesia, the Philippines (where he was involved in easing Ferdinand Marcos out of office along with his exfiltration of billions of dollars in cash, gold bullion and gems), the Middle East, and elsewhere would be rewarded on March 16, 2005 when George W. Bush nominated him to be President of the World Bank.

The Night the Lights Went Out in Georgia

Like an urban SWAT team, a force of young gung-ho British and American men descended upon a country's capital city and seized control over the electric power system of the entire na-

---

[10] "Decree Was Gus Dur's Last Futile Effort," *Jakarta Post*, August 6, 2001.

tion. Soon, British and American control of the system resulted in widespread power failures, a breakdown in critical infrastructures and industrial output, and widespread public anger.

While this could very well have been an accurate description of U.S. and British occupation troops in Baghdad or Basra in Iraq, these events occurred "peacefully" in the former Soviet Republic of Georgia in 1999. However, in this case, it was not American and British troops who took over the country's power system, but employees of Applied Energy Services (AES) of Arlington, Virginia, a company that bills itself as the "largest owner of power in the world." AES, not unlike the now-defunct Enron, is politically connected to the GOP. And AES nearly went the way of Enron; teetering on bankruptcy, the company chalked up a $2 billion debt in 2002.

Formed in 1981 by two ex-Department of Energy officials, Roger W. Sant and Dennis Bakke, AES's current Board Chairman is Richard Darman, the Office of Management and Budget director under Bush the Elder and partner of the GOP influence-peddling venture firm, The Carlyle Group. More important, Darman's job at Carlyle meshes in nicely with his AES duties: he is Carlyle's Senior Advisor for Global Energy & Power. Another AES board member, and also an adviser to Carlyle, is Republican Charles Rossotti, the former Internal Revenue Service Commissioner under Bill Clinton.

In Georgia, AES was teamed with Black and Veatch, a Kansas City-based engineering and construction company with operations in Saudi Arabia, Kuwait, and Bahrain. On its board is H.P. Goldfield, a long-time GOP fund-raiser who worked for Presidents Reagan and George H.W. Bush and also served on the Bush-Cheney 2000 National Finance Committee.

With the help of Florida's Governor Jeb Bush, AES won a lucrative "fast track" contract to build an undersea natural gas pipeline from the Bahamas to Florida.[11] AES had other connections with the Bush family's global business empire. After AES defaulted on a $1.2 billion loan from the National Development Bank of Brazil to help finance AES's investment in Sao Paulo's Eletropaulo Metropolitana SA, the largest power distribution company in Latin

---

[11] Robert Trigaux, "Going on offense for the defense industry," *St. Petersburg Times*, June 21, 2004, p. 1D.

America, there were charges that AES conspired with Enron to devalue the price of the Brazilian company.[12] Brazilian authorities claimed they would investigate the charges, but after Enron's collapse the investigation ground to a halt.

AES's Web site proclaims that its "businesses consist of competitive generation, distribution, and retail supply businesses in 27 countries. Our generating assets include interests in 116 facilities totaling over 45,000 megawatts of capacity. We also operate 17 electric distribution companies that deliver electricity to approximately 11 million end-use customers." Given that corporate resume, it is not surprising that AES muscled its way into the unsuspecting Republic of Georgia.

* * * *

In 1999, Georgia sold its state-owned power company, Telasi, to AES, on the recommendation of Merrill Lynch, its chief consultant on privatization. *Power Trip*, an award-winning documentary by director Paul Devlin, chronicles the effects of the takeover of Telasi by a team of young American and British managers and consultants, who attempted to teach the Georgians that electricity, as they had known it under the Soviets, was not free. In their exuberance to force Georgia to change its business ways practically overnight, the AES team plunged the country into economic and social chaos.

AES-Telasi, the name of the privatized company, began installing meters in apartment buildings, businesses, and homes throughout Georgia. Soon, Georgians who earned an average of $15 a month were receiving electric bills for $45. For those unable to pay, including a number of fixed-income pensioners, AES-Telasi simply cut off power until their bills were paid.

Soon, the company discovered that 40 percent of the electric lines that tapped into its own lines were illegal. Georgians, desperate for power for heat and light, had begun hooking up their own lines to poorly grounded electrical switches and exposed overhead lines. The results were disastrous. In areas of Tbilisi, Georgians were electrocuted when attempting such dangerous hookups.

---

[12] Martha McNeil Hamilton, "AES's New Power Center; Struggling Utility Overhauls Corporate (Lack of) Structure, *Washington Post*, June 2, 2003, p. E01.

Apartment block electrical rooms, replete with live wires and un-grounded hookups, were turned into death traps for unsuspecting children and others. AES-Telasi would simply cut off power to entire neighborhoods where payment was lagging.

The American-British team carried on blithely. Supplied with their own generators and back-up batteries, they were unaffected by the widespread blackouts that they, themselves, were creating as a form of group punishment for the tardy Georgians. To make matters worse, AES-Telasi lost the records of customers who had scraped enough money together to pay their bills, yet these customers were cut off in the same manner as their "deadbeat" neighbors.

Despite the outrage, AES-Telasi persisted in their strong-arm tactics. In one case, the company cut off power to Tbilisi airport while a plane was landing. In other cases, power was cut to the Chinese embassy and the National Philharmonic. In one amazing case, they cut off power to a major Georgian army base essential to fighting Chechen and Al Qaeda-allied guerrillas in the Pankisi Gorge. Corporate officials laughed off the incidents.

The Georgian government, then headed by Eduard Shevard-nadze, drew the line on AES-Telasi when it threatened to cut off power to cash-strapped industries, including the Rustavi Water Supply Company and Azoti Chemical Company. Georgia's government continued to control the National Dispatch Center, so when factory managers received a threat from AES-Telasi to cut off their power, they simply bribed dispatch center and Ministry of Fuel and Energy officials to keep their power on.

Shevardnadze, who survived an attempted assassination during AES-Telasi's occupation of the energy sector, blamed the company for the constant blackouts. After Georgian television's *60 Minutes* began looking into the whole affair, its anchorman was found shot to death in his apartment.

Shevardnadze's comment about AES-Telasi was echoed by one in-flamed Georgian who, upon noticing the camera filming the *Power Trip* documentary, shouted, "What do these Americans care? In the Soviet Union no one paid for electricity. Americans and British are occupiers! They're conquering us little by little." They were prophetic words, and now might easily be heard in Basra, Baghdad, or Mosul.

* * * *

Eventually, after all the upheaval and economic shock, AES pulled out of Georgia, selling its assets to the state-owned Russian company, UES. But it did not did not sit well with the Bush administration, and the right-wing elements it had groomed there, that Georgia, a major transit route for the Baku, Azerbaijan to Ceyhan, Turkey pipeline, being built by a consortium that includes Halliburton, would have its electrical system owned by Russians. The Caspian Pipeline Consortium had the full backing of George W. Bush, with many of its shareholders being huge Bush campaign contributors: Amoco, Chevron, Exxon, Mobil, Occidental, and Unocal. Shevardnadze, who had been a major ally of the United States, became a major liability to Big Oil, as had been other erstwhile U.S. allies and friends, including Mullah Omar of Afghanistan, Saddam Hussein of Iraq, Mobutu of Zaire, and Jonas Savimbi of Angola. Shevardnadze would have to go.

On November 23, 2003, demonstrators, who were trained with the help of the United States by Serbian activists who had overthrown Slobodon Milosevic, stormed Parliament and forced Shevardnadze to flee. They claimed he had been re-elected in a rigged vote. A young American-trained lawyer named Mikhail Saakashvili assumed control of the country. Stamping his own imprimatur on Georgia, the new president scrapped the old non-sectarian and traditional Georgian flag and replaced it with the Christian, St. George's Cross flag of his right-wing coalition, the Georgian National Movement. Rubbing salt in the wounds of the majority Muslim population of autonomous Adjaria, Saakashvili ordered its flag replaced with one featuring the Christian St. George's cross after the 2004 overthrow of Adjarian president Aslan Abashidze. The use of the Christian cross as a symbol for a majority Muslim former autonomous republic was not lost on the population.

In December 2003, following the coup against Shevardnadze, Secretary of Defense Donald Rumsfeld, on a surprise trip to Georgia, warned the Russians to exit from their two military bases in that country

Saakashvili's "election" was certified in early January 2004, with an overwhelming, Soviet-style, 97 percent of the vote. U.S. special operations forces in Georgia, originally there only temporarily to assist in stamping out terrorist activity in the Pankisi Gorge, announced that their presence would be permanent. In February 2004, Saakashvili's takeover was lauded by George W. Bush during the Georgian president's visit to the White House.

But Georgian Defense Minister David Tevzadze scoffed at claims from Washington and neoconservative circles that Al Qaeda was operating in the Pankisi Gorge. He told the American defense magazine, *Defense Week*, "It is very difficult to believe that [about Al Qaeda in Pankisi] ... they would have to cross at least six or seven countries."[13] Tevzadze was rewarded for his honesty by being dismissed by Saakashvili from his post as ambassador to NATO. Tevzadze was also accused by the Georgian government of having assisted a group of Chechen rebels to cross from Pankisi to Abkhazia in September and October 2001, and faced criminal charges.[14]

* * * *

From Washington, Deputy Secretary of State Richard Armitage, who once headed the U.S.–Azerbaijan Chamber of Commerce, a virtual shill for Halliburton and other U.S. oil companies, congratulated Ilham Aliyev, the son of Azerbaijan's long-reigning dictator, upon his election in 2003 to the presidency, in a totally rigged election. In a world where the "only remaining superpower" was in the hands of an "oilgarchy," and after a series of Washington-inspired coups and phony elections in Georgia and Azerbaijan, the Caspian Region became safe for Halliburton to begin its pipeline construction. Former Secretary of State James Baker III opened an office of his Baker Botts law firm in Baku, Azerbaijan. His son, James Baker IV, served as general counsel for the U.S.–Azerbaijan Chamber of Commerce.

Ceyhan would soon be awash in oil from both Azerbaijan and northern Iraq. In May 2005, work was completed on the Baku-Tbilisi-Ceyhan (BTC) pipeline just weeks after President Bush visited Tbilisi and heralded Saakashvili's "democracy." A dedication ceremony was held in Baku. The presidents of Azerbaijan, Geor-

---

[13] Frida Berrigan, "George in Georgia," *In These Times,* June 20, 2005, p. 21.
[14] Georgia Daily Digest, Eurasianet.org, June 29, 2004 < http://www.eurasianet.org/resource/georgia/hypermail/200406/0085.shtml>

gia, Turkey, and Kazakhstan attended the ceremony along with oil company moguls from BP Amoco, UNOCAL, ConocoPhillips, Amerada Hess, and Halliburton. The pipeline would carry over one million barrels of oil a day, and would eventually be extended from Azerbaijan to the Kazakh oil fields. Saakashvili said that the Halliburton BTC pipeline was crucial to his nation, and he put the Russians on notice that they would soon be ejected from what he said was a more pro-Western Georgia.

* * * *

A mystery surrounded AES's founder Bakke, who had given up his position as AES Chairman at the end of 2003. According to a Securities and Exchange Commission filing, between March 3 and March 19, 2003, Bakke gave away 3.1 million shares of AES stock in five separate transactions, retaining 28.9 million shares.[15] The beneficiary or beneficiaries of Bakke's largess remains a mystery.

However, Bakke is a strong supporter of a shadowy and wealthy group of fundamentalist Christians known as the "Fellowship" and the "Family." Bakke lives on the same quiet North Arlington, Virginia street where the Fellowship maintains a secretive estate known as The Cedars. The Cedars attracts a steady stream of members of Congress, Pentagon brass, chiefs of defense contractors, foreign heads of state and ambassadors. The Fellowship also sponsors the annual National Prayer Breakfast, which is attended by the President of the United States and national and world dignitaries.

The politically-connected Fellowship and its largely Republican and Wall Street supporters are mainstays of the global push for privatization of critical public utilities. Although these modern-day brigands were ultimately unsuccessful in completely emptying the purses of poor pensioners in Georgia, one can only wonder how long it will be before the AESes of the world return to Georgia and, once again, order "lights out!"

—§—

02000599

Carol,

I am so sorry for this. I feel I just
can't go on. I have always tried to
do the right thing but where there
was once great pride now it's gone.
I love you and the children so much.
I just can't seany good to you or
myself. The pain is overwhelming.
Please try to forgive me.

Cliff

J. Clifford Baxter

Did J. "Cliff" Baxter, a former
Enron vice chairman, who had
sold 577,436 shares for $35.2
million committ suicide in his
Mercedes or … ?

Joye M. Carter, M.D., FCAP
Chief Medical Examiner

(713) 796-9292
(713) 796-6815
FAX: (713) 796-6844

OFFICE OF THE MEDICAL EXAMINER OF HARRIS COUNTY
JOSEPH A. JACHIMCZYK FORENSIC CENTER
1885 OLD SPANISH TRAIL
HOUSTON, TEXAS 77054-2098

AUTOPSY REPORT

OC 2002 - 34

January 25, 2002

ON THE BODY OF

John C. Baxter
5211 Palm Royale Boulevard
Sugar Land, Texas

CAUSE OF DEATH: Penetrating gunshot wound to
                   the head

MANNER OF DEATH: Suicide

Joye M. Carter, M.D., FCAP   01/31/02
Chief Medical Examiner   MMDDYY

RIP: Cliff Baxter

On January 25, 2002, the body of former Enron Vice Chairman Cliff Baxter was found near his suburban Houston home. The police in Sugar Land, Texas ruled Baxter's death a suicide from a gunshot wound. Baxter left a suicide note. Case closed? Not quite.

Baxter, who was in a position to finger George W. Bush's close friend, Enron Chairman Kenneth ("Kenny Boy") Lay in the Enron Ponzi scheme that largely funded Bush's 2000 election campaign, was due to provide testimony to the U.S. Congress and a federal grand jury investigating the Enron collapse. All of a sudden, the government was absent its star witness.

Baxter had abruptly left Enron in May 2001. Those familiar with the Enron scandal felt that Baxter had stumbled across the company's illegal activities and wanted to distance himself from the firm before it totally collapsed.

Enron's official media statement regarding Baxter's death would have been fitting for a far more junior ex-"colleague":

We are deeply saddened by the tragic loss of our friend and colleague, Cliff Baxter. Our thoughts and prayers go out to his family and friends.

Some of Baxter's friends questioned Baxter's suicide note, which was written in block letters, claiming that all of his notes to them were written in cursive letters. When his body was found, in his car, Baxter was wearing his bedclothes, but was without shoes, socks, or even slippers.

A toxicology report disclosed that Baxter had ingested five Ambien tablets within a day of his death. Ambien is a powerful non-narcotic sedative, with two being the maximum to be taken at any one time. Baxter also had taken Norpropoxyphene, a narcotic pain medication, and Citalopram, an anti-depressant. The strong cocktail of the drugs that Baxter allegedly had in his system would have made it impossible for him to drive his car to the spot where he supposedly shot himself, using untraceable ammunition known as "rat shot" (a Teflon coated bullet containing small pellets that is normally used to shoot at rodents and snakes).

As with other "suicides" involving people in a position to bring down the powerful clique surrounding Bush and Cheney, police in Sugar Land ruled Baxter's death a suicide before all the facts were in: the toxicology report, the autopsy, and the official police report. There was also the unusual nature of the suicide note.

Many Houstonians did not believe the suicide story. They reasoned that Baxter was surprised in bed, may have been force-fed drugs, shot, and then propped over his steering wheel to give the impression that he had taken his own life. And Houston and Enron insiders also realized something else: the Harris County Medical Examiner Office was replete with people with close ties to the Bush family.

According to people in Houston who tracked the Enron scandal and Baxter's mysterious death, the Harris County Texas Medical Examiner Joye Carter and her Laboratory Director and chief toxicologist, Ashraf Mozayani, both of whom were involved in the Baxter autopsy, had such strong conflicts of interests with Bush and Cheney that they should have turned over the case to an independent panel of experts.[1]

Although the conflicts of interests of Carter and Mozayani appear, at first glance, to be circumstantial, there were more than enough reasons for them to recuse themselves from the Baxter autopsy and lab tests. In fact, Attorney General John Ashcroft recused himself from the Enron prosecution when his own receipt of campaign contributions from the firm were revealed. At the time of Baxter's death, Mozayani sat on the board of Drug Free Business (DFB) Houston along with William Bedman, a 24-year Halliburton veteran and the company's in-house labor counsel.

Carter and Mozayani are also linked to ex-House of Representatives Majority Leader Tom DeLay (who represented Sugar Land) through Justice for All, a conservative Texas victim rights' group that ardently supports the death penalty.[2]

---

[1] Confidential sources in Houston.
[2] Letters on the Enron Collapse, op. cit.

* * * *

Enron executives were also involved with DFB Houston, which was tied to the Drug Free America Foundation (DFAF), an organization founded by the Sembler family of Florida. The Semblers are strong Bush and Cheney financial supporters, to the tune of hundreds of thousands of dollars.[3]

Melvin Sembler, a shopping center magnate and the founder of Straight Foundation, Inc., an organization that treats adolescents for drug addictions, has been rewarded handsomely for his support of the GOP. While the elder Bush had appointed him ambassador to Australia, George W. made him ambassador to Italy. Once there, he was at the center of a number of neoconservative plots and machinations, including the laundering of bogus Niger government documents alleging that Iraq was shopping for yellowcake uranium in that West African nation. Sembler, whom this author referred to as "Dissembler" in an interview with the Italian magazine *Oggi*, appeared to have been a central player in the cover-up by the Bush administration and its allies in the Italian government in the March 2005 shooting death by U.S. troops of Italian SISMI military intelligence deputy chief Nicola Calipari. The Italian intelligence official was accompanying freed Italian hostage Giuliana Sgrena to Baghdad International Airport when U.S. troops opened fire on their vehicle, killing Calipari and wounding Sgrena.[4]

As a result of Straight, Inc. being sued for questionable legal and ethical acts, Sembler founded DFAF to avoid further legal difficulties.[5] DFAF, which includes Mozayani as a "Forum member," received money from the right-wing Carthage Foundation, controlled by extreme conservative troublemaker Richard Mellon Scaife.

* * * *

There is no doubt that Baxter was someone who knew about how Enron scammed the world. While the Bush administration was

---

[3] Letters on the Enron Collapse, "DB," February 7 letter, World Socialist Web Site, February 13, 2002. <http://www.wsws.org/articles/2002/feb2002/corr-f13.shtml>

[4] Umberto Pascali, "Calipari e il 'Teorema di Madsen,'" *Oggi*, May 8, 2005, p. 3.

[5] Pete Brady, "Straight, Incorporated," *Cannabis Culture*, November 12, 2001. <http://www.cannabisculture.com/articles/2072.html>

freezing the accounts of terrorist groups, including Irish and Latin American groups having no known ties to the Bin Laden organization, it allowed the Enron pirates who pocketed the financial holdings of its stockholders and employees—in the biggest financial scam in the history of the world—to keep their holdings safe in offshore sanctuaries.

Through a Byzantine network of offshore subsidiaries, Enron was able, with the assistance of its auditor, the now-defunct accounting giant Arthur Andersen, to squirrel away hundreds of millions of dollars through 2,832 subsidiaries, including 874 registered in tax havens like the Cayman Islands, Turks and Caicos Islands, Bermuda, and Mauritius.

The Financial Crimes Enforcement Center (FINCEN), a computerized financial intelligence unit that is run by the Treasury Department at a secure facility in Tyson's Corner in northern Virginia, supposedly monitors international financial scams through cooperative agreements with the CIA, National Security Agency (NSA), FBI, and financial intelligence units around the world. Yet Enron's criminal activities seem to have gone undetected by FINCEN.

Oversight of Treasury was once controlled by Senate Banking Committee Chairman Texas Senator Phil Gramm, whose wife Wendy, sat on the board of Enron. Sweetening the deal for Enron, Arthur Andersen had the contract to revamp the FBI's computer system (and look at its files).

—§—

TRUST AGREEMENT

8th July, 1976

I, Salem M. Binladen, do hereby vest unto James Reynolds Bath, 2330 Bellefontaine, Houston, Texas, full and absolute authority to act on my behalf in all matters relating to the business and operation of Binladen-Houston offices in Houston, Texas, located at 1405 and 1109 Fannin Bank Bldg., Houston, Texas, 77030.

James Reynolds Bath shall have full authority to disburse funds for Company, or Binladen family expenses, and shall have discretion to disburse funds for all other expenses related to the Binladen-Houston office, or the Binladen family, or any other purpose as directed by Salem M. Binladen.

Witness _____   _____
                                            Salem M. Binladen

Witness _____

This is to certify that the signatures herewith above are true and actual.

Notary _____

MARTY LITTLE
Notary Public in Harris County, Texas
My Commission Expires September 17, 1979

Copy of a check for $6,667 drawn on the Saudi American Bank, which was used by the Saudis to funnel money to the "Zakat Committee Tulkarm," a group associated with Palestinian terrorists, particularly Hamas.

CHAPTER FOUR

DEALING WITH THE DEVIL

Never in the history of the United States has a president and his family been so closely involved with the family of a sworn enemy of America as George W. Bush, his father, and brothers with the Bin Laden family. After his inauguration in 2001 George W. Bush all but ignored the threat posed by Al Qaeda. Moreover, Bush's brothers were carrying on a robust business with businessmen who crossed paths with the Bin Ladins and some of the most extreme members of the Wahhabi sect in Saudi Arabia and other countries. The President's Daily Brief (PDB) of August 6, 2001 was titled "Bin Laden Determined to Attack inside the United States," and it specifically addressed the potential for hijacking airliners in order to bargain for the release of prisoners arrested for terrorist activities between 1998 and 1999. For the record, here it is, with the usual security redactions:

PRESIDENT'S DAILY BRIEF
AUGUST 6, 2001

OSAMA BIN LADEN DETERMINED TO STRIKE IN US

CLANDESTINE, FOREIGN GOVERNMENT, AND MEDIA REPORTS INDICATE OSAMA BIN LADEN SINCE 1997 HAS WANTED TO CONDUCT TERRORIST ATTACKS IN THE US. BIN LADEN IMPLIED IN US TELEVISION INTERVIEWS IN 1997 AND 1998 THAT HIS FOLLOWERS WOULD

FOLLOW THE EXAMPLE OF WORLD TRADE CENTRE BOMBER RAMZI YOUSEF AND "BRING THE FIGHTING TO AMERICA."

AFTER US MISSILE STRIKES ON HIS BASE IN AFGHANISTAN IN 1998, BIN LADEN TOLD FOLLOWERS HE WANTED TO RETALIATE IN WASHINGTON ACCORDING TO A XXXXXX SERVICE.

AN EGYPTIAN ISLAMIC JIHAD (EIJ) OPERATIVE TOLD AN XXXXXX SERVICE AT THE SAME TIME THAT BIN LADEN WAS PLANNING TO EXPLOIT THE OPERATIVE'S ACCESS TO THE US TO MOUNT A TERRORIST STRIKE.

THE MILLENNIUM PLOTTING IN CANADA IN 1999 MAY HAVE BEEN PART OF BIN LADEN'S FIRST SERIOUS ATTEMPT TO IMPLEMENT A TERRORIST STRIKE IN THE US.

CONVICTED PLOTTER AHMED RESSAM HAS TOLD THE FBI THAT HE CONCEIVED THE IDEA TO ATTACK LOS ANGELES INTERNATIONAL AIRPORT HIMSELF, BUT THAT BIN LADIN [*SIC*] LIEUTENANT ABU ZUBAYDAH ENCOURAGED HIM AND HELPED FACILITATE THE OPERATION. RESSAM ALSO SAID THAT IN 1998 ABU ZUBAYDAH WAS PLANNING HIS OWN US ATTACK.

RESSAM SAYS BIN LADEN WAS AWARE OF THE LOS ANGELES OPERATION.

ALTHOUGH BIN LADEN HAS NOT SUCCEEDED, HIS ATTACKS AGAINST THE US EMBASSIES IN KENYA AND TANZANIA IN 1998 DEMONSTRATE THAT HE PREPARES OPERATIONS YEARS IN ADVANCE AND IS NOT DETERRED BY SETBACKS. BIN LADEN ASSOCIATES SURVEILLED OUR EMBASSIES IN NAIROBI AND DAR ES SALAAM AS EARLY AS 1993, AND SOME MEMBERS OF THE NAIROBI CELL PLANNING THE BOMBINGS WERE ARRESTED AND DEPORTED IN 1997.

AL-QAIDA MEMBERS—INCLUDING SOME WHO ARE US CITIZENS—HAVE RESIDED IN OR TRAVELED TO THE US FOR YEARS, AND THE GROUP APPARENTLY MAINTAINS A SUPPORT STRUCTURE THAT COULD AID ATTACKS. TWO AL-QAIDA MEMBERS FOUND GUILTY IN THE CONSPIRACY TO BOMB OUR EMBASSIES IN EAST AFRICA WERE US CITIZENS, AND A SENIOR EIJ MEMBER LIVED IN CALIFORNIA IN THE MID-1990S.

A CLANDESTINE SOURCE SAID IN 1998 THAT A BIN LADEN CELL IN NEW YORK WAS RECRUITING MUSLIM-AMERICAN YOUTH FOR ATTACKS.

We have not been able to corroborate some of the more sensational threat reporting, such as that from a XXXXXX service in 1998 saying that bin Laden wanted to hijack a US aircraft to gain the release of "Blind Shaykh" 'Umar 'Abd al-Rahman and other US-held extremists. Nevertheless, FBI information since that time indicates patterns of suspicious activity in this country consistent with preparations for hijackings or other types of attacks, including recent surveillance of federal buildings in New York. The FBI is conducting approximately 70 full field investigations throughout the US that it considers bin Laden-related.

CIA and the FBI are investigating a call to our Embassy in the UAE in May saying that a group of bin Ladin [sic] supporters was in the US planning attacks with explosives.

* * * *

According to two articles in the *Progressive Populist* written by investigative journalist Margie Burns, Marvin Bush served on the board of Securacom (since renamed Stratesec), a company registered in Delaware, from 1993 to 2000. The chairman of the board of Stratesec was Wirt D. Walker III, a cousin of Marvin and George W. Bush. Others associated with the firm included former Reagan Star Wars chief General James Abrahamson and another Reagan administration official, Barry McDaniel, who served as Stratesec's chief executive officer. Securacom had contracts to provide security for Dulles International Airport (the airport from which American Airlines Flight 77, which crashed into the Pentagon, originated) and the World Trade Center in New York. A videotape released just prior to the dissemination of the 9-11 Commission report showed four of the five hijackers of American Airlines Flight 77 being pulled aside by Securacom personnel at Dulles.

Although it was believed the hijackers used box cutters to overpower the crew and passengers, the security personnel fail to find any weapons. Two hijackers, Khalid al Mihdar and Majed Moqed, are seen setting off a metal detector and Moqed undergoes a hand held metal detector search. Two other hijackers, Nawaf al Hazmi and his brother Salem al Hazmi, are seen undergoing a hand check of their carry-on luggage. Hani Hanjour, the pilot of the aircraft, walks through security unimpeded.[1]

The company's important security work did not prevent the American Stock Exchange from delisting the company in 2002. Stratesec appealed the decision, but for unknown reasons suddenly withdrew its appeal.

Stratesec filed for bankruptcy in September 2003 after its major investor, E.S. Bankest, an obscure Miami financial services firm, was sued by Portugal's Bank Espirito Santo International, a bank with $40 billion in assets. The Portuguese bank accused E.S. Bankest of absconding with $170 million of its investment money. Espirito Santo's Cayman Islands branch had maintained a partnership with E.S. Bankest since April 1998; however, the original agreement was made by Espirito Santo's Nassau, Bahamas branch. The U.S. Attorneys Office in Miami opened a criminal investigation of E.S. Bankest's two principals, Hector and Eduardo Orlansky of Key Biscayne, Florida.[2]

Securacom's backers included a number of Kuwaitis, through a company called KuwAm Corp (Kuwaiti-American Corp.). Stratesec also has Saudi investments. Wirt Walker served as a managing director of KuwAm, which maintained offices within the Watergate complex with Riggs Bank, on whose board Bush's uncle Jonathan Bush sat.[3] Saudi Princess Haifa al Faisal, the wife of Saudi Ambassador to the U.S. Prince Bandar, used a Riggs account to funnel money to Omar al Bayoumi and Osama Basnan, two Saudi students in California who were associated with two of the 9-11 hijackers. A former employee of the Saudi embassy in Washington reported that the embassy also used the Saudi American Bank (SAMBA), located in the Watergate complex across the street from the embassy, as a conduit in which to funnel money to questionable groups located at several mosques in northern Virginia.[4]

---

[1] John Solomon and Ted Bridis, "Dulles video shows hijackers setting off metal detectors on Sept. 11," Associated Press, July 22, 2004.

[2] Gregg Fields, "Missing millions at center of bank fight," *Miami Herald*, September 7, 2003.

[3] Margie Burns, "Bush-Linked Company Handled Security for the WTC, Dulles and United," *Prince George's Journal*, February 4, 2003. < http://www.commondreams.org/views03/0204-06.htm>

[4] Private conversation.

In April 2002, when Israeli troops stormed into the West Bank to put down the Intifada, the files of a number of banks operating in the West Bank were seized by Israeli intelligence. One record, provided to me during a visit to Israel, clearly indicates that the Saudi American Bank was used by the Saudis to funnel money to the "Zakat Committee Tulkarm," a group associated with Palestinian terrorists, particularly Hamas.

In April 2004, U.S. banking regulators announced that they planned to impose fines on Riggs Bank for engaging in "suspicious transactions" via its embassy banking division. The plan for fines against the bank came amid separate investigations by the FBI, congressional committees, and banking regulators of Riggs's role as the chief bankers for the Saudi embassy in Washington for some twenty years.[5]

Until November 2002, Marvin Bush served on the board of HCC Insurance Holdings, Inc., (formerly Houston Casualty Company), a re-insurer for the World Trade Center. Bush still serves as an adviser to the firm. Wirt Walker served as chief executive officer of Aviation General, an aircraft company backed by KuwAm. Aviation General, formerly Commander Aircraft, brokered the sale of airplanes to the National Civil Aviation Training Organization (NCATO), located in Giza, Egypt, the hometown of lead hijacker Mohammed Atta and the only civilian pilot training school in Egypt. NCATO has a training agreement with Embry-Riddle University in Daytona Beach, Florida, the flight school that was investigated by the FBI for possibly training at least one of the 9-11 hijackers.[6]

In 1993, Marvin Bush co-founded Winston Partners Group, a private investment company that manages a $780 million portfolio, and which once headquartered in Alexandria, Virginia but relocated to McLean, Virginia, whose biggest employer is the CIA. Bush's partner in the venture was A. Scott Andrews, WorldCom's former chief financial officer who left the firm in 1994. Winston Partners provided Bush with yet another link to Dulles Airport.

---

[5] "U.S. moving to sanction Riggs Bank, top officials," *Houston Chronicle*, April 18, 2004.

[6] Margie Burns, "Security, Secrecy and a Bush Brother," January 13, 2003. <http://www.scoop.co.nz/mason/stories/HL0301/S00032.htm>

The investment firm had a financial stake in AeroLink Transportation, the contractor that operates both Dulles and Reagan National airport parking lots, parking lot shuttles, and the large shuttles that move passengers from Dulles's main terminal to the separate boarding terminals. AeroLink is a division of Tourmobile Sightseeing, the company that operates the tour buses that transport tourists around all of Washington, DC's major tourist attractions.[7]

Marvin Bush also has control over a network of affiliated companies, including Winston Growth Fund, Winston International Growth Fund, and Winston Small Cap Growth Fund. Sources who have investigated the Bush family's finances said the name "Winston" stems from the deep admiration the Bush family has for Winston Churchill. The business name "Winston" is used as a virtual "wink and a nod" code word to signal to investors that a limited liability partnership using the name has the full backing of the Bush family. Winston Partners Group was part of a larger investment firm called the Chatterjee Group, a conglomerate with business addresses in the Cayman Islands, Netherlands Antilles, and the Isle of Man.[8]

It is obvious the Bushes are sensitive about their global Winston enterprises. On May 6, 2005, the Web site for the *Calcutta Telegraph* in India posted a story about Marvin Bush's Winston Partners' parent group Chatterjee Group teaming with Access Industries, Inc., to outbid the Iranian National Petrochemical Company in the purchase of multinational Royal Dutch Shell affiliate, plastics manufacturer Basell Polyolefins, for $5.7 billion. Chatterjee's spokesman denied any connection between Winston Partners and Chatterjee: "There's no connection between [Chatterjee Group] and the Bush family.... It's a total coincidence that there are two entities using the name Winston Partners."[9]

But other media sources reported that Purnendu Chatterjee, the U.S. citizen head of the Chatterjee Group, who maintains an office

---

[7] Margie Burns, "Marvin Dips into the Security Pie: Another Fortunate Bush Brother," *CounterPunch*, December 5, 2002. <http://www.counterpunch.org/burns1205. html>

[8] Margie Burns, "Marvin Dips into the Security Pie: Another Fortunate Bush Brother," *CounterPunch*, December 5, 2002. <http://www.counterpunch.org/burns1205. html>; "Shell bows to US pressure on Basell sale," *Energy Compass*, May 13, 2005.

[9] Frank Esposito, "Bush not linked to plastics deal," *Plastics News*, May 16, 2005, p. 27.

on Mumbai's Nariman Point, had close links to George W. Bush through Marvin Bush's Winston Partners. Notwithstanding the attempt by Chatterjee Group to distance itself from the Bushes, SEC filings indicate that Winston Partners companies are part of the firm. According to those filings, the Chatterjee Group is composed of Winston Partners, LP; Chatterjee Fund Management, LP; Winston Partners II LDC, based in the Cayman Islands; Winston Partners II LLC; Chatterjee Advisors LLC; Chatterjee Management Co.; and Furxedown Trading Ltd., based in the Isle of Man. The corporate address for Winston Partners II LDC is listed in the Netherlands Antilles.[10] Purnendu Chatterjee continues to deny any relationship with Marvin Bush. He told an Indian business magazine, "I've also read about it ... the confusion arises from the fact that I had floated a fund called Winston Partners LP in 1991. It has nothing to do with Marvin Bush and we have no business connections whatsoever."[11]

The Cayman Islands, in particular, have been an attractive destination for the Bushes, not as a vacation spot, but for their dubious business operations. Two weeks before 9-11, a Cayman radio station received an anonymous warning letter that three Afghans detained earlier in the Islands for immigration violations had been planning a "major terrorist act against the U.S. via an airline or airlines." The letter's author stated, "I have been convinced that they [Nez Nazar Nezary, Mohammad Raza Hussani and Ali Sha Yusufi] are agents of Osama Bin Laden—one of the world's greatest terrorist operating out of Afghanistan." The three, who were traveling on Pakistani passports and arrived in the Caymans from Cuba, were held in protective custody by the Cayman police until they were ordered released by the Cayman Grand Court on June 5, 2001. The court ruled that "there is no evidence that they are a danger to the public and fears as to their possible links with a terrorist organization have long since been dispelled." After 9-11, Donovan Ebanks, the islands' Deputy Chief Secretary, said he regretted the decision to release the Afghanis, "I would be the first to acknowledge that had I the benefit of 20/20 vision that

---

[10] "Shell bows to US pressure on Basell sale," *Energy Compass*, May 13, 2005; "Bush Family Linked to Sale of Shell Unit," *International Oil Daily*, May 10, 2005.

[11] Arnab Mitra, "Purnendu's Big Deal," *Business Today*, June 5, 2005, p. 62.

only hindsight brings, I would have certainly made a different decision."[12]

Marvin Bush had other connections to shadowy firms connected to the Middle East. He served on the board of Fresh Del Monte Produce, Inc., a New York Stock Exchange-listed company that is headquartered in the Cayman Islands. Claiming to grow bananas in Guatemala and pineapples in Mexico (half the world's supply of pineapples, in fact), the firm is half-owned by Mohammed Abu Ghazaleh and IAT Group of Chile. Ghazaleh is the head of a Palestinian chicken producing family based in Jordan. Del Monte Produce's U.S. office is located in Coral Gables, Florida. As with many businesses involving Marvin Bush, the SEC opened an investigation of the company but provided few details, except that it paid little in the way of taxes to the U.S. government in 2002, although it netted *$2.09 billion* in profit from its North American operations, most of it in the United States. Shortly after the SEC investigation began, Marvin Bush left the company's board.[13]

In 2002, shortly after Bush left Fresh Del Monte, a group of Fresh Del Monte's original investors sued the firm for what it claimed was a fraudulent 1996 sale to the current owners. One of the defendants in the suit is Eduardo Bours Castelo, the Institutional Revolutionary Party (PRI) Governor of the Mexican state of Sonora. The plaintiffs argue that Bours sold the firm in a low bid in return for a $321,000 bribe from IAT, whose chairman was Ghazaleh and who is also a defendant in the suit.[14]

Marvin, like others in his family, has an interest in Florida with a spacious home in Boca Grande, Florida, the same town on Florida's Gulf coast where the patriarch and matriarch of the family, George H.W. "Poppy" and Barbara Bush, spend their winters. The Latin American, Florida-based activities of Marvin and Jeb Bush, along with those of Poppy, provide the reason Panamanian ex-dictator Manuel Noriega is sitting in a Federal prison in Florida serv-

---

[12] "Island Warned Two Weeks Before Terror," *Evening News* (Edinburgh), September 21, 2001, p. 4.

[13] Christopher Byron, "Spoiling The Produce - Probe, Suits and Bush Tie Help Del Monte Rumors Spread," *New York Post*, June 16, 2003, p. 35; Robert Trigaux, "Another suspect deal, another Bush brother in the mix," *St. Petersburg Times*, January 3, 2003.

[14] Brenon Daly, "A tale of pineapples, a fugitive and a Bush," *Corporate Control Alert*, October 23, 2004.

ing a 98-year sentence for homicide, drug trafficking, and corruption. Noriega is oddly considered a prisoner of war, even though no declared war ever existed between the United States and Panama. Like Saddam Hussein, Noriega knew too much about the criminal activities of the family Bush, especially in Latin America. The Bush family saw to it that if Noriega and Hussein could not be assassinated, they should be jailed and remain muzzled.

A Houston businessman who worked closely with the Bush family over the years confided that Marvin Bush and Wirt Walker appeared to have taken over the Saudi real estate investment and aircraft brokerage business once run in Texas by Houston-based James Bath in association with Salem Bin Laden, the late brother of Osama Bin Laden, and Khalid Bin Mahfouz, the billionaire Saudi banker. Salem Bin Laden's aviation enterprises included ownership of the single-runway Houston Gulf Airport and murky brass plate operations, including Socrates, Ltd., headquartered in Florida and HGA Investments and Binco Investments, both sheltered in the Netherlands Antilles.[15]

Salem bin Laden was killed in a mysterious crash of a BAC 1-11 he was piloting near San Antonio in 1988. Immediately after the crash there was a mystery about the type of airplane that Salem Bin Laden was, in fact, piloting. Another report had him flying an ultra-light aircraft that became entangled in power lines. The Bexar County medical examiner ruled Salem Bin Laden's death a "freak accident." Nevertheless, Bin Laden was said to have been a very experienced pilot. He was pronounced dead by military doctors at the U.S. Army's Brooke Medical Center in San Antonio.[16]

In July 1976, James Bath had been authorized by Salem bin Laden to handle all business activities for the Bin Laden family in the United States. This included Binladen Aviation, a Texas-chartered company that managed Bin Laden's aircraft.[17] The Bin Laden-Bath trust agreement, dated July 8, 1976, stated,

I, Salem Binladen, do hereby vest unto James Reynolds Bath, 2330 Bellefontaine, Houston, Texas, full and absolute authority to act on

[15] Mike Ward, "Binladen family business damaged by Osama," Cox News Service, November 8, 2001.

[16] Ibid.

[17] Bud Kennedy, "The Strange Death of Bin Laden's Brother in Texas," *Fort Worth Star Telegram*, September 27, 2001.

my behalf in all matters relating to the business and operations of Binladen-Houston offices in Houston, Texas, located at 1405 and 1109 Fannin Bank Bldg., Houston, Texas, 77030.

James Reynolds Bath shall have full authority to disburse funds for Company, or Binladen family expenses, and shall have discretion to disburse funds for all other expenses related to the Binladen-Houston office, or the Binladen family, or any other purpose as directed by Salem M. Binladen.

Witness:
Witness: /Signed/
                                       Salem M. Binladen
                                  Notarized: Marty Little
                        Notary Public in Harris County, Texas

In 1979, Bath purchased a 5 percent stake in George W. Bush's first oil venture, Arbusto Oil of Midland, Texas. Meanwhile, following the Soviet invasion of Afghanistan in 1979, Osama bin Laden made his first trip to the border area of Pakistan and Afghanistan, a region he would become familiar with after he ordered the September 11, 2001 attacks on Washington and New York.

Bath was also George W. Bush's Texas Air National Guard colleague and friend. Ironically, according to one of Bath's old colleagues, Bath was a member of the Louisiana Civil Air Patrol (CAP) in the mid-1950s. It was in the CAP that he learned how to fly. One of the other members of the Louisiana CAP during the time Bath was a member (and who was around his same age) would dramatically change the history of the presidency of the United States. He was Lee Harvey Oswald.[18]

George W. and Bath maintained a number of business relationships with one another after their Guard service. In 1994, Bath's ex-wife Sandra was sued by Bath and Khalid bin Mahfouz's National Commercial Bank of Saudi Arabia. Ms. Bath claimed that Bin Mahfouz and her ex-husband were trying to take possession of Southwest Airport Services, over which she had gained ownership as part of her divorce settlement with Bath. Southwest Airport provided support and fuel services to Houston's city-owned El-

---

[18] Houston business source.

lington Field, which serviced and fueled transiting military aircraft and even Air Force One. According to *Time* magazine and the *Houston Post*, when Bath ran Southwest Air Services, the company had charged the military and White House a 60 percent markup on the sale of fuel to military planes and Air Force One.[19] Sandra Bath, in countering the lawsuit, claimed, "Mr. Mahfouz, as owner of National Commercial Bank, hopes to accommodate Mr. Bath's desire to assume control of Southwest Airport Services Inc., and treat it as his personal piggy-bank as he has done over the preceding several years."

In 1993, Mahfouz and his associate Haroon Kahlon paid a $225 million settlement to the Federal Reserve Board and the New York District Attorney's office for their and National Commercial Bank's role in defrauding the depositors and investors of the Bank of Commerce and Credit International (BCCI), which was based in Luxembourg and collapsed in the worst banking collapse in modern history.[20] The late Democratic House Banking Committee Chairman, Henry Gonzalez of Texas, often stressed that BCCI was a slush fund for Bush family money laundering and smuggling activities. Given the later Enron collapse, Gonzalez was surely right on the money when he stated that BCCI was a slush fund for the Bushes—Enron having later served the same purpose for the Bush family and its political allies.

Senator John F. Kerry's investigation of BCCI also discovered that the bank was used to fund terrorist activities and covert intelligence operations. Strangely, Kerry never brought up details of the criminal enterprises of the Bush family during his 2004 presidential run against George W. Bush. However, after a campaign speech in Chicago, Kerry was picked up by an open microphone describing the Bush administration accurately: "These guys are the most crooked, you know, lying group I've ever seen. It's scary."[21]

The Cayman Islands firm that incorporated Bath's four Skyways enterprises also established the Iran-Contra money-laundering

---

[19] Jonathan Beaty, "A Mysterious Mover of Money and Planes," *Time*, October 28, 1991, p. 80.

[20] Jerry Urban, "Banking scandal figure seeks claim to airport contract," *Houston Chronicle*, September 10, 1994.

[21] Marlon Manuel, "Kerry not the first whose bluntness went public," *Atlanta-Journal Constitution*, March 12, 2004, p. 12.

front company for Oliver North.[22] Furthermore, some of the financial and legal principals involved in the Iran-Contra scandal would later re-emerge as key players in the Enron bankruptcy.

The involvement of Khalid bin Mahfouz and James Bath with Ellington Field in Houston took on an ironic twist when George W. Bush's Texas Air National Guard status became a recurring issue in both the 2000 and 2004 presidential campaigns. Ellington Air Force Based received the following order from Washington, DC in 1972:

> 29 September 1972
> Verbal orders of the Comdr on 1 Aug 72 suspending 1STLT GEORGE W. BUSH, ANGUS (Not on EAD), TX ANG, Hq 147 Ftr Gp, Ellington AFB, Houston, TX, from flying status are confirmed, exigencies of the service having been such as to preclude the publication of competent written orders in advance. Reason for Suspension: Failure to accomplish annual medical examination. Off will comply with para 2-10, AFM 35-13. Authority: Para 2-29m, AFM 35-13....
> Verbal orders of the Comdr on 1 Aug 72 suspending MAJ JAMES R. BATH, ANGUS (Not on EAD), TX ANG, Hq 147 Ftr Gp, Ellington AFB, Houston, TX, from flying status are confirmed, exigencies of the service having been such as to preclude the publication of competent written orders in advance. Reason for Suspension: Failure to accomplish annual medical examination. Off will comply with para 2-10, AFM 35-13. Authority: Para 2-29m, AFM 35-13....
>
> BY ORDER OF THE SECRETARIES OF THE ARMY AND THE AIR FORCE FRANCIS S. GREENLIEF, Major General, USA Chief, National Guard Bureau

* * * *

Richard Armitage, a major figure in the Iran-Contra scandal, traveled to Burma in 1997 on a trip sponsored by the Burma/Myanmar Forum, a Washington-based entity heavily funded by UNOCAL. At that time UNOCAL was negotiating a pipeline deal with the

---

[22] Beaty, op. cit.

Taliban government of Afghanistan, while Osama bin Laden was being harbored by the radical fundamentalist regime. After Bush II came to power in 2001, the links between UNOCAL and the Taliban were resumed, with a number of Taliban and Pakistani Inter Service Intelligence (ISI) officials visiting Washington and talking to people like Armitage. In December 2002, the CentGas pipeline deal with Afghanistan was cemented between Afghan leader Hamid Karzai, a one-time UNOCAL consultant, and officials of Pakistan and Turkmenistan. UNOCAL stood to benefit handsomely from the deal.

First brother Neil Bush was also cozy with some of the Saudi circles that supported fundamentalist Wahhabism. Neil found lucrative comfort in Saudi Arabia. After his brother's inauguration as President, Neil's company, Ignite!, Inc., an e-learning educational software company, began finding clients in the educational community of Saudi Arabia and the United Arab Emirates. It is always a great thing to find better ways to teach children. But many of the schools in Saudi Arabia and the UAE were financed and influenced by the Wahhabi clerical structure. It was astounding that Neil Bush would be trying to sell software to schools that could then put vile and extremist religious ranting online and accessible to more students, madrasahs, and potential future terrorists throughout the Middle East. But then again, when have the Bushes ever cared about the consequences of their business dealings? Neil Bush, of course, in typical Bush fashion, denied that he was trying to do any business in the UAE, which begs the question: Why he was there just a few weeks after 9-11 in the first place?[23]

In fact, so-called "homeland security" is also made to order for the Bushes. From 1994 to 1999, Neil ran Interlink Management Corporation from 10000 Memorial Drive in Houston, the same building where his father has his office. Interlink was a venture capital firm that funded start-up companies in the biotech fields, including many that were engaged in bio-war defenses involving people, animals, and crops. In the wake of the anthrax attacks, companies like Interlink were in high demand.

---

[23] Associated Press, "President's brother travels world promoting online education venture," April 8, 2002.

Neil Bush also was involved in an enterprise with Jamal Daniel, a Syrian American Orthodox Christian who established the Foundation for Interreligious and Intercultural Research and Dialogue in Geneva, Switzerland in 1999 to "promote ecumenical understanding." Among the board members of the foundation were Cardinal Joseph Ratzinger (now Pope Benedict XVI), Jordan's Prince Hassan (who was a close friend of Iraqi con man turned Oil Minister and Deputy Prime Minister Ahmad Chalabi), Jamal Daniel, and inexplicably, Neil Bush. Daniel and Bush were co-investors in Crest Investment Company, based in Dallas.[24] Daniel also was a principal in New Bridge Strategies, a company that made a handsome profit from the U.S. invasion of Iraq. Daniel's biographical blurb on New Bridge's Web site states, "Jamal has extensive experience in structuring investing in energy and oil and gas projects throughout the U.S., Europe and the Middle East."[25]

One of Neil Bush's best friends and advocates in the Middle East was the Crown Prince of Dubai, Shaikh Mohammed bin Rashid al Maktoum, an individual who often crossed paths with the Taliban and Al Qaeda on his frequent hunting and falconing trips to eastern Afghanistan, and just so happened to be in charge of a project to put computers in UAE schools. Rashid, who is also the Defense Minister of the United Arab Emirates, said the following in the wake of 9-11: "The United States must not to act in haste, it must give diplomacy and legal means every opportunity before launching a military strike on Afghanistan, it must not rush to accuse people without hard evidence." The UAE had been only one of three countries to recognize the Taliban, which acquiesced to the financing of Al Qaeda and other terrorist groups.

In October 2001, while visiting Dubai just weeks after 9-11, Neil Bush praised Shaikh Rashid as a man with "foresight and vision." In the same speech, Neil Bush said something that should chill the bones of every American—he said the following about his learning-disabled son Pierce, "My father was the 41st president and my brother is 43rd. I think that if Pierce finishes high school, he'll be

[24] Knut Royce and Tom Brune, "Neil Bush, Ratzinger co-founders; President's younger brother served with then-cardinal on board of relatively unknown ecumenical foundation," *Newsday*, April 21, 2005.

[25] < http://www.newbridgestrategies.com/bios.asp>

the 50th president of the United States."[26]-Bush's other escort was Shaikh Hamdan bin Rashid al Maktoum, the Finance Minister of Dubai and someone who certainly had his radar on the millions of dollars sent through the emirate to the Taliban, Al Qaeda, and Pakistani madrasahs and assorted Islamic "charities."[27]

Internal documents from the UAE Central Bank in Dubai detail huge money laundering operations in the UAE. The Sharjah branch of HSBC Holdings PLC was tied to international arms trafficker Victor Bout, indicted in Belgium for money laundering and named in various UN reports as a chief embargo buster in Africa and Taliban-controlled Afghanistan. American citizen Iqbal Hakim was the chief examiner for the UAE Central Bank. Hakim, yet another whistleblower who has been ignored by the Bush administration and threatened by its Persian Gulf potentate friends, discovered a suspicious $343 million per year money flow through an HSBC personal account in Dubai. The transactions were investigated by the FBI and the Bureau of Immigration and Customs Enforcement, but no prosecutions resulted.[28]

UAE banking insiders have revealed that accounts used to fund the Taliban and Al Qaeda involved members of the Dubai royal family. Banking insiders in Dubai report that in March 2002, U.S. Secretary of Treasury Paul O'Neill visited Dubai and asked for documents on a $109,500 money transfer from Dubai to a joint account held by hijackers Mohammed Atta and Marwan al Shehhi at Sun Trust Bank in Florida. O'Neill also asked UAE authorities to close down accounts used by Al Qaeda and affiliated partners like Victor Bout. The UAE complained about O'Neill's demands to the Bush administration. O'Neill's pressure on the UAE and Saudis contributed to Bush firing him as Treasury Secretary in December 2002.[29]

O'Neill's successor at Treasury, John Snow, was later identified as a key player in the decision by the Bush administration in early

---

[26] Jay Hilotan, "Application key to learning —Neil Bush," *Gulf News,* January 23, 2002; "Neil Bush happy with IT progress," *IT Porta*l, January 24, 2002. <http://www.itep.ae/english/News/PressRoomDetails.aspx?ID=729

[27] Rasha Owais, "UAE Denounces Terrorism," Gulf News Online, October 15, 2001. < http://www.gulf-news.com/Articles/news.asp?ArticleID=29262>

[28] Glenn R. Simpson and Erik Portanger, "UAE Banks Had Suspect Transfers," *The Wall Street Journal,* September 17, 2003, p. A10.

[29] Confidential sources in Dubai.

2006 to assign control of a number of U.S. ports to Dubai Ports World from Britain's Peninsular and Oriental Steam Navigation Company (P&O). Dubai Ports World was an entity controlled by the Dubai Royal family and government, and The Carlyle Group also had its fingerprints on the deal. After Treasury Secretary John Snow left CSX Corporation as its chairman, CSX Lines was sold to Carlyle, which renamed it Horizon Lines. David Sanborn, who was a CSX executive under Snow, became director of European and Latin American operations for Dubai Ports World and arranged to sell to the Dubai state-owned firm CSX's port operations in South America and Asia. Sanborn was then appointed Assistant Secretary of Transportation for Maritime Administration (MARAD), the oversight agency for U.S. shipping and ports. The Dubai Ports World deal to take over U.S. port operations was "approved" by the Committee on Foreign Investment in the United States (CFIUS), chaired by Sanborn's old CSX boss Snow. Perhaps not coincidental to the lucrative port deals, the Dubai Investment Corporation invested $100 million in The Carlyle Group.

Moreover, the Dubai Ports World deal involves taking over operations at more than just the widely-reported six or seven U.S. ports—New York, Newark, Philadelphia/Camden, Baltimore, Miami, and New Orleans. The Web site of "Great British" P&O stated that the Dubai Ports World deal involved stevedore operations at *twenty-two* U.S. ports: New York; Newark; Philadelphia/Camden; Baltimore; Miami; New Orleans; Portland, Maine; Boston; Davisville, Rhode Island; Wilmington, Delaware; Baltimore; Newport News, Norfolk and Portsmouth, Virginia; Lake Charles, Louisiana; Gulfport, Mississippi; Beaumont, Corpus Christi, Freeport, Galveston, Houston and Port Arthur, Texas. Amid an explosive political and congressional backlash to the deal, the Bush administration announced that Dubai Ports World would sell the port operations to a U.S. firm. There were suspicions that the ubiquitous Carlyle lurked in the background in the negotiations for a change in the port operations deal.

* * * *

CIA Director George Tenet, speaking about the Clinton administration's moves to kill Osama bin Laden before the 9-11 Commission hearing, said that on four occasions between December 1998 and May 1999 the CIA thought about launching cruise missiles against Al Qaeda forces in Afghanistan, but changed its mind when they considered the possibility that a strike might inadvertently kill members of the royal family of the United Arab Emirates, who frequented a nearby Afghan hunting camp. Richard Clarke, the counter-terrorism coordinator for Clinton and George W. Bush, who later broke with the latter, drafted a plan to take out Al Qaeda with pinprick military strikes. The plan was called OPERATION DELENDA (Latin for "to destroy").[30] The UAE royal family members who helped nix the plan to take out Al Qaeda in Afghanistan were some of the same individuals with whom Neil Bush was doing business and praising.

Members of the Bush administration and its neoconservative cheerleaders continued to have a love affair with some former Taliban leaders even after 9-11. According to German intelligence sources, the ex-intelligence chief for the Taliban, Mullah Kakshar, who defected from the Taliban after the U.S. invasion of Afghanistan in late 2001, began making prolonged visits to Washington, DC under the tutelage of neoconservative circles. The neoconservatives wanted to provide further evidence that the Saudi government, particularly former Saudi intelligence chief and current ambassador to the UK, Prince Turki al Faisal, negotiated a mutual non-aggression pact with the Taliban and Al Qaeda and provided Saudi financial assistance to both Al Qaeda and the Taliban. Turki was reported to have met with Taliban leader Mullah Omar and Al Qaeda figures in 1998. Turki admitted that he had met Omar but denied he ever met Kakshar, an amazing claim when it is considered that Kakshar was then Turki's counterpart as chief of intelligence for the Taliban.

In 2002, Kakshar provided a sworn statement in support of a $15 trillion class action lawsuit brought by the families of the victims of 9-11 against key members of the Saudi Royal Family, including Turki, for their alleged involvement in the 9-11 attacks. On No-

---

[30] David Johnston and Todd S. Purdum, "Missed Chances in a Long Hunt for bin Laden," *New York Times*, March 25, 2004.

vember 14, 2003, U.S. District Judge James Robertson dismissed the lawsuits against Turki and Saudi Defense Minister Sultan bin Abdulaziz al Saud, citing a lack of U.S. jurisdiction in matters concerning acts "allegedly done in their official capacities."

* * * *

In 1999, the DEA may have stumbled across a major conspiracy involving a Saudi prince's Colombian cocaine smuggling from Venezuela to support some "future intention" involving Koranic prophecy. In fact, the failure to pursue the Saudi drug connection was another failure of U.S. intelligence and law enforcement to possibly prevent the 9-11 attacks. The DEA operations were contained in a "Declassification of a Secret DEA 6 Paris Country Office" memorandum dated June 26, 2000, which coincided with the height of 9-11 hijacker activity in the United States. In June 1999, 808 kilograms of cocaine had been seized in Paris. The DEA was conducting a major investigation of the Medellin drug cartel called OPERATION MILLENNIUM.

Through an intercepted fax, the Bogota Country Office of the DEA learned of the Paris cocaine seizure, and linked the drug smuggling operation to the Saudis. The DEA investigation centered around Saudi Prince Nayif al Saud, whose alias was El Principe (the Prince). Nayif traveled in his own Boeing 727 and used his diplomatic status to avoid customs checks. The DEA report stated that Nayif studied at the University of Miami, Florida, owned a bank in Switzerland, spoke eight languages, was heavily invested in Venezuela's petroleum industry, regularly visited the United States, and traveled with millions of dollars of U.S. currency.

Nayif was also reported to have met with drug cartel members in Marbella, Spain, where Saudi King Fahd and the Saudi royal family maintained a huge palatial residence. The report states that when a group of cartel members traveled to Riyadh to meet Nayif, "they were picked up in a Rolls Royce automobile, belonging to Nayif, and driven to the Riyadh Holiday Inn hotel. The next day they were met by Nayif and his brother [believed to be named Saul].... The second day they all traveled to the desert in terrain vehicles

[Hummers]. During this desert trip they discussed narcotics trafficking. UN [the DEA informant] and Nayif agreed to conduct the 2,000 kilogram cocaine shipment, which would be delivered to Caracas, VZ, by UN's people, where Nayif would facilitate the cocaine's transport to Paris, France. Nayif explained he would utilize his 727 jet airliner, under Diplomatic cover, to transport the cocaine."

Nayif told UN that he could transport up to 20,000 kilograms of cocaine in his jet airliner, and propositioned UN "to conduct 10-20,000 kilogram shipments in the future." UN wondered why Nayif, supposedly a devout Muslim, would be involved with drugs. Nayif's response, especially in light of what is now known about Saudi funding of terrorism, is worth a close perusal. During the Riyadh meeting, Nayif responded to UN's question by stating that "he is a strict advocate of the Muslim Corran [sic]." UN stated, "Nayif does not drink, smoke, or violate any of the Corran's [sic] teachings. UN asked Nayif why he [Nayif] wanted to sell cocaine and Nayif stated that the world is already doomed and that he has been authorized by god to sell drugs. Nayif stated that UN would later learn of Nayif's true intentions for trafficking narcotics although Nayif would not comment further." The Saudi prince's drug smuggling operation was smashed by the DEA and French police in October 1999,[31] and Nayif remains a free man.

There has never been any explanation by the Saudis of what Nayif's ultimate intentions were and what he was planning to do with the cash from the illegal cocaine shipments. In light of the funding for 9-11 and other terrorist incidents, the DEA report on OPERATION MILLENNIUM takes on greater significance.

* * * *

Another company involved in the Taliban-U.S. CentGas pipeline was the now-defunct Enron, a company that defrauded billions of dollars from its stockholders, employees, and business partners. As with Halliburton and Richard Armitage's AALC, a number of former U.S. intelligence officers turned up on Enron's payroll. The

---

[31] Drug Enforcement Administration, Memorandum, Declassification of Secret DEA 6 for Paris Country Office, June 26, 2000.

firm had at least three ex-CIA agents on its payroll. These included Andre Le Gallo, who later became a business intelligence consultant based in California, and David M. Cromley, a former CIA clandestine services officer who served in civil-war ravaged Somalia and Liberia and who, after serving as Enron's chief competitive analysis officer, went to work with three other former CIA/Enron officials at Secure Solutions International. The company was formed from the remnants of the security division at Enron after the financial collapse.[32]

There were reportedly secret meetings held between Enron and the Taliban in Tashkent on September 7, 1996 (also attended by representatives of the Uzbek government and UNOCAL) and at the Houstonian Hotel in Houston in the spring of 1997. Prior to the Tashkent meeting, the sum of $10 billion was moved from a Cyprus bank, through Barclay's Bank in London, and on to Enron in Houston. Saudi financier Adnan Khashoggi, the billionaire arms dealer and veteran of the BCCI and Iran-Contra scandals, reportedly attended the 1996 meeting in Tashkent.[33]

Frank Wisner Jr., who served on Enron's board, used his links with the CIA station chief in New Delhi (while he was ambassador to India in the mid-1990s) to secure Enron's acquisition of the Dabhol power plant. Wisner assured that Enron would be guaranteed $30 billion in revenue from the government of Maharashtra state, with about half of that net profit. During his stint as the U.S. ambassador to the Philippines from 1991-1992, Wisner clinched Enron the contract to manage two Subic Bay power plants. Wisner's father was a CIA agent who committed suicide in 1965, after a career that included assisting the overthrow of democratically elected governments in Iran and Guatemala. Another Enron director was Henry "Pug" Winokur, who, from 1988-1997 was Chairman of Dyncorp, a favorite CIA "carve out" contractor in Latin America, the Balkans, and Africa. Ken Lay had his own ties to the intelligence community, having worked in the Pentagon during the Vietnam War.[34]

---

[32] "A Closer Look at Enron's Collapse," *Intelligence Online*, January 17, 2002; Alan Bernstein, "The fall of Enron; Security team leaves Enron to form firm; Group to continue working through consulting contract," *Houston Chronicle*, January 23, 2002, p. 13.

[33] Confidential information from a high-placed Enron source.

[34] Vijay Prashad, "The Parochial Coverage of Enron," *Z Net Commentary,* February

Other questions about the oil industry's ties to the U.S. military-intelligence complex were raised when Michael Trumpower, the owner of Prescott, Arizona-based company Matco, Inc., filed for corporate bankruptcy shortly after George W. Bush's inauguration. In questionable financial moves similar to those of Enron, Matco traded on a lucrative oil concession it was granted for all offshore exploration in the Emirate of Fujairah in exchange for unsecured loans for equipment and services. Fujairah, one of the poorest of the emirates, is led by Sheik Hamad bin Mohammed al Sharqi, one of the more fundamentalist Wahhabi Muslims in the UAE leadership. Al Sharqi patronizes the Fujairah Islamic Call and Guidance Center, which has recruited a number of foreign adherents to Wahhabi Islam. These include Filipinos, British, Americans, Russians, and Sri Lankans. Moreover, all their native countries are targets of Bin Laden's Al Qaeda. In addition, a number of Pakistani nationals who worked at the National Bank of Fujairah were known by international law enforcement to be sympathetic to the Taliban.

Trumpower's close ties to Sheikh Hamad are only rivaled by his close ties to the CIA. Although he became strapped for cash after his company tanked, Trumpower, like Enron's Kenneth Lay, was a major contributor to the Bush campaign and those of other Republican candidates, including that of powerful House Rules Committee member, Representative Thomas Reynolds of New York. Reynolds was in a position to derail any House investigation of the GOP-CIA-oil industry ties.

In the mid-1980s, Trumpower was an associate of Iran-Contra figure Oliver North. North claims Trumpower was instrumental in helping to free U.S. hostages in Lebanon. That affair was the heart of the Iran-Contra scandal, in which several current Bush administration officials took part. These include National Security Council Middle East adviser Elliot Abrams, former Defense Department Information Awareness Office chief Admiral (retired) John Poindexter, and Assistant Secretaries of State for Latin American Affairs Otto Reich and Roger Noriega. The old Iran-Contra fraternity largely remains intact. In 2000, North and Trumpower jointly appeared at a Republican fund-raising dinner in Arizona.[35]

15, 2002.
[35] James Norman, "Petrodollars," *Platt's Oilgram News*, April 9, 2001, p. 3.

Trumpower was also close to the reigning Emir of Sharjah, who granted the shadowy ex-CIA agent of influence rights to drill in a strip of ocean bordering Fujairah.[36] Sharjah was a major base of operations for Al Qaeda and the Taliban, which used the emirate to smuggle weapons and drugs under Ariana Afghan Airlines security credentials. Sharjah was a base of operations for Viktor Bout's Air Cess operations, which was accused of running weapons to the Taliban and of gun-running activities in Africa, especially the Democratic Republic of Congo.

Next door to Sharjah is Dubai, the center of CIA spying in the region, according to U.S. intelligence sources. Dubai's Dolphin Energy Ltd., was one quarter-owned by Enron before the firm's collapse. Dolphin's CEO was UAE Foreign Minister Sheikh Hamdan bin Zayed Al Nahayan. In July 2001, Osama bin Laden was reported to have received kidney treatment at the American Hospital in Dubai with the blessing of the Dubai and UAE governments. At the time of his hospitalization, Bin Laden was reported by the French newspaper *Le Figaro* and Radio France International to have been visited on July 12, 2001, by Larry Mitchell, the CIA chief in Dubai, who was said to have had close contacts with all the Gulf royal families. Mitchell was reportedly called back to CIA headquarters in Langley, Virginia on July 15, 2001.[37] Oddly, Carlyle owned a 42 percent stake in *Le Figaro* at the time it reported on the Bin Laden meeting with the CIA in Dubai.[38]

The magazine *In These Times* reported yet another former CIA officer who had ties to the Gulf and who was heavily involved with the oil industry. He is Stephen "Satch" Baumgart of Reston, Virginia. He reportedly helped funnel arms to Sadaam Hussein in the 1980s with the approval of the CIA, which had, at the time, tilted to Baghdad in its war with Iran. Baumgart was linked to another Republican contributor and oil mogul, Pierre Falcone of Scottsdale, Arizona. Falcone was implicated in a complex guns-for-oil scandal involving Angola and Vice President Cheney's old company, Halliburton, a major player with the Luanda regime. Falcone

---

[36] Ibid.

[37] UPI, "CIA Officer Said to Have Met With Bin Laden Last July, November 1, 2001.

[38] "Carlyle Will Not Sell 'Figaro' Stake," *La Tribune*, October 15, 2001.

was also closely linked to Arizona Republican State Senator Scott Bundgaard, who ran for the House of Representatives' Second District in Arizona in 2000.[39]

* * * *

Dick Cheney's Halliburton also had more than a vested interest in pre-9-11 Afghan politics, considering the importance of the Cent-Gas pipeline. It was apparent from the outset that Hamid Karzai was the preferred alternative to the Taliban as far as pipeline politics was concerned. There were increasing reports that pro-Taliban elements in Pakistan's Inter Services Intelligence (ISI) and their pro-Taliban colleagues in the Bush administration tipped off the Taliban about the presence of mujaheddin opposition commander Abdul Haq in Afghanistan. After 9-11, Haq entered Afghanistan without the knowledge of either the Pakistani or American governments to organize resistance against the Taliban. According to Haq's main American backers, who included wealthy Chicago financiers James and Joseph Ritchie and former Reagan National Security Adviser Robert McFarlane, Haq and his group of former mujaheddin commanders received absolutely no support from the Bush administration.[40]

According to U.S. government sources, the same Bush administration elements that promoted the Taliban over the Northern Alliance may have tipped off Pakistan about Haq's presence near Jalalabad on October 26, 2001. The ISI, in turn, notified their Taliban allies. Haq and his party were surrounded by Taliban military units, captured, tortured, and executed. Haq's use of two satellite telephones while inside Afghanistan also meant his exact location was known to the National Security Agency's overhead signals intelligence (SIGINT) satellites—intelligence that would have been available to the Pentagon.

The CIA claimed it tried to vector an armed Predator UAV to assist Haq but that it arrived too late. Oddly, the Pentagon claimed

---

[39] Ken Silverstein, "The Arms Dealer Next Door: International billionaire, French prisoner, Angolan weapons broker, Arizona Republican. Who is Pierre Falcone?" *In These Times*, December 22, 2001.

[40] Molly Moore and Kamran Khan, "Slain Rebel's Brief but Disastrous Foray; Pakistani Intelligence Blames Death on CIA; Friends Cite Frustration with U.S.; *Washington Post*, October 28, 2001, p. A20.

it never received any requests to assist Haq. What was later discovered about the neoconservative Office of Special Plans in the Pentagon made the capture and execution of Haq even more suspicious. Haq was widely believed to have been the number-one contender to head a future post-Taliban government in Afghanistan. Haq was an opponent of Karzai, who enjoyed close relations with Taliban leader Mullah Mohammed Omar. Haq was also a bitter enemy of Pakistan, all the more understandable when it is recalled that Haq's wife and daughter were assassinated in Peshawar in 1999 in a plot believed to have been carried out by the ISI.

More perplexing was the presence of the ISI chief, General Mahmud Ahmed, in Washington, DC on the morning of 9-11. The Northern Alliance spokesman in Washington, Haron Amin (who became Hamid Karzai's ambassador to the United States), and Indian intelligence, in an apparent leak to *The Times of India*, confirmed reports that General Ahmed ordered a Pakistani-born British citizen—and known terrorist—named Ahmed Umar Sheik to wire $100,000 from Pakistan to the U.S. bank account of Mohammed Atta, the lead hijacker on American Airlines Flight 77 that crashed into the World Trade Center.

When the FBI traced calls made between General Ahmed and Sheik's cellular phone—the number having been supplied by Indian intelligence to the FBI—a pattern linking the general with Sheik clearly emerged. According to *The Times of India*, the revelation that General Ahmed was involved in the Sheik-Atta money transfer was more than enough for a nervous and embarrassed Bush administration. It pressed Musharraf to dump General Ahmed. Musharraf eventually mealy-mouthed the announcement of his general's dismissal by stating Ahmed "requested" early retirement.[41]

Sheik was well known to the Indian police. He had been arrested in New Delhi in 1994 for plotting to kidnap four foreigners, including an American citizen. Sheik was released by the Indians in 1999, in a swap for passengers on board New Delhi-bound Indian Airlines flight 814, hijacked by Islamic militants from

---

[41] Manoj Joshi, "India helped FBI trace ISI-terrorist links, *The Times of India*, October 9, 2001.

Kathmandu, Nepal to Kandahar, Afghanistan. India continues to believe the ISI played a part in the hijacking, since the hijackers were affiliated with the pro-bin Laden Kashmiri terrorist group, Harkat-ul-Mujaheddin, a group only recently and quite belatedly placed on the State Department's terrorist list. The ISI and bin Laden's Al Qaeda reportedly assisted the group in its operations against Indian government targets in Kashmir.

The FBI, which assisted its Indian counterpart in the investigation of the Indian Airlines hijacking, says it wants information leading to the arrest of those involved in the terrorist attacks. Yet, no move was made to question General Ahmed or those U.S. government officials, including Richard Armitage, who met with him in September 2001. Clearly, General Ahmed was a major player in terrorist activities across South Asia, yet still managed to maintain very close ties to the U.S. government.

CIA veteran Milt Bearden, who headed up the support network for the Afghan mujaheddin during the Afghan war against the Soviets, represented the pro-Taliban view within the military-intelligence complex. He said he foresaw an Afghanistan headed by a "reformed Taliban." After 9-11, Bearden was signed up as an on-air consultant for CBS News. Officials of the unofficial embassy of the Islamic State of Afghanistan (the Northern Alliance) in Washington cited Bearden, along with INR's Marvin Weinbaum, as the chief promoters of the Taliban within the United States government. According to knowledgeable sources, after the Bush administration came to power, Bearden and Weinbaum prevailed on the National Security Council to tilt toward the Taliban. In fact, a written prohibition by Secretary of State Colin Powell on any discussions with the Taliban without his authorization was nixed by the White House.[42]

Former White House Counter-terrorism coordinator Richard Clarke said that he and CIA director George Tenet had come up with a plan prior to September 11 to arm the Northern Alliance against the Taliban. Since he and Tenet were holdovers from the Clinton administration, their plan was quickly nixed by National Security Adviser Condoleezza Rice and the neoconservative cabal.

---

[42] U.S. State Department sources.

Clarke maintained that pre-9-11 warnings he and Tenet passed to Rice and the administration about an impending large scale attack on the United States were ignored.[43] Apparently, the Bush administration was not even fazed by the September 9, 2001 Al Qaeda assassination of Northern Alliance military leader Ahmed Shah Massoud. That came amid terror warnings about an Al Qaeda strike on the United States just two days before the attacks on New York and Washington. On dealing with the Taliban, Secretary of State Powell was outflanked by his own deputy, former CIA/Special Forces veteran Richard Armitage, who was also a veteran of the CIA-supported war in Afghanistan and whose old colleague, Christina Rocca, was involved in pre-9-11 negotiations with the Taliban.

Outwardly, Armitage was considered a loyalist of former Afghan King Mohammed Zahir Shah. However, there were definite links between the King and Taliban leader Mullah Omar. They were both ethnic Pashtuns and hailed from the same Afghan tribe. The Taliban was represented in the United States by Laili Helms, a relative of Zahir Shah and the niece-in-law of the late Richard Helms, the former CIA director and old colleague of Armitage. The pro-Taliban faction in Washington was also aided by the head of the Voice of America's Pashto service, who was called "Kandahar Rose" by her critics and colleagues alike, recalling the wartime "Tokyo Rose," an American defector who broadcast propaganda for Imperial Japan.

During the presidential campaign of 2000, there were a number of contacts between Bush staffers and moderate Taliban elements in Afghanistan. The Bush officials were seeking ways for moderates in Afghanistan to stem support for terrorism in exchange for U.S. investment in the CentGas pipeline. There were even earlier meetings between moderate Taliban officials and U.S. oil executives in Houston. Dick Cheney, the CEO of Halliburton, was said to have attended one such meeting in 1998. After these meetings, links were established with some in the Taliban leadership.

In fact, things were quite cozy between the Houston oil barons and the Taliban. In December 1997, eight Taliban officials, led by Mullah

---

[43] Richard Clarke appearance, *Meet the Press*, March 28, 2004

Ghows and including of one Pakistani ISI agent, visited Houston as the guests of UNOCAL. They were even permitted to visit NASA's Johnson Space Center. Afterward, part of the delegation went to the University of Nebraska where they were the guests of the UNOCAL-funded Center for Afghanistan Studies and its pro-Taliban head, Thomas E. Gouttierre. Two of the members of the group visited Mount Rushmore as if the spirit of Washington, Jefferson, Lincoln, and the anti-oil monopoly President, Theodore Roosevelt, would have some effect on the brutal, twelfth century-thinking Taliban.[44]

* * * *

The idea of the U.S. oil industry coming to Afghanistan did not sit well with conservative Saudi Wahhabi clerics who saw Afghanistan as the "perfect Islamic society." They did not want a pipeline built. The Saudi clerics, allied with wealthy Saudi financial backers of Bin Laden, reportedly planned the terrorist attacks on New York and Washington as revenge for attempting to gain access to Afghanistan. One report claimed Bin Laden might have received up to $50 million from wealthy Saudi donors until the Saudi government uncovered and stopped the donations.[45]

The situation became worse when OPEC met in a secret session in Vienna to discuss the "moderate Taliban solution" in Afghanistan and continuation with the pipeline plan. This inflamed the Saudi clerics, Osama bin Laden's followers, and his Saudi and other Persian Gulf financial backers even more. These factions saw such plans as an attempt by the oil industry to "break Islamic control in Afghanistan"—certainly something for which it was worth waging a "jihad."

A senior State Department official revealed the name of a fourth key player involved in UNOCAL's discussions with the Taliban to build the CentGas pipeline. He was Charles Santos, a Partner with SBS Associates in New York City. Santos was the Political Adviser

---

[44] Anthony Shadid, and John Donnelly, "America Prepares Shaping Strategy; A Courtship; U.S. Tried To Woo Taliban In '90s," *Boston Globe*, September 20, 2001, p. A32; Jennifer Van Bergen, "Zalmay Khalilzad and the Bush Agenda, Truthout, January 13, 2002. <http://www.truthout.org/docs_01/01.14A.Zalmay.Oil.htm>

[45] "Arab Businessmen Donate Millions to Aid Bin Laden: Money is Allegedly Used To Renew Anti-U.S. Effort," *Baltimore Sun*, July 7, 1999, 8A.

to the United Nations Special Mission to Afghanistan. In 1995, he had also been the first member of the mission to meet the Taliban Council in Kandahar. In October 2001, Santos told the House International Relations Committee that he lived near Osama bin Laden's residence in central Kandahar.[46] Moreover, after his stint as a UN envoy, Santos became an executive with Delta Oil, the Saudi firm that was negotiating the CentGas deal with UNOCAL.[47]

Santos, in an article written for the neoconservative and "Moonie" magazine, *Insight on the News*, later called for a federalized Afghanistan consisting of eight regions centered in Heart; Mazar-i-Sharif; Bamian (Hazarastan); Faizabad (Badakhshan); Kabul; Jalalabad; the eastern provinces of Khost, Paktia, and Paktika; and Kandahar.[48] For those who feared a resurgent Islamic radical regime in Afghanistan, what could be a better way to keep the Taliban alive and kicking than to create a loose-knit Afghanistan with semi-autonomous regions in areas with a history of supporting the Taliban? The proposed federal Afghan plan was very much like the Kansteiner plan for a fractured Congo and Sudan in Africa, and also the Bush administration's plan for a federalized and decentralized Iraq. Divide the targeted country into various semi-independent statelets and deal directly with local political chieftains. To many in Asia and Africa, the emerging "Bush Doctrine" was a return to the days of European colonialism.

In 1996 and 1997, Santos had worked with Zalmay Khalilzad, the Afghani-American Bush National Security assistant and subsequent U.S. ambassador to Afghanistan; Hamid Karzai; and former U.S. ambassador to Pakistan Robert Oakley on a UNOCAL-Delta Oil (Saudi Arabia) Advisory Group working with the Taliban to prepare the groundwork for the CentGas pipeline. A State Department source revealed that the entire Taliban pipeline operation was shepherded and supported by senior members of the Bush administration, including Cheney and Rice. Moreover, Enron, a chief cash cow for the Bush-Cheney 2000 campaign, conducted the feasibility study for the CentGas pipeline.

---

[46] Testimony, House Committee on International Relations, October 3, 2001.

[47] Damien Cave, Max Garrone and Daryl Lindsey, "After the Fall," Salon.com, November 14, 2001.

[48] Charles Santos, "Let U.S.-inspired federalism balance the competing interests of a wide range of ethnic factions," *Insight on the News*, March 25, 2002, p. 40.

Washington permitted the Taliban to maintain a diplomatic office in Queens, New York headed by Taliban diplomat Abdul Hakim Mojahed. In addition, U.S. officials, including Assistant Secretary of State for South Asian Affairs Christina Rocca, who is also a former CIA officer and a close friend of Richard Armitage, visited Taliban diplomatic officials in Islamabad. The visits of Islamist radicals did not end with the Taliban. In July 2001, the head of Pakistan's pro-bin Laden Jamiaat-i-Islami Party, Qazi Hussein Ahmed, also reportedly was received at the George Bush Center for Intelligence (aka, CIA headquarters) in Langley, Virginia. According to the *Washington Post,* the Special Envoy of Mullah Omar, Rahmatullah Hashami, even came to Washington bearing a gift carpet for President Bush from the one-eyed Taliban leader. When asked what became of the carpet, Bush's White House gift office refused to provide any information, claiming that the only person to whom they could disclose the information was the gift presenter, Mr. Hashami. An official with the Clinton gift office said that such stonewalling was outrageous when considering that gifts to the President of the United States should be in the public record. The *Village Voice* reported that Hashami, on behalf of the Taliban, offered the Bush administration to hold on to Bin Laden long enough for the United States to capture or kill him but, inexplicably, the administration refused.

The pro-Northern Alliance faction in Washington was supported by the Pentagon's Joint Intelligence Staff (J-2) and the Defense Intelligence Agency. The public affairs representative for the Northern Alliance in Washington was Otilie English, the sister of Pennsylvania Republican Congressman Phil English. Ironically, English filled the seat after his predecessor, Tom Ridge—later the first Secretary of Homeland Security—successfully ran for Governor of Pennsylvania. But the Bush administration took a hostile attitude toward the Islamic State of Afghanistan, otherwise known as the Northern Alliance. Even though the United Nations recognized the alliance as the legitimate government of Afghanistan, the Bush administration, with oil at the forefront of its goals, decided to follow the lead of Saudi Arabia and Pakistan and curry favor with the Taliban mullahs of Afghanistan.

Julie Sirrs, a Defense Intelligence Agency (DIA) analyst and graduate of the Georgetown School of Foreign Service, oversaw developments in Afghanistan and Iran and had some knowledge of Pashto and Farsi. An analyst for DIA since 1995, she traveled to Afghanistan twice on her own time, once in 1997 and again in 1998. The trips were made at her own expense and with the knowledge of her DIA superiors. She met with the Northern Alliance chief Massoud, saw an Al Qaeda terrorist training camp, and was given a "treasure trove" of information on the Taliban and Al Qaeda, including Bin Laden's earnest desire to assassinate Massoud. When she returned to the United States, Sirrs was met by a DIA security officer at Reagan National Airport and her photos were confiscated. She lost her top secret/compartmented security clearance. She eventually resigned, in 1999.

No one in the DIA was interested in what she saw and heard in Afghanistan—they merely determined Sirrs did not follow procedures in traveling to a restricted country. However, she said she had received all the proper permissions, but pressure had been brought to bear by State Department elements who wanted Sirrs to be fired by the DIA. "The State Department didn't want to have anything to do with Afghan resistance," Sirrs said, "or even, politically, to reveal that there was any viable option to the Taliban." A DIA colleague of Sirrs said, "The State Department called the director of DIA repeatedly, demanding her [Sirrs'] 'execution.'" The CIA was not even interested in interrogating the Northern Alliance's prisoners.[49]

Another faction in Washington represented the Israeli view as it pertained to the Taliban. It is centered around the Defense Policy Board (DPB), chaired by former Reagan-era national security official Richard Perle. Considered by many a virtual mouthpiece and representative for the Israeli government within the U.S. defense establishment, Perle advocated a quick military strike on Iraq after an assault on Afghanistan. Other members of the DPB supporting this position included former Secretary of State Henry Kissinger, former Defense Secretary James Schlesinger, former Vice President Dan Quayle and former House Speaker Newt Gingrich.

---

[49] Diane Sawyer, ABC News, Good Morning America, February 18, 2002; Gail Sheehy, "What Julie Sirrs Knew, " *San Antonio Current*, April 1, 2004.

Visiting former Israeli Prime Minister Benjamin Netanhayu, who made several trips to Washington before and after 9-11, advocated, in addition to invading Iraq, U.S. strikes against terrorist camps and cells in Syria, Lebanon, and Iran. But Middle East experts warned against advancing the agenda of Israel in singling out Shi'a Islamic groups. They pointed out that as Shi'as, Iranian backed Islamic groups such as Hizb Al Da'wa (active in Iraq) and the Lebanese Hezbollah were the sworn enemies of Sunni Wahhabis like Bin Laden and his loyalists. "It is clear that Israel is using the terrorist attacks on the United States to draw us into their wars," claimed one U.S. government insider.

Israeli and U.S. military forces also held a series of joint air and naval exercises unprecedented in scope and frequency—OPERATION JUNIPER STALLION, OPERATION JUNIPER COBRA, and OPERATION NOBLE SHIRLEY. Israel's military incursion into the West Bank was code named OPERATION ENDURING STORM. Not coincidentally, the U.S. invasion of Iraq was code named OPERATION ENDURING FREEDOM. U.S. mercenary companies also entered the fray in the Israeli-Palestinian conflict. Palestinians in the Gaza Strip killed three Dyncorp contractors in October 2003.[50]

* * * *

Although UNOCAL claimed it abandoned the CentGas pipeline project in December 1998, a series of meetings between U.S., Pakistani, and Taliban officials after 1998 indicated the project was never really off the table. After 9-11, and the Taliban's total fall from grace with the Bush administration, there were stepped-up meetings between U.S. Ambassador to Pakistan Wendy Chamberlain and that country's oil minister, Usman Aminuddin. Chamberlain, who maintained close ties to the Saudi ambassador to Pakistan (a one-time chief money conduit for the Taliban), pushed hard for Pakistan to begin work on its Arabian Sea oil terminus for the pipeline.

Speaking at a news conference at the National Press Club on April 6, 2004, U.S. ambassador to Afghanistan Dr. Zalmay Khalil-

---

[50] Jim Krane, "Private Firms to U.S. Military's Work," Associated Press, October 29, 2003.

zad studiously avoided discussing the details of the planned Cent-Gas pipeline. Khalilzad, the Afghan-American Republican and neoconservative stalwart, who arrived in Ceres, California near Modesto as an exchange student in 1966, said the pipeline was "a good thing economically," adding that Afghanistan was in a "good location to serve as a regional hub to ports in Pakistan and Iran from central Asia." Prior to working for the Bush administration, Khalilzad also worked for Rand Corporation. As a consultant for Cambridge Energy Research Associates, Khalilzad provided consultation to the team that included UNOCAL, Enron, Halliburton, and the team's consultant, Hamid Karzai, which was negotiating with the Taliban for the pipeline project. Not surprisingly, Khalilzad's State Department biography made no mention of Cambridge Energy.

Responding to a question about the role of private military companies in Afghanistan, Khalilzad stated that no private security companies were providing security for any private sector activities in the country. He admitted that in addition to providing protection for Hamid Karzai, the U.S. security firm Dyncorp also handled his own security. Khalilzad, instead of replying fully to questions concerning the Afghan pipeline and the military situation in Afghanistan, devoted a great amount of time to discussing potential Afghan exports to the Persian Gulf region. He specifically mentioned almonds, walnuts, carpets, rose oil, flowers, mulberries from Badakhshan, raisins and grapes, dates, pomegranates, melons, and saffron.

Khalilzad was promised by President Bush that his role as Special Presidential Envoy to Afghanistan would continue after his assignment as U.S. ambassador ended. However, Bush would eventually decide to send Khalilzad to Baghdad to serve as ambassador at the largest U.S. Embassy in the world. Khalilzad replaced John Negroponte, the former U.S. ambassador to Honduras who was involved in running death squads during the Contra war against Nicaragua. Negroponte was named the Director of National Intelligence, a new "intelligence czar" position created to govern the U.S. intelligence community. Before becoming ambassador to Afghanistan in September 2003, Khalilzad was the

National Security Council's Senior Director for Islamic Outreach and Southwest Asia Initiatives and Special Presidential Envoy and Ambassador-at-Large for the Free Iraqis, where he coordinated activities with Ahmad Chalabi and the Iraqi National Congress. Khalilzad also headed the Bush-Cheney transition team for the Defense Department. Interestingly, Khalilzad used the term "we" when he referred to the Afghan government of Karzai. Also, in a breach of diplomatic protocol, both the U.S. and Afghan flags were displayed behind him at the news conference at the National Press Club, even though Khalilzad was a U.S. citizen and the U.S. ambassador to Afghanistan.

Bush's promise that Khalilzad would remain as his envoy to Afghanistan indicated that the Bush administration planned to install various pro-U.S. "governors-in-residence" in countries where it had an economic interest: Khalilzad and Karzai in Afghanistan; L. Paul Bremer and, subsequently, Ahmad Chalabi in Iraq; Gerard Latortue in Haiti; Reza Pahlavi II (the former Shah's son) in Iran; Farid N. Ghadry in Syria, and others. However, when Iraq began to descend into civil war, Khalilzad was quickly dispatched to Baghdad as ambassador and Afghanistan's "success" story for Bush soon became a disaster. A resurgent Taliban and opium-growing independent warlords ensured that Hamid Karzai's political power did not extend beyond the suburbs of Kabul.

—§—

RIP: Dale Solly

In February 2002, after news broke of a major Israeli spy operation in the United States that was summarized in a leaked Drug Enforcement Administration report, no television news reporters touched the story except for local Washington, DC ABC affiliate anchorman and special investigations reporter, Dale Solly.

In December 2001, Fox News' Carl Cameron reported the story before the leak of the full DEA report, but Fox quickly took the story down from its Web site. On March 5, Solly led off the evening WJLA Channel 7 news, which was anchored by Kathleen Matthews, the wife of NBC political talk show host Chris Matthews, with the story of the Israeli spy scandal, stating, "Eleven months before the attacks on Washington and New York, a hundred-twenty young Israelis, posing as art students, came to this country. Once here, however, what they painted was a very different picture…. The students were probing for information at various government agencies. It was an intelligence gathering operation in this country that this country knew nothing about. And it seemed aimed at the men who would ultimately carry out the 9-11 attacks."

Solly, 53, was found dead at his Silver Spring, Maryland home on April 27, 2002, after suffering a reported heart attack. Friends and colleagues expressed shock that a person in such excellent physical condition and with no reported history of family heart ailments could have succumbed to heart failure.

At the time of Solly's untimely death, WJLA's broadcast facilities in northwest Washington, DC were virtually next door to the Israeli embassy. In late 2001, Solly went to Israel to cover its war on terrorism, but infuriated the Israelis by insisting on also covering the Palestinian situation on the West Bank. He told me he had been rebuked by the Israelis for deciding to travel into the West Bank.

On March 5, 2002, I drove to the Channel 7 studios in Northwest Washington for an interview with Solly about the espionage story. I arrived a bit late because, as bad luck would have it, I mistakenly turned into the driveway of the Israeli embassy instead of making a right turn onto International Drive, the street that would take me to the entrance of the studio. Solly and I joked that if I had gone into the embassy by mistake and they noticed a copy of the DEA Report in my hand, I probably would not have made it for the interview at all.

WJLA ran Solly's story and interview with me as a video stream file for a few months after his death. But like the Fox News and other news Web sites carrying stories of Israeli espionage activities in the United States, the story was abruptly removed. However, the teleprompters used by WJLA fortunately contain computer memory. Thanks to someone at WJLA, I was able to recover the full teleprompter version of Solly's report:

ISRAELI SPIES 5PM NEWSCAST 03/05/02 17:00
KATHLEEN:
TONIGHT, ABC 7 NEWS HAS OBTAINED DETAILS OF A MAJOR SPY RING THAT HAS TIES TO SEPTEMBER ELEVENTH. GOOD EVENING, I'M KATHLEEN MATTHEWS...

DEL:
AND I'M DEL WALTERS...
ONLY ON SEVEN TONIGHT, A DISTURBING REPORT THAT ALLEGES, ISRAELI SPIES, HOT ON THE TRAIL OF AL QAEDA TERRORISTS, WERE OPERATING IN THIS COUNTRY PRIOR TO SEPTEMBER 11TH WITHOUT THE GOVERNMENT'S KNOWLEDGE. AS ABC SEVEN NEWS REPORTER DALE SOLLY TELLS US

DALE:
IT'S BECOME A QUESTION NOW OF WHAT DID THEY KNOW AND WHEN DID THEY KNOW IT:
ELEVEN MONTHS BEFORE THE ATTACKS ON WASHINGTON AND NEW YORK, A HUNDRED-TWENTY YOUNG ISRAELIS, POSING AS ART STUDENTS, CAME TO THIS COUNTRY. ONCE HERE, HOWEVER, WHAT THEY PAINTED WAS A VERY DIFFERENT PICTURE:

MADSEN\INTELIGENCE SPECIALIST:
WHAT THEY WERE DOING WAS GOING DOOR-TO-DOOR VISITING DEA, FBI, INS AGENTS...

DALE:

INTELLIGENCE SPECIALIST, WAYNE MADSEN, SAYS D-E-A GOT SUSPICIOUS...

AND THIS D-E-A REPORT, OBTAINED BY ABC SEVEN NEWS, SAYS THE STUDENTS WERE PROBING FOR INFORMATION AT VARIOUS GOVERNMENT AGENCIES. IT WAS AN INTELLIGENCE GATHERING OPERATION IN THIS COUNTRY THAT THIS COUNTRY KNEW NOTHING ABOUT.

AND IT SEEMED AIMED AT THE MEN WHO WOULD ULTIMATELY CARRY OUT THE 9-ELEVEN ATTACKS:

MADSEN:

THE ISRAELI ART STUDENTS WERE LOCATED IN THE SAME NEIGHBORHOODS WHERE THE SEPTEMBER 11TH ARAB HIJACKERS WERE ALSO LIVING.

IN ONE CASE IN HOLLYWOOD, FLORIDA THE ISRAELI TEAM LEADER WAS RENTING AN APARTMENT LITERALLY TWO BLOCKS FROM A MAIL BOX RENTAL PLACE THAT WAS BEING USED BY MOHAMMED ATTA, THE LEAD HIJACKER AND SOME OF THE OTHER HIJACKERS.

DALE:

BUT WHAT, IF ANYTHING, DID THEY LEARN? AT WORST, MADSEN SAYS, THEY HAD ADVANCE KNOWLEDGE OF THE ATTACKS AND EITHER DIDN'T SHARE ALL OF IT WITH U-S INTELLIGENCE OR WERE IGNORED IF THEY DID:

DALE TO MADSEN:

SO ISRAEL HAS 120 AGENTS, ALL OF THEM CAUGHT BEFORE 9-11. WHAT'S HAPPENED TO THEM?

MADSEN:

THEY WERE ALL ARRESTED AND DEPORTED SO THEY'RE PROBABLY BACK IN ISRAEL.

DALE:

LATE TODAY THE F-B-I AND D-E-A CONFIRMED THE ARRESTS. THE FRENCH NEWSPAPER LE MONDE, CALLED THIS THE BIGGEST ISRAELI SPY CASE IN THIS COUNTRY SINCE THE JONATHAN POLLARD CASE IN 1986.

Following my interview with Solly, he indicated he would be following up on the art student story. The next thing I heard about him was in late April 2002 when I was in a cyber-cafe in Paris checking my e-mail and shockingly read his obituary notice.

On May 9, 2002, reporter Christopher Ketcham wrote in an article in *Salon* that he was told by a high-level U.S. intelligence agent using the code name STABILITY that people involved in the investigation of the Israeli spies were at personal danger of being killed. The agent told Ketcham, "There are a lot of people under a lot of pressure right now because there's a great effort to discredit the [Israeli art student] story, discredit the connections, prevent people from going any further... There are some very, very smart people who have taken a lot of heat on this—have gone to what I would consider extraordinary risks to reach out. Quite frankly, there are a lot of patriots out there who'd like to remain alive. Typically, patriots are dead."[1]

—§—

---

[1] Christopher Ketcham, "The Israeli 'Art Student' Mystery," Salon.com, May 10, 2002. <http://www.salon.com/news/letters/2002/05/10/ketcham>

AL-QUAEDA

Some evidence has emerged that where organised crime and its adherents leads-----Al-Quaeda exists and operates. Verification from several sources partially indicate the purchase on a large scale of Sierra Leone diamonds through Liberia (and in particular Liberian corporations) and using local addresses in Liberia. No 'returns' are made here.

Some of the characters involved in this trade have been identified and notified to the press and the United Nations. Others, though not known, appear to have a 'charmed' and 'untouched' existence.

A 2002 private British risk analysis assessment reported that Liberia has served as an important nexus between diamond smuggling and terrorist financing.

Diamonds are also a smuggler's best friend, here is $1,000,000 worth of gold versus the same amount in investment-grade diamonds. (1979 US dollars)

CHAPTER FIVE

DIAMONDS ARE A
TERRORIST'S BEST FRIEND

C learly, U.S. law enforcement and intelligence, along with agencies from scores of other countries, have, since 9-11, managed to prevent horrific terrorist attacks launched by Al Qaeda and other groups like Jemaah Islamiyah. However, one troubling aspect remains—the unwillingness to vigorously shut down the Russian-Israeli mafia operations that have facilitated the purchase and transport of SAMs, other weapons, and radiological material. And even more perplexing was the presence of pardoned-by-Clinton arms dealer Marc Rich's former attorney, Lewis I. "Scooter" Libby, inside the power structure of Washington. Before his indictment and resignation over the Valery Plame affair, Libby was the Chief of Staff to Vice President Cheney.

Rich's network has strong links to Russian oligarch Boris Berezovsky, who sought asylum in Israel, and Natan (formerly Anatoly) Sharansky, the Israeli Settlements Minister and one-time Soviet Jewish refusenik, whose book, *The Case for Democracy: The Power of Freedom to Overcome Tyranny and Terror*, became bedside reading for George W. Bush and required reading for his Cabinet.

* * * *

The first widely reported link between terrorist organizations like Al Qaeda and the international diamond smuggling and associated money laundering trade was the arrest in New York in August 2003 of an Israeli-American and Afghanistan-born diamond dealer with business links to the Saudi government. The diamond dealer, Yehuda Abraham, working alongside an Indian-born arms dealer with links to Al Qaeda and a Muslim courier from Malaysia, attempted to facilitate the purchase of fifty Russian shoulder-launched missiles for a possible attack on Air Force One.

But the nexus of the Russian mafia with diamonds, money laundering and weapons had long been known to investigators. In 1997, according to the *Washington Post*, Jim E. Moody, who was a lead FBI investigator of Russian-Israeli mob activities from 1971 until his retirement in 1996 as the Deputy Assistant Director of the Criminal Division, stated that the Russian-Israeli mafia is unique in that it will deal with anyone: "When they overlap with other criminal groups, they tend to set up cooperative efforts.... They learn from the other groups, and they work together. No one else does that."[1]

Testifying before the House of Representatives Trade Subcommittee of the Ways and Means Committee on September 12, 2000, Virginia Congressman Frank Wolf revealed that the CIA and other U.S. intelligence agencies have "a wide array of evidence" that Sierra Leone diamonds were being trans-shipped via Liberia, Cote d'Ivoire, Burkina Faso, and Togo to diamond centers in Antwerp, the Netherlands, Israel, India, and New York. The intelligence included information on the diamond smuggling activities of Liberia's former President Charles Taylor and his regime.[2]

Wolf urged the subcommittee members to look at the intelligence. Wolf and Representatives Tony Hall, Cynthia McKinney, and Donald Payne were testifying on behalf of the Consumer Access to a Responsible Accounting Trade (CARAT) Act that would have required the diamond industry to verify where diamonds originate. Hall stated that the primary purpose was to let consumers know where diamonds were mined so they could make their own decisions about what to buy. Without such action, Wolf said, the diamond industry would face a certain boycott that will harm

---

[1] Douglas Farah, "Russian Mob, Drug Cartels Join Forces," *Washington Post*, September 29, 1997, p. A01.

[2] Testimony U.S. Congressman Frank R. Wolf, Hearing on Conflict Diamonds, House Subcommittee on Trade, September 13, 2000.

legitimate diamond-producing nations like Botswana and South Africa. Hall added, "In Sierra Leone, this otherwise respectable industry happily did business with rebels—who used the profits from their trade to turn children into their parents' murderers, and then into soldiers and sex slaves."[3]

Hall also revealed that Lazare-Kaplan, the diamond brokerage firm owned by Maurice Tempelsman, earned nearly 40 per cent more in profits in 1999. Hall added that 30 per cent of the profits came from Sierra Leone, Angolan, and Congolese so-called "conflict diamonds."[4] According to well-informed sources, Tempelsman enjoyed a close social and personal relationship with then-Secretary of State Madeleine Albright. Knowledgeable observers claimed that this close relationship enabled Tempelsman to have undue influence over America's policy on Africa, including the Clinton administration's lukewarm support for a ban on the trade in conflict diamonds. The CARAT Act went nowhere, and diamonds continued to be used by the Israeli-Russian mafia and Al Qaeda to finance their international activities.

A wiretap transcript from the Taormina, Sicily Carabinieri pointed to the increased role of the "new mafia" which was moving into the home turf of the Italian mafia. The transcript involved a wiretap of a conversation of Cosa Nostra figures in Sicily who complain that the *nuovo mafia* had recently taken over a hotel in Taormina, conducting operations from it, and that records of the hotel's sale to the newly-arrived organized crime figures had disappeared. According to the transcript, the Russian-Israeli mafia was using the Sicilian hotel to run various illicit operations.[5]

* * * *

The target of the 2003 sting, Hemant Lakhani, had shown up on the FBI and FSB radar screens before. Like Abraham, he maintained close connections to Arabian Peninsula ruling elites, in Lakhani's case, the ruling families of the United Arab Emirates.

[3] Ibid.

[4] Testimony U.S. Congressman Tony Hall, Hearing on Trade in African Diamonds, Subcommittee on Trade of the House Committee on Ways and Means. September 13, 2000.

[5] Regione Carabinieri Sicilia Compagnia di Taormina, Wiretap 0942/24656.

Shortly before 9-11, Lakhani, who lives in Hendon, in north London, a primarily Orthodox and Hasidic Jewish community, served as a weapons sales agent for the Ukrainian state-owned trading company, UKRSPETSEXPORT and reportedly for ROSOBORONEXPORT, Russia's state-owned weapons export agency. Both companies remained silent on any past relationships with Lakhani.[6] Law enforcement considers Ukraine to be a primary base of operations for the Russian-Ukrainian-Israeli mafia.

Lakhani, a self-described "textile merchant" who hailed from Mumbai's prosperous cloth-trading Kutchi Lohana community, and whose Multitrade, Ltd., "import" business had previously gone bankrupt in 1999, was busy filling orders for Sri Lanka's army, which, at the time, was waging a ferocious guerrilla war against Tamil separatists on the island nation. According to *India Today*, Lakhani supplied the Sri Lankans with MIG-27 warplanes, cannons, shells, and rocket launchers from Ukrainian military warehouses and factories. Lakhani considered ammunition a cheap commodity and not worth his time.

Lakhani also had an interest in selling arms to feuding factions in East Africa because, as reported by *India Today*, he said it was merely a case of "kalus [blacks] killing kalus." It was Lakhani's numerous trips to Kenya that first raised the eyebrows of Kenyan law enforcement authorities. It was there he met a significant international arms dealer, Sanjivan Ruprah, an ethnic Indian and Kenyan citizen.[7]

Ruprah, in turn, was associated with the notorious Viktor Bout, a Tajikistan-born arms dealer who has been associated with the reputed Israeli-Georgian mafia boss Grigori Loutchansky, and Leonid Minin, a Ukrainian-Israeli citizen and leader of the "Odessa mafia" who was also supplying arms to Liberia's Charles Taylor via Burkina Faso.

Italian police arrested Minin in a hotel room in Monza, outside of Milan, in August 2000. In his room, police found $500,000 worth of uncut diamonds, files on illegal weapons shipments to

---

[6] Simon Saradzhyan, "Doubts Linger Over the Igla Sting," *Moscow Times*, August 15, 2003.

[7] Anil Padmanabhan and Sandeep Unnithan, "Hemant Lakhani: Trading In Terror," *India Today*, September 1, 2003, p. 34.

Sierra Leone, Liberia, and the Ivory Coast, and a banking document showing a $10,263.02 payment to international financier and reputed Russian-Israeli-American mafia don Marc Rich, pardoned in January 2001 by President Clinton in the eleventh hour of his administration.[8] Italian police knew Minin as the head of the *neftemafija* or "oil mafia" of Odessa.

In April 2004, details emerged that a number of companies were profiting from the UN's Iraq oil-for-food program by receiving cash payments from Saddam Hussein. Among those investigated was Patrick Maugein, a past associate of Marc Rich. Maugein said the principals of two companies involved in the Iraqi payments—Trafigura and Ibex—were involved with Rich.[9] According to the Public Broadcasting System's news show *Frontline*, Rich's Glencore International AG and Minin's Galaxy Management once shared the same London office telephone number. Loutchansky's company, NORDEX, was also linked to Rich when Interpol discovered that he was one of its founders.

In June 2002, in Operation Spiderweb, European police and FBI agents arrested fifty individuals, twenty of them Russian-Israeli dual citizens, and all linked to Israeli-Russian mafia money laundering. The investigation of the mobsters began in 1999, when it was discovered that millions of dollars were being laundered from Russia through the Bank of New York (BONY). One of the banks that blew the whistle on BONY was Republic National Bank of New York, founded by Edmond Safra, a Lebanese-Syrian Jew, one time head of American Express, and international financier who lived in Monte Carlo. In December 1999, Safra and his granddaughter's nanny had died of smoke asphyxiation after two masked men set fire to his penthouse in Monaco. It was reported that the Russian-Israeli mafia put a contract out on Safra and his family. Safra's wife and granddaughter survived the attack.[10]

---

[8] Matthew Brunwasser, "Leonid Efimovich Minin: From Ukraine, A New Kind of Arms Trafficker," Frontline World, May 2002. <http://www.pbs.org/frontlineworld/stories/sierraleone/minin.html>

[9] Kenneth R. Timmermann, "Documents Prove UN Oil Corruption," *Insight On The News*, April 13, 2004.

[10] John Litchfield, "Billionaire Who Blew Whistle On Russian Cash Scandal Is Killed In Monte Carlo," *The Independent*, December 4, 1999, p. 3.

Federal investigators discovered that one of BONY's clients was the Russian bank Menatep, a bank tied up with a criminal investigation of the European Union Bank, an "Internet" bank licensed in Antigua. The bank turned out to be a huge cyber-fraud orchestrated by the Russian-Israeli mafia.[11] OPERATION SPIDERWEB also uncovered the fact that another Rich company, Benex, was connected to the BONY money laundering scandal.[12] Benex's office, located on Queens Boulevard in Forest Hills, New York, shared the office building with two companies connected to Grigori Loutchansky.

In February 2002, the diamond and arms smuggler Sanjivan Ruprah was arrested by Belgian police for using a false passport. The *Washington Post* reported that Ruprah had secretly provided the United States information about Viktor Bout's network before his arrest by Belgian police.[13] The U.S. Customs Service had initiated PROJECT SHIELD AMERICA after 9-11 to cut off the flow of illegal arms. *Frontline* reported that Ruprah, "was directly involved in the operations of Leonid Minin's arms sales to Liberia, and owns diamond mines in Liberia."[14] According to an article by Peter Landesman in the *New York Times* magazine, Bout admitted that Minin was one of his clients.[15]

On November 30, 2005, the UN Security Council Committee on Liberia identified Minin as one of Bout's associates, and provided details on the Odessa crime lord:

MININ, Leonid Yukhimovich
Aliases: BLAVSTEIN, BLYUVSHTEIN, BLYAFSHTEIN, BLUVSHTEIN, BLYUFSHTEIN, KERLER, Vladamir (Vladimir) Abramovich (DOB: 18 OCT 1946), POPILO-VESKI, POP-ILOVESKI (POPELA/POPELO), Vladimir Abramovich (DOB: 18 OCT 1946, BRESLAN, Wulf DOB: 10 JUL NK), OSOLS, Igor (DOB: 14 DEC 1947)

---

[11] Jeffrey Robinson, "Russian Villains Clean Up; Bank of New York Staff Are At The Centre of a Probe into the Laundering of $ 10bn Of Eastern European Mob Money," *The Independent*, August 22, 1999, p. 2.

[12] Nick Paton Walsh, "$9bn money laundering ring broken," *The Guardian*, June 16, 2002.

[13] Douglas Farah, "Arrest Aids Pursuit of Weapons Network; Dealer Supplied Taliban, Al Qaeda, Officials Say," *Washington Post*, February 26, 2002, p. A01.

[14] Brunwasser, Frontline, op. cit.

[15] Peter Landesman, "Arms and the Man," the *New York Times Magazine*, August 17, 2003, p. 28.

DOB: 14 DEC 1947 in Odessa, USSR (18 OCT 1946) (10 JUL NK) (14 DEC 1947)

Nationality: Israel

Bolivian Passport: 65118. Forged German Passports: 5280007248D, 18106739D (MININ), Greek Passport: no details, Israeli Passports: 6019832 valid 06/11/94-05/11/99, 9001689 valid 23/01/97-22/01/02, 90109052 issued on 26/11/97, Russian Passport: KI0861177

Owner of Exotic Tropical Timber Enterprises. Key financier for [Liberian ex-dictator Charles] Taylor [S/2001/1015, para. 346]. Arms dealer in contravention of UNSC resolution 1343. Supported former President Taylor's regime in effort to destabilize Sierra Leone and gain illicit access to diamonds.[16]

The exploits of Bout and Ruprah in Africa's worst killing fields are the subject of numerous United Nations reports on mercenary activity, diamond smuggling, and arms trafficking in Angola, Sierra Leone, the Democratic Republic of the Congo, Liberia, Uganda, and Rwanda. According to the *Sub-Equatorial Africa Defense Monitor*, Ruprah has been tied to Al Qaeda training activities in Afghanistan, Somalia, and Eritrea and illicit mining operations in the Democratic Republic of the Congo that involve Rwandan President Paul Kagame, former Rwandan External Security Organization director Colonel Patrick Karegeya, former Rwandan military intelligence chief Col, Jack Nziza, and businessman Faustin Mbundu. The United States was reported to have "investigated" the link.[17] Rwandan Patriotic Army (RPA) forces had a significant experience with the downing of a presidential aircraft by a Russian-made SAM. On April 6, 1994, two Russian SAM 16 IGLA series missiles, captured from Iraqi caches by U.S. forces during Operation Desert Storm, were used by the RPA to shoot down the presidential aircraft flying Rwandan President Juvenal Habyarimana and Burundian President Cyprien Ntaryamira back from a peace summit in Dar es Salaam, Tanzania.[18]

---

[16] UN Security Council SC/8570, "Security Council Committee on Liberia Updates Freeze List," November 30, 2005.

[17] Periscope Daily Defense News Capsules, "Kagame, Officials Alleged To Have Al-Qaida Ties," September 11, 2002.

[18] Bernard Debre, Le retour du Mwami (The Return of the Mwami), (Paris: Edition Ramsay, 1998), pp. 90-91: Paul Barril, Guerres Secrets a l'Elysee (Secret Wars of the

It was in Sierra Leone that Ruprah and Bout discovered the convenience and secrecy of swapping arms for diamonds. Not only could diamonds be sold easily on the international black market, but the financial trails of the transactions would be virtually non-existent, and virtually undetectable by law enforcement. The *Los Angeles Times* reported that Lakhani also arranged the sale of Russian and Ukrainian-made BTR-80 armored personnel carriers to Angola's government, which was waging a bloody civil war against UNITA guerrillas who were occupying some of Angola's most prized diamond mines.[19]

Another reputed Russian-Israeli mafia figure involved in arming Angola's government was Arkadi Gaydamak. He told the paper *Yediot Aharanot* that he initiated a weapons-for-oil agreement with Angola in which oil concessions were used as capital to buy Eastern European weapons.[20] The front company in the deal was Brenco International, run by Pierre Falcone, Jr., whose wife, Sonia, a health and beauty company owner based in Arizona, has been linked politically to George W. Bush. She donated $100,000 to the Republican Party during the 2000 presidential election campaign. Pierre Falcone's oil interests in Angola were reported by the NGO Global Witness to be linked to Halliburton, Inc., during the time the company was headed by Vice President Dick Cheney.[21]

Kenyan police told London's *Sunday Times* that Lakhani and Ruprah were "suspected of being involved in the seeking of arms for diamonds to rebel group movements in the Great Lakes region, in the eastern Democratic Republic of Congo and Burundi."[22] Both Lakhani and Ruprah had owned airlines that were possibly involved in arms and diamond smuggling. Ruprah's airline, Simba Airlines, which is based at Nairobi's Wilson Airport, has been linked to diamond smuggling involving Israeli companies. Lakhani's airline, Gujarat Airways, went bankrupt in 1999 and was forced to return

Elysee), (Paris: Albin Michel, 1996), p. 176.

   [19] Richard B. Schmitt, John J. Goldman and Ken Silverstein, "Details of Sting Tell of Wider Threat," *Los Angeles Times*, August 14, 2003, p. 1.

   [20] Center for Public Integrity, "The Influence Peddlers," *Africa News*, November 13, 2002.

   [21] Center for Public Integrity, "Angola; Greasing the Skids of Corruption," *Africa News*, November 4, 2002.

   [22] "Trail of 'amateur' missile trader leads to Al-Qaeda," *Sunday Times*, August 17, 2003, p. 10.

its leased Beechcraft airplanes to Raytheon. Kenyan police also reported that Lakhani was under investigation in Kenya for selling arms to various Al Qaeda groups, including one group arrested in Mombassa on August 10, two days before Lakhani and Abraham's arrest. It is particularly significant what Kenyan police discovered in the Al Qaeda weapons cache: five IGLA missiles, similar to the one purchased by Lakhani from the Russians.[23]

The world of international diamond trading operations is masked in secrecy. Jewish diamond dealers, known as *yahalom manin*, strike deals based on a handshake, and, as with the Islamic *hawalahs*, payments for diamonds are wired around the world through a variety of pass-through companies and middlemen. A major center for diamond smuggling and money laundering is in Hatton Garden, a heavily Hasidic and Orthodox community reachable by the London "Tube" from Lakhani's neighborhood of Hendon. In 1998, Solly Nahome, an international drug smuggler, money launderer, and diamond merchant tied to an Israeli-Russian mafia diamond smuggling ring operating out of Tel Aviv, Antwerp, and Hatton Garden, was shot to death outside his Finchley, north London home.[24] British police reported that joint diamond and heroin smuggling activities by some of Britain's Orthodox and ultra-Orthodox Jews have spread to northern London neighborhoods such as Stamford Hill and Golders Green, historically Jewish areas that have, heretofore, been free of criminal activity.

A former chief of Mossad confirmed to me in a meeting in Herzliya, north of Tel Aviv, that terrorist groups like Al Qaeda, Hamas, and Hezbollah launder money through diamonds in places like West Africa in order to buy weapons without detection by international financial surveillance authorities. On a visit to the spot where the late Israeli Prime Minister Yitzhak Rabin was gunned down by a right-wing Jewish extremist, the former chief warned of the agenda by the right-wing elements that were part of the Ariel Sharon government to destroy the Arab-Israeli peace process.

* * * *

---

[23] Padmanabhan and Unnithan, op. cit.

[24] Jason Bennetto and Paul Lashmar, "Two shot dead in suspected 'hits,'" *The Independent*, December 1, 1998, p. 7.

The arms-diamonds-cash smuggling operation that was the object of the sting was hatched some four months after the September 11 terrorist attacks in New York and Washington. While U.S. and allied forces were hunting down Al Qaeda and Taliban troops in Afghanistan, a shadowy network of Al Qaeda, Jemaah Islamiyah, and international arms smugglers linked to the Russian-Israeli mafia began planning another massive 9-11 style terrorist attack.

Although the eastern European mafia is referred to by many in the media and law enforcement as the Russian mafia, it is important to note that in the book *Red Mafiya: How the Russian Mob Has Invaded America*, author Robert Friedman describes the close connections between the so-called Russian Mafia and Israel. Friedland quotes Jonathan Winer, a former Assistant Secretary of State for International Law Enforcement, who revealed, "There is not a major Russian organized crime figure who we are tracking who does not also carry an Israeli passport."[25] According to Winer, a former aid to Senator John Kerry's investigations of BCCI and international drug smuggling, all 75 top Russian and Ukrainian Mafia figures carry Israeli passports.[26]

While links between Saudi Arabian businesses and charities and Al Qaeda have been highlighted by law enforcement and the media, very little attention has been paid to the long-term association of terrorist groups like Al Qaeda with the Russian-Israeli mafia. A 23-year veteran of the CIA's counterterrorism division told me in July 2004 that one of the most overlooked aspects of the 9-11 attacks was the role of Russian-Israeli organized crime in facilitating the attack. (He added that Pakistan's role was also a major driving force behind 9-11.)

Russian policeman Kiril Kagner points out that some, but not all, Russian mobsters are Jewish. He says many Russian mobsters claim Jewish roots in order to obtain an Israeli passport. He estimates that the Russian-Israeli mafia has pumped some $4 billion into the Israeli economy. According to Britain's *Independent*, some of this money is kept in religious banks in Israel, which are tax

---

[25] Robert I. Friedman, *Red Mafiya: How the Russian Mob Has Invaded America* (Boston, Little, Brown and Co., 2000), p. xvii.

[26] Strategic Forecasting (Stratfor), "Russian Ukrainian Crime Groups Set to Corner Global Drug Market," April 8, 2002.

exempt.[27] Making matters worse is the fact that there is no law against money laundering in Israel.

* * * *

Sixty-seven year old Yehuda H. Abraham, an Orthodox Jewish resident of Forest Hills in Queens, New York City, might once have seemed a most unlikely individual to serve as a money launderer for shady arms dealers tied to Al Qaeda and Jemaah Islamiya. However, as a native of Afghanistan and fluent in Urdu (also a major language of Pakistan and India), as a merchant with a store called "New York Jewels" in the lobby of the posh Sheraton Hotel in Jeddah, Saudi Arabia, and as a self-described provider of gems to the Saudi royal family, Abraham would normally be identified as a "person of interest" in any number of U.S. intelligence and law enforcement databases. Thus, and adding the fact that Abraham's gem trading company, Ambuy International Corporation, sits right in the middle of Manhattan's 47th Street "Diamond District" and also has locations in Antwerp, Milan, Bangkok, and Jeddah, it is indeed odd that he was not included on any "watch list" profiles created by the FBI or CIA. According to Israeli intelligence sources, Afghan-born Jews are highly prized by the Mossad, which had reportedly used them to infiltrate the Taliban in Afghanistan.

Abraham, along with a 68-year-old Indian-born and Hindu British arms smuggler named Hemant Lakhani (some spellings had his first name as Hekmat [possibly his Muslim alias] and Hemad) and an Indian resident of Malaysia named Moinuddeen Ahmed Hameed, were arrested by federal agents and local police in the New York metropolitan area on August 12, 2003. The arrests capped a lengthy investigation into how terrorist groups like Al Qaeda obtain weapons and fund their purchases on the international black market. Lakhani was attempting to procure a number of IGLA man-portable air defense systems (MANPADS) and C-4 explosives from Russian sources reportedly connected to organized crime.

---

[27] Paul Lashmar, "Heroin trail that led to the heart of London's Jewish community," *The Independent,* July 25, 1998, p. 3.

Lakhani first approached Russian contacts in St. Petersburg sometime at the end of 2001 and asked about purchasing the portable missiles. The two factories that produce the IGLA missile are the Moscow-based Kolomna Engineering Design Bureau and the Vladimir-based Degtyarev Plant. According to the *Moscow Times*, officials of both plants subsequently denied any knowledge of Lakhani. But someone reported the contact, and soon Russian President Putin reported to the White House that Lakhani was a British citizen who was known by Russian intelligence to be connected to arms rings supplying both Chechen and Al Qaeda cells. Lakhani's attempts to purchase Russian SAM missiles were also reported by Putin to the White House. An FBI team was soon sent to St. Petersburg to further investigate the proposed arms deal.

Sometime between Lakhani's trip to St. Petersburg around December 2001 and January 2002, the FBI was able to place an informant inside the arms smuggling network. This is where the official story gets somewhat murky. The FBI maintained that an informant, code named "CW," or "confidential witness," met Lakhani in New Jersey. CW's cover story was that he was representing the Ogaden Liberation Movement in Ethiopia and Somalia. It was later reported that CW was Mohammed Habib Rehman, also known as "Haji," and said by detractors of the government's case against Lakhani and Abraham to be a "small time swindler."[28]

However, Rehman had been recruited by the Drug Enforcement Administration in Pakistan around 1993. Rehman was highly prized by the DEA, and he helped crack a major Pakistani heroin smuggling ring, an act that caused the DEA to relocate him and his family to the United States for their personal safety. Later, Rehman acted as an informant for the FBI in terrorist investigations in Minneapolis, the city where Zacarias Moussaoui allegedly planned his part of the 9-11 attacks. Rehman was in high demand by the FBI after 9-11.[29]

But, the "fix" was in. The FBI's star witness and informant was viciously portrayed as a con man in a carefully crafted character

---

[28] John P. Martin, "Was sting target kingpin or tool? Doubts raised in terror 'triumph,'" *Times Picayune*, April 6, 2004, p. 1.

[29] John P. Martin, "Missile Sting: Closer Look Dims Anti-Terror 'Victory,'" Newhouse News Service, April 5, 2004.

assassination campaign in an attempt to absolve both Abraham and Lakhani. Court papers filed by the government characterized Rehman as a worthless deadbeat with many outstanding debts.

Lakhani and Rehman had had their first meeting in Dubai in October 2001, providing yet another link between international arms traffickers, Israeli money launderers, and Al Qaeda. The Dubai meeting was arranged by Abdul Qayyum, an Indian terrorist leader with reported links to Al Qaeda who carried out a series of deadly terrorist bombings in Mumbai, India in 1993.[30] Qayyum told Lakhani that "Haji" (Rehman) had good ties to rich Saudis. Qayyum was a well-known figure in Dubai, a major financial hub for Al Qaeda and the Taliban.

Lakhani provided Rehman with an arms brochure and business cards from three employees of a Russian arms company. Lakhani, according to the U.S. government charges against him, offered to supply Rehman with anti-aircraft guns and missiles. Rehman and Lakhani conducted their conversations in Urdu and Hindi.

Lakhani obviously was not aware that Rehman was rigged with sophisticated audio and video recording equipment. Nevertheless, Lakhani and Rehman continued their relationship while the FBI secretly audiotaped and videotaped some 200 conversations between the two in Urdu and Hindi. During a meeting between Lakhani and Rehman on January 17, 2002, the FBI discovered that Lakhani praised Osama bin Laden, saying he [Bin Laden] "straightened them [the Americans] all out" and that 9-11 was "a good thing."

On or about April 25, 2002, Lakhani and Rehman met again. After Lakhani described the types of MANPADs available, Rehman changed his cover story, and said their use was for a "jihad" against airplanes in the United States. According to the FBI's tapes of Lakhani's conversations with Rehman, the arms dealer suggested conducting a coordinated attack aimed at passenger planes at ten or fifteen locations simultaneously. Lakhani offered to sell Rehman 200 of the missiles, but Rehman said he initially only wanted one sample.

From May to September 2002, Lakhani worked out the deal with his supplier in Russia. On May 2, Lakhani phoned Rehman and

---

[30] *NBC Nightly News*, May 2, 2004.

said he had met with the Russian supplier. On May 16, Lakhani faxed Rehman a brochure on the IGLA series missile. The Russian IGLA-S series SAM was agreed upon. The price of the missile and launcher was also set.

On August 17, Lakhani explained to his Russian suppliers that delays in delivery were unacceptable, since delivery of the weapon was required by Rehman for "the anniversary," a reference to the first anniversary of the previous year's September 11 terrorist attacks. On August 21, Lakhani gave Rehman more technical details about the missile. Eight days later, Lakhani told Rehman his Russian suppliers said that shipping just one IGLA was too risky, and they wanted a minimum purchase of twenty missiles. On September 17, from his window at the Wyndham Hotel overlooking Newark's Liberty International Airport, Lakhani said that attacking airplanes taking off and landing could "shake the economy" of the United States.

On October 8, 2002, a fax from Lakhani demanded a down payment for the first IGLA. He told Rehman that his agent must be paid $30,000, and would confirm his identity with the serial number F836160631J on a U.S. one dollar bill that would be shown to Rehman. Lakhani said the total price for the missile was $85,000. Rehman discussed payment arrangements with a Lakhani associate in Britain who was referred to in court papers as "the Individual." The Individual, later identified as Manthena or "Vijay" Raja, informed Rehman that he would be dealing directly with a contact in New York City, and he gave him the phone number of the agent.

Yehuda Abraham turned out to be the agent in question, and the two Urdu speakers met on October 16 at Abraham's New York City diamond trading office, where $30,000 in $100 bills was paid by Rehman to Abraham after the dollar bill serial number code was confirmed. After counting every bill, Abraham gave Rehman his business card, which stated he was Yehuda H.A. Abraham, President of Ambuy Gem Corp., 580 Fifth Avenue, New York. Abraham later charged Lakhani a $1500 fee for the transaction.

Federal prosecutors said Abraham wired the $30,000 to a bank account in Europe as a show of "good faith" to the Russian arms dealers. In court papers filed by prosecutors, Abraham's financial transfer network was described as an Islamic *hawalah* cash transfer system. The papers also indicated that Abraham's financial network had a good reputation among past customers.

From November 2002 to February 2003, Lakhani insisted upon full payment for the missile. Rehman wanted to make the payment to a bank account. At first, Lakhani resisted dealing with a bank, but finally agreed that a phony invoice for $60,000 in medical equipment and a foreign bank account number would be supplied. During a meeting with Rehman in December 2002, Lakhani also claimed that the quality of the IGLAs was much better than the older Russian-made STRELA SAM-7s fired at an Israeli charter jet in Mombassa the previous month; the two STRELA missiles fired at the Israeli jet had merely bounced off the ascending aircraft without exploding.

In February 2003, Lakhani faxed Rehman an invoice for $60,000 from Laberia Corporation, a company in Cyprus with branches in Ukraine, for "spare parts for medical facilities" and a "laboratory bench" with the country of origin listed as Russia. Cyprus is a favored money laundering location for the Russian-Israeli mafia. In March, Lakhani informed Rehman that the IGLA would be shipped to the United States from St. Petersburg, and the contents on the shipping manifest would be listed as "spare parts."

On July 12, 2003, Lakhani flew to Moscow to finalize the weapons deal. He met with two agents for the supplier who, unbeknownst to Lakhani, were Russian FSB agents. Lakhani agreed to a payment of $70,000 for the missile (making only $15,000 as a commission) and informed the two Russian agents he wanted to buy 50 more missiles and a supply of several tons of C-4 plastic explosive (the same type of explosive used in the deadly bombing of night clubs in Bali in October 2002 that killed over 200 people).

That month, Lakhani informed Rehman that the cost for the fifty additional IGLAs would be $500,000; $56,500 was wired to Lakhani's foreign account.

On August 12, Lakhani flew on a British Airways flight from London's Heathrow Airport to Newark to meet Rehman at their traditional rendezvous spot, the Wyndham Hotel. An FBI agent trailed Lakhani on the same flight from Heathrow. The IGLA had already arrived in the United States by ship from St. Petersburg to the port of Baltimore. From there, it was transported to Newark. The shipment had a false bill of lading indicating the shipment was "dental equipment." The recipient was listed as Rehman's company, the House of Rice, an import company located in Avenel, New Jersey.[31] However, Russian agents had already rendered the SAM inoperable. On August 13, FBI special agent William Evanina, said, "Lakhani saw it [the IGLA] in Moscow, and he saw it again in the hotel room yesterday."

At the Wyndham Hotel, which was already crawling with FBI, DIA, Bureau of Immigration and Customs Enforcement, Secret Service, FSB, and British MI-5 operatives, agents with the FBI Joint Terrorism Task Force placed Lakhani under arrest. Other Federal agents and New York City police entered Abraham's office in suite 1206 at his office building at 1 47th Street and 580 Fifth Avenue in Manhattan. There, Abraham and Ahmed Hameed, who were awaiting the delivery of the $500,000 missile payment, were arrested and Abraham's computers and files were seized. The one-dollar bill with the serial number used in previous transactions was found in the possession of Hameed in Abraham's office. Hameed told Rehman the bill had been kept in Abraham's office.

U.S. law enforcement officials reported that Abraham had brought Hameed to the United States from Malaysia to facilitate the laundering of the $500,000 for the additional 50 IGLAs. The government also had evidence that Lakhani and Abraham had worked together in the past. Court papers indicate that Rehman conversed with Hameed, Lakhani, and Abraham in Urdu. Lakhani is reported to have told Rehman that Abraham was "very trustworthy."[32]

Oddly, the Bergen County (New Jersey) *Record* reported that Lakhani and Hameed were taken by U.S. Marshals Service agents

---

[31] John P. Martin, "How 2-year sting brought down missile deal," *Star-Ledger* (Newark), April 4, 2004.

[32] Michael Slackman, "Threats and Responses: The Plot; Gem Dealer Is Said to Aid Scheme on Terrorist Funds," *New York Times*, August 14, 2003, p. A16; Amy Klein, "U.S. details terror plot; Trafficker's plan: Sell 50 missiles," *The Record* (Bergen, NJ), August 14, 2003, p. A01.

to the Passaic County jail in New Jersey; Abraham's detention location was never revealed.[33]

At Abraham's arraignment, Assistant U.S. Attorney Jeffrey Clark argued against any release of the diamond dealer. Clark said that although the government could not prove beyond a reasonable doubt that Abraham knew he was involved in an arms smuggling ring, he remained "willfully blind" to "the nature of what he was involved in." However, Federal Judge for the District of New Jersey Joel Pisano agreed with an earlier decision by Federal Judge Andrew Peck that Abraham was not knowingly engaged in a weapons smuggling ring.

Clark argued that with relatives in Israel, Italy, and England, Abraham remained a "significant flight risk." And according to Abraham's local newspaper, the *Forest Hills Ledger*, Abraham spent a good time of the year away from his home.[34] *Jewish Week* reported that Abraham's neighbor said the diamond merchant made frequent trips to Thailand,[35] and Abraham reportedly spent enough time in Bangkok to help start a synagogue and open a kosher kitchen.[36] Abraham's attorney argued for bail based on the fact that his client had high blood pressure and suffered from stomach cancer. He also said Abraham was a respected member of his Forest Hills community and the founder of his local Bukharian synagogue, where he had donated a Torah five years earlier.[37] But Assistant U.S. Attorney Michael Purpura was having nothing of that argument: "Yes, this elderly gentleman in poor health significantly helped broker the sale of a surface to air missile."[38]

Nonetheless, Abraham was treated in an entirely different manner from either Lakhani or Hameed. While bail was refused for the

[33] Klein, Ibid.

[34] Tien Shun-Lee, "Borough jeweler charged with financing terrorists," *Forest Hills Ledger*, August 21, 2003. <http://www.zwire.com/site/news.cfm?newsid=10038677&BRD=1079&PAG=461&dept_id=506462&rfi=8>

[35] Eric J. Greenberg, "Diamond Merchant Awaits Bail," *The Jewish Week*, August 22, 2003. <http://www.thejewishweek.com/news/newscontent.php3?artid=8337&offset=0&B1=1&author=Eric J. Greenberg&issuedates=&month=04&day=09&year=2004&issuedate=20031009&keyword=Yehuda Abraham>

[36] <http://www.amyisrael.co.il/asia/thailnd>

[37] Neil Graves, Jennifer Fermino and Gersh Kuntzman, "Suburban 'Terrorists' - Neighbors Stunned At 'Mr. Average' Arrests," *New York Post*, August 14, 2003, p. 4.

[38] Slackman, op. cit.

two Indians, Abraham's lawyer successfully argued for his client's release on $10 million bail. Abraham was permitted by a Federal judge in Newark to post a $10 million promissory note guaranteed by ten co-signers and a $5 million secured property bond. However, a former Justice Department prosecutor, speaking on conditions of anonymity, said that promissory notes are virtually unheard of in Federal bail proceedings. "It's always been cash on the barrel head," he said. The value of an international diamond dealer with links to an arms smuggling network connected to the Israeli-Russian mafia and Al Qaeda may explain why Abraham was confined to house arrest with electronic monitoring, while Lakhani and Hameed remained in prison in New Jersey.

On March 30, 2004, Abraham pleaded guilty to the charge that he laundered money for Lakhani. He told Judge Katharine Hayden that he "wasn't aware of what the money was used to buy."[39] Hameed pleaded guilty to the charge of "conspiracy to operate an unlicensed money transmitting business." In what was clearly a plea bargain, Hameed agreed to testify against Lakhani. Lakhani's business associate in London, "the Individual" (Manthena Raja) also agreed to cooperate in the government's case against Lakhani. Raja later pleaded guilty to a single money laundering charge, Raja admitting that on October 17, 2002, at Lakhani's request, he had arranged a transfer of $30,000 to Lakhani in London, and that on March 4, 2003, using a Swiss bank account, he had transferred $56,500 to Lakhani.[40]

* * * *

The sting of Lakhani, Abraham, and the Malaysian courier Hameed came just hours after the CIA, FBI, and Thai security police bagged one of the biggest fish in Jemaah Islamiyah (JI), the notorious Hambali (aka Riduan Isamuddin, born, Encep Nurjaman), who was wanted for his role in the bombing of the Bali nightclubs and the Marriott Hotel in Jakarta. Thai Prime Minister Thaksin

---

[39] Amy Klein. "Guilty plea in missile sting; Merchant had financial role," *The Record* (Bergen, NJ), March 31, 2004, p. A03.

[40] U.S. Fed News, "Information Issued By U.S. Attorney's Office For New Jersey On Sept. 10: Indian National Admits Transfer Of Funds For Purchase Of Shoulder-Fired Missile," September 10, 2004.

Shinawatra later said that Hambali and his confederates were planning several bombings to coincide with the APEC summit in Bangkok. The CIA and Thai police were alerted to the presence of Hambali in Thailand based on information derived from captured JI member and moneyman, Wan Min Wan Mat, in Malaysia. He told Malaysian police that Hambali was living in Phnom Penh, Cambodia, so police were looking for him there. Cambodia was a center for JI activity. In June 2003, in Phnom Penh, Cambodian police nabbed Malaysian JI chief of finances, Zulkifli Marzuki, and turned him over to U.S. interrogators.[41]

Zulkifli and Hambali met in Bangkok in February 2002 to discuss the planned Bali bombing with two other Malaysian JI members, Azahari Hussin, the number one bomb maker for JI, and Noor Din Mohammed Top. The latter two are at large and are thought to have aided the Marriott bombing. According to Agence France-Presse, Malaysian Deputy Prime Minister Abdullah Ahmad Badawi brushed aside questions at an August 19, 2003 news conference in Kuala Lumpur. When asked if Abraham's partner Hameed was linked to Hussin or Top, Badawi claimed that Hameed was not a Malaysian.[42] However, the U.S. Attorney's Office in Newark confirmed that Hameed had arrived in the United States from Malaysia.

When Hambali was arrested in the Thai city of Ayuthaya on August 12, he was carrying a fake Spanish passport bearing the name Daniel. Although Hambali had entered Thailand numerous times from Cambodia, where he lived for seven months, and Myanmar, his passport had him always entering through the Thai-Laotian border town of Chiang Kong. Thai police discovered that although Hambali did not enter Thailand from Laos, he frequently traveled to Chiang Kong. The Thai-Laotian border is a favored smuggling route for the Russian-Israeli mafia. In addition, Cambodia, a country awash in Russian- and Chinese-made weapons from its long civil war, is a major center for Russian-Israeli mafia arms smuggling, as well as trafficking in blue zircon gems.[43] Bangkok was also

---

[41] "Hambali Arrest: US, Aust missions targeted," *The Nation* (Bangkok), August 22, 2003.

[42] "Malaysian who reportedly led to Hambali arrest now in US custody," Agence France Presse, August 19, 2003.

[43] Fabiola Desy Unidjaja, "Hassan seeks U.S. permission to question Hambali," Ja-

where 9-11 hijackers Khalid Al Miidhar and Nawaf Al Hamzi stayed after attending an Al Qaeda terrorist planning summit in Malaysia in January 2000. The CIA was never able to locate the two men while they were in Thailand. The connections between Israeli organized crime smuggling and similar Al Qaeda activities in Southeast Asia are much more than coincidental.

Hambali's arrest was the result of a tip following the arrest of two Malaysian Al Qaeda members, code-named "Li Li" and "Zubair," who were arrested in June 2003 in Bangkok and turned over the U.S. investigators. Li Li apparently gave the CIA Hambali's location.[44]

After Hambali was arrested, he was suspected of smuggling a large cache of explosives and weapons into Thailand, including surface-to-air missiles, to be used against the APEC summit in October 2003.[45] The first indication that IGLA missiles might be used against Air Force One came from BBC reporter Tom Mangold, who broke the story on the BBC 1's *Ten O'Clock News*, much to the consternation of the FBI, which wanted to bag others involved in the missile smuggling operation. Mangold reported that Lakhani was part of a smuggling ring that wanted to shoot down Air Force One. Although Bangkok was not mentioned as the venue, the links between the Lakhani operation and Hambali's JI group in Thailand, and the fact that Hambali was arrested just hours before Lakhani's arrest, point to a connection between the two cases.

Newsweek magazine, which is owned by The Washington Post Company, claimed Mangold was incorrect in his account of Air Force One being a target. However, British intelligence and law enforcement knew that passenger jets were vulnerable to attack by Al Qaeda. Earlier in 2003, 1700 British policemen surrounded London's Heathrow Airport amid fears that Al Qaeda had procured SAMs. According to the *Guardian*, Mangold totally refuted *Newsweek's* charge that his story about Air Force One was false. Whoever in the U.S. government tipped off Mangold before the FBI could complete its investigation, they helped deter further in-

---

karta Post, August 27, 2003; 'Top-Secret' Report Confirms Botched Visa Run Led To Hambali's Arrest, *World News Connection*, August 17, 2003.

[44] "Capture of last four terror suspects will wipe out JI in Malaysia: official," Agence France Presse, August 20, 2003.

[45] Boonradom Chitradorn, "Thailand hunting for smuggled portable missiles ahead of APEC summit," Agence France Presse, October 1, 2003.

vestigation of the Russian-Israeli mafia links to the missile smuggling ring. *Newsweek* claimed Mangold's scoop foiled the FBI's investigation, and Mangold then began legal proceedings against the magazine.[46]

* * * *

Hong Kong police revealed that they had shared key intelligence with Thai authorities about Hambali before his arrest. This revelation was significant in linking the Hambali arrest to the Lakhani-Abraham case, because Hong Kong had been the scene of a past attempt by Al Qaeda-linked traffickers to buy SAMs, and Abraham had extensive business dealings in Hong Kong.

The first indications that Jemaah Islamiyah(JI) was planning one or more radiological bombings in Bangkok came after Narong Penanam, a respected citizen of his village, Praokala, along the Thai-Cambodian border, was arrested on June 13, 2003, in a sting operation at the Royal Pacific Hotel in Bangkok for possession of 70 pounds of Cesium-137. Penanam later claimed that a U.S. intelligence agent, known simply as Pattanapong, previously asked him to procure a "radioactive" substance.[47] The U.S. Customs Service, which had been active in identifying supply lines for illegal SAM shipments from Russia and Ukraine, was in on the sting operation. The *Bangkok Post* reported that Gary Phillips, the U.S. Embassy's deputy customs attaché in Bangkok, was present during Penanam's interrogation.

Penanam admitted that the Cesium was to be used by a terrorist group for the production of dirty bombs. He then added that the Cesium in his possession was from Russia, and that the deal involved an international network of weapons dealers who were using a military base in Laos close to the Thai border to store the material. Penanam said his Cesium batch was to fetch $350,000

---

[46] Andrew Johnson, "BBC Journalist To Sue U.S. Magazine Over Foiled FBI Plan Story," *The Independent*, August 16, 2003; Tom Mangold, "Make no mistake, this was a real threat to kill the President," *Evening Standard*, August 13, 2003; Michael Isikoff and Mark Hosenball, "The bust of arms dealer was supposed to be kept secret and another step in the hunt for Al Qaeda operatives," *Newsweek*, August 13, 2003.

[47] "CIA's role In Seizure Of Cesium-137 Arouses Interest Of Southern Thai Muslims," *World News Connection*, June 26, 2003.

and that more was available from the storage location in Laos. Thai police suspected that Penanam's buyers were JI, and that they planned to use the Cesium in dirty bombs to be set off during the APEC summit.[48] The day after Penanam's arrest, Georgian police discovered two metal boxes containing Cesium 137 and Strontium 90. Inside another container was one of the ingredients needed to produce mustard gas. The deadly containers were being transported by a taxi driver, who said he was paid to deliver them to individuals in central Tbilisi.[49]

A few days before 9-11, Thai police discovered that thieves had stolen from a Bangkok public works facility humidity detection equipment containing deadly Cesium-137, Amerithium-124, and Beryllium.[50] In May 2002, Lithuanian police arrested six men tied to the Russian-Israeli mafia for trying to sell a large quantity of Cesium-137.[51] The same month, four Israeli-Russian mafiosi were arrested in Bulgaria for trying to smuggle plutonium from Russia. The next month, Jose Padilla (aka Abdullah Al Mujahir) was arrested at Chicago's O'Hare Airport on charges that he was planning to blow up a radioactive dirty bomb in an American city. If Padilla was involved with Israeli-Russian mafia suppliers, the public may never know, because after being held incommunicado in a Navy prison in Charleston, South Carolina, where U.S. citizen Padilla was prevented from talking to a lawyer, the Bush administration decided to indict him in Federal Court on unrelated charges, thus avoiding a test of Presidential power, which the Supreme Court had signalled it was likely to lose.

U.S. law enforcement officials, charging Lakhani with providing material support to terrorism, also tied Lakhani to an attempt to procure a dirty bomb for his "clients." On December 18, 2003, federal prosecutors accused Lakhani of admitting during the sting operation that he could obtain a radiological dirty bomb as well as C-4 explosives. Prosecutors also alleged that the targets of the SAMs being procured by Lakhani would be 15 U.S. airliners.[52]

---

[48] Terry Frederickson, "Dirty Dealings," *Bangkok Post*, June 24, 2003. < http://www.bangkokpost.net/education/site2003/wnjn2403.htm

[49] "Georgian police foil 'dirty bomb' plot: official," Agence France Presse, June 16, 2003.

[50] <http://fun.supereva.it/polarsun/it/archives/P_news_0901_att.html?p>

[51] "Vilnius Police Seize Record-Size Amount Of Radioactive Cesium," Baltic News Service, May 30, 2002.

[52] "US indicts British man of Indian descent on attempting to aid terrorists," Agence France Presse, December 19, 2003.

A week after Hambali's arrest, Prime Minister Shinawatra announced that another seven Muslims were arrested in Chiang Mai province and Phuket in southern Thailand for ties to terrorist activities. Those arrested included three Pakistanis, two Burmese, and a Thai citizen. Two of the Pakistanis arrested in Chiang Mai had fake Israeli and Portuguese passports in their possession.[53] As a result of the fear that terrorists might be planning a truck bomb in Bangkok and other cities, Thai police began controlling the movement of large vehicles near sensitive buildings, including hotels and embassies.

The United States kept Hambali detained in a secret location, widely believed to be Guantanamo Bay, Cuba. Australian, Philippine, and Indonesian law enforcement officials were thus unable to gain direct access to the JI figure for interrogation. Meanwhile, U.S. government officials began to downplay the importance of Lakhani as a major arms trafficker and terrorist figure.

* * * *

It is clear that the FBI had bigger fish to fry in the sting operation and that someone in a position of authority successfully interfered with the investigation of an arms ring that had ties to both Russian-Israeli mafia figures and Al Qaeda. Abraham's "highly discerning clientele" in Saudi Arabia and his operations in Jeddah and Bangkok would have been of immense interest to law enforcement. The BBC reported that about the same time the sting was being launched against Abraham and Lakhani in the United States and Jemaah Islamiya leader Hambali was being arrested in Thailand, Saudi police seized a truckload of SAMs on a desert road near Jeddah. The truck was apparently en route from the Yemeni border to the Saudi port city. The confiscation prompted Saudi Arabia to issue a terrorist warning, resulting in British Airways temporarily suspending its flights to Riyadh. The London *Evening Standard* reported another interesting facet of the Lakhani-Abraham investigation—that the Russian FSB had not become involved in the case until March 2003, which means the FBI was hesitant to tip

---

[53] "7 Held for Questioning: Detainees in Phuket and Chiang Mai suspected of links with terrorists," *The Nation* (Bangkok), August 24, 2003.

off Russian authorities until it had identified the key Russian suppliers of the weapons requested by Lakhani.[54]

U.S. intelligence sources report that Yehuda Abraham's neighborhood of Forest Hills and adjoining Rego Park is a nest of Russian-Israeli mafia money laundering by figures tied to terrorist
arms suppliers and drug dealers. Abraham's home is a few blocks
from the 11821 Queens Boulevard building that housed the office of the major joint money laundering operation involving the
Bank of New York's East European Division, Marc Rich's Glencore, Loutchansky's Benex International, and three other firms involved in money laundering for the Israeli mafia: Becs, Torfinex,
and Lowland, Inc., (the last based in Jersey City, New Jersey).[55]
Ironically, Queens was also the location of the office of the Taliban
prior to 9-11.

* * * *

Before the Lakhani-Abraham-Hameed SAM smuggling ring was
broken, U.S. law enforcement had success in breaking up similar
attempts by Russian-Israeli mafia-connected groups to smuggle
SAMs into the United States. In 1997, U.S. Customs agents in
Miami arrested two Lithuanians, Alexander Progrebeshki and
Alexander Darichev, for attempting to smuggle forty SAM-14
STRELAs and SAM-16 IGLAs into Puerto Rico from the state-
owned Bulgarian arms exporter, ARMIMEX. A group of Florida-
based mobsters, known as "redfellas," and who were tied to the
Russian-Israeli mafia syndicate, had been under investigation by
a joint Federal-local police task force code-named OPERATION
ODESSA. The missiles, to be purchased for $1 million, were to be
shipped from the Bulgarian city of Bourgas, a favorite out-ship-
ment location of Bout, Minin, and Ruprah, to Puerto Rico aboard
the Equatorial Guinea flagged ship *Al Fares*. The missiles were
manifested as machinery and "general cargo."[56]

---

[54] "'Del Boy' trader out of his depth in arms world," *Evening Standard*, August 14,
2003, p. 7.

[55] Dan Morrison, "Couple Admits Money Scheme / Laundered $7 Billion From
Russia," *Newsday*, February 17, 2000, p. A07.

[56] Tammerlin Drummond, "Enter the Redfellas; Are Russian Mobsters Dallying
with Drug Lords?" *Time*, July 14, 1997, p. 36.

Another law enforcement success came just after 9-11. Peter Landesman reports in his *New York Times* article on Bout that a few weeks following 9-11, a Hungarian customs inspector discovered a shipment by a Budapest trading company to a buyer in Macon, Georgia, of 300 Ukrainian SAMs, along with 100 launchers. The Ukrainian shipper, ERI Trading and Investment Company, was thought by investigators to be a front operation, likely one of many set up by the Russian-Ukrainian-Israeli mafia. There are obvious similarities between this incident, involving 300 missiles and Lakhani's deal involving up to 200 missiles. Lakhani dealt with both Russian and Ukrainian weapons suppliers.[57]

After Ruprah's arrest in Belgium he provided law enforcement with even more information about his international arms smuggling network. This was shortly after his associate, Lakhani, began meeting with the FBI undercover agent to discuss the terms for the IGLA missile deal. After Ruprah was released on bail, he jumped bond and fled Belgium. Ruprah was re-arrested in Italy in August 2002 for "criminal association" and carrying a false passport.[58] Italian authorities released Ruprah from jail in September 2002. That same month, the Italian Court of Cassation ordered Minin released from jail, ruling that Italy had no jurisdiction over a case involving arms trafficking in other countries.

On September 20, 2002, Ilyas Ali, an Indian-born U.S. citizen from St. Paul, Minnesota, and two Pakistani citizens, Muhammad Abid Afridi and Syed Mustajab Shah, were arrested in Hong Kong for trying to procure four U.S.-made Stinger SAMs. They were caught by undercover San Diego-based FBI agents for trying to trade five tons of hashish and 600 kilograms of heroin for the missiles—missiles the FBI claimed were to be used to "shoot down airplanes" in the United States.[59]

The similarities between this case and the Lakhani-Abraham-Hameed sting are significant. The Hong Kong sting occurred at the same time Lakhani was dealing with Rehman. In court depositions by the government, the FBI claimed that the Afridi and his two

---

[57] Landesman, op. cit.

[58] Agence France Presse, "Italian police arrest man suspected of al-Qaeda arms link," August 3, 2002.

[59] Peter Michael, "Duo admit HK drug-missile deal; Pair seized by FBI in plea bargain over terror charges," *South China Morning Post*, March 5, 2004, p. 3.

colleagues said they were going to sell the Stingers to Taliban members associated with Al Qaeda. Hong Kong deputy police commissioner Dick Lee Ming-kwai later admitted that terrorists had been using Hong Kong to launder money.[60] According to the *South China Morning Post* of September 21, 2001, Abraham's Ambuy International firm participated in that week's Hong Kong Jewelry and Watch Fair at the Fine Design Pavilion. Abraham's company, according to its Web site, also maintains an office in Hong Kong.[61]

* * * *

In November 2002, Uwe Jensen, a Danish-born U.S. citizen and former right-wing Progress Party member of the European Parliament, and three Colombians identified as Carlos Ali Romero Varela, Cesar Lopez, and someone referred to merely as "Commando Emilio," were arrested in Houston for trying to procure 9000 AK-47s, 300 pistols, grenade launchers, SAMs, 53 million rounds of ammunition and 300,000 grenades from Ukrainian-Israeli mafia sources in Eastern Europe. The deal, worth $45 million in cash and cocaine, was said to involve the right-wing paramilitary Colombian terrorist group, the United Self-Defense Forces. The four were arrested after a 13-month long FBI sting code-named OPERATION WHITE TERROR that coincided for nine months with the sting operation against Lakhani, and used a Ukrainian undercover policeman who posed as a mafia arms trafficker during an April 28, 2002 meeting in a St. Croix warehouse.[62] The FBI operation involved its agents, as well as Drug Enforcement Administration agents, in London, Panama City, Costa Rica, and St. Croix. Along with Jensen's three Colombian colleagues, Costa Rican police arrested two other Colombians, Elkin Arroyave Ruiz and Edgar Fernando Blanco Perta, for trying to trade $25 million in cocaine for Eastern European arms for the Colombian paramilitaries.

Arroyave was identified by the Colombian newspaper *El Espectador* as having been trained in Israel. Jensen and Romero

---

[60] Niall Fraser, "HK is not a terrorist base, police chief insists after warning from FBI," *South China Morning Post*, November 24, 2002, p. 3.

[61] Wong Joon San, "Fair boasts bigger show of fine jewelry," *South China Morning Post*, September 21, 2001, p. 9.

[62] Associated Press, "Officials Target Two Drug, Terrorism Rings," November 7, 2002.

said they were able to send drugs to Russia via Israeli mafia safe routes established in Venezuela and Brazil.[63] Other venues prized for meetings between Colombian drug figures and the Russian-Israeli Mafia are Antigua, Aruba, St. Vincent, and the Dutch half of St. Martin, where diamonds smuggled from mafia operations in Amsterdam do not have to pass through customs.

In May 2000, Colombian intelligence agents in Cali arrested two Israelis, Isaac Richter and Ofer Zusmanovith, and a Colombian who were trying to smuggle weapons, including rifles, machine guns, grenade launchers, rocket-propelled grenade launchers, ammunition, and Scorpio SAMs, to leftist guerrillas in the country. As part of the round-up, code-named OPERATION NEFER, Israeli police arrested two other Israelis, Yaron Cohen and David Lipman Birnbaum, a licensed arms dealer, for their role in the operation. The smuggling operation involved the Israeli-Russian mafia. Colombian police suspected the Israelis were linked to the notorious former Israeli commando, Yair Klein, who was identified in the past with providing training for the Medellin drug cartel. The Israeli smuggling ring was reported to operate from Russia and Austria with support bases in Ecuador, Nicaragua, Peru, and Venezuela.[64]

The Colombian link to the Israeli-Russian mafia is apparently as strong as ever. In June 2003, as the FBI was involved in the sting against Lakhani and Abraham, six jewelry store owners from 47th and 46th Streets in New York's diamond district were arrested in OPERATION MELTDOWN for assisting Colombian drug dealers in laundering $1 million in gold. The gold was to be melted down to make plated tools, which would then be sent to the Colombian drug dealers.[65] On the evening of May 20, 2004, Eduard Nektalov, one of the jewelers linked to the money laundering operation, was shot execution style as he walked near the Diamond District. Like Abraham, Nektalov was a leader of the Bukharian Jewish community in Queens. On December 17, 2003, Alik Pinhasov, Nektalov's

[63] BBC Monitoring International Reports, "Men Arrested By FBI Implicate Paramilitary Leader In Drug Trafficking," November 11, 2002.

[64] David Adams, "Police tell of smashing arms ring," *St. Petersburg Times*, June 20, 2000, p. 2A.

[65] John Lehmann and Marianne Garvey, "Colombian Gold - N.Y. Jewelers Molded Metal For Drug Lords: Feds," *New York Post*, June 6, 2003, p. 9.

cousin, had been shot in Rego Park. Pinhasov had survived, and Nektalov had been contacted before his death by someone who demanded he persuade his cousin to drop the charges in the Rego Park shooting.[66]

* * * *

A week after the Lakhani-Abraham sting operation in New York, on August 23, 2003, Vladimir Guzinsky, the former Russian media and oil magnate, was arrested at Athens airport after a flight from Tel Aviv. Greek police said Guzinsky's name was on an Interpol wanted list for fraudulent activities totaling $250 million. Guzinsky was a dual Russian-Israeli citizen who had been linked by law enforcement officials to Israeli mafia activities.[67]

On August 20, a few days before Guzinsky's arrest, Latvian police had stopped a 28-ton air cargo shipment of "agricultural technical products" to Tehran. The cargo actually contained military equipment and weapons. Latvian police said the cargo was bound for terrorists in Iran, and that because of the age of the weapons the Iranian government would not have been a buyer. The shipment involved a number of offshore companies linked to the Israeli-Russian mafia and Bulgarian criminal elements. However, the United States, Russia, and Bulgaria refused to reply to a Latvian request for assistance in the case.[68]

The investigation of Israeli government ties to the mafia reached a new level on November 11, 2005, when Israel's ambassador to Britain, Zvi Hefetz, was questioned by Israeli police about his involvement in money laundering through Bank Hapoalim accounts controlled by Guzinsky. Before being named ambassador, Hefetz had been Guzinsky's agent in Israel. The bank's Hayarkon branch in Tel Aviv was accused of laundering as much as $250 million.

---

[66] "Money laundering suspected as motive in NYC killing," *National Jeweler*, June 16, 2004.

[67] Ioanna Mandhrou, "Russian extradition request for Guzinsky," *World News Connection*, September 23, 2003.

[68] Baltic News Service, "Bulgarians Involved in Arms Contraband Case Investigated in Latvia," April 5, 2004; Baltic News Service, "Investigation of Arms Contraband in Latvia Stalls over Inefficiency of Foreign Authorities," March 13, 2004; Baltic News Service, "Latvian Security Police Launch Criminal Case on Arms Smuggling to Iran," August 29, 2003.

Among Hapoalim officers arrested was the chief of the bank's Commonwealth of Independent States branch.[69]

* * * *

Wadih el Hage, a top assistant to Osama bin Laden who is serving a life sentence for his role in the 1998 U.S. Embassy bombings in Kenya and Tanzania, visited Hatton Garden in the lead up to 9-11 to raise funds for Al Qaeda by smuggling tanzanite gems from Tanzania.[70] The *Sunday Express* reported that Al Qaeda financial front men associated with the Islamic charity, Mercy International Relief Agency, used Irish bank accounts to transfer money to Warsaw. The transactions were ultimately traced to a bank associated with Russian-Israeli mafia chief Semion Mogilevich, who was linked to the Marc Rich Benex-BONY scandal. A senior FBI agent said, "Mogilevitch is into more bullshit than you can shake a stick at."[71] Some of the funds transfers, picked up by National Security Agency and British Government Communications Headquarters (GCHQ) intercepts, were likely used to fund part of the 9-11 attacks.[72]

Perhaps the diamond smuggling network was what Osama bin Laden referred to when, in an interview with the Pakistani newspaper *Ummat*, he said Al Qaeda uses "three alternate financial systems" that are "separate and independent," adding any attempt to remove them "won't succeed."[73] It must be conceded that Bin Laden may not have been simply bragging, since one of his money launderers traveled under the name "Cyril Jacob" and was involved with Hasidic diamond dealers in London.

The nexus of diamond dealers and weapons smuggling was highlighted in *Yediot Aharonoth*, which detailed the links between the notorious Israeli arms smuggler Yair Klein and Daniel Gertler, an

---

[69] Jonathan Lis, "Israeli envoy to UK questioned in money -laundering probe," *Ha'aretz*, November 14, 2005.

[70] Maxim Kniazkov, "Regulations for African gems trade approved after report of terror links," Agence France Presse, February 10, 2002.

[71] Jeffrey Robinson, *The Independent*, op. cit.

[72] Tim Shipman, "Face Up To Terror Threat At Home, Security Chiefs Tell Blair; 1,000 Of Bin Laden's Men 'Active' In UK," *Sunday Express*, August 25, 2002, p. 2.

[73] Jeffrey Robinson, "The Terrorist Dollar: 'follow the money'" is the battle cry in the 21st century's first war," *Playboy*, January 1, 2002, p. 70.

Israeli diamond mogul. The paper described Klein's role as a field agent for Gertler in Sierra Leone and Liberia, the two countries a former Mossad chief described as major laundering centers for Islamic terrorist groups. *Yediot Aharonoth* reported that the Israeli diamond merchants hoped that by providing "friendly" guerrilla groups in Sierra Leone and Liberia with money, weapons, and military training, if their leaders achieved power, they would give the Israelis "power over the diamonds in their countries."[74]

One of Israel's major diamond kingpins is Tashkent-born Lev Leviev, the son of Hasidic Jews who migrated to Israel from Uzbekistan. According to *Le Monde*, Roman Abramovich, a wealthy Russian oligarch tied to the investigation of Russian oligarch Mikhail Khodorkovsky, and the Liechtenstein money laundering activities of Russian-Israeli citizen Mikhail Chernoy, helped Leviev secure a monopoly on the export of diamonds from Angola. Illegal diamond smuggling from that country helped fund the operations of various guerrilla groups in Angola and neighboring countries, including UNITA.[75]

According to a 2002 private British risk analysis report on Liberia, that nation has served as an important nexus between diamond smuggling and terrorist financing: "Some evidence has emerged that where organized crime and its adherents leads—Al Quaeda [*sic*] exists and operates. Verification from several sources partially indicate the purchase on a large scale of Sierra Leone diamonds through Liberia (and particular Liberian corporations) and using local addresses in Liberia.... Some of the characters involved in this trade have been identified and notified to the press and the United Nations. Others, though not known, appear to have a 'charmed' and 'untouched' existence."[76]

The risk analysis report also accused the Liberian International Ship & Corporate Registry (LISCR) of involvement with the Liberian government's questionable activities. A copy of an e-mail message accompanying the risk analysis report indicated

[74] Nicole Gaouette, "Inside Israel's diamond trade: a family affair," *Christian Science Monitor*, February 21, 2002, p. 1.

[75] "Roman, friends and countrymen; Penetrating Russia (and Britain) steppe by steppe: Part Two," *London Calling!* July 8, 2003. < http://www.minesandcommunities. org/Aboutus/londoncall25.htm

[76] "Republic of Liberia: Liberian Corporate & Maritime Programs, Liberian 'Court' Systems & 'Judges.'" May 14, 2002.

the originator was the well-respected London risk analysis firm Drum Cussac. The document states that the "Registry is imploding even faster as the unbeatable combination of organized crime, diamonds, Al-Quaeda [*sic*], a corrupt and incompetent judiciary, a corrupt brutal and greedy 'government' is highlighted."

The LISCR, which maintains offices in New York and Vienna, Virginia, and other offices in London, Hong Kong, Piraeus, Rotterdam, Zurich, etc., is accused of having a murky ownership, with shipping and corporate fees it collects largely unaccounted for. LISCR's operations in Piraeus and London are reported to be "opaque." The report suggests that LISCR's opaqueness has attracted "organized crime and Al-Quaeda." The report also indicates that the U.S. State Department has been covering up for LISCR, with "no comment" being the usual State Department response to inquiries about the operation.[77]

The risk analysis report is consistent with information received from a former head of Israel's Mossad, that West African diamond smuggling is key to the financial operations of Al Qaeda. He also revealed that Al Qaeda's funding eventually involves money laundering by the six largest U.S. banks in New York City. Individuals involved in the diamond trade in West Africa have revealed that the actual reason U.S. Marines and Special Operations forces went ashore in Liberia in July 2003, was to secure Liberian government documents proving the links between Charles Taylor, the Russian-Israeli Mafia, and Al Qaeda. As part of OPERATION SHINING EXPRESS, U.S. and Israeli intelligence agents reportedly took possession of or destroyed a number of incriminating documents, especially those maintained at Liberian government offices at 80 Broad Street in Monrovia.

After the Liberian document seizure was completed, U.S. Marines were summarily pulled out of Monrovia on August 24, 2003.[78] In their place came a private military company named Pacific Architects and Engineers to provide logistical support for Nigerian peacekeepers. Another U.S. private military company, Intercon Security, protected the U.S. Embassy in Monrovia.[79] The onset of the

---

[77] Ibid.
[78] Confidential source.
[79] Jim Krane, "Private Firms do U.S. Military's Work," *Associated Press*, October

Monrovia operation followed by only two days the arrest of Abraham and Lakhani. Lakhani's partner Ruprah was also a diamond smuggling agent of Charles Taylor, one who traveled on a Liberian diplomatic passport under the name of Samir M. Nasr. Ruprah also served as an agent of the LISCR.

Most of the "establishment" foreign policy community consistently ignores the Israeli connection to diamond smuggling and the funding of terrorists. For example, the Center for Strategic and International Studies (CSIS) stated in a report on transparency in the African oil sector that "Lebanese trading communities, long-standing support networks for Hizbillah [*sic*], some of which are reportedly engaged in illicit diamond trafficking, money laundering, and the movement of lethal material."[80] The same charges could have easily been leveled against the Israeli mafia. but CSIS studiously avoided that issue.

In 1999, the Israeli weapons smuggler Yair Klein was jailed by the Sierra Leone government for selling arms to the RUF guerrillas, who were also being armed by Ruprah and Bout. Klein, a former Israeli military commando, is still wanted by U.S. law enforcement for training members of the Medellin drug cartel in Colombia. In 1991, Klein, who ran a security company called Spearhead, Ltd., had been convicted by an Israeli court for exporting military expertise and technology without a license, but was merely given a suspended sentence.

* * * *

In 1990 Arik Afek, a colleague of Klein, who was a partner in First Paragon, Inc., a Miami "flower importing" business, was found dead in the trunk of a car at Miami International Airport with multiple gunshot wounds. Afek had reportedly begun cooperating with the U.S. Secret Service and CIA about Israeli activity in Colombia, and a plan by Israeli-backed drug dealers to assassinate President George H.W. Bush while he was on a state visit to Colombia. Is-

---

29, 2003.
   [80] Center for Strategic and International Studies, *Promoting Transparency in the African Oil Sector: A report of the CSIS~Task Force on Rising U.S. Energy Stakes in Africa*, March 2004, p. 14.

raeli television reported that Afek was given a U.S. passport by the CIA in return for information about Israeli military and drug operations in Colombia.[81]

There is a very long history of Israeli weapons smuggling in Latin America, particularly to drug cartels. On April 7, 1988, *ABC World News Tonight* reported that from 1983 to 1986, Israeli agents bought weapons from the Communist bloc using American money and on behalf of the United States. The weapons were delivered by a joint U.S.-Israeli airlift to Panama. Michael Harari, a former Israeli Mossad agent and assassin who was also a security adviser to Manuel Noriega, arranged to ship the weapons to Nicaraguan bases in Costa Rica and El Salvador. The last part of the deal was to fly cocaine from Colombian Medellin cartel sources to the United States. As Richard Threlkeld reported,

> After dropping off their weapons, the planes and contract pilots of this makeshift Israeli-American airlift went back to business as usual, smuggling illegal Colombian cocaine across the U.S. border. If U.S. officials who'd sponsored this airlift knew it was drug dealing, they did nothing to stop those cargo planes.[82]

A convicted money launderer named Ramon Milian-Rodriguez testified about the CIA–Vice President Bush–Noriega drug and weapons smuggling operation before Senator John Kerry's Senate hearings on drug smuggling and terrorism in Central America. Milian-Rodriguez testified that he set up a meeting between Jeb Bush and a Guatemalan presidential candidate named Alfonso Cabrera, who was backed by the Medellin cartel. Soon after, Cabrera visited Washington and met with President George H.W. Bush.[83]

The Russian-Israeli mafia actually used a strip club owned by a Russian-Israeli mobster named Ludwig Fainberg, nicknamed

---

[81] Michael Isikoff, "Slain Israeli Reportedly Advised Bush Security; Secret Service Questioned Businessman About Medellin Cartel's Military Capabilities," *Washington Post*, January 29, 1990, p. A14; Wolf Blitzer, "Miami Vice - Mystery Shrouds Slaying Of Israeli," *Jerusalem Post*, January 28, 1990; Michael Wines, "Israeli Slain in Miami Was Under U.S. Scrutiny," *New York Times*, January 27, 1990, p. 9.

[82] *ABC World News Tonight with Peter Jennings*, ABC News Transcripts, April 7, 1988.

[83] Connie Bruck, "How Noriega Got Caught and Got Away," *The American Lawyer*, July/August 1988, p. 35.

"Tarzan" to arrange for Russian weapons sales to South American drug cartels. From "Porky's," a club near Miami International Airport, Fainberg and his associates negotiated the sale of two Soviet-era military helicopters, and even a Tango-class Russian diesel submarine, to the Cali cartel. In the mid-1990s, the FBI indicted Fainberg and Vyacheslav Ivankov, nicknamed Yaponchik or "Little Japanese," a notorious Russian mobster based in New York City, who was heavily involved in weapons, drugs, and diamond smuggling especially from business fronts located in New York's primarily Russian community of Brighton Beach.[84]

* * * *

An interesting link between the Israeli-Russian mafia and the Donald Rumsfeld's and Douglas Feith's Office of Special Plans was revealed in early August 2003, when F. Michael Maloof was stripped of his security clearance for links with a Lebanese businessman thought to have ties with Israeli Mafia gun runners in Guatemala. The businessman, Imad el Hage, was arrested by Bureau of Immigration and Customs Enforcement agents at Dulles International Airport for possession of a .45 caliber pistol. The gun was registered to Maloof. El Hage had already been under investigation for arms trafficking. Inexplicably, law enforcement authorities released el Hage shortly after his arrest, and specific charges relating to the gun incident have not been filed.

At the time, a Bush administration official told *Newsday*, "It's unclear whether his [Maloof's] involvement with him [el Hage] was official rogue duties or unofficial rogue duties." El Hage is linked to the Lebanese Christians allied with General Michel Aoun, who enjoys the support of Israel's Sharon government and its neoconservative allies in the United States. According to *Newsday*, Maloof was investigated for leaking classified material while working at the Pentagon during the Clinton administration. According to Pentagon insiders familiar with Maloof, his specialty in improperly obtaining access to Sensitive Compartmented Information (SCI) had been highly prized by Richard Perle and Douglas Feith during

---

[84] Robert Friedman, "Land Of The Stupid; When you need a used Russian submarine, call Tarzan," *New Yorker*, April 10, 2000, p. 40.

their stints in the Pentagon during the Reagan administration. His operation even had a code name: "the Batcave."

During the Clinton administration, Maloof's security clearance was stripped when investigators discovered financial improprieties. However, after assuming the job of Undersecretary of Defense for Policy, Douglas Feith quickly restored Maloof's clearance.[85] Maloof also restored the Batcave to full operations.[86]

U.S. law enforcement sources report that Maloof and el Hage were tied to an Israeli arms smuggling ring that was broken up by Guatemalan police. Three Israeli employees of the Guatemalan-registered company, GIRSA, Oris Zoller, Uzi Kisslevich, and Shimon Yelinek Shrem were ordered arrested by a Guatemalan court for illegally trying to smuggle Russian-made weapons to Colombia's right-wing paramilitaries. Yelinek was later arrested at Panama City's Tocumen International Airport after a flight from Venezuela. The original source of the weapons was reported to be Nicaragua. Yeliek is also the owner of a Panamanian-registered company, Inversiones Digal SA, also implicated in the smuggling operation. The incident involving Maloof and El Hage preceded by days the arrest of Lakhani and Abraham for weapons smuggling involving similar mafia-connected Russian suppliers.[87]

In addition, according to U.S. law enforcement officials, the Pentagon and FBI were investigating the activities of a Panamanian-registered but Israeli-owned company called ICS for illegally receiving Pentagon contracts for unspecified "security" work in Iraq. Some of ICS's employees in Iraq who were involved in interrogations of Iraqi detainees were reportedly discovered to be on loan from Israel's "special techniques" interrogation center, Unit 1391. One of the names that surfaced in the investigation was that of Israeli soldier of fortune Yair Klein.[88]

---

[85] Knut Royce, "Pentagon Official's Clearance Stripped; Linked to businessman under federal probe," *Newsday*, August 3, 2003, p. A4.

[86] Confidential information.

[87] James Wilson, "Nicaragua promises tighter controls on arms stockpiles," *Financial Times*, January 22, 2003, p. 2; *El Nuevo Diario* Web site, "Nicaraguan army spokesman explains army's role in arms shipment," BBC Monitoring Latin America, May 11, 2002; Juan O. Tamayo, "Huge weapons shipment gets diverted to Colombia rebels," *Miami Herald*, June 17, 2002.

[88] Confidential information.

* * * *

U.S. investigations of top arms smugglers connected to the Russian-Israeli mafia have often met with stonewalling by senior officials of the Bush administration. According to a number of former Clinton administration officials, anytime a law enforcement or intelligence investigation leads to anything or anyone connected to the mafia, such as Viktor Bout and his network, the Bush administration shuts down the operation. Some law enforcement officials also suspect that the Russian-Israeli Mafia was behind a mysterious shorting of airline and insurance stocks shortly before 9-11.

According to the Landesman article in the *New York Times Magazine*, during the final months of the Clinton administration, U.S. intelligence began tracking Bout's activities and his network (which included Ruprah and Lakhani). From his base in Sharjah in the Gulf, Bout was servicing Ariana Afghan Airline flights to Kandahar, Afghanistan. These flights were believed to be ferrying weapons and Al Qaeda and Taliban volunteers to Afghanistan, and the Clinton National Security Council believed Bout was aiding terrorism. Belgium had an international arrest warrant out for Bout for money laundering and diamond smuggling. Clinton White House counter-terrorism czar Richard Clarke wanted an arrest warrant issued for Bout, but the U.S. had no legal jurisdiction abroad. Gayle Smith, Clinton's National Security Council Africa bureau chief, along with CIA and British MI-6 agents, kept a wary eye on Bout's activities in Africa's conflicts. But when the Bush administration took over, Landesman reports, National Security Adviser Condoleezza Rice told U.S. intelligence to "look but don't touch."[89]

Bout would get yet another free pass from the Bush administration and its allies at Number 10 Downing Street. In May 2004, the French government complained that Washington and London were not supporting a move by the UN to freeze Bout's assets for his role in supporting Liberia's dictator Charles Taylor. Paris also alleged that the U.S. and Britain were permitting Bout's firms to operate freely in occupied Iraq, including his air cargo companies being involved in supplying coalition forces.[90] When Britain ap-

---

[89] Landesman, op. cit.
[90] Mark Huband, Andrew Parker, and Mark Turner, "UK snubs France over arms

peared ready to agree to put the squeeze on Bout's operations, the Bush administration pressured London to relent.

When Sharjah police sent a special police unit to capture Bout and give him to U.S. authorities, the White House declined. After 9-11, Rice inexplicably called off all operations aimed at Bout. Law enforcement and intelligence agents considered such a move amazing, given Bout's direct links to arms smuggling to the Taliban and Al Qaeda, as well as to other areas rife with Islamist terrorist groups. E.J. Hogendoorn, a former UN weapons inspector, told Landesman that Bout was "being protected by highly influential people." Lee Wolosky, the director of transnational threats in the Clinton and George W. Bush National Security Council, told *India Today*, "Lakhani is a very insignificant fish in the overall market. Also, it is a sting operation and hence entirely staged. Contrast this with Bout who lives openly in Moscow. There seems to be a clear disconnect."[91]

According to *Der Spiegel*, Bout also reportedly helped arrange the sale of up to 200 Russian T-55 and T-62 tanks to the Taliban. The deal was reportedly supported by Vadim Rabinovich, an Israeli-Ukrainian, and a former director of the Ukrainian secret service. The Russian SVR intelligence agency discovered that Pakistan's Inter Service Intelligence (ISI) agency was in on the arms smuggling deal, a violation of UN sanctions against the Taliban.

Bout was reported by the UN to be using Flying Dolphin Airlines, which operated scheduled flights between Dubai and Kandahar between October 2000 and January 2001, to ship arms to the Taliban. Flying Dolphin was owned by Shaikh Abdullah bin Zayed bin Saqr al Nahayan, a former UAE ambassador to the U.S. and a relative of the President of the UAE, who is also the ruler of Abu Dhabi. Flying Dolphin was registered in Bout's favored Liberia, although its main office was in Dubai.[92] Part of the reason why the Bush administration was hesitant to lean on Bout and his Abu Dhabi partners was the presence of a secret U-2 spy plane base at Al Dhafra, just outside Abu Dhabi. Al Dhafra was a key base in the war in Iraq and intelligence overflights of Iran.

---

trafficker: Bid to help dealer linked to coalition avoid sanctions," *Financial Times*, May 17, 2004, p. 1.

[91] Padmanabhan and Unnithan, op. cit.

[92] Phillip van Niekerk and André Verlöy, "Africa's 'Merchant of Death' Sold Arms to the Taliban," Center for Public Integrity, Washington, DC.

On April 26, 2005, the U.S. Treasury Department's Office of Foreign Assets Control (OFAC) froze the assets of Bout's companies, although some both on and off the freeze list were continuing to provide logistical services to U.S. and allied military forces and private contractors in Iraq. Some services to and from Baghdad International Airport were provided by a Bout-controlled firm called British Gulf.[93] Although British Gulf was not on the Treasury Department freeze list, Bout's Transavia was. However, between March 6 and 9, 2005, Transavia transported British armored vehicles and troops to Iraq from RAF Brize Norton in Oxfordshire. Another airline connected to Bout, Jet Line International, based in Chisinau, Moldova, was reported to have made flights on behalf of the British Ministry of Defense to Kosovo. Jet Line's Moldova address is the same as another Bout firm, Aerocom, which was accused by the UN of smuggling arms to Liberian rebels. In fact, Jet Line and Aerocom used the same planes.[94]

Bout's Texas-based Air Bas had rights to refuel at U.S. bases in Iraq. One of Bout's airfreight companies, Airbus, was subcontracted through another firm called Falcon Express of Dubai, by Kellogg, Brown and Root, the subsidiary of Halliburton. Air Bas also had links to Falcon Express.[95] Vega Airlines, a Bulgarian-based airline connected to Bout, had one of its Antonov AN-12 transports seized by Indian police at Ahmedabad airport in Gujarat. On board police found military equipment destined for Nepal's government, which was battling leftist guerrillas.

The U.S. Embassy in New Delhi and the State Department admitted that the equipment was for the Nepal police "to develop anti-terrorist capability and the plane was carrying the equipment to support this training [and] simulated ammunition for the training exercises and arms intended for training and equipping the Nepalese anti-terrorist police unit." After the United States was caught red handed smuggling weapons into Nepal, U.S. Embassy in Kathman-

---

[93] Julio Godoy, "Un Aides Say U.S. Is Protecting Global Arms Dealer," IPS-Inter Press Service, May 20, 2004.

[94] "How can Britain still use the Merchant of Death?" *Evening Standard* (London), May 9, 2005, p. 16.

[95] Gareth Walsh, "UK aid flights linked to arms dealer," *Sunday Times* (London), December 26, 2004, p. 9; Michele Keleman, "U.S. Ties to Russian Arms Dealer," Morning Edition, National Public Radio, December 24, 2004; Michael Isikoff, "Government Deal With a 'Merchant of Death?'" *Newsweek*, December 20, 2004, p. 8.

du spokesperson Constance Codling Jones, proceeded to lie about the military shipment, "The U.S. has already provided $22 million in assistance to Nepal in the last three years to fight terrorism, but as far as today's delivery is concerned, it is not military assistance."[96]

Neither Aerocom nor Airbus was included on Treasury's freeze list, an indication that Bout continued to have protectors in the Bush administration.

* * * *

One arrest in January 2004 pointed to the potential links between Israeli entrepreneurs and Islamist groups bent on producing weapons of mass destruction, including nuclear weapons. FBI and U.S. Customs agents arrested Asher Karni, a Hungarian-born Orthodox Jew, Israeli citizen, and resident of Cape Town, South Africa, at Denver International Airport for illegally exporting 200 electrically triggered spark gaps—devices that send synchronized electrical pulses—to Pakistan via a New Jersey export company called Giza Technologies of Secaucus (owned by Zeki Bilmen and which listed the equipment as electronics gear [lithotripters used to break up kidney stones] for the Baragwanath Hospital in Soweto) and Karni's Top-Cape Technology of Cape Town, South Africa, which, in turn sent them to AJKMC Lithography Aid Society in Islamabad, Pakistan through Dubai.[97]

Although AJKMC said it merely printed copies of the Koran, U.S. investigators pointed out the initials also stand for the All Jammu and Kashmir Muslim Conference, an Islamist opposition party that supports groups allied to Al Qaeda in Kashmir.[98] Top-Cape reportedly traded military and aviation electronics equipment. The triggering devices were eventually sent to a company in Islamabad, Pakistan called Pakland PME, using what the U.S. government said were falsified documents, and could be employed in the production of nuclear weapons.[99]

---

[96] *UPI Hears*, October 4, 2004.

[97] Peter Fabricius, "The man who used hospitals to trade in nukes," *The Independent Online*, February 15, 2004.

[98] Farah Stockman and Victoria Burnett, "From Salem to Pakistan, An Atomic Smuggler's Plot," *Boston Globe*, March 14, 2004, p. A1.

[99] Associated Press, "Israeli held in U.S. over nuclear parts sales to Pakistan," January

According to FBI insiders, wiretaps of phone calls in the Giza-Bilmen-Karni smuggling ring yielded the name Douglas Feith, the Undersecretary of Defense for Plans and Policy and one of Donald Rumsfeld's chief advisers, and of Turkish MIT intelligence members of the Turkish American Council.[100] South African agents had reportedly tipped off the United States about Karni's activities.

In a move similar to how Yehuda Abraham's case was handled by the federal judiciary, a Federal Judge in Denver said Karni could be released on $75,000, bail but the government appealed the decision to Judge Thomas Hogan of the U.S. Court of Appeals in Washington, DC.[101] Hogan was the judge who handled the appeal of convicted Israeli spy Jonathan Pollard, who is serving a life sentence and who unsuccessfully sought a reduction in his sentence at a hearing held on November 14, 2003. As with the U.S. prosecutors in Newark, the federal prosecutors' appeal failed, and Karni was released on bail into the custody of Rabbi Herzel Kranz. Like Abraham, Karni was ordered to wear an electronic monitor and, in his case, to remain at the Hebrew Sheltering Home in Maryland. And as with Abraham, a Malaysian link was discovered in Karni's network.[102]

* * * *

U.S. intelligence sources reported that the arrest of Abraham, Lakhani, and Hameed, the detention of el Hage, and the revocation of Maloof's security clearance were all tied to rogue activities of the Pentagon's former Office of Special Plans, now renamed the Office of Northern Gulf Affairs. One source said the "arrest of Lakhani and Abraham is part of something very big," and that "Abraham is a plug in to the Russian Mafia and there is a link to Hambali." It is interesting that Abraham struck a plea agreement with Justice Department prosecutors in which he agreed to plead guilty to lesser charges in return for his testimony against his two accomplices, Lakhani and Hameed. In his initial court appearance,

---

13, 2004; Fox News, "Arrest Ties Pakistan to Nuke Black Market," January 15, 2004.

[100] Confidential information.

[101] Associated Press, "Israeli held in U.S. over nuclear parts sales to Pakistan," January 13, 2004. Fox News, "Arrest Ties Pakistan to Nuke Black Market," January 15, 2004.

[102] Fabricius, op. cit.

Lakhani's attorney argued that his client had been entrapped by overzealous U.S. government agents. On April 27, 2005, a federal jury in New Jersey convicted Lakhani of attempting to provide material support to terrorists for his role in trying to sell an anti-aircraft missile to a person he knew to be a person representing a terrorist group.

Lakhani was also convicted of one count of unlawful brokering of foreign defense articles, two counts of money laundering, and one count of attempting to import merchandise into the U.S. by means of false statements. U.S. Attorney Christie said, "The jury understood that Lakhani was a persistent and willing arms broker, relentless in his attempt to bring shoulder-fired anti-aircraft missiles into the U.S."[103] On September 12, 2005, the day after the fourth anniversary of the terrorist attacks on the United States, Lakhani received the maximum sentence: 47 years in prison.

The Lakhani-Abraham caper would not be the last thwarted attempt to smuggle shoulder-launched surface-to-air missiles into the United States. On November 10, 2005, two naturalized Chinese-American citizens, Chao Tung Wu and Yi Qing Chen, were indicted by a Federal grand jury for attempting to smuggle such missiles into the United States. They were arrested by the FBI in a special investigation, code named Operation Smoking Dragon, that was linked to a related investigation in New Jersey.[104] The FBI did not say whether the New Jersey investigation involved the Lakhani and Abraham case.

With very few intelligence assets in Africa and inside the diamond businesses of Europe, Israel, and Asia, Western intelligence has been slow to comprehend the importance of diamond smuggling to the financing of terrorist groups like Al Qaeda. One European law enforcement investigator told the *Washington Post*, "I now believe that to cut off al Qaeda funds and laundering activities you have to cut off the diamond pipeline…. We are talking about millions and maybe tens of millions of dollars in profits and laundering."[105] If Israeli law enforcement officials are to be believed,

---

[103] <http://www.usdoj.gov/usao/nj/publicaffairs/NJ_Press/files/lakh0427_r.htm>

[104] Peter Bowes, "US lays missile smuggling charges," BBC News, November 10, 2005.

[105] Douglas Farah, "Al Qaeda Cash Tied to Diamond Trade," *Washington Post*, November 2, 2001, p. A1.

the European investigator underestimated the potential money involved in diamond and related commodities smuggling—with billions of ill-gotten dollars being pumped by into the Israeli economy alone by the Russian-Israeli mafia.

RIP: John Kokal & Dr. Gus W. Weiss

A former top official of the CIA, speaking on the condition of anonymity, said two alleged suicide deaths of high-ranking U.S. intelligence officials in November 2003 (both of whom died in the same manner—falls from Washington, DC buildings—and only weeks apart) appeared to be "more than coincidental."

On November 7, State Department Bureau of Intelligence and Research Near East and South Asian division (INR/NESA) Iraqi analyst John J. Kokal, 58, was found dead outside the State Department building. Washington police reported the case a suicide resulting from Kokal's jumping from the roof of the headquarters building.

According to State Department sources, Kokal was said to be despondent over a "problem" with his security clearance, and had thrown himself head first out of a window at the State Department headquarters, landing in a 20 foot-deep window well at the bottom of the building. Others stated that the manner of his fall was to ensure that Kokal would "land on his head."

He was not wearing shoes or a jacket when he was found. The story was only reported by Fox News and a local all-news cable station.[1] The *Washington Post* made a short three-paragraph entry on the death in the Metro section on November 8, 2003. However, the *Post* entry stated that Kokal did not work in intelligence.[2] Another news report had Kokal jumping off the roof. Not mentioned in any of the news reports was the fact that access to the roof of the State Department is secured, and that the windows are secured as a countermeasure against bomb blasts.

State Department officials told Washington, DC police that although Kokal worked in INR, he "was not involved in intelligence analysis." However, a senior State Department official has revealed that Kokal was not only the top Iraqi analyst within INR, but that he "regularly briefed the Secretary," a reference to Colin Powell.

---

[1] Fox News, State Dept. Worker Found Dead Outside Agency," November 8, 2003; Associated Press, "Police Investigate State Department Worker Death," November 8, 2003.< http://www.news8.net/news/stories/1103/109563.html>

[2] In Brief, Metro, *Washington Post*, November 8, 2003, p. B03.

Kokal's INR/NESA bureau was at the forefront of confronting claims that Iraq possessed weapons of mass destruction. A colleague of Kokal's told me that the Iraq analyst was despondent over "problems" with his security clearance. Washington police never ruled out homicide as the cause of his death.

Kokal's wife, Pamela, before being transferred to the State Department's Bureau of Western Hemisphere Affairs, worked in the Bureau of Consular Affairs, where she was charged with tightening up visa controls following the September 11 attacks. During the time that Kokal was said to have been committing suicide, around 5:00 P.M., Pamela was waiting for him in the State Department parking garage. They lived in Arlington, Virginia. It was unusual that the *Northern Virginia Journal*, the local Arlington paper, never published an obituary notice on Kokal. State Department officials report that the "official story" is that Kokal's alleged suicide had "nothing to do with work." However, a chill has set in among State Department employees, with many individuals questioning the official explanation but afraid to speak out.

There was no secret that there was plenty of dissension within Kokal's office. Another INR official, Greg Thielmann, said INR was largely ignored by Undersecretary of State for Arms Control and International Security, John Bolton, and his deputy, David Wurmser, both neoconservatives. Thielmann was backed up by his colleague, Christian Westermann. They both claimed that the neoconservatives in the Bush administration were "grossly distorting" intelligence on Al Qaeda's links to Iraq and Iraq's alleged possession of nuclear weapons.[3] Wurmser later became Vice President Cheney's Middle East policy adviser.

Kokal's former boss, Carl W. Ford, said that Bolton often exaggerated information to steer people in the wrong direction. In later testimony before the U.S. Senate Foreign Relations Committee on the nomination of Bolton to be U.S. ambassador to the UN, Ford, a conservative Republican, called Bolton a "a quintessential kiss-up, kick-down sort of guy." Other witness statements during the nomination hearings revealed that Bolton, over his entire ca-

---

[3] Robert Dreyfuss and Jason Vest, "The lie factory: only weeks after 911, the Bush administration set up a secret Pentagon unit to create the case for invading Iraq," *Mother Jones*, January 1, 2004, p. 34.

reer, often became abusive and psychologically unhinged around his colleagues and subordinates.

A former INR employee revealed that some one-third to one-half of INR employees are either former intelligence agents with the CIA or are actually detailed from the CIA. The employee also said it would have been impossible for Kokal to gain entry to the roof on his own, as INR occupies a Sensitive Compartmented Information Facility (SCIF) on the sixth floor that has no windows. It also has a structure on the roof that has neither windows nor access to the roof. Other windows at the State Department have been engineered to be shatter proof from terrorist bombs and cannot be opened.

* * * *

On November 25, 2003, former National Security Council official Dr. Gus W. Weiss, an outspoken critic of the Bush administration's war in Iraq, was found dead outside a service entrance to Washington's Watergate East residential building where he lived. Police ruled that Weiss had committed suicide by jumping from the roof of the Watergate building. Weiss was a former Assistant Secretary of Defense for Space Policy under President Carter and served on the Signals Intelligence Committee of Carter's Intelligence Board. Weiss also served as an adviser to the CIA and as a member of the Defense Science Board. The CIA Web site stated that "Gus W. Weiss has served as a Special Assistant to the Secretary of Defense and as Director of International Economics for the National Security Council." Weiss was awarded the French Legion of Honor in 1975 and the CIA's Medal for Merit.

Weiss had been a colleague of arch-neoconservatives Richard Perle, Paul Wolfowitz, and Frank Gaffney when he worked with them in the office of Senator Henry "Scoop" Jackson in the late 1970s. However, unlike his colleagues, Weiss was a vocal opponent of the Iraq war, something his friends said was surprising considering his low-key manner. One of his friends told the *Nashville Tennessean,* "He was very interested in diplomatic strategy and was very, very opposed to the Iraq war. It was the first military action he ever opposed, but he believed we shouldn't go to war in the Middle East without knowing what we were getting into."

Weiss's friends expressed shock at the manner of the former intelligence official's death. Weiss' neighbor, Audrey Wolf, who grew up with Weiss and was his neighbor in the Watergate, said, "He was a brilliant, brilliant guy and was always very focused."[4]

* * * *

It is noteworthy that Audrey Wolf was the head of the Audrey A. Wolf Literary Agency in Washington and the agent for the book written by former U.S. ambassador Joseph Wilson, whose revelations about his CIA-sponsored investigation and Niger not being a source for Iraqi uranium earned him the wrath of the Bush White House.

The White House then proceeded to name Valerie Plame (Wilson), as a CIA agent, and her employer, Brewster Jennings & Associates, a consultancy brass plate firm—with only a post office box and a telephone located at 101 Arch Street in Boston and a non-existent chief executive officer named Victor Brewster—as a CIA front.[5] The outing of Mrs. Wilson resulted in a criminal investigation of the White House by a Justice Department special prosecutor. To date, Lewis "Scooter" Libby has been the only Bush administration official indicted in the matter, but Bush insiders remain apprehensive that other heads may role.

Brewster Jennings was the President of Socony-Vacuum, the forerunner of Mobil Oil. Intelligence sources were sketchy about a link between Brewster Jennings of Mobil and Brewster Jennings & Associates. However, according to U.S. intelligence sources, Brewster Jennings & Associates was either established from scratch, or revived with a new mandate, in 1994: that being the collection of intelligence on the development and proliferation of weapons of mass destruction (WMDs).

The outing of Valerie Plame by Bush White House operatives resulted in the rolling up of Brewster Jennings & Associates, a

---

[4] Holly Edwards, "Nashville native Gus Weiss, adviser to 4 presidents, dies," *Nashville Tennessean*, December 1, 2003.

[5] Ross Kerber and Bryan Bender, "Apparent CIA front didn't offer much cover," *Boston Globe*, October 10, 2003.

severe blow to a relatively legitimate covert operation that helped to establish decades of contacts between the firm's agents and top international political and business leaders having connections to or knowledge of the proliferation of WMDs. According to former CIA counter-terrorism chief Vince Cannistraro, other CIA agents also used Brewster Jennings for cover, and their work had also been put at risk. Former CIA and State Department intelligence agent Larry Johnson said, after the CIA conducted its internal damage assessment, that the effect of the Brewster Jennings and Valerie Plame disclosures could have been much worse, though "at the end of the day, [the harm] will be huge and some people potentially may have lost their lives."[6] A CIA source told me in July 2004 that at least one anonymous star added to the CIA's Wall of Honor during the previous year had been a covert agent killed as a result of the White House disclosure of Plame's identity.

Brewster Jennings & Associates had developed an impressive array of contacts in the ten years before its cover was blown by White House operatives. It was particularly successful in penetrating the nuclear material sales ring led by Pakistani nuclear scientist Dr. Abdul Qadeer ("AQ") Khan, the "father of Pakistan's atomic bomb," and his associates. Khan's proliferation network extended to Iran, Libya, North Korea, and Saudi Arabia. Now, around the world, diaries and rolodexes were checked by corporate and intelligence officials to find out who had been in contact with the CIA firm. In addition to covers being revealed, inside sources were likely compromised. U.S. intelligence-targeted companies and entities that were involved in the nuclear technology export business could backtrack and find out what information may have been passed to Brewster Jennings representatives, and who within their firms may have passed it. Sensitive CIA investigations were either abandoned or severely compromised.[7]

A Swiss citizen named Urs Tinner was arrested by German authorities in October 2004 and was accused of supervising the manufacture of centrifuge components in Malaysia. The United States demanded Tinner's release, which led to speculation that Tinner

---

[6] Warren Strobel, "CIA leak may have caused more damage; Work of others using front company name may be at risk, *Milwaukee Journal Sentinel*, October 19, 2003, p. 2A.

[7] Confidential U.S. intelligence sources.

was a U.S. intelligence asset who had penetrated the A.Q. Khan network, and that he may have been part of the exposed Brewster Jennings operation.[8] In May 2005, *Der Spiegel* magazine reported that Tinner was, in fact, a CIA agent. Germany announced that Tinner would be extradited to Switzerland, something that *Der Spiegel* reported was a "deal" cut between Germany and the United States.

A February 2004 Malaysian police report named both Urs Tinner and his father, Friedrich, as principal engineers in overseeing the machining of uranium-enrichment centrifuge components at a Scomi Precision Engineering (Scope) plant in Malaysia. Friedrich Tinner, owner of a Swiss firm named PhiTec AG, was named in an International Atomic Energy Agency (IAEA) report as one of many Swiss individuals involved in shipping nuclear components to Libya and Iran. Swiss authorities had previously cleared Friedrich Tinner of charges that he shipped centrifuges to Iraq.[9] Friedrich Tinner's other son, Marco, owned a firm called Traco that was also reported as a supplier of equipment and services to Scomi.[10]

If the Tinners were working for the CIA, one subject of interest was a Sri Lankan businessman named B.S.A. Tahir, who arrived in Malaysia via Dubai in the mid-1990s. In a February 2004 speech at the National Defense University in Washington, DC, President Bush stated that Tahir was A. Q. Khan's "chief financial officer and money launderer." Investigators discovered that Tahir made several trips to Turkey and Germany to meet with suppliers for the Khan network.[11] Turkey is a nexus for smuggling operations that link Israeli-connected intelligence and organized crime operations to nuclear activities in countries like Pakistan and Iran.

* * * *

---

[8] Juergen Dahlkamp, Georg Mascolo and Holger Stark, "The First Accomplices Head to Trial," *Der Spiegel*, March 14, 2005.

[9] BBC Monitoring International Reports, "Swiss Engineer in Libya Nuclear Probe to be Extradited from Germany," Swiss Radio International, May 13, 2005.

[10] Raymond Bonner, "Multinational network aided Pakistan's nuclear help to Libya, report says," *New York Times*, February 23, 2004, p. 6.

[11] Ray Bonner, "Salesman From Nuclear Circuit Casts Blurry Corporate Shadow," *New York Times*, February 18, 2004, p. A4.

Khan had been monitored by the CIA for decades. There are indications that Khan became a "person of interest" to U.S. intelligence as early as 1972, when he began working for the Physics Dynamic Research Laboratory (FDO) in Amsterdam. Khan worked under contract to URENCO, a British-Dutch-West German consortium that developed gas centrifuges to enrich uranium for European nuclear power plants. Because Khan had applied for Dutch citizenship, he was not required to undergo a security background check as required for employees who were not citizens of the Netherlands, Britain, or West Germany. However, Khan never followed through with his request for Dutch citizenship.

Khan had already been directed to develop Pakistan's nuclear arsenal by then Pakistani President Zulfiqar Ali Bhutto, the father of the later female President Benazir Bhutto. When Khan began to inquire about obtaining various nuclear technologies at industry shows across Europe, the Dutch intelligence service became suspicious. Dutch intelligence wanted to arrest Khan, but the CIA warned them off. Former Dutch Prime Minister Ruud Lubbers confirmed that the CIA told the Dutch to back off arresting Khan, preferring to let him quit his job with FDO/URENCO and move back to Pakistan.

Lubbers said that another attempt by the Dutch to seize Khan in 1986 was met with opposition from the CIA, even though it had concluded that the scientist had enriched uranium to 93 percent, ample for a powerful atomic bomb. The Reagan administration, at the time, was using Pakistan as a conduit for supplying weapons and training for the anti-Soviet Afghan *mujaheddin*.

By 1987, Khan had expanded his nuclear proliferation network from "buyer" to "seller" status. Khan arranged to sell centrifuge technology to Iran for that nation's embryonic nuclear weapons program. Khan's network soon expanded to selling nuclear components and material to Libya and North Korea. As a vendor of nuclear components, Khan supplied ring magnets from Pakistan; non-corrosive pipes and valves from Pakistan, South Africa, Switzerland, and Dubai; aluminum or maraging steel from Turkey, Pakistan, Malaysia, and Singapore; flow-forming or balancing equipment from South Africa, South Korea, Switzerland, and Pakistan; end caps and baffles from Dubai, Malaysia, and Pakistan; vacuum pumps from Pakistan and South Africa; and power supplies from Turkey and Dubai.[12]

The Turkish and South African connections would have been of particular interest to Brewster Jennings and Associates, because of the intersection in these supplier countries with networks tied to the Israelis.

* * * *

During the early 1990s, the time period that Brewster Jennings began to ramp up its counter-proliferation activities, it was discovered that a company called Mainway International, with offices in Bad Homburg, Germany and Hong Kong, was involved in the smuggling of nuclear, biological, and chemical weapons and missile components to Iran. The company's principals were Gerhard Merz (a German mercenary and off-and-on resident of Israel who was killed during the Equatorial Guinea coup attempt in 2004), an Austrian named Manfred Felber, and an Australian, Luciano Moscatelli. In November 1994, President Clinton included Merz's name on a blacklist of individuals known to have sold nuclear, biological, and chemical weapons from China to Iran. It was later revealed that an Israeli diamond and gold trader named Moshe Regev was involved with Mainway as a principal member.

In the 1970s, Regev ran afoul of Swiss and Austrian authorities because of fraudulent activities involving First International Bank. George H.W. Bush was the chairman of Houston-based First International Bank from 1977 to 1980. Mainway maintained a direct link to Unit 105 of the Iranian Defense Ministry, the element responsible for acquiring chemical weapons and missile components. Unit 105 was headed by Dr. Majid Abbaspour, who met several times with Merz, Felber, and another Israeli businessman, Nahum Manbar, in Vienna.

As the headquarters for the International Atomic Energy Agency, the Austrian capital was of particular interest to the Brewster Jennings counter-proliferation team. Manbar was later arrested and sentenced by an Israeli court in 1997 to 16 years in prison for

---

[12] Douglas Frantz, "From Patriot to Proliferator," *Los Angeles Times*, September 23, 2005.

security offenses involving the illicit trade with Iran. Regev was later arrested by South African, Swiss, and German authorities for fraud. However, Manbar and Regev revealed something very significant about Israel's role in Iran's acquisition of WMD materials: both businessmen had earlier reported their Iranian business dealings to Israel's domestic security service, the Shin Bet.[13]

* * * *

Among the highlights of a long and distinguished intelligence career was Gus Weiss' involvement in a controversial CIA scheme to sabotage equipment sent from the West to the Soviet Union. After French intelligence informed the Reagan administration in 1981 that the Soviets were both buying and stealing sophisticated systems from third parties (in the "Farewell Dossier"), Weiss helped hatch a plan to place a "Trojan horse" software program in a computer control system stolen by the Soviets from a Canadian company for a Siberian to Europe natural gas pipeline. In June 1982, after the software corrupted the pipeline system's software, there resulted the biggest non-nuclear explosion and fire ever seen from space. The plan had involved tricking a number of Soviet purchasing agents in Western Europe, Canada, and Japan.

Whether the operation involved another incarnation of Brewster Jennings & Associates is not known, but what is known is that the mastermind of the operation died in a very unusual and suspicious manner. All *New York Times* columnist William Safire wrote in his overview of Weiss and Farewell was the following understatement, "Gus Weiss died from a fall a few months ago."[14] Weiss obviously was one of those pre-neoconservatives who had advocated a tough line with the Soviets. The fact that he broke with his old colleagues over the Iraq invasion makes his fall from the top of the Watergate triply suspicious.

In a manner similar to its handling of the suspicious automobile crushing death of Marvin Bush's babysitter on September 29, 2003,

---

[13] Yossi Melman, "Equatorial Guinea: Death of a Mercenary and a Private Army," *Haaretz*, April 15, 2005.

[14] William Safire, "The Farewell Dossier," *New York Times*, February 2, 2004, p. 21A.

the *Washington Post* waited until December 7 to report Weiss's suspicious death. A number of journalists in Washington opined that the *Post* had become nothing more than a vassal propaganda arm of the Bush White House, hesitating to cover politically embarrassing stories in order to protect its high-level access to senior Bush administration officials. For example, the *Washington Post* was one of the few media outlets to have been granted permission to fly on Air Force One with Bush on the controversial 2003 Thanksgiving trip to Baghdad.

Then the paper gave very little coverage to the stagecraft by the White House in mounting the trip, including a fake turkey held up by Bush for a photo op, a non-existent British Airways passenger plane allegedly encountered during the flight, and another non-existent German charter plane that "saw" Air Force One en route to the Middle East. Nor was there reporting of the fact that the troops that "dined" with Bush were all pre-selected. When a newspaper compromises its independence, such oversights and self-censorship become the rule rather than the exception.

The fact that both Kokal and Weiss had been critics of the Bush administration's Iraq policy should have resulted in much more media attention, but there seemed to be a blackout on coverage of these suspicious deaths. One seasoned Washington intelligence expert said that the possibility of official or semi-official "death squads" carrying out assassinations of Bush administration critics could not be ruled out. "Remember that the Watergate scandal began with the discovery of a single tape," said the expert, "and that brought down an entire administration."

—§—

John Negroponte

Elliott Abrams

Porter Goss

The retrogressive nature of the Bush administration, packed with Iran-Contra "stars" like Otto Reich, John Negroponte, and even Elliott Abrams and John Poindexter, sends a clear message to Latin America that America does not countenance leaders who get out of line. And then there is the recent CIA Director Porter Goss, whose earlier SE Asian and Latin American forays in cladestine operations are still secret …

Otto Reich

John Poindexter

CHAPTER SIX

COUPS 'R' U.S.

The George W. Bush administration enhanced the time-honored tradition of the U.S. government overthrowing leaders it found not to its liking. The easiest way for a foreign leader to arouse its ire was to preside over an oil-rich region and resist domination by Big Oil.

VENEZUELA, APRIL 2002

The left-leaning government of Venezuela's President Hugo Chavez Frias was an early target for the Bush coup plotters, many of whom were part and parcel of the Iran-Contra scandal of the 1980s. However, speaking after the April 2002 attempted coup against President Chavez, President Bush said his administration had made known to the Venezuelan opposition that it was "very clear ... that we support democracy and did not support any extra-constitutional action." Bush's exclamation of ignorance about the coup seemed to borrow liberally from the movie *Casablanca*, in which Claude Raines, playing the French police inspector, proclaimed how shocked he was at finding gambling in Rick's Bar.

The facts never supported Bush's claim of the United States being an innocent bystander to the constitutional upheaval in Venezuela that began in earnest on April 11. Since June 2001, the CIA had had a U.S. Special Operations Forces field grade officer on the ground in Venezuela to start "rounding up the usual suspects" to support a coup against the irksome Chavez. As soon as the CIA decided on what was in store for Chavez, it was a mere matter of time before Venezuela's business syndicates, pro-U.S., military officers, Catholic Church hierarchy, and selected leaders in the oil workers' unions launched their uprising.

U.S. mercenary companies were also involved in the coup attempt. From bases in eastern Colombia, CIA and U.S. mercenary contractors, ostensibly used for counter-narcotics operations, stood by to provide logistics support for the leading members of the two-day coup. Patrol aircraft operating from the U.S. Forward Operating Location (FOL) in Manta, Ecuador also provided intelligence support for the military move against Chavez.[1] Military contractor Dyncorp's Web site lists Manta as one of its operating locations.[2]

The retrogressive nature of the Bush administration, packed with Iran-Contra "stars" like Otto Reich, John Negroponte, and even Elliott Abrams and John Poindexter, sends a clear message to Latin America that America does not countenance leaders who get out of line. Chavez's forays to Cuba, Iraq, Iran, and Libya made him an honorary member of Bush's Axis of Evil. But terrorists and "evil" are not endemic to Venezuela or its OPEC allies. A quick check of Otto Reich's dossier reveals his own close ties to a brutal Cuban terrorist named Orlando Bosch.

While U.S. ambassador to Venezuela, Reich, who became Assistant Secretary of State for Latin America over the objection of the U.S. Senate and after a recess appointment, helped pressure the government to release Bosch from jail after he was found guilty for masterminding the 1976 bombing of a civilian Air Cubana Boeing 707. The plane had blown up shortly after it took off from Bridgetown, Barbados. Ironically, U.S. Navy divers and medical personnel from the small naval facility on the island were called

---

[1] Richard Bennett and Wayne Madsen, "U.S. Support for the April coup in Venezuela," *Peacework*, April 13, 2002. <http://www.afsc.org/pwork/0205/020519.htm>
[2] <http://www2.dyncorp.com/internetactive/contact/map.asp?c=Ecuador>

upon to help recover the bodies from the Caribbean. There were no survivors among the 73 men, women, and children on board.

For the Reagan-era members of the Bush II administration it must have been like old times in gearing up for the Venezuelan coup. In scenes harkening back to the days of U.S. support for the Nicaraguan Contras and the Salvadoran death squads, the coup plotters began visiting the U.S. Embassy in Caracas; the armed forces chief Gen. Lucas Rincon met with the Pentagon's Latin America affairs chief, Rogelio Pardo-Maurer; and the CIA's one-time shadowy network of continually whoring and hard-drinking American and foreign expatriates began their mischief making, albeit in the name of counter-narcotics, along the Colombian-Venezuelan border. They were intent on finding trucks crossing the border carrying weapons to Colombia's FARC guerrillas and then blaming Chavez.

A U.S. private military contractor, the Phoenix Consulting Group, was mentioned by the Chavez government as being involved with supporting the coup.[3] Phoenix was founded by former CIA agent John Nolan, a veteran of the Vietnam War. The company had contracts with the Defense Intelligence Agency and was based in Huntsville, Alabama.

But like the failed coup, the attempt to tag Chavez as a FARC supporter—along the same lines as Hitler branding Poland as an aggressor in 1939—crumbled. Chavez was not sending arms to the FARC, and the Bush administration operatives lost their chance to create a "border incident."

When Chavez replaced the directors of Venezuela's state-owned oil company with his own men, he had triggered a trip wire for the Bush administration, as when anyone threatens the international oil cabal. The Bush people—many of whom are, of course, veterans of the U.S. oil industry—went into red alert. Days after Chavez shook up Venezuela's oil monopoly, he found himself besieged in his own presidential palace by upper- and middle-class demonstrators, not the usual people found battling police in the streets. Oddly, anti-Chavez "demonstrators" attempted to break into the embassies of Cuba, Iraq, and Iran. Intelligence sources

---

[3] Business Intelligence and Lobbying, *Intelligence Online*, October 11, 2002.

reported that these "demonstrators" were U.S.-hired teams led by U.S. Special Operations forces who were instructed to ransack the embassies for intelligence and other sensitive documents. Behind the scenes, the right-wing and proto-fascist Catholic sect, Opus Dei, was also working to bring about Chavez's downfall.

Shortly after being sent to temporary exile on the island of La Orchila, Chavez, a former Venezuelan paratrooper, spotted a civilian executive jet with U.S. markings parked on the apron near his detainment room. And Chavez must have known about the large U.S. Navy carrier task force, led by the USS *George Washington*, steaming just north of Venezuela as part of two naval exercises in the Caribbean, Joint Task Force Exercise (JTFEX) and Comptuex (Composite Training Unit Exercise). Students of the coup against Chile's Salvador Allende in 1973 are painfully aware of the key role played by the U.S. Navy in helping that coup along; Chavez must have quickly put two and two together.

However, the ultra-conservatives in the Bush administration miscalculated. Extreme rightists within the Venezuelan military forced the interim President Pedro Carmona to dissolve the National Assembly and Supreme Court. Support for the coup quickly faded, and even Bush's "closest friend," Mexico's President Vicente Fox, condemned it. Washington kept blaming Chavez for all the events until it became clear the plan for installing a pro-business puppet government in Caracas had no chance for success.

As for the Bush administration, its mouthpieces claimed that any reports of its involvement in the coup were "utter nonsense." Yet, during the coup, one of the U.S.'s top operatives in Caracas sent e-mail to the United States containing upbeat language on the coup's progress, only to be quickly followed by disappointment that the "coup didn't stick." As I told a reporter for the *Guardian*, "I first heard of Lieutenant Colonel James Rogers [the assistant military attaché then based at the US embassy in Caracas] going down there last June to set the ground.... Some of our counter-narcotics agents were also involved." Rogers had been seconded to the embassy from his U.S. Army Special Operations unit at Fort Bragg, North Carolina. A Venezuelan congressman, Roger Rondon, also told the *Guardian* that U.S. military officers, whom he named as (James) Rogers and (Ronald) MacCammon, had been at the Fuerte Tiuna military headquarters with the coup leaders during the night of April 11-12, 2001.[4]

After the fact, Bush offered Chavez some sage advice: "When the pressure gets on, leaders should not compromise those institutions that are so important for democracy." Very interesting words from a person, who, lacking a majority of the votes of the American people, took every opportunity in the wake of September 11 to compromise America's most valued democratic traditions.

The second-term George W. Bush administration showed no signs of lessening the pressure on Chavez, who successfully beat an American-inspired and supported recall referendum in 2004. In May 2005, Bush met in the White House with one of the architects of the recall move against Chavez, conservative opposition leader Maria Corina Machado. Machado faced criminal conspiracy charges in Venezuela after it was discovered that her Sumate organization received $31,000 from the National Endowment for Democracy, an organization that had been subsidized by Republican right-wingers to foment electoral disruption in countries like Venezuela, Nicaragua, Haiti, and Bolivia. At the same time Bush met Machado, his administration was rejecting a Venezuelan request for the extradition of Cuban-born terrorist Luis Posada Carriles, who was wanted by Venezuela for his role in the 1976 bombing of the Cubana Airlines passenger plane off the west coast of Barbados. As noted, all 73 passengers and crew aboard the aircraft were killed. Posada had escaped from a Venezuelan prison in 1985.

President Chavez claimed on several occasions that Bush was trying to assassinate him. Chavez's charges were bolstered when Felix Rodriguez, a former CIA agent, Iran-Contra provocateur, and prominent Bush supporter in Florida, told Miami's Channel 22 that he had detailed information about the Bush administration's plans to "bring about a change" in Venezuela by "military measures." Rodriguez was tied to the CIA operation that executed Cuban revolutionary Che Guevara in Bolivia in 1967, and to various plots to assassinate Cuba's president, Fidel Castro.[5]

---

[4] Duncan Campbell, "American 'navy helped Venezuelan coup,'" *The Guardian*, April 29, 2002.

[5] Jefferson Morley, "Venezuela's 'Anti-Bush' Fears Assassination," *Washington Post*.

President Chavez also maintained that Venezuelan intelligence had uncovered a secret U.S. plan, code named OPERATION BALBOA, to invade Venezuela. Chavez said he had instructed Venezuela's forces to develop a counter-BALBOA plan.

In April 2006, it appeared that the Bush administration was dusting off its playbook from April 2002. A task force led by the USS *George Washington* was dispatched to the Caribbean for a two-month long naval exercise code-named OPERATION PARTNERSHIP OF THE AMERICAS. Not coincidentally, U.S. and British and Dutch NATO forces were in Jamaica "training" English-speaking Caribbean paramilitary forces as part of OPERATION TRADEWINDS.

The Bush administration also relied on its neocon allies in the Dutch government to accuse Chavez of having designs on the Netherlands Antilles. Dutch Defense Minister Henk Kamp called Chavez a "fanatic populist" who wanted to invade Aruba, Bonaire, and Curacao (the "ABC islands"). Venezuelan political and military leaders called the Dutch charges ridiculous and pointed out that the U.S. Southern Command was issuing policy documents clearly stating that populist movements spreading from Venezuela, Uruguay, and Bolivia to Peru, Ecuador, Nicaragua, and Mexico were threats to national security.

The Bush administration slightly changed its 2002 Venezuela destabilization template by encouraging border problems for the country. Chavez accused Zulia state's right-wing governor, Manuel Rosales, of working with the United States and American oil interests to promote independence for the oil-rich western state on the Colombian border. A new right-wing and pro-business group called "Own Road" (*Rumbo Propio*) began pushing for an independence referendum for the state. There was evidence that the group received support from intelligence elements operating from within the U.S. embassy in Caracas. U.S. ambassador to Venezuela William Brownfield even referred to the state as the "Republic of Zulia." He later claimed he was joking. U.S. intelligence sources also reported that U.S. Special Forces were training Guyanese rebels in Guyana for cross-border incursions into the eastern part of Venezuela, an area disputed by Guyana and Venezuela.

---

com, March 17, 2005.

HAITI, FEBRUARY 2004

State Department sources began to report in late 2003 that right-wing elements in the State Department and National Security Council were going to employ the same coup template in trying to oust Haitian President Jean-Bertrand Aristide from power.

Otto Reich—who went to the National Security Council (NSC) after the Senate blocked his nomination at the State Department, was replaced by Roger Noriega—and his NSC colleague, Elliott Abrams, an Iran-Contra felon, were coordinating and applying the same pressure against Aristide that was used against Chavez. According to congressional Democratic sources, Noriega, a former chief of staff for right-wing Republican Senator Jesse Helms, and a supporter of death squads in El Salvador, visited Port-au-Prince on a supposed "peace" mission, but actually tried to force Aristide to resign. When Aristide refused to resign, and acceded to a coalition government with the rebels, his opponents, especially rebels in northern Haiti, vowed to continue their insurgency.

On February 19, 2004, Pentagon spokesman Lawrence Di Rita would only admit that a 3- to 4-person U.S. Southern Command team was being assembled to go to Port-au- Prince to discuss options with the U.S. ambassador. After their visit, the Pentagon announced that a 50-man U.S. Marine Corps FAST (Fleet Anti-terrorism Security Team) team would secure the U.S. embassy against any problems arising from what was expected to be a final assault against the Haitian capital by U.S.-backed rebels. The operation against Aristide had the full support of Republicans on the House of Representatives International Relations Committee, and anti-Aristide propaganda was being spread by the extreme right-wing Heritage Foundation.

In fact, funds from the National Endowment for Democracy, funneled through the International Republican Institute (IRI) (chaired by Senator John McCain), the same channel used to steer money to anti-Chavez forces in Venezuela, were used to "rent" mobs who stoked the anti-Aristide flames with Republican Party-generated picket signs that read, oddly, "Down With Bill Clinton" and "Down With Jesse Jackson."

Using the U.S. Southern Command's forward base for the Special Operations Command, South (SOCSOUTH) at Naval Station Roosevelt Roads, Puerto Rico, its new headquarters at Homestead Air Force Base in Florida, and units at the nearby Guantanamo Bay Naval Station in Cuba (which went into total security lockdown prior to the launch of the coup against Aristide), the Noriega-Reich-Abrams team used ex-supporters of the Duvalier dictatorships, Duvalier's paramilitary Ton Ton Macoutes, exiled military coup leaders who originally ousted Aristide in a Bush I-inspired coup in 1991, right-wing Front for the Advancement and Progress of Hati (FRAPH) members, rebel units within the Haitian military, and wealthy business leaders, to foment the rebellion against Aristide.

The coup against Chavez had been supported by U.S. Special Operations and private military contractor personnel in neighboring Colombia. In Haiti, the rebellion was supported by SOC-SOUTH psyops and military training personnel in the neighboring Dominican Republic. And as with the coup against Chavez, the Haitian coup was supplemented by electronic eavesdropping being conducted from the National Security Agency signals intelligence station at Sabana Seca, Puerto Rico.

According to knowledgeable US and Haitian sources, some of the Dominican troops and Spanish and English-speaking paramilitaries trained by the United States during Operation Jaded Task's initial phase in the Dominican Republic during 2003 were fighting alongside Haitian rebels in Cap Haitien and Gonaives in the north of the country and Les Cayes on the southern coast. In addition, Spanish and English speaking commandos and private military contractor paramilitaries, believed to have been trained by U.S. Navy SEAL Special Boat Teams and other U.S. Special Forces in the Dominican Republic, landed at Les Cayes on February 25. Similar boats carrying Spanish and English speaking militias earlier landed at Cap Haitien.

Some English and Spanish speaking military advisers to the Haitian rebels also engaged in sniper attacks, a highly specialized capability in which Dominican troops were trained during Jaded Task. Shortly after the United States began training Dominican troops, Haitian government authorities intercepted vans carrying new M-16s across the border from the Dominican Republic. "We are now running the serial numbers on the M-16s from the DR to ascertain their origin," said one Haitian official.[6] During 2003, the U.S. military delivered 20,000 M-16s to the Dominican army.

The Steele Foundation, a San Francisco-based security firm modeled on the international investigative and security firm, Kroll Associates, provided VIP security for Haitian President Jean-Bertrand Aristide. Steele Foundation officials demurred at Aristide's revelations that he had been kidnapped at gunpoint by a U.S. military team at his home in the Tabarre neighborhood of Port-au-Prince and whisked off in a U.S. Air Force plane to the Central African Republic (CAR) via Antigua. They claimed their VIP bodyguards, consisting of ex-US Special Forces and State Department VIP protection detail bodyguards would have fired on U.S. troops if they tried to apprehend Aristide. That contention was dismissed by a number of U.S. military specialists as ridiculous, because ex-US military members would never fire on U.S. troops.

ISTO's Richard Armitage weighed in with his own take on the situation and defended Steele. He said of Aristide's charge that he had been kidnapped, "His own bodyguards, The Steele Foundation, were on the plane with him with all of their weapons, and they've said it was not true; he was not kidnapped; they wouldn't have allowed it." Armitage added that Aristide would not be allowed to return to Haiti.[7]

Later, it was reported that a number of Steele's bodyguards in Haiti had abandoned Aristide as the rebellion against him grew, and a company called Richmond Group International of Woodbridge, Virginia had declined an offer to replace Steele's bodyguards with its own.[8] However, some Steele bodyguards accompanied Aristide's U.S. military escort to Bangui, CAR in what appeared to be a joint effort between the firm and the U.S. Special Operations team.

From Bangui, Aristide continued to maintain that U.S. forces kidnapped him, a charge that White House press secretary Scott McClellan brushed aside as a "conspiracy theory."[9] It should be

[6] Confidential information.

[7] "Armitage: Aristide Can't Return," UPI, March 9, 2004.

[8] Bryan Bender, "Change In Haiti / Private Security; Firms' Worldwide Role Concerns Some Specialists," *Boston Globe*, March 4, 2004, p. A20.

[9] "U.S. denies forcing Aristide's retreat," *Marin Independent Journal*, March 2, 2004.

noted that McClellan's father, Barr McClellan, a one-time lawyer for Lyndon Johnson, claimed in a book, *Blood, Money & Power: How LBJ Killed JFK,* that Johnson was behind the assassination of John F. Kennedy!

Steele was very close to the Pentagon and State Department, the two departments at the center of organizing the rebellion against Aristide. Steele maintained a Secure Operations Center in Baghdad and offices in Saudi Arabia, Kuwait, and Jordan. Steele also maintained an office in Miami, the home of the headquarters of the U.S. Special Operations Command, which was also involved heavily in training the rebels who ousted Aristide. Steele had not been hired by Aristide, but by his predecessor Rene Preval.

In 1995, Preval's government had contracted with a number of U.S. companies close to U.S. intelligence and military circles to provide security services, including Kellogg, Brown & Root, which Dick Cheney headed at the time. Preval, a favorite of the U.S., defeated Aristide in the 1995 presidential election. But in 1999 Preval began to rule by decree, and, after the Haitian armed forces were disbanded, Dyncorp (now owned by Computer Sciences Corporation) was brought in to establish and train the new Haitian National Police. Dyncorp recruited former Ton Ton Macoutes of the Duvalier regimes and pro-US former members of the military junta as policemen. According to U.S. congressional sources, some of these Dyncorp-trained police served as a virtual fifth column in the 2004 coup against Aristide.

The Bush administration wasted no time in appointing an unelected puppet regime to replace Aristide. From Miami, the United States flew Gerard Latortue, a former Haitian government official, international business "consultant," resident of trés chic Boca Raton, and Miami talk show host, to Haiti to serve as interim prime minister and to head a U.S.-imposed contrivance called the "Council of Wise Men," as inaptly named as the U.S.-installed "Governing Council" in Iraq.

Caribbean leaders rejected the Haitian puppet regime and refused to recognize it or to invite its members to Caribbean Community meetings. Regional leaders decried the arrogance of the Bush administration, joining leaders in Europe, Asia, the Middle

East, Latin America, and Africa who made similar pronouncements. In typical neoconservative fashion, the Bush administration warned Jamaica not to give Aristide asylum, and threatened reprisals. Jamaica refused to be intimidated and did grant Aristide temporary asylum, to which the commander of the U.S. Southern Command, General James T. Hill, another in a long parade of arrogant U.S. pro-consuls for Latin America, reacted by stating that Jamaica should make sure Aristide kept "his mouth shut."[10]

In March 2004, General Hill told the House Armed Services Committee that the U.S. faced a "terrorist" threat from "emerging terrorists" in Latin America, whom he described as "radical populists" who capitalize on "deep-seated frustrations of the failure of democratic reforms to deliver expected goods and services." Observers regarded Hill's comments as being directed against Venezuela's Chavez and Bolivia's then-peasant leader, now-president, Evo Morales. Hill represented yet another U.S. military leader who espoused the extreme right-wing political agenda promoted by the Bush administration.[11]

In the Pentagon, Hill had the support of Rogelio Pardo-Maurer, the Deputy Assistant Secretary of State for Western Hemisphere Affairs. Pardo-Maurer was the conduit for the Pentagon neoconservatives in launching attacks against democratically elected populist leaders in Venezuela, Brazil, and Uruguay. Pardo-Maurer was no stranger to right-wing circles that influenced Republican Latin American policy. A dual U.S.-Costa Rican citizen, he was the head of the Nicaraguan Contra office in Washington during the Iran-Contra scandal.

Also supporting the Haitian coup were a number of U.S.-owned companies that had set up sweatshops in the outskirts of Port-au-Prince, such as Andy Apaid's Alpha Industries and Cintas. On September 27, 1999, President Preval charged Apaid with defrauding Haiti's state-owned Teleco phone company by allowing customers to bypass Teleco and make phone calls via Apaid's Alpha Communications Network and its high-speed satellite connection. Apaid refused to pay a $120,000 government fine.[12]

[10] Justin Felux, "U.S. and Haiti: Imperial Arrogance at its Worst," *Dissident Voice*, March 25, 2004. <http://www.dissidentvoice.org/Mar04/Felux0325.htm>

[11] Jack Epstein, "General Seeks Boost for Latin American Armies," *San Francisco Chronicle*, April 30, 2004.

[12] Joel Dreyfuss, "How Haiti Became Unwired," *Fortune*, January 24, 2000, p. 30.

The underpaid workers at textile and electronic equipment factories owned by Apaid, a U.S. citizen born of Haitian parents, were at the core of Aristide's political base. From the sweatshops, electronic parts flowed to the factories of IBM, Unisys, and Honeywell. Apaid's "Group of 184 Civil Society Organizations" was linked to the death squads of Guy Philippe and his band of U.S.-trained and supported murderers and brigands.[13] Secretary of State Powell, whose parentage is Jamaican, not only threatened the island of his family's origin for granting Aristide asylum, but also coordinated his efforts against Haiti's democratically elected government by speaking directly to Apaid.[14] Apaid, a resident of Massachusetts, was a supporter of the Republican Party.

On February 16, 2006, Rene Preval was elected president in a very close election. Preval distanced himself from Aristide's Lavalas Party. During a March 2006 visit to the United Nations, Preval was asked by Joe Lauria of the *Boston Globe* if he was aware of OPERATION JADED TASK, the U.S. destabilization operation conducted against Haiti from the Dominican Republic. Preval astonishingly responded that he never heard of JADED TASK and could not respond to the issue of U.S. involvement in the ouster of Aristide. It was a clear sign that Preval was not interested in investigating the coup against Aristide, and would continue the role of numerous Haitian leaders as a marionette of the United States..

Sao Tome & Pricipe, July 2003

Speaking at a seminar on the African Oil Sector at the Center for Strategic and International Studies (CSIS) in Washington DC on March 30, 2004, Sao Tome and Principe President Fradrique De Menezes revealed an amazing but all-too-typical story about how a well-known diamond company, with past links to Executive Outcomes activities in Sierra Leone and Angola, attempted to land a deal for a joint venture between DiamondWorks' subsidiary, Energem Petroleum, Ltd., and the government of Sao Tome and Principe on the commercialization of the hydrocarbon products to be produced from the Sao Tome's Joint Development

---

[13] Businessman and Bitter Aristide Critic: Andy Apaid, Jr." *Jamaica Observer*, March 14, 2004.
[14] State Department Press Briefing, February 23, 2004.

Zone with Nigeria in the Gulf of Guinea. DiamondWorks' wholly owned subsidiary, Otterbea International (Proprietary) and its 50 percent owned subsidiary, PetroPlus Africa, were seeking the lucrative Sao Tome oil contracts. According to DiamondWorks, the firms are involved in "commodities trading, the supply and sale of crude oil and refined petroleum products and procurement and logistics for the mining industry in Africa." The Sao Tome deal was to have involved marketing refined crude oil products from Sao Tome to Nigeria. DiamondWorks mining operations were located in Sierra Leone, Central African Republic, and Angola.

De Menezes, who admitted that Sao Tome has not a single native oil engineer, revealed that recent negotiations with PetroPlus, the DiamondWorks firm registered in South Africa, which negotiated the deal through the Vancouver, Canada-based DiamondWorks, were canceled after a business center computer and printer at Sao Tome's Hotel Miramar were found to contain copies of DiamondWorks' proposal, which failed to contain basic transparency requirements compliant with Sao Tome's laws and regulations regarding the nascent oil industry.

The proposal was prepared by DiamondWorks personnel who were staying at the Miramar, a favorite hotel for the oil industry personnel who were flooding into the country. An employee of the American military training firm MPRI (a subsidiary of L-3 Communications, a leading intelligence and defense contractor), who was also staying at the Miramar with other members of an MPRI training team, "found" the copies of the proposals in the hotel's computer and printer and gave them to Steve Cowper, the Democratic Governor of Alaska from 1986 to 1990, who was an oil adviser to the Sao Tome government and who also happened to be staying at the Miramar.

The leak of the proposal created a scandal in the Sao Tome government, with Natural Resources Minister Tome Vera Cruz resigning for making the deal with DiamondWorks. De Menezes's oil adviser Patrice Trovoada, who is the son of Sao Tome's former President Miguel Trovoada, was also in favor of the DiamondWorks deal and, according to De Menezes, originally agreed to the deal with DiamondWorks. De Menezes, who represents the Democratic Movement of Forces for Change, is a political opponent of Miguel Trovoada, who led the Liberation Movement of Sao Tome and Principe. DiamondWorks had past links to South African mercenary firms, some of which were linked to the July 2003 coup against de Menezes. Three other ministers, including the Foreign Minister, also resigned in the scandal. De Menezes revealed that it was Patrice Trovoada who originally agreed to deal with DiamondWorks. De Menezes canceled the Memorandum of Understanding with DiamondWorks.

The involvement of MPRI in "finding" the DiamondWorks documents is all the more interesting considering the fact that two U.S. oil companies, Exxon-Mobil and Environmental Remediation Holdings Corp. (ERHC) stood to benefit from the locking out of DiamondWorks. Arcadia, a Nigerian-Japanese company backed by Mitsui, retained a contract to transport Nigerian crude to Sao Tome.

Not much is known about ERHC. It had one full-time employee, was based in an office building in Houston, had $21,000 in cash, and had no experience in offshore drilling. In 1996, ERHC was spun from a Colorado-based company called Regional Air Group Corporation. Its first CEO was Sam L. Bass, Jr. In 1999, ERHC's CEO Geoffrey Tirman of Talisman Capital in Little Rock, Arkansas, accused the Sao Tome government of demanding bribes in return for oil concessions. The government accused Tirman of seditious actions, and he was forced to flee the island nation.[15]

In 2001, Tirman sold his stake in ERHC to Emeka Offor, a wealthy Nigerian entrepreneur and one-time associate of Nigerian dictator Sani Abacha. The new owner relocated the company's headquarters from Lafayette, Louisiana, to Houston. In 2004, ERHC teamed up with Pioneer Natural Resources of Dallas (the head of its Tunisian office, Hashim al Khersan, was appointed by the Department of Defense to the four member post-Saddam Iraqi Oil Industry Advisory Board), Devon Energy of Oklahoma City (politically connected to the Bush family and James Baker III), and Noble Energy of Houston to exploit Sao Tome's offshore drilling blocks. A ten percent stockholder in ERHC, Nigeria's First At-

---

[15] Ken Silverstein, "Sinking Its Hopes Into a Tiny Nation; Obscure Texas oil firm, amid claims of bribery, secures a deal with poor Sao Tome and Principe, *Los Angeles Times*, May 24, 2003, p. 1.

lantic Bank, charged Offor with fraud and sued for repayment of a $57 million loan. ERHC's financial problems resulted in Exxon Mobil's desire for its small partner to "go away."[16]

De Menezes, responding to my question regarding the March 26, 2004, revelations by Equatorial Guinea President Teodoro Obiang that the mercenary-led coup against him was also going to target the Democratic Republic of the Congo (DRC) and Sao Tome and Principe, said he was confident that his Defense Minister Oscar Sousa, who remained in Sao Tome, "had everything under control." Two days after Obiang's warning, on March 28, there was an attempted coup—code named OPERATION PENTECOST—against President Joseph Kabila in the DRC by former Zairean armed forces and Mobutu Sese Seko presidential security forces, who arrived in new boats from Brazzaville armed with new weapons.

De Menezes that said the July 16, 2003 coup in Sao Tome had been carried out by "the same people who were involved in the [subsequent] Equatorial Guinea affair." He thanked Portugal, Angola, Mozambique, and Nigeria for helping to restore Sao Tome's democracy. De Menezes had been attending a Corporate Council on Africa summit in Washington and the Leon Sullivan Summit in Abuja when the coup against him was launched. It is noteworthy that De Menezes did not mention either South Africa (the point of origin for the mercenaries who temporarily ousted him) or the United States, whose President, George W. Bush, had just completed a visit to South Africa prior to the coup.

Following De Menezes' remarks, the EUCOM's General Charles Wald said that during the coup in Sao Tome, U.S. ambassador to Gabon Kenneth Moorefield (who was also accredited to Sao Tome but resided in Libreville) just happened to be in Sao Tome at the time and that he "ensured the stability of the country during the coup." But Wald later joked, "I don't know if Moorefield caused the coup or prevented it."

De Menezes said that fortunately the Equatorial Guinea coup plotters had been found out, but he remained very worried about security matters in the Gulf of Guinea region. He added he was hopeful the U.S. would do something to improve the region's security.

[16] David Ivanovich, "Tiny player strikes gold in huge oil deal," *Houston Chronicle*, March 13, 2005, p. 2005.

De Menezes may have more security than he ever bargained for. On March 30, 2004, the Center for Strategic and International Studies (CSIS) used the occasion of De Menezes's visit to issue a report on "Transparency on Africa's Oil Industry." It is significant that those who participated in drafting the report included individuals close to Vice President Dick Cheney, including his adviser Robert Wells and James Andrews of Kellogg, Brown & Root/ Halliburton. Others involved in the report's preparation included representatives of Chevron Texaco, where Condoleezza Rice was once a board member, and Shell Oil.

The report requested that Bush name a special adviser to the President for Africa Energy Diplomacy, and called for expanded International Military Education and Training (IMET) support, further expansion southward of the EUCOM military activities in Ghana, Senegal, Gabon, Angola, Sao Tome and Principe, and Nigeria, and increased effort for EUCOM's counterterrorism Pan Sahel Initiative in Chad, Mali, Niger, Mauritania, Algeria, and Morocco. The report also emphasized the need for a maritime security program to protect offshore oil rigs maintained by Exxon Mobil, Chevron Texaco, Devon, Amerada Hess, Marathon Oil, and UNOCAL, and further military programs to protect the Exxon Mobil-led Chad-Cameroon pipeline and the Chevron Texaco-led West Africa Gas Pipeline from Nigeria to other West African countries, including Benin, Togo, and Ghana. In May 2004, a consortium of oil companies attended a seminar in London that, in part, assessed recent oil finds off the coasts of Mauritania and Guinea-Bissau, two nations wracked by incessant coups and coup attempts.

MPRI's military assessment in Sao Tome and Principe was completed in March 2004, and Wald prognosticated that the final report would call for a national gendarmerie and coastal/maritime security program. He added that former colonizer Portugal agreed to assist in the defense projects, and that a retired U.S. Coast Guard officer on the MPRI team would be involved in the maritime security program, which Wald stressed, encompassed the entire west coast of Africa.

Sao Tome and Principe became a major oil producer in its own right, which further had helped put it on the map of the Bush administration. The Sao Tome coup was partly successful, with allies of 32 Battalion holding key government positions in the administration of a restored President de Menezes. Some of the mercenaries later arrested for their part in the attempted Equatorial Guinea coup were Sao Tomean veterans of 32 Battalion and the coup against de Menezes.

De Menezes viewed the discovery of oil in the territorial waters of his two-island state as a mixed blessing. He said when Sao Tome and Principe achieved independence from Portugal in 1975, all that was left was a few run-down cocoa plantations and no capital or investments. Nonetheless, on March 30, 2004, he said, "The recent discovery of mercenaries in Zimbabwe, supposedly bound for a coup attempt in Equatorial Guinea, demonstrates how oil wealth can destabilize an entire region."

De Menezes also said that the activities of oil companies should be governed by transparency and accountability. He thanked George Soros's Open Society Institute for its work in addressing the problem of oil industry corruption through his international "Publish What You Pay" campaign.[17] That obviously does not sit too well with the Bush and Cheney administration, which favors operating in the shadows in the style of Enron and Halliburton. And De Menezes's praise for Soros, an ardent financial supporter of soon-to-be Democratic presidential nominee John Kerry, must have especially angered the Bush defense, foreign policy, and commerce apparatchiks.

EQUATORIAL GUINEA, MARCH 2004

In March 2004, Zimbabwe authorities detained and arrested the passengers and crew of a plane suspected of carrying mercenaries to oil-rich Equatorial Guinea to stage a coup. Although the American embassy in Harare, Zimbabwe and the U.S. State Department disavowed any American connection to the Boeing 727-L100 seized at Harare International Airport transporting 67 mercenaries—mainly South African—and specialized commando equipment, a database search of the aircraft's registration number, N4610, revealed that the owner was, at one time, the U.S. Air Force. The plane first flew in

---

[17] Fradrique de Menezes, Speech made at Center for Strategic and International Studies (CSIS), March 30, 2004.

the U.S. Air Force fleet in 1964. After the plane's seizure in Harare, State Department spokesman Richard Boucher said, "We have no indication this aircraft is connected to the U.S. government."[18]

Federal Aviation Administration Records traced the registration number N4620 to Dodson Aviation, Inc., of Rantoul, Kansas. Dodson claimed it sold the airplane to Logo Logistics Ltd., a murky South African company, a few days before it was seized in Zimbabwe. Logo later claimed the plane was on its way to the eastern Democratic Republic of the Congo (DRC), where huge arms caches had recently turned up. Central and southern African governments were edgy about the movements of mercenaries. A major offensive by ethnic Congolese Tutsi and Rwandan troops against the Kinshasa government and its allies was expected at any time by observers on the ground in the DRC.

Not much was known about Logo, which was reportedly based in Pretoria, but incorporated in Guernsey. Logo's Web site, www.logo-4log.com, claimed that the firm was involved in Venezuela, Guyana, Sierra Leone, Liberia, Congo (Brazzaville), Democratic Republic of the Congo, Angola, Zambia, Mozambique, Pakistan, and China. Logo Logistics was also reported to also have an office in the British Virgin Islands.

Dodson had been a regular supplier to the South African Air Force. Of greater interest was the individual who was named the administrative contact for the firm when it was officially registered on Sept. 4, 2000:

MANN, SIMON (SMS902) DNS-ADMIN@MWEB.CO.ZA
LOGO
18 DUCKITT AVENUE, CONSTANCIA,
CAPE TOWN, CAPE 7800
SOUTH AFRICA

In 1993, Simon Mann, along with fellow Briton Tony Buckingham, registered the mercenary company Executive Outcomes, which was headquartered in London. Executive Outcomes was corporately linked to both DiamondWorks and Branch Energy, two firms involved in a number of covert activities in Africa.

---

[18] "U.S. Aircraft Seized in Africa," Reuters, March 9, 2004.

Logo claimed that it had chartered N4610 from a firm called Systems Design. Systems Design appeared to be as murky as Logo Logistics.

In fact, the aircraft appeared to have had many owners. U.S. Air Force records had the following information about the aircraft: "83-4610/4617 Boeing C-22B. Ex-commercial 727-100 operated by ANG 4610 (c/n 18811) was formerly N4610 of National Airlines. Sold Jan 11, 2002 to Dodson International Parts, Inc., and then to Dodson Aviation Jan 14, 2002. Registered to Dodson Aviation as N4620."

Dodson had been involved with clandestine activities in the past, mostly involving private military contractor activities. In September 1998, the Economic Community of West African States Military Observer Group (ECOMOG) identified a plane in Liberia that it reported was registered to Dodson Aviation Maintenance and Spare Parts, a South African company. The plane was spotted at Roberts Field in Monrovia: a Gulfstream 14-passenger jet, leased to Greater Holdings, Ltd. (Liberia), a gold and diamond mining company.

Dodson Aviation Maintenance and Spare Parts was owned by Fred Rindel, but was shut down on December 31, 1998. Rindel was a former South African Air Force officer and defense attaché to the United States. He trained a multinational security force for then-Liberian President Charles Taylor and was also connected to arms smuggling to warring parties in Sierra Leone. Rindel was also named by the United Nations as being involved in the smuggling of 68 tons of weapons from Bulgaria to the Revolutionary United Front (RUF) of Sierra Leone in July 1999. The arms smuggling was facilitated, according to the UN, by Zief Morganstein, an arms and diamond smuggler based in Sierra Leone. The arms carrier was a Dakar-based charter company called Continental Aviation.

Dodson's Web site claimed that a follow-on company, Dodson International Parts SA (Pty.) Ltd., was the African division of two U.S.-based companies: Dodson International Parts Inc., and Dodson Aviation. The Web site stated that the company had been established in 1998 and was based at Wonderboom Airport, Pretoria. Wonderboom is where the Boeing N4620 took off before it stopped at Harare via Polokwane International Airport in South

Africa. The plane was said to have been en route to Bujumbura, Burundi.

On January 6, 2004, Dodson was sued in the Tenth U.S. Circuit Court of Appeals in Denver by Aerotech Resources for improper business practices over the sale of a Dodson Boeing 727 and another aircraft to the Air Military Transport of Ecuador (TAME). Ecuador is a country rife with U.S. Special Operations forces and private military contractors.

It was in Ecuador that U.S. Special Operations forces trained Haitian rebel leader Guy Philippe and his colleagues in 1996. The U.S. also maintained a Forward Operating Location military airbase at Manta, Ecuador, which was reportedly involved in the April 2002 coup against Venezuelan President Chavez. The presence of Logo, Ltd., a firm with close ties to Dodson, in both Venezuela and neighboring Guyana, raised suspicions about the role of both companies in efforts to launch another coup against Chavez. U.S. intelligence sources pointed out that Yair Klein, the Israeli mercenary, was active in arms sales to Ecuador and to guerrillas in neighboring Colombia, as well as diamond and arms smuggling in Liberia and Sierra Leone, two areas where Dodson Aviation and Logo had also been active.

The Boeing captured by Zimbabwe was en route to Equatorial Guinea to mount a coup d'etat against President Teodoro Obiang Nguema and send him off to exile in Las Palmas, Canary Islands. Obiang suspected Spain of using naval exercises in his waters in February as a pretext for the coup against him, so he cancelled the Spanish Navy's request to dock at Malabo.

Interestingly, this was the same scenario used by the Bush administration when it helped launch the April 2002 coup against Venezuelan President Chavez. A major U.S. Navy exercise was being conducted off Venezuela's coast at the time of that coup. In 1994, Gambia's democratically elected President Dawda Jawara was ousted in a military coup while he was being entertained on board the visiting USS *La Moure County*. And Chilean President Salvador Allende was overthrown by the right-wing military coup on September 11, 1973 while U.S. Navy ships were conducting "training" off the Chilean coast and providing support to the coup leaders. America's covert operators rarely depart from their play-book.

U.S. oil companies also had significant installations in Equatorial Guinea. In addition, a new U.S. embassy had been opened in Malabo in 2003. Obiang, whose human rights record was every bit as bad, if not worse, than that of Saddam Hussein, met with a number of Bush administration officials, including Colin Powell and Energy Secretary Spencer Abraham.

Frank Ruddy, who was Ronald Reagan's ambassador to Equatorial Guinea during the 1980s, condemned Bush's policy towards the Obiang regime. He accused the Bush administration of being "big cheerleaders for the government—and it's an awful government." During a Senate hearing on Equatorial Guinea's questionable business deals with U.S. oil companies, Michigan Senator Carl Levin told Exxon Mobil officials, "I know you're all in a competitive business ... but I've got to tell you, I don't see any fundamental difference between dealing with an Obiang and dealing with a Saddam Hussein."[19]

Shortly before the Boeing 727's detention in Harare, Equatorial Guinea arrested fifteen mercenaries it said were connected to the coup attempt. Four Kazakh pilots working for the Pan African Airlines Company were also questioned in Malabo, although the Kazakhstan government denied they were part of the coup attempt.[20]

Immediately, the international news media, particularly in Africa, were subjected to false leads and disinformation. There were suggestions that the plane may have been en route to Ivory Coast to aid in the civil war there, or to the DRC to mount a coup against President Joseph Kabila, whose father had been assassinated in a U.S. and Angola-inspired coup just four days before George W. Bush was inaugurated, and forty years from the date of the assassination of Congolese Prime Minister Patrice Lumumba, a murder that was sanctioned by the CIA.

Northbridge Services Group, a British private military contractor, reported that its information pointed to the mercenaries' use

[19] Maass, "A Touch of Crude," op. cit., pp. 51, 86.
[20] BBC Monitoring Service, "Secret service denies Kazakhs engaged in illegal activities in Africa," March 28, 2004.

of Equatorial Guinea as a jumping off point to capture former Liberian President Charles Taylor from exile in Calabar, Nigeria and deliver him to the UN War Crimes Tribunal for Africa. The Bush administration had posted a $2 million reward for the capture of Taylor. Northbridge's president, Bob Kovacic, claimed that his representative in the United States, Pasquale Dipofi, "did know a couple of the guys on the plane and one or two in the target country [Nigeria], but we had nothing to do with the mission." Interestingly, Kovacic revealed this Liberian connection from Kuwait, where he was seeking security contracts in Iraq.[21]

This points to the big problem with private actors playing on the international foreign policy stage. Whether a group of mercenary companies connected to security work in Iraq were trying to capture a deposed leader in Nigeria without that country's approval, or they were trying to launch a coup d'état in Equatorial Guinea, the ramifications of such freelancers acting either independently, or with a "wink and a nod" from government interlocutors, are indeed chilling.

President Obiang added to the intrigue when he later suggested, on March 26, 2004, that after the mercenaries overthrew him, they were to launch coups in the DRC and Sao Tome and Principe: "We have learned that after Equatorial Guinea, the mercenaries also wanted to overthrow the governments of Sao Tome, the Democratic Republic of Congo, and maybe other countries."[22] Ironically, two days after Obiang's revelation, Congolese troops put down an attempted coup in Kinshasa, said to have originated from neighboring Brazzaville across the Congo River, and reported to have had the backing of American interests that wanted to get rid of Joseph Kabila.

* * * *

The Equatorial-Guinea plot took on greater intrigue when links between the coup plotters and high-powered Western politicians were disclosed. On August 25, 2004, South African police arrested Sir Mark Thatcher, the son of former British Prime Minister Baroness Margaret Thatcher, at his posh home in Constantia, a

[21] Reuters, "Paper says 'mercenaries' wanted reward for Taylor," March 24, 2004.
[22] Reuters, "Soldiers of fortune had more than one plan," March 27, 2004.

wealthy neighborhood of Cape Town, shortly before he was to fly to Dallas to join his American wife and children. Thatcher's family had fled Cape Town shortly before his arrest; his wife, Diane Burgdorf Thatcher, is a wealthy heiress to a Dallas car dealership fortune. Mark Thatcher had been dogged by allegations involving dubious contracts with Oman and Saudi Arabia in the 1980s.

He was also charged with aiding the Equatorial-Guinea coup attempt. In a plea bargain, Thatcher admitted to "unwittingly" bankrolling the coup plot, and he was ordered to pay a $500,000 fine before he could leave South Africa. In April 2005, while Thatcher was waiting in London for a U.S. visa, he was informed that he was ineligible to enter the United States due to his criminal conviction. Equatorial Guinea continued to maintain an arrest warrant for Thatcher.

It was discovered that Thatcher paid $275,000 to charter two helicopters to be used in the coup against Obiang. South Africa's special law enforcement "Scorpions" unit discovered a tangled web of influential Britons associated with the coup. They included Jeffrey H. Archer (Lord Archer), the ex-convict disgraced peer and former deputy leader of the British Conservative Party; David Hart, Prime Minister Thatcher's adviser and a close friend of Ronald Reagan's CIA chief William Casey; Nigerian-born Lebanese businessman and oil trader Elie (or Ely) Calil; businessman Greg Wales, once associated with Simon Mann's Executive Outcomes; Gary Hersham, a London property agent; British businessman David Tremain, based in South Africa; and close Tony Blair confidant and European Union Trade Commissioner Peter Mandelson.

A report written by the Conservative Party think tank, the Center for Policy Studies, and which was obtained by South African investigators, disclosed that Mandelson and Calil discussed the plot at a chic Lebanese restaurant in London's Belgravia district. Nigel Morgan, a former member of the Irish Guards, wrote the report. Mandelson previously served as Northern Ireland Secretary in Blair's government. Simon Mann used the code names "Smelly" for Calil and "Scratcher" for Mark Thatcher.

After the coup plotters were arrested in Zimbabwe and Equatorial Guinea, British Foreign Secretary Jack Straw denied prior knowledge of the coup. Straw was later forced to retract his original denials under pressure from the Opposition in the House of Commons. Straw admitted Blair's government "received detailed reports about the conspiracy from a *foreign intelligence service* and was bound by a duty of confidentiality not to disseminate the information" (emphasis added).[23]

* * * *

More information was revealed that indicated what role U.S. black ops may have played behind the scenes in the coup attempt against Obiang. *Africa Analysis* reported in March 2004 that when Obiang visited Riggs Bank in Washington, DC in February 2004, he was abruptly told to close his account, opened under the corporate named Otong SA, and worth some $300 million.

Riggs's Vice President for International Banking (African and Caribbean operations), Kenyan-born Simon Kareri was suddenly fired by Riggs along with many of his colleagues. Soon, FBI agents arrived at the bank asking about the finances of the Equatorial Guinea president's family. *Africa Analysis* also reported that the FBI had raided Kareri's Washington home while he was in Malabo. The agents, never known for their manners, asked his Senegalese wife, Nene Fall Kareri, about files Kareri had regarding Equatorial Guinea, and seized his computers. Upon his return to Washington, Kareri contacted the FBI, but they said he was not a target of their investigation, and they declined to talk to him.

Riggs, meanwhile, froze Obiang's funds. Oddly, Riggs did not freeze Haitian President Aristide's funds after he was ousted from power.[24]

---

[23] Kim Sengupta and Karyn Maughan, "The Thatcher Dossier; Yet again, Mummy appears to have saved Mark Thatcher, paying his fine and playing a key role in the plea bargain, according to South African police sources," *The Belfast Telegraph*, January 14, 2005; David Leigh and Rory Carroll, "Poolside plots: the chronicle of a coup foretold: Christmas party took place at crucial stage of plan," *The Guardian*, January 13, 2005, p. 4; Anthony Barnett, Martin Bright and Patrick Smith, "Investigation: How much did Straw know and when did he know it?: The Foreign Secretary is facing new questions on the alleged coup in Equatorial Guinea. Why didn't the government decide to act sooner?" *The Observer*, November 28, 2004, p. 8; Antony Barnett, "The tale of an ex-SAS hero and his chums Smelly and Scratcher: It sounds like an adventure story: a group with links to senior establishment figures has been drawn into the fall-out from a plot to oust an African president," *The Observer*, July 18, 2004, p. 11.

[24] "Who was Really After Obiang," *Africa Analysis*, March 2004. <http://217.199.1

In January 2005, Riggs pleaded guilty to Federal government charges that it failed to prevent money laundering by Equatorial Guinea government officials and former Chilean dictator General Augusto Pinochet. The Office of the Comptroller of the Currency was also investigating suspicious transactions involving Saudi Arabia and Riggs.

The FBI expanded the investigation to examine ties between Riggs transactions, Saudi officials, and the 9-11 hijackers.[25] Particular attention was being paid by Federal investigators to an Obiang personal slush fund, a mysterious shell company called Abayak SA, headquartered in an empty seven story office building in Bata, on the Equatorial-Guinea mainland. Abayak's accounts routinely received large deposits of cash from U.S. oil companies.[26]

Also suspicious was the role of Israel in protecting Obiang. Israeli troops trained Obiang's personal security detail in the president's hometown of Mongomo while Israel Military Industries sold Equatorial Guinea's embryonic Coast Guard two Shaldag MK11 fast patrol boats. Israel's Aeronautics Defense System was also active in providing security hardware and training to Obiang's dictatorship.

Subsequently, PNC Financial Services Group bought Riggs, a bank which once billed itself as the "bankers to the Presidents" and "most important bank in the most important city in the world," and counted Abraham Lincoln, Ulysees Grant, Dwight Eisenhower and eighteen other presidents, as well as Jefferson Davis and Douglas MacArthur among its clientele.

But Riggs' most valued recent patrons had been the Bush family. Jonathan Bush, George W. Bush's uncle and George H.W. Bush's brother, ran a New Haven, Connecticut-based Riggs subsidiary called J. Bush & Co., a money management firm that later morphed into Riggs Investment Management Company (RIMCO). Federal investigators discovered that Riggs set up phony and deceptive accounts and dummy corporations in offshore locations like the Bahamas.[27] Riggs was caught up in the Russian mafia money

68.239/040.html>

[25] Andrew Zajac, "Bank fined $16 million for hiding accounts; Pinochet among Riggs' suspect customers," *Chicago Tribune*, January 28, 2005, p. 11.

[26] Maass, "A Touch of Crude," op. cit.

[27] Ibid.

laundering scandal through its stake in a Channel Islands company called Valmet. That scandal involved jailed Russian oil tycoon Mikhail Khodorkovsky and the Bank of New York, as well as key Russian mafia figures.[28]

In May 2005, after Khodorkovsky and his partner Platon Lebedev were convicted of tax evasion and fraud by a Russian court and sentenced to nine years in prison, President Bush came to the defense of these gangsters: "Here [in the U.S.], you're innocent until proven guilty and it appeared to us—at least to people in my administration—that it looked like he had been judged guilty prior to having a fair trial."[29] Bush did not name who in his administration thought Khodorkovsky's trial had been unfair, but the close ties of Scooter Libby and other leading neoconservatives like Jack Abramoff to the Russian mafia network would suggest likely sources of the angst about the verdict.

Before he stepped down as Riggs' Chief Executive Officer in 2002, Washington power broker and media magnate Joe Albritton, a transplanted Houstonian and political backer of the Bushes, counted Saudi ambassador Prince Bandar as one of his most valued clients. The Saudis maintained sizeable accounts in Riggs.[30]

In May 2005, Simon Kareri and his wife were arrested at their Silver Spring, Maryland home after Mr. Kareri attempted to wire $1 million from the sale of his home. The government discovered that the Kareris attempted to wire this $1 million, just prior to the seizure of their home by the U.S. government, to Jadini Holdings Ltd., a shell company owned by the Kareris in the Bahamas, on through to a bank account in Luxembourg. Mrs. Kareri served as Jadini's president to mask her husband's ownership of the firm. Simon Kareri maintained other suspicious accounts in the Canary Islands, the place of exile selected by the Equatorial Guinea coup plotters had their ouster of Obiang been successful. Kareri was also charged with trying to overbill the government of Benin for construction work on its Washington, DC embassy.[31]

---

[28] Timothy O'Brien, "A Washington Bank in a Global Mess," *The New York Times*, April 11, 2004, p.1

[29] Catherine Belton and Lyuba Pronina, "Khodorkovsky, Lebedev Sentenced to Nine Years in Camp," *St. Petersburg Times* (Russia), June 3, 2005.

[30] O'Brien, op. cit.

[31] Terence O'Hara, "Former Riggs Executive, Wife, Charged With Fraud and Con-

As might be expected after a scandal where the Bush name arises, J. Bush & Company/RIMCO was sold in May 2005 to Waterbury, Connecticut-based Webster Financial Corporation. The purchase price was not disclosed.[32]

With the sale of Riggs and J. Bush/RIMCO, the post-scandal house cleaning was complete.

* * * *

Part of the planning for the Equatorial Guinea coup involved financing from the Canary Islands, Spanish islands off the African coast. Using laundered Iraqi money to finance a coup in Africa was reminiscent of the Iran-Contra scandal, which saw money earned from the illegal sale of weapons to Iran by the Reagan-Bush administration used to illegally purchase weapons for the Nicaraguan Contras.

The coup involved ex-members of 32 (Buffalo) Battalion, a South African apartheid-era Special Operations unit. 32 Battalion members were also involved in a 2003 coup against Sao Tome and Principe's government. That coup took place after George W. Bush's visit to South Africa and a visit by then-Assistant Secretary of State for African Affairs Walter Kansteiner III to Sao Tome to discuss the setting up of a U.S. Navy base in the country. Kansteiner was the Director of the Strategic Minerals Task Force under then-Secretary of Defense Cheney in the first Bush administration.

He was also a close associate of U.S. oil companies operating in Africa. A former adviser to the Corporate Council on Africa (CCA), Kansteiner continued to maintain a close relationship with the consortium of multinational companies doing business in Africa after he assumed his duties as Assistant Secretary of State for Africa. In November 2002, prior to the coups in Sao Tome and Equatorial Guinea, Kansteiner spoke at a Houston meeting of the CCA, where he and CCA boss Maurice Tempelsman gathered together an array of oil men and politicians from West Africa, including Sao Tome and Equatorial Guinea.

---

spiracy, *The Washington Post*, May 25, 2005, p. E01; O'Brien, op. cit.; Sarah Kelley, "Former Riggs officer to remain jailed," *The Examiner* (Washington, DC), June 1, 2005, p. 4.

[32] Steve Higgins, "Webster Bank buys investment management firm," *New Haven Register*, May 19, 2005.

The gathering, called the West Africa Oil & Gas Forum, was opened by Kansteiner with an emphasis on the following economic baseline: "The West African region supplies almost 15 percent of United States energy needs and imports are expected to rise to nearly 25 percent by 2005." With that in mind, Kansteiner and his oil friends ominously presented the Bush administration's real priority for Africa, which was not AIDS abatement or quality of life improvement, but "A Public-Private Partnership for Economic Growth, African Oil and U.S. Priorities." Speakers included James Andrews, a Vice President of Kellogg, Brown and Root and Rayna Milkova of Kroll Associates, a firm involved with a number of murky off-the-shelf activities in trouble spots around the world. Another participant was Andre "Action" Jackson, the Chairman of DRC-based JFPI Corporation, and an individual reportedly involved in a number of dubious financial and political activities in the DRC and other countries. In reality, the Bush administration's approach to Africa, Latin America, Southeast Asia, the Middle East, and every region where Big Oil and its allies want to extend their influence and exploitation, should be titled, "A Private Partnership with Minimal Public Involvement for Maximized Profits, Oil, and Bush Cartel Priorities."[33]

But oil was not Kansteiner's only interest. After leaving his State Department job, he joined the board of Sierra Mineral Holdings, Ltd., a firm active in mining in Sierra Leone, and which was owned by Sam Jonah, whose other company, Ashanti Goldfields Co., Ltd., was linked by a secret UN report to various guerrilla activities in the Ugandan-controlled part of the Democratic Republic of the Congo.[34] Anglo American, an international mining mega-corporation, acquired Ashanti Goldfields in April 2004, and Jonah became a non-executive director of the new Anglo Gold Ashanti.

Human Rights Watch accused Anglo Gold Ashanti of backing Ugandan and Rwandan trained Hema and Lendu militia in the DRC's northeast Ituri province in return for lucrative gold mining

---

[33] U.S. State Department Press Release, "Major West Africa Oil and Gas Conference Opens in Houston," November 20, 2002.

[34] David Pallister, "UN names forces in struggle for Congo gold fields; Secret report on militias' backers could embarrass Britain," *The Guardian*, December 4, 2003.

concessions.[35] Negotiating deals with fractured virtual statelets in the DRC was a long-range plan for the neoconservatives (including Kansteiner) and their allies in Israel and central Africa. Kansteiner is also on record, in a paper written while he was an employee of the Scowcroft Group (run by the first President Bush's National Security Adviser), as favoring the "Balkanization" of Congo into various smaller, ethnically-based independent states, including a Tutsi-majority state in eastern Congo.[36]

Kansteiner was an ardent supporter of the South African apartheid regime, and lived in that country under the auspices of the International Republican Institute (IRI), an organization funded by the National Endowment for Democracy to advance the conservative political agendas and to foment revolts against populist governments (its most recent activities having been in Haiti and Venezuela). Kansteiner's support for South Africa's "Bantustan" policy for the country's African population made his support for dividing the Congo into ethnic-based statelets all the more understandable.

The Balkans, the Caucusus, and Beyond

Nikola Gruevski, the leader of the Macedonian nationalist conservative opposition party—the Internal Macedonian Revolutionary Party (VMRO-DPMNE)—and a favorite of the Bush administration, met with senior Bush administration officials in Washington in early February 2004, but he declined to discuss details of his visit and with whom he actually met. Gruevski, a former Finance Minister in the previous conservative government, favored more privatization of Macedonian state-owned enterprises and more free market reforms: a major goal of the Bush administration in countries around the world.

Actually, Gruevski had been on the payroll of the U.S. government, acting as a privatization adviser to the Serbian government under contract to USAID, an agency that was led by Andrew Natsios, a figure who had long been seen as a pass-through for U.S. intelligence operations in Iraq, Sudan, and Afghanistan, both

---

[35] "Ashanti to Continue Exploring in Congo," Associated Press, June 21, 2005.
[36] Walter Kansteiner, "Eastern Zaire," Issue Brief, Forum for International Policy, November 15, 1996.

as a U.S. Army reserve officer and assistant administrator for the Bureau for Food and Humanitarian Assistance, where he played an important part in the dispatch of U.S. troops to Somalia during the first Bush's lame-duck period.

After 9-11, U.S. Special Operations forces landed at Hargeisa airport in Somaliland to procure hangars and warehouses at the airport to store "security equipment." The forces were operating under cover of a USAID team, since the U.S. did not officially recognize the independence of Somaliland.[37] But there may have been another reason for the Bush administration's sudden interest in Somaliland. In March 2004, Somaliland's President Daher Riyale Kahin made an unprecedented non-state visit to London, where he addressed the House of Commons and paid homage to the Queen.

A little known oil company named DNO Britain, Ltd. had begun to show an interest in Somaliland after U.S. Special Forces arrived.[38] The company's parent DNO ASA of Oslo was also active in Yemen, Norway (in a Norwegian Sea exploration effort called the Jurassic Project), Syria, and Equatorial Guinea. DNO ASA also owned a subsidiary named Island Petroleum Developments, which had interests in oil platforms off the coast of Ireland. The company's Web site reported that DNO sold its share in both DNO Britain and Island Petroleum Developments. An affiliate U.S.-based company named DNO Widrusco was active in Mozambique. The murky nature of oil company relationships adds to the opaque nature of their international deals causing untold problems for international investigators.

Covert U.S. paramilitary teams also went into Somalia proper to meet with leaders of the Rahanwein Resistance Army, a guerrilla group supported by Ethiopia that is battling the central government in Mogadishu. Before Somalia fractured in 1991, U.S. oil companies, including Mobil and Conoco were actively exploring for oil in the country.

By 2003, the operations of USAID and other foreign affairs offices were subsumed by Big Oil and covert operations interests.

---

[37] U.S. Explores Sands of Hargeisa, *The Indian Ocean Newsletter*, No. 980, January 19, 2002.

[38] "Hargeisa lobbying marks points in London," *The Indian Ocean Newsletter*, March 20, 2004.

Macedonian sources reported at the time Gruevski was in Washington that he was being groomed by neoconservative elements in the State Department, National Security Council, and Pentagon to eventually take over either the presidency of Macedonia or the prime ministership.

After the Feb. 26, 2004 death of Macedonian President Boris Trajkovski in a suspicious plane crash near Stolac, Croatia, U.S. ambassador to Macedonia Lawrence Butler quickly met with Gruevski. Trajkovsky had been en route to a Balkan investors' conference in Mostar, Bosnia.

Butler was viewed as one of a new breed of Bush administration interventionist ambassadors, and he has been likened to the U.S. ambassador to Georgia Richard Miles, ambassador to Haiti James Foley, ambassador to Venezuela Charles Shapiro, and ambassador to Bolivia Manuel Rocha. All were involved in U.S.-sponsored regime changes in the countries they were assigned.

Although Trajkovski, a Methodist minister, was a member of the conservative VMRO-DPMNE, he had been seen as less than accommodating to international demands for internal reform in Macedonia. Crvenkovski, a Social Democrat, was considered much more amenable to Western demands to speed up privatization.

Trajkovski's moderate allies in VMRO suggested that the plane crash that took his life, and that of his aides and the flight crew, might not have been an accident. Prime Minister Crvenkovski quickly blamed NATO's Stabilization Force (and, in particular, a French air controller) for interfering with the plane's flight control, and with causing communications problems in the subsequent investigation of the plane crash.

Macedonian and Bosnian officials claimed that they had been kept in the dark about NATO's investigation of the plane crash. There was confusion about who was to have access to the two black boxes of the U.S.-made Beechcraft King Air 200 plane; a team of U.S. Federal Aviation Administration officials arrived in Bosnia to investigate the crash, but some Macedonian officials were opposed to bringing the U.S. in on the probe. Others in Macedonia, particularly Crvenkovski loyalists, were opposed to sending the black boxes to France, suggesting Germany as an alternative.

The generally pro-U.S. Crvenkovski was elected in April 2004 in a special election to replace Trajkovski as President. VMRO-DPMNE officials charged that there was massive ballot box stuffing in the election and refused to accept the results. Thus, as a result of an unexplained air crash, Macedonia became another firm vassal state of the Bush administration, its presidency safely in the hands of a trusted U.S. ally, with the badly-fractured opposition led by a former U.S. government employee. It was "the perfect storm" for the neoconservative policy-makers in Washington.

* * * *

Anchoring its European defense strategy to what U.S. Defense Secretary Donald Rumsfeld calls "New Europe," the U.S. ramped up plans to establish a large combined air and naval base in Albania. According to a former high-ranking White House security official, the base was to provide security for the Adriatic Sea terminus of a planned trans-Balkan natural gas pipeline connecting Albania to a trans-Turkish pipeline, which, in turn, would be linked to huge natural gas reserves in the Caspian-Caucusus region and northern Iraq.

The Pentagon wasted no time in laying the groundwork for a permanent U.S. military presence in Southeast Europe and the Caucusus to protect its pipelines and other oil installations. The NATO Membership Action Plan (MAP) was initiated to see rapid NATO membership for Croatia, Macedonia, and Albania. A parallel project, called the Southeast Europe Clearinghouse, brought Bosnia-Herzegovina, Serbia-Montenegro, and Ukraine onto the deck for eventual NATO membership. A third entity, called the South Caucusus Clearinghouse, provided a similar launching pad for NATO membership for Azerbaijan, Armenia, and Georgia.

The former White House official said that the upheavals in Kosovo, in Georgia's Adjaria autonomous republic, and in Macedonia were part of an attempt by the Bush administration to quell any potential ethnic problems and establish a series of pro-U.S., leaders in the countries the pipeline will transverse. The Bush administration tilted to the Albanians because of their support for the future pipeline, the base agreement, and support for the U.S. coalition in Iraq.

In a 2004 meeting with Azerbaijan Defense Ministry officials, Deputy Assistant Secretary of State for European and Eurasian Affairs Steven Pifer, a former ambassador to Ukraine, negotiated for U.S. military base rights at Abiyev, Azerbaijan, and, more ominously, at three bases along the Armenian-Azeri border that are currently under Armenian military occupation: Cabrayil, Fuzuli, and Zangilan.[39]

* * * *

The Bush administration also wanted its new ally, Georgia President Mikhail Saakashvili, who had replaced Eduard Shevardnadze in a November 2003 U.S.-inspired coup, dubbed the "Rose Revolution, to consolidate his hold over a fractured country. Saakashvili immediately cracked down on the near-independence of two pro-Russian autonomous Georgian republics, Adjaria and Abkhazia, and on the autonomy of a third, South Ossetia. The three statelets were near the strategic Baku-Tbilisi-Ceyhan oil pipeline route. Saakashvili came to an agreement with the Adjarian leadership preventing an armed conflict, but it was clear that one of the preconditions was a scaling down of Adjaria's ties to Russia and a scaling back of its autonomy. To protect its interest in the Azerbaijan-Turkey pipeline, the U.S. used U.S. Marines and private contractors with Cubic Corporation to train Georgia's armed forces. When Adjaria's government sealed the border with Georgia, the Georgian armed forces held a major military exercise just north of the border. And it was clear that another leader who failed to obey orders from Washington was targeted for overthrow

Adjaria's pro-autonomy president Aslan Abashidze, who was called "Babu" (grandfather) by the Adjarians and had led the majority Muslim region ever since Soviet days, was finally forced from power by Saakashvili on May 5, 2004. Abashidze also had a connection to former President Clinton and Senator Hillary Rodham Clinton. Senator Clinton's brothers, Hugh and Tony Rodham

---

[39] UPI Hears, October 4, 2004.

(Tony is married to California Senator Barbara Boxer's daughter), entered into a lucrative hazelnut business deal with Abashidze, but had abandoned it after pressure was applied by Clinton's National Security Adviser Sandy Berger.[40]

Entering Adjaria after Abashidze fled into exile, Saakashvili addressed a crowd of his supporters from a window at Abashidze's former presidential residence in Batumi, the republic's capital. The supporters waved Saakashvili's Christian cross and Georgian and U.S. flags. It was clear that Saakashvili had been ordered by his masters within the Bush administration to stamp out Adjaria's autonomous government, a furtherance of the "creative destruction" doctrine of the neoconservatives. The reason was simple. Batumi was a major oil transshipment port and figured prominently in Big Oil's plans for the Caucusus and Black Sea.

Saakashivili also announced that Adjaria's autonomy was over, and he said he would also repeal the autonomy of Georgia's two other republics, South Ossetia and Abkhazia. From the State Department, spokesman Richard Boucher gave the Bush administration's predictable reaction to the Adjarian coup: "The United States welcomes the peaceful restoration of Tbilisi's authority; [it is a] historic day for all the people of Georgia."[41]

In early 2002, even before Shevardnadze's overthrow, Georgian military officers being trained by U.S. instructors had made it clear that Abkhazia was the target of the United States and Georgia. As one Georgian Special Forces officer admitted, "We are doing something much more serious. We are training for an operation in Abkhazia." One Georgian guerrilla leader who led armed incursions into Abkhazia to attack Abkhaz and Russian forces said, "Let Americans come and help us ... but tell the American government that 200 advisers are not enough. We need them to send at least 2,000 troops."

However, other Georgian guerrillas fighting against Abkhazia on behalf of the Georgians and United States received direct support from Chechen and Arab fighters, including a few Al Qaeda-linked elements. A member of one Georgian guerrilla group called

[40] Ed Helmore, "Hillary's trouble with men: With a husband and brothers like hers, who needs enemies?" *The Observer* (London), February 25, 2001, p. 17.

[41] Tamazi Gendzhekhadze, "Georgians Celebrate Warlord's Ouster," Associated Press, May 6, 2004.

the Forest Brotherhood said that 500 Chechen and Arab fighters helped them in their attempted invasion of Abkhazia in October 2001, a month after the 9-11 attacks by Al Qaeda on the United States. Zurab Lipartia of the Forest Brotherhood said, "They offered to help us, and we accepted.... Why not?" Fearing the loss of his republic's autonomy to a U.S.-backed government in Tbilisi, Abkhaz President Vladislav Ardzhinba appealed to President Vladimir Putin to recognize his republic's independence or annex it to Russia as an autonomous republic.[42]

The connections between Al Qaeda and U.S.-supported regimes and agendas was not limited to Georgia. It was common in places ranging from the diamond exchanges of Tel Aviv, London, and New York to shadowy nuclear component exporters in New Jersey and South Africa and Big Oil headquarters in Houston and London.

The autonomy of the Abkhazians, Adjarians, and Ossetians had been honored since the days of the first Soviet leader, Vladimir Lenin. But under American tutelage, Georgia stamped out the principle of ethnic autonomy.

* * * *

Speaking to the Center for Strategic and International Studies (CSIS) on March 30, 2004, General Charles Wald, U.S. Air Force, the Deputy Commander of the U.S. European Command (EUCOM) in Stuttgart, Germany, was frank about his military priorities for the Caucusus and the Balkans. Wald stated that EUCOM's security initiative for the Caucusus region is centered on OPERATION CASPIAN GUARD, which seeks to counter the proliferation of weapons of mass destruction and to assist Azerbaijan and Kazakhstan to develop a command and control system for the Caspian Sea to "protect hydrocarbon pipelines to the Mediterranean Sea and natural gas pipelines across Turkey [and the Balkans] in order to bypass the Russian natural gas pipeline to Europe." As part of CASPIAN GUARD, Wald said the U.S. was training the Azerbaijan Border Guard and U.S. Special Operations forces were training Azerbaijan Special Forces.

---

[42] Anna Badkhen, "Georgia has its own agenda; U.S. trainers seen as allies against secessionists," *San Francisco Chronicle*, March 21, 2002, p. A1.

Wald also said that in Georgia, the U.S. Georgia Train and Equip (GTEP) program was being carried out by U.S. Marines, who took over the function in 2003 from U.S. Special Operations Forces. He said the major goal of the program is to provide "pipeline security." Wald admitted that the U.S.-trained and advised Georgian armed forces specifically refused to battle with protesters and coup leaders during the 2003 "Rose Revolution," which toppled the democratically elected President Eduard Shevardnadze and replaced him with the young, U.S-trained lawyer Saakashvili, who has given his full backing to the Baku-Ceyhan oil and Caucusus-Balkans natural gas pipelines which will both run through Georgia. The United States established the Georgia Sustainment and Stabilty Operations Program (SSOP) to ensure a continued Georgian military presence in Iraq.

* * * *

The "Made in America" events in Georgia and Adjaria would not stop in the Caucusus. Ukraine's former prime minister and opposition leader Viktor Yuschenko and his supporters cried foul after November 2004 rigged elections that handed the Ukrainian presidency to Russian-backed candidate Viktor Yanukovich. The Opposition launched massive street demonstrations using the color orange. The so-called "Orange Revolution" mimicked Georgia's Rose Revolution. America's hidden hand behind the events in Ukraine ignored the fact that Yanukovich's predecessor and supporter, Leonid Kuchma, sent Ukrainian troops to bolster Bush's "Coalition of the Willing" in Iraq; similar action by Georgia had done nothing to save Shevardnadze from the U.S.-backed Rose Revolution.

Yuschenko's American-born wife of Ukrainian descent, Katerina Yuschenko-Chumachenko, worked in the Reagan White House, a fact that was a lightning rod for Ukrainian and Russian nationalists, who smelled a neoconservative plot by the Opposition and their Bush administration allies to take over Ukraine, in an effort to deny Vladimir Putin the traditional Russian sphere of Belarus, Ukraine, and Kazakhstan. According to files held at the Reagan

Library, "Katherine" or "Kathy" Chumachenko performed White House liaison work between 1985-1988 with such right-wing groups as the Heritage Foundation, American Security Council, Council for National Policy, Council for Inter-American Security (linked to the World Anti-Communist League of retired General John Singlaub), Nicaraguan Freedom Campaign, and Committee on the Present Danger.[43]

After revelations that Ukrainian security agents poisoned Yuschenko during the campaign, the fate of the Russian-backed Yanukovich was sealed. The Ukrainian Supreme Court ordered another election held. Yuschenko won handily. But in what represented a setback for his allies in the Bush administration, Yuskchenko also played the nationalist card and promised to withdraw Ukrainian troops from Iraq.

* * * *

The massive street demonstrations in Kiev did not go unnoticed by a group of Kyrgyz pro-democracy observers funded by Americans. In a little over three months, some of these observers took to the streets of Bishkek, Kyrgyzstan after disputed elections in that Central Asian nation. In what was alternately called the "Tulip Revolution" and the "Daffodil Revolution," the opposition forced President Askar Akayev from office. Like Shevardnadze, Akayev had supported the U.S. wars in Afghanistan and Iraq. He permitted the U.S. to establish a military base at Manas. And like Shevardnadze, this U.S. ally was forced to flee his nation by a revolution inspired by the neoconservative think tanks and policy makers in Washington.

However, the "color-hued revolution" did not pan out in Moldova, where elections gave the anti-Russian Communist Party (they switched their allegiance from Moscow to the West) a clear majority. Winning only 9.7 percent of the vote, the Moldovan "Orange Revolution" hoped for by the Christian Democrats failed to gain the support of either Georgia or Ukraine. The failure of an Orange Revolution in Moldova was largely due to Washington's desire for

---

[43] Chumachenko, Katherine: Files, 1985-1988 – Reagan Library Collections. <http://www.reagan.utexas.edu/resource/findaid/chumache.htm>

the Communists to win, because they were the most promising party to help create the pro-United States GUUAAM (Georgia, Ukraine, Uzbekistan, Armenia, Azerbaijan, and Moldova) (sometimes limited to GUUAM—with the exemption of Armenia) alliance as an alternative to Putin's Russian-dominated economic sphere of Russia, Belarus, Ukraine, and Kazakhstan. If there were going to be popular revolutions in former Soviet states, they were going to have the imprimatur of the Bush global agenda—an agenda dedicated to throwing security cordons around China and Russia, and to ensuring that new "democratic" leaders answered to the dictates of Washington.

* * * *

Attempts by the Bush administration global manipulators to spread their thematic "popular" revolutions to the Middle East also met with failure, notwithstanding the pronouncements of the corporate media and the neoconservative spinmeisters in Washington.

On February 28, 2004, Bush's Undersecretary of State for Global Affairs Paula Dobriansky said, "As the president noted in Bratislava just last week, there was a Rose Revolution in Georgia, an Orange Revolution in Ukraine and, most recently, a Purple Revolution in Iraq. In Lebanon, we see growing momentum for a 'Cedar Revolution' that is unifying the citizens of that nation to the cause of true democracy and freedom from foreign influence."[44] Dobriansky had been a longtime supporter of the Lebanese Christians through her membership in the U.S. Committee for a Free Lebanon—a group that included other notorious neoconservatives, including Richard Perle, Paul Wolfowitz, Elliott Abrams, Douglas Feith, Frank Gaffney, and David Wurmser.

Bush coined the term "Purple Revolution" from the purple ink into which Iraqi voters were required to dip their index fingers to ensure they did not vote more than once. Nonetheless, there were charges that the massive vote for the Sh'ia slate of candidates was reduced from over 60 percent to 48 percent by American authorities, in order to ensure that the Sh'ias were prevented from having

[44] Timothy Garton Ash, "Mideast Democracy: Thank Bin Laden," *Los Angeles Times*, March 3, 2005.

an absolute majority in the provisional legislative assembly. The Carter Center had refused to monitor the Iraqi elections, because it said the elections did not meet internationally accepted standards for transparency and proper polling procedures. The Iraqi Turkmen Front and the Sunni Iraqi Islamic Party charged that the election was marked by fraud.[45]

The so-called "Cedar Revolution" in Lebanon followed the suspicious and sophisticated car-bomb assassination in Beirut of former Lebanese Prime Minister Rafik Hariri. The Cedar Revolution—marked by crowds of demonstrators waving Lebanese flags in the streets of Beirut—was not so much aimed at instituting democracy in Lebanon, but at forcing the withdrawal of Syrian forces from the country.

The same neoconservative cells in the Bush administration and its media outlets that championed the war against Iraq praised the Cedar Revolution. Paul Wolfowitz hailed the Cedar Revolution as evidence of the spread of Western democracy in the region, and was joined in his praise by another arch-neoconservative, Ken Adleman of the Defense Policy Board.

Oddly, one of the neoconservatives' new "darlings" in Lebanon, Walid Jumblatt, the head of the anti-Syrian Druze Party, upon hearing in 2004 that Iraqi insurgents had fired rockets at the Baghdad hotel where Wolfowitz was staying, expressed his disappointment that the attack had not killed Wolfowitz. Jumblatt was punished by the Bush administration by being denied a U.S. visa.[46]

The Cedar Revolution backfired when Hezbollah, the major Sh'ia political movement in Lebanon, was able to turn out even more Lebanese flag waving demonstrators in the streets of Beirut who were supporting the Syrian presence in the country.

Another so-called "democratic revolution," the "Olive Tree Revolution," was touted in Washington when Mahmoud Abbas of Fatah was elected Palestinian President in January 2005, after the suspicious death (strongly rumored to be poisoning) of Palestine's long-time leader Yassir Arafat on November 11, 2004. Abbas, an

---

[45] Aaron Glantz, "Non-Kurds Allege Vote Fraud in North," Inter Press Service, February 8, 2005.

[46] Gwynne Dyer, "Towards a 'Cedar Revolution,'" Dawn (Pakistan) Internet Edition, March 15, 2005 <http://www.dawn.com/2005/03/15/op.htm>

investor in a Jericho casino—was known to be a moderate with financial links to Sharon allies: Dov Weisglass, an adviser to Sharon, represented the casino's investors.[47]

However, not unlike Lebanon, free elections in Palestine would not favor pro-U.S., or pro-Israeli candidates, but candidates of Hamas, a party detested by the Bush administration. Both Hamas and Hezbollah were labeled as terrorist organizations by the Bush administration and Ariel Sharon's government.

It was also clear that the Bush administration hope for a "popular" movement against the Bashar Assad regime in Syria was ephemeral. On March 24, 2005, Vice President Cheney's daughter, Elizabeth Cheney, the new "democracy czar" at the State Department, hosted a meeting with the Syrian opposition. The only Syrian political party represented was the very small and U.S.-funded Syrian Reform Party, a carbon copy of the Iraqi National Congress of Ahmad Chalabi. In fact, the Washington, DC-based head of the Syrian Reform Party, Farid Ghadry, was called the "Syrian Chalabi" by Middle East experts who doubted the strength and motives of the party. Murhaf Jouejati, director of the Middle East Studies Program at George Washington University, said of the Syrian Reform Party, "Its membership is extremely thin and is not taken seriously. It's almost unheard-of in Syria."

This was the same charge that had been leveled against the Iraqi National Congress by U.S. intelligence and foreign policy experts prior to the U.S. invasion of Iraq. Cheney and her Syrian "opposition" were joined at the Foggy Bottom conclave by noted Bush administration neoconservatives: John Hannah, the Vice President's deputy chief of staff; Robert Danin of the National Security Council and a former scholar-in-residence at the pro-Israeli Washington Institute for Near East Policy (WINEP) and also formerly with the State Department's Bureau of Intelligence and Research; and David Schenker from the Pentagon, who also had been with WINEP.[48]

* * * *

---

[47] Caroline B. Glick, "Then peacemongers are back," *Jerusalem Post*, February 4, 2005, p. 24.

[48] Robin Wright and Glenn Kessler, "Bush Administration Probes Syria's Future With Assad's Opposition," *Washington Post*, March 26, 2005, p. A11.

In his praise for the Cedar Revolution, Paul Wolfowitz likened the event to the Orange Revolution in Ukraine, and to the anti-Marcos "Yellow Revolution" in the Philippines in 1987.[49] Not surprisingly Wolfowitz failed to mention his own special role in the latter, as Assistant Secretary of State for East Asia not only helping to spirit Ferdinand Marcos out of the Philippines, but also his immense cache of gold, diamonds, and rubies, much of which ended up in offshore coffers controlled by the Bush family.

Philippine businessman Enrique Zobel produced credible evidence of Marcos's international disbursement of billions of dollars in looted Philippine wealth before a 1999 Philippine Senate hearing in Honolulu. Zobel entered into evidence a copy of a U.S. Federal Reserve note worth $161 million. The note bore the name "Mr. Ferdinand Marcos" and had the transaction number 65089793422199675.F.L. Zobel also told of Marcos showing him, in 1988, gold certificates worth $35 billion, deposited in the United States, Solomon Islands, Switzerland, Portugal, Vatican City, and Spain. Philippine Senate Committee Chairman Aquilino Q. Pimentel, Jr., stood by Zobel's testimony.[50]

Wolfowitz always seems to be associated with the theft of gems and precious metals from developing countries. After the Taliban fell in 2002, the new government discovered that ten tons of the blue gemstone lapis lazuli vanished from vaults at the former presidential palace. The gems, amassed during the long reign of King Mohammed Zahir Shah, had gone untouched through Soviet occupation, civil war, and Taliban rule ... that is, until the American invasion.[51] After the U.S. invasion of Iraq, Baghdad museums were similarly looted of priceless artifacts dating back to Ottoman, Persian, Babylonian and Sumerian rule. Some 6000 museum pieces were stolen from the National Museum of Antiquities in a "cherry picked" manner indicating "inside knowledge."[52]

—§—

---

[49] Roula Khalaf, "Lebanon Government Quits," *Financial Times*, March 1, 2005, p. 1.

[50] "Senate blue ribbon committee head stands by Zobel's testimony," *Business World* (Philippines), November 1, 1999, 11.

[51] Elliot Blair Smith, "Mystery Swirls Around Missing Afghan Gems," *USA Today*, December 9, 2002, p. 4B.

[52] Guy Gugliotta, "Looters Stole 6,000 Artifacts; Number Expected to Rise as Officials Take Inventory in Iraq," *Washington Post*, June 21, 2003, p. A16.

Bertha Champagne's car pinned her against a security structure of Marvin Bush's Alexandria, VA family compound.

Mystifying is the fact that the *Washington Post* waited almost an entire week to publish the story about the death Bush's babysitter. The incident occurred on September 29 but the *Post* had not covered it until October 5, and then buried it on page 3 of the Metro section of the newspaper.

RIP: Bertha Champagne

At around 9:00 P.M. on September 29, 2003, Fairfax County police responded to what might only be described as a freak accident. But on closer examination, the police discovered they were dealing with the mysterious death of an employee of the 47-year-old brother of President George W. Bush, venture capitalist Marvin Bush.

Sixty-two-year-old Bertha Champagne, described as a long time "baby sitter" for Marvin and Margaret Bush's two children, son Walker, 13 years old, and daughter Marshall, 17 years old, was found crushed to death by her own vehicle in a driveway in front of the Bush family home at 6202 Fort Hunt Road in the Alexandria section of Fairfax County, Virginia. Champagne reportedly lived at the Bush family home, or at least that is what they told police.

But a simple search of the Internet White Pages turned up a Bertha Champagne living at 5912 Wescott Hills Way, Alexandria, VA. A phone call to the house confirmed that Ms. Champagne did, in fact, live there. A relative was adamant that no one should ever "talk about the case" and "not to call again." Later, Ms. Champagne's daughter said that her mother had never worked for Bush, but worked at the Belle Haven Country Club, and that the "accident" had in fact happened there, not in the Bush driveway.[1]

But the police story of the incident did not change. Champagne had left the residence to retrieve something (later discovered from the police report to be a videotape of her with President Bush) from her SUV, which police say had somehow been left in gear. According to the Web version of the police report, the vehicle rolled forward and pinned the woman between it and a small building next to the driveway. The car then crossed a busy two-lane street, Fort Hunt Road, coming to rest in a wooded area across the street that adjoins the prestigious Belle Haven Country Club.

---

[1] Interview with confidential source who interviewed Bertha Champagne's daughter.

Champagne was pronounced dead on arrival at Inova Mount Vernon Hospital. Courtney Young, a spokesperson for the Fairfax County police was surprised when asked about the circumstances surrounding Champagne's death. The media was primarily focused on another story, the kidnapping and holdup of the wife of New Hampshire Senator Judd Gregg on October 7, and Young said police still did not know the exact cause of Champagne's death. More mystifying is the fact that the *Washington Post* waited almost an entire week to publish the story about Bush's babysitter's death. The incident occurred on September 29 but the *Post* had not covered it until October 5, and then buried it on page 3 of the Metro section of the newspaper.[2]

Spokesperson Young said that the police department had posted the incident on its Web site the very same day the incident occurred, although the Web version of the police report makes no mention of Marvin Bush. Though the police could have been aware of Marvin Bush's controversial role in serving on corporate boards for companies associated with the 9-11 terrorist attacks, they emphasized that Champagne's death was merely a quirky accident and that no foul play had been involved.

A further call to Young did not meet with the same level of cooperation as the first. She said the official paper version of the police report, usually available to insurance agents and anyone else who asked for it, was a "restricted document," and only available to the Fairfax County police "accident reconstruction team."

The police report was finally obtained as a result of a special request to a Fairfax County official.

A Houston business source, who has dealt personally with the Bush family in Texas for a number of years, said mysterious deaths of Bush family associates, like that of Champagne at Marvin Bush's residence, appear to be accidents but usually are not. The source related that Champagne might have been privy to some sensitive information that the Bush family wanted kept secret.[3]

Some observers wondered if Secret Service agents might have been able to assist Champagne when her car pinned her, however, according to the Secret Service in Washington, the agency only

---

[2] Bush Family Babysitter Killed in Fairfax, *Washington Post*, October 5, 2003, p. C03.
[3] Private conversations.

provides protection to presidential siblings if an Executive Order authorizes such action. A Secret Service spokesperson said there was no protection for Marvin Bush at the time of Champagne's death. But there remains a question of why private security agents posted at the Bush compound could not have responded to Champagne's dilemma.

—§—

Three excerpts from a four-page Fairfax County police report showing the movement of the deadly car and the investigative officers statements. The complete report is available online at:
http://www.waynemadsenreport.com/marvinbush.htm

CAPTION   The driver of vehicle #1 started the engine and place the vehicle in drive. After the vehicle moved a considerable distance forward she attempted to exit the vehicle. She exited the vehicle and then attempted to get back in the vehicle as it struck a building at the end of the driveway. As she attempted to get back in the vehicle she got pinned between the driver door and the B-pillar area of the vehicle. Vehicle #1 continued to roll approximately 100ft. down the driveway.

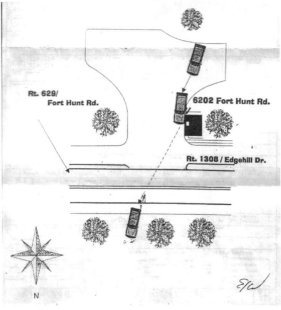

September 09-29-03 at approximately 2130 hours I was contacted by the on duty PSCC supervisor to respond to 6202 Ft. Hunt Rd. for a single vehicle fatality. While on scene I discovered a black Olds Bravada in the tree line and two small blood pools in the drive way. There was also blood and glass debris in the driveway. The operator of the vehicle was tansported by ground to Mt. Vernon Memorial Hospital and identified as Bertha Champagne. Bertha was a maid for Marvin Bush who resides at 6202 Ft. Hunt Rd. By the time I arrived on scene the body was already transported to Mt. Vernon Hospital by ground. During the course of my investigation I interviewed Marvin Bush. Marvin stated that he arrived home at approximately 2045 hours. He advised me that he had a brief conversation with Bertha in the kitchen. Bertha then tells Marvin that she wants to show him a video tape of her and President Bush. She then leaves the residence to take out the family dogs and to retrieve the video tape. There are no witnesses to the crash. There were no signs of any other type of crime involved with this event. The victim had all her money in her wallet and all her personal belongings such as jewelry and a watch in her possession. According to the Medical Examiner, Bertha's injuries were related to this crash. There were no blunt injuries or injuries related to a robbery or a carjacking.

During the course of my investigation I found several paint scrapes on the building located at the end of the driveway. Sgt. Wimberly directed me to take several samples of evidence at the scene. The following evidence was taken from the crash scene, vehicle involved, and Bertha's shoes:

The United States stands in the way of various international initiatives to limit or outright ban the activities of mercenaries or "private military companies" (PMCs). There are many reports of various nefarious acts committed by "PMC employees," such as this U.S. government account:

23. ON MAY 12, 2000, THE COLOMBIAN NATIONAL POLICE INTERDICTED A PARCEL PACKAGE FROM THE FED/EXPRESS SERVICE AT THE EL DORADO INTERNATIONAL AIRPORT IN BOGOTA, COLOMBIA. THE PARCEL NUMBER ▮▮▮▮▮ CONTAINED TWO (2) SMALL BOTTLES OF A THICK LIQUID. THE THICK LIQUID HAD THE SAME CONSISTENCY AS MOTOR OIL. THE LIQUID SUBSTANCE TESTED POSITIVE FOR HEROIN. THE ALLEGED HEROIN LACED LIQUID WEIGHTED APPROXIMATELY 250 GRAMS. THE SENDER WAS IDENTIFIED AS: ▮▮▮▮▮, DYNCORP SITE, COLOMBIA, ENTRADA NO. 2, INT.7, LINEAS AEREAS SURAMERICANS, BOGOTA, COLOMBIA. THE RECIPIENT WAS LISTED AS: DYNCORP, BUILDING 330 (SW CORNER 9) SPACE, ADDRESS: LIFT AVENUE PATRICK AIR FORCE BASE, FLORIDA.

from: corpwatch.org/

DEA document recently obtained under the Freedom of Information Act, stating that on May 12, 2000 the Colombian National Police intercepted a FedEx parcel at the airport. It was sent from the Bogota DynCorp site and destined for DynCorp's office on Patrick Air Force Base in Florida. The name of the sender has been blacked out. The 250 Gram liquid "tested positive for heroin," according to the DEA.

"My understanding is that was a faulty test result," DynCorp spokesperson Wineriter told CorpWatch.

CHAPTER SEVEN

MERCENARIES INC.

At a March 1998 seminar co-sponsored by the South African Institute of Strategic Studies and the Canadian Council for International Peace and Security, increased government sanctioned mercenary activities around the world were described as ushering in a new "multinational neocolonialism for the 21st century."[1] Rather than condemn mercenary activities, the United States, under both the Clinton and Bush II administrations, has chosen to embrace so-called "private military companies" (PMCs) and recognize them as virtual extensions of the U.S. military. Only in a world where George Orwell's dire prediction of a government-sanctioned politically-correct language, which he called "Newspeak," has come to fruition, are mercenaries permitted to label themselves as "PMCs." Regardless of their expensive tailor-made business suits and posh office furniture, these soldiers of fortune are, and will continue to remain, mercenaries in both word and deed.

Past U.S. administrations made no secret of their opposition to mercenaries when they were used on behalf of countries like France, Portugal, and South Africa. When mercenaries were used

---

[1] Philippe Chapleau and François Misser, Mercenaires S.A. ("Mercenaries S.A."), (Paris: Desclée de Brouwer, 1998), 41-42.

to threaten the sovereignty of countries like Seychelles, Comoros, Benin, and Dominica, the United States condemned foreign support for such freelancing brigands.

But now the United States stands in the way of various international initiatives to limit or outright ban the activities of mercenaries. As the Bush II administration adopts new policies of unilateralism and unhindered force projection around the globe, PMCs are viewed as central to the new evolving American foreign policy doctrine.

One international initiative to curtail mercenaries, the International Convention against the Recruitment, Use, Financing and Training of Mercenaries, continues to languish in the United Nations. With 24 member states having ratified the accord, the United States is determined that the convention never becomes an effective international treaty, even though it entered into force in October 2001.[2]

The military-industrial complex that President Dwight Eisenhower warned the United States about in his 1961 Farewell Address has now discovered the incredible profit margins in subsuming American foreign policy and striking separate military and economic contracts with sovereign states.

The chief American companies that have been involved in the international mercenary and "security" business include Dyncorp (now a wholly-owned subsidiary of Computer Sciences Corporation and formerly known as California Eastern Airways), Military Professional Resources Inc. (MPRI, a wholly-owned subsidiary of L-3 Communications, Inc.), Kellogg, Brown & Root (a subsidiary of Halliburton), Air Scan, Aviation Development Corporation, California Microwave Systems (a subsidiary of Northrop Grumman), Eagle Aviation Services and Technology, Inc. (EAST), Vinnell Corporation (a subsidiary of Northrop Grumman), The Carlyle Group (which maintained a partnership with Vinnell in Saudi

---

[2] The following states have ratified or acceded to the convention: Azerbaijan, Barbados, Belarus, Belgium, Cameroon, Costa Rica, Croatia, Cyprus, Georgia, Italy, Libya, Maldives, Mali, Mauritania, Qatar, Saudi Arabia, Senegal, Seychelles, Suriname, Togo, Turkmenistan, Ukraine, Uruguay, and Uzbekistan. A number of these countries, however, are customers for PMC services. These include Croatia, Georgia, Qatar, and Saudi Arabia. Ukraine is a provider of mercenary services.

Arabia),[3] Armor Group (also known as Armor Holdings), Dili-
gence (headed by Richard Burt, a Carlyle Group consultant and
former U.S. ambassador to Germany, and Joseph Allbaugh, former
head of the Federal Emergency Management Agency (FEMA)
and George W. Bush's 2000 presidential campaign manager), New
Bridge Strategies (headed by Allbaugh and Republican strategists
Ed Rogers and Lanny Griffith—Rogers and Griffith are partners
of the powerful Republican law firm Barbour [Haley Barbour, former Republican National Committee Chairman and current Governor of Mississippi], Griffith & Rogers), Century Arms, Maytag
Aircraft Corporation, Science Applications International Corporation (SAIC), Sytex, Ronco, Parsons Corporation (whose board
members have included Elaine Chao, George W. Bush's Labor
Secretary and wife of Kentucky Republican Senator Mitch Mc-
Connell and retired Admiral R.J. Zlaptoper, former Command-
er-in-Chief of the U.S. Pacific Fleet), Logicon, Blackwater USA,
MZM, Inc., Titan, U.S. Investigation Services (USIS), EOD
Technology, Cochise Consultancy, Zapata Engineering (based in
Charlotte, North Carolina and started in 1991 by Manuel Zapata,
a Chilean immigrant to the United States), Vance International,
Virginia Electronics, Betac, Custer Battles, International Charter,
Inc. of Oregon (ICI), CACI, Tetra Tech, Sayeret Group, Triple
Canopy, Booz Allen Hamilton, Man-Tech, Premier Technology
Group, Critical Intervention Services, Trojan Securities Interna-
tional, Ground Zero USA, and Phoenix Consulting Group.

* * * *

America's mercenaries can generally be divided into two groups.
One group is largely composed of military veterans or law enforcement personnel who were lured away from low-paying police and
other jobs by companies offering lucrative salaries and benefits. Not
a small number of these individuals became discouraged by working
for PMCs and returned to the United States to their previous jobs.

The other group can best be described as career expatriate mercenaries. They have been in the mercenary business for a number of

---

[3] Tim Shorrock, "Crony Capitalism Goes Global," *The Nation*, April 1, 2002.

years and are true "soldiers of fortune." Some served with shadowy CIA-front companies, including Air America and Southern Air Transport, in Indochina and Central America, respectively. Most of these freelancing expats are fairly conversant in at least one other language. Many have foreign wives (or concubines) and families. Other, more unsavory expats live non-descript existences in small hamlets and towns throughout Latin America, Africa, and Southeast Asia. In Colombia, employees of Dyncorp have been accused of smuggling drugs, including cocaine, heroin, and amphetamines.[4]

A Drug Enforcement Administration report from 2000 stated that on May 12, 2000, the Colombian National Police intercepted a U.S.-bound Federal Express package at Bogota's international airport that "contained two (2) small bottles of a thick liquid" that "had the same consistency as motor oil." The report went on to state that the liquid, which weighed 250 grams, "tested positive for heroin." The package was sent from a Dyncorp employee in Colombia to the firm's Andean operations center at Patrick Air Force Base in Florida.[5] That same year, the wife of U.S. Army Colonel James Hiett, the commander of the U.S. counter-narcotics program in Colombia, used the U.S. embassy's mail system in Bogota to send drugs from Colombia to New York. Although Army officials cleared Hiett of any wrongdoing, he later pleaded guilty to failure to inform authorities of his wife's drug-money-laundering activities.

Illegal activity involving the U.S. military and paramilitary presence in Colombia erupted once again in 2005. In March 2005, Colombian authorities detained five U.S. military personnel for attempting to smuggle 35 pounds of cocaine from Colombia to the United States on a U.S. military transport plane. In May 2005, U.S. Army Chief Warrant Officer Allan N. Tanquary and Sergeant Jesus Hernandez were arrested by Colombian authorities for trying to sell 42,900 rounds of ammunition to the right-wing terrorist paramilitary group United Self Defense Forces of Colombia (AUC). Although the Colombian chief prosecutor wanted the two detained in Colombia, President Alvaro Uribe, an ally of the Bush admin-

---

[4] Robert Lawson, "Dyncorp: Beyond the Rule of Law," *Colombia Report*, August 27, 2001.< http://www.colombiareport.org/colombia78.htm>

[5] Jason Vest, "Dyncorp's Drug Problem," *The Nation*, July 10, 2001. <http://www.alternet.org/story.html?StoryID=11162>

istration, quickly overruled him, and they were turned over to U.S. custody. The Bogota magazine *Semana* referred to U.S. military and civilian advisers in Colombia as "criminal rogues." The U.S. military personnel were in Colombia to support a Colombian government offensive against leftist guerrillas code-named the "Patriot Plan."[6]

* * * *

In Bosnia, Dyncorp employees were accused of involvement in the white slave trade and child prostitution. Rather than face criminal courts, Dyncorp simply fired the accused employees and sent them home to the United States. Apparently, the Dayton Peace Accords on Bosnia gave the employees immunity from prosecution under Bosnian law, and U.S. laws did not apply.[7] Although some PMCs claim they try to vet their personnel, many employees of mercenary companies are foreign nationals with criminal backgrounds. Yet others are clearly incompetent and have problems with alcohol.

Ben Johnston, a former Dyncorp employee in Bosnia who sued his former employer under the Racketeer Influenced Corrupt Organization Act (RICO), a stature normally used by federal prosecutors against organized crime syndicates, said the following about some of the Dyncorp personnel assigned to Bosnia: "I noticed there were problems as soon as I got there, and I tried to be covert because I knew it was a rougher crowd than I'd ever dealt with. It's not like I don't drink or anything, but Dyncorp employees would come to work drunk. A Dyncorp van would pick us up every morning and you could smell the alcohol on them. There were big-time drinking issues."[8]

* * * *

---

[6] Marcela Sanchez, "What happens to U.S. soldiers charged with aiding and abetting an international terrorist organization?" *Seattle Post-Intelligencer,* May 15, 2005, p. D3; John Otis, "Uncertainty, Costs Weigh on U.S. in Colombia," Houston Chronicle, May 15, 2005, p. 1.

[7] Kelly Patricia O'Meara, "Dyncorp Disgrace," *Insight,* January 20, 2002. <http://www.insightmag.com/main.cfm/include/detail/storyid/163052.html>

[8] Ibid.

Two PMCs, Titan of San Diego and CACI of Arlington, Virginia, were implicated in the torture and abuse of Iraqi prisoners at the Abu Ghraib prison in Baghdad. In addition, members of the 372nd Military Police Company were also charged with participating in the abuse. According to a secret U.S. Army report prepared by Major General Antonio Taguba and leaked to the media in early May 2004, male prisoners were forced to conduct simulated sexual acts and were sodomized with chemical glow lights and broomsticks during their captivity. Moreover, guards raped female and young male prisoners. The report stated that the abuse included:

> ...breaking chemical lights and pouring the phosphoric liquid on detainees; pouring cold water on naked detainees; beating detainees with a broom handle and a chair; threatening male detainees with rape; allowing a military police guard to stitch the wound of a detainee who was injured after being slammed against the wall in his cell; sodomizing a detainee with a chemical light and perhaps a broom stick, and using military working dogs to frighten and intimidate detainees with threats of attack, and in one instance actually biting a detainee.

Taguba recommended that two CACI employees, Steven Stephanowicz and John Israel, be disciplined, with a particular recommendation that Stephanowicz be fired. Israel, who was later identified as John Benjamin Israel and reported to be an Iraqi-American Christian from Santa Clarita, California, is identified in the Taguba report as being with both CACI and Titan and not having a security clearance, an indication that his actual immigration status was undetermined by investigators.[9] It was later discovered that Israel actually worked for a sub-contractor called SOS Interpreting, a firm with offices in New York City and northern Virginia.

The CIA's Inspector General conducted an internal investigation of the role of its interrogators in reported deaths of inmates at Abu Ghraib. Ironically, Abu Ghraib was the central site where Saddam Hussein's regime carried out torture and execution of political prisoners. In May 2005, the Pentagon released its findings of wrongdoing by senior officers in Iraq relating to the Abu Ghraib

---

[9] Seymour Hersh, "Torture at Abu Ghraib," *New Yorker*, May 4, 2004.

scandal. Lt. Gen. Ricardo S. Sanchez, the commander of Combined Joint Task Force 7 (CTJF7) was found innocent of dereliction of duty and failure of communicating interrogation policies. Sanchez's deputy, Maj. Gen. Walter Wojadowski was found innocent of dereliction of duty. Sanchez's chief intelligence officer, Maj. Gen. Barbara G. Fast, was found innocent of dereliction of duty, making a misrepresentation to an investigating officer, and failure to obey a direct order. Colonel Marc Warren, the chief Judge Advocate for CTJF7 was found innocent of professional impropriety and dereliction of duty.

Brig. Gen. Janis Karpinski, the one-time Commander of the 800th Military Police Brigade, was found guilty of dereliction of duty and, in what was the top non-sequitur of the entire Abu Ghraib scandal, shoplifting! Karpinski was reduced in rank to Colonel.

In reality, Karpinski's only infraction was in telling the truth. She was the highest-level military officer to expand upon what Taguba referred to as third-country parties being involved in the prisoner abuse in Iraq. Karpinski admitted that on one occasion she witnessed an Israeli national involved in the interrogation of Iraqi prisoners, telling the BBC about a man she saw at a Baghdad intelligence center that was not part of the Abu Ghraib complex: "I saw an individual there that I hadn't had the opportunity to meet before, and I asked him what did he do there, was he an interpreter—he was clearly from the Middle East.... He said, 'Well I do some of the interrogation here. I speak Arabic but I'm not an Arab; I'm from Israel.'... I was really kind of surprised by that.... He didn't elaborate any more than to say he was working with them and there were people from lots of different places that were involved in the operation."[10] For that truth-telling, Karpinski earned the wrath of the pro-Israeli cabal operating from its base in the Pentagon, and was made a scapegoat.

* * * *

The involvement of unsavory personnel in mercenary and private militia firms has also earned the United States the suspicion of a

---

[10] "Report: Former head of Abu Ghraib says Israelis involved in probing Iraqis," Al Bawaba, July 3, 2004.

number of nations around the world that have ratified the International Criminal Court (ICC). The Bush administration, these nations reason, withdrew from the ICC and is engaged in signing exemption treaties for its citizens with other nations because it realizes it will be depending more and more on mercenary personnel, and does not want them prosecuted for crimes in the full glare of the international spotlight. The Bush administration cut off all military aid programs to nations that refused to sign exemption treaties.

American mercenary firms consistently seek to avoid the spotlight, although their presence is undeniable in some of the world's most violent trouble spots. For example, the May 13, 2003 bombing of four expatriate compounds in Riyadh, Saudi Arabia was a clear embarrassment for America's mercenary presence in the kingdom. One of the compounds blown up housed the employees and families of Vinnell, which has had a contract to train Saudi Arabia's National Guard since 1975. Never before had American civilians been permitted to train a foreign army. Vinnell's Saudi contract would open the way for other U.S. mercenary firms to seek similar contracts from nations around the world.

Vinnell was owned by the secretive Carlyle Group from 1992 to 1997, when it was sold to TRW. In 1995, during the time Carlyle owned Vinnell, the company had oversight of the Saudi National Guard during an incident that allowed a known terrorist to escape arrest. The FBI planned to arrest Imad Mughniyah, wanted for his role in the 1983 barracks bombing in Beirut that killed 241 Marines, at a Saudi airport. The Saudi National Guard personnel at the airport waved off the plane, allowing Mughniyah to escape capture by the FBI.[11]

Carlyle had some interesting connections to the Saudi Bin Laden Group. Prior to 9-11, the Bin Laden family owned, at least since 1994, an interest in Carlyle, primarily through Carlyle Partners II, a corporate buyout fund. Carlyle board members and advisers, including former Secretary of State James Baker III, and former President George H.W. Bush, were frequent visitors to the Bin Laden family's corporate headquarters in Jeddah, Saudi Arabia.

---

[11] "Doing the Saudi Dirty Work," *Rocky Mountain News*, April 9, 1997, p. 40A.

After 9-11, the Bin Laden Group quickly divested itself of its financial interests in Carlyle.[12]

Carlyle represents a textbook study of a firm that operates in the shadows and whose operations remain largely out of the spotlight of government regulators and investigators, the Congress, and the media. In addition to its U.S. political heavyweights, Carlyle counts former British Prime Minister John Major, former Philippine President Fidel Ramos, and former Thai Prime Minister Anand Panyarachun among its foreign advisers.

Carlyle was formed in 1987 by a group of businessmen, who included T. Rowe Price director Edward Mathias, former Jimmy Carter assistant David Rubenstein, Marriott executives Stephen Norris and Daniel D'Aniello, MCI's chief financial officer William Conway, Jr., and New York investment financier Greg Rosenbaum. It was formed with a large pool of seed money from T. Rowe Price, Alex. Brown & Sons (now Deutche Bank Alex. Brown), First Interstate Bank, and the Mellon family of Pittsburgh. The name came from Manhattan's prestigious Carlyle Hotel, but the company decided to establish its headquarters in Washington, DC. In 1989, former Reagan Defense Secretary Frank Carlucci joined the firm.[13]

Carlucci was a controversial CIA veteran, whose name often came up in association with the 1961 assassination of Congolese Prime Minister Patrice Lumumba (Carlucci was the Second Secretary at the U.S. embassy in then-Leopoldville) and the 1980 mysterious plane crash death of Portuguese Social Democratic Prime Minister Francisco Sa Carneiro while Carlucci was the U.S. ambassador to Portugal. Carlucci had often bitterly feuded with Sa Carneiro.[14]

Carlucci oversaw some large acquisitions by Carlyle. They included Coldwell Banker's real estate operations and Marriott's airline food services company, Caterair International. George W. Bush served on the board of Caterair in the early 1990s. By the time Carlyle sold Caterair, it was worth just four cents for every dollar originally paid for it. Carlyle also invested in a number of

[12] Kurt Eichenwald, "Bin Laden Family Liquidates Holdings With Carlyle Group," *New York Times*, October 26, 2001.

[13] Hoover's Database, "The Carlyle Group," 2004.

[14] Ronald Koven, "Portugal's Premier, 'The Fighting Cock,' Thrived on Conflict," *Washington Post*, December 5, 1980, p. A21.

military and intelligence-related companies, including BDM International and United Defense Industries.[15]

On the fatal morning of September 11, 2001, Carlyle was holding its annual investors' conference at the Ritz Carlton Hotel in downtown Washington. Ensconced with Carlucci and James Baker were representatives of the Bin Laden family, including Shafiq Bin Laden, Osama's brother.[16] Also in Washington at the same time was General Mahmud Ahmed, the head of Pakistan's Inter Service Intelligence, the prime backer of the Taliban, and, as revealed by the Northern Alliance and the Indian press, Al Qaeda. After 9-11, the financial worth of Carlyle's defense and intelligence contracts skyrocketed.

George H.W. Bush had been at the Carlyle conference the day before 9-11. He left Washington sometime after his meetings with Carlucci, Baker, and the Bin Laden representatives at the Ritz Carlton on September 10, but before all planes were grounded soon after the September 11 plane impacts in New York and Washington.[17] When the FAA grounded all aircraft, the elder Bush's plane, which was en route to St. Paul, Minnesota, where the former president was to speak to an insurance company meeting, was diverted to Milwaukee, where it was grounded.[18]

A passenger manifest obtained by New Jersey Senator Frank Lautenberg showed that Carlyle investor Shafiq bin Laden was flown out of the country on September 19, 2001, along with twelve of his relatives and a number of other Saudis, on a special Boeing 747 charter DB Air/Ryan International aircraft. The same plane, (tail number N521DB) had previously been used by the White House for the press corps. A Ryan partner company called Sport Hawk was contracted by the Saudi embassy in Washington to organize the flight.[19]

[15] John Mintz, "So What Would Your Company Do with These Guys on Your Team?" *Washington Post*, April 7, 1996, p. H01.

[16] Lawrence Kaplan, "'Joined at the hip'; Dissecting Washington's relationship with Saudi Arabia," Review of Robert Baer's Sleeping With the Devil, *Houston Chronicle*, August 17, 2003, p. 19.

[17] Greg Schneider, "Connections And Then Some; David Rubenstein Has Made Millions Pairing the Powerful With the Rich," *Washington Post*, March 16, 2003, p. F01.

[18] Robert Hager, "Air Traffic Controllers Recount September 11," MSNBC, December 15, 2001.

[19] Dana Milbank, "Plane Carried 13 Bin Ladens; Manifest of Sept. 19, 2001, Flight From U.S. Is Released," *Washington Post*, July 22, 2004, p. A07.

* * * *

The secretive nature of mercenary companies also results in questionable business deals with the government. An obvious potential conflict of interest arose when retired General Jay Garner, the head of the Pentagon's Office of Reconstruction and Humanitarian Assistance, a creation of Rumsfeld, was appointed to take over Iraq's civil administration pending the creation of an Iraqi interim authority. Garner formerly worked for SY Coleman, a subsidiary of L-3 Communications, the same company that owns MPRI. It was also anticipated that MPRI would bid on contracts to retrain the Iraqi armed forces. It was advantageous for Garner to have as his chief of staff in Iraq, retired General Jared Bates, who also happened to have worked for MPRI.

Although Garner was abruptly terminated as the civil administrator of Iraq in May 2003, and Vinnell was awarded a $48 million contract in June 2003 to train the nucleus of the new Iraqi army, MPRI retains tremendous influence over the American policy makers dealing with Iraq's future.[20] As an example of the lack of cultural awareness by the U.S. civil administration in Iraq, it was initially announced that the name for the new Iraqi army was "New Iraqi Corps," the English acronym for which ("NIC") is also an Arabic synonym for fornication.[21]

Garner later revealed that he was forced from his Baghdad post by Rumsfeld and the neoconservative cabal surrounding him. He cited the fact that he wanted early elections and rejected the Bush administration's quick privatization scheme for Iraq's state-owned enterprises. After he called for early elections, Garner told the BBC the following occurred: "The night I got to Baghdad, Rumsfeld called me and told me he was appointing Paul Bremer as the presidential envoy.... The announcement ... was somewhat abrupt."[22]

* * * *

[20] Contract Announcement, US Department of Defense, issued June 25, 2003.

[21] Agence France Presse, "US authorities in Iraq learn embarrassing lesson in Arabic," June 24, 2003.< http://www.spacewar.com/2003/030624124136.1v7vm0kv.html>

[22] David Leigh, "Iraq: one year on: General sacked by Bush says he wanted early elections, *The Guardian*, March 18, 2004, p. 11.

The Pentagon clearly favors the use of mercenaries for three major reasons.

First of all, fatalities and injuries of mercenaries do not carry the same political onus as flag-draped military coffins arriving at U.S. air bases. Myles Frechette, a former U.S. ambassador to Colombia, a country where a number of U.S. mercenary firms operate, said, "It's very handy to have an outfit [that is] not part of the U.S. armed forces, obviously. If someone gets killed or whatever, you can say it's not a member of the armed forces."[23]

Second, the contracts awarded to mercenary companies can be veiled as "company proprietary information," thus avoiding probes from congressional investigators, non-governmental organizations, and journalists. Colonel Bruce Grant of the U.S. Army War College in Carlisle, Pennsylvania takes the side of those skeptical about the cloak of secrecy surrounding privatized military firms. He said the use of such companies by the military is "a way of going around Congress and not telling the public."[24] Similarly, the late retired Rear Admiral Eugene Carroll and former deputy director of the Center for Defense Information said that private mercenary companies "put the U.S. Military Assistance Program one reach removed from government agencies."[25] Retired U.S. Army Colonel David Hackworth, a highly decorated veteran of the Vietnam War, said such "guns for hire" are, in fact, mercenaries operating without a popular mandate. Echoing Grant and Carroll, he said, "These new mercenaries work for the Defense and State Department and Congress looks the other way … it's a very dangerous situation. It allows us to get into fights where we would be reluctant to send the Defense Department or the C.I.A. The American taxpayer is paying for our own mercenary army, which violates what our founding fathers said."[26]

Third, the use of mercenaries is claimed to be more cost-effective for the Pentagon, but this is debated. Retired U.S. Army Major

---

[23] Joshua Kurlantzick, "Warfare Inc.," *Military Officer*, April 24, 2003. <http://www.moaa.org/magazine/may2003/f_warfare.asp>

[24] Center for Public Integrity, "Conflict and Security; Privatizing Combat, the New World Order," *Africa News*, October 28, 2002.

[25] Wayne Madsen, "Mercenaries in Kosovo: The U.S. Connection to the KLA," *The Progressive*, August 1999, p. 30.

[26] Leslie Wayne, "America's For-Profit Secret Army," *New York Times*, October 13, 2002, Sect. 3, p. 1.

General Andrew Cooley, a Dyncorp Vice President referred to the cost advantage in a 1999 military conference. Cooley coordinated Dyncorp's activities in Somalia during OPERATION RESTORE HOPE in the early 1990s. Cooley said then-Joint Chiefs Chairman General Colin Powell asked him, "Andy, when are you going to take over so I can bring my people home?" Cooley replied, "We're too expensive." Powell dismissed the cost argument, "No, there's a difference—you're cheaper because I don't have to go to the president and ask for reserves."[27]

Powell's predisposition to use mercenaries has also been embraced by Donald Rumsfeld, who hailed the success of Pentagon outsourcing and said he would "pursue additional opportunities to outsource and privatize."[28] Speaking about the lucrative market for modern-day privateers, the head of the Defense Security Cooperation Agency, D.B. Des Roches, said, "The war on terrorism is the full employment act for these guys."[29]

Andy Messing, Jr., a 17-year Special Forces veteran, agreed with Colonel Hackworth on the control of mercenaries. Addressing the role of companies like Dyncorp in Colombia, Messing said, "You can't control them as well as you can American military … when they wind up getting whacked, it only adds to the confusion." And countering claims, such as that made by Powell, that using Dyncorp contractors is cheaper, Messing said, "They're way too expensive," indicating that although U.S. Special Forces can do the job more inexpensively, the use of private soldiers is a political consideration and not a financial one.[30]

A report prepared by the International Consortium of Investigative Journalists (ICIJ) confirms the lucrative nature of the mercenary business. From 1994, the Pentagon signed 3,061 contracts with 12 of the 24 private military firms based in the United States. The contracts totaled more than $300 billion, and over 2700 of the contracts were awarded to just two firms, Kellogg, Brown & Root

---

[27] Wayne Madsen, *Genocide and Covert Operations in Africa 1993-1999* (Lewiston, NY: Mellen Press, 1999), p. 340.

[28] Center for Public Integrity, op. cit.

[29] Esther Schrader, "US Companies Hired to Train Foreign Armies," *Los Angeles Times*, April 14, 2002. <http://www.globalpolicy.org/security/peacekpg/training/pmc.htm>

[30] Daniel Burton-Rose and Wayne Madsen, "Corporate Soldiers: The US Government Privatizes the Use of Force," *Multinational Monitor, Vol. 30, No. 3*, March 1999. <http://multinationalmonitor.org/mm1999/mm9903.07.html>

and Booz Allen Hamilton. The exorbitant cost of these contractors flies in the face of a 1995 Defense Science Board report that suggested the Pentagon could save $6 billion a year by 2002 if it contracted out all support services except for core war-fighting functions.

* * * *

But even combat is sometimes contracted out. In 1998, when ICI of Oregon provided emergency transport and medical services to the Economic Community of West African States Monitoring Group (ECOMOG) forces defending Freetown, Sierra Leone from a siege by Revolutionary United Front (RUF) guerrillas, ICI personnel, many of whom were former U.S. Special Forces troops, returned fire when attacked by the RUF. Their right to retaliate was specifically authorized in writing by the U.S. ambassador to Sierra Leone, Joseph Melrose. ICI has also engaged in similar operations in Liberia and Haiti.[31] In 1991, when Saddam Hussein's army invaded the Saudi town of Khafji, Vinnell employees accompanied Saudi National Guard units into battle.[32]

Of course Iraq presented mercenary firms with new lucrative business possibilities. However, Iraq was also riskier for companies wishing to keep their personnel safe and under the radar screen of media publicity. On March 31, 2004, four American private military contractors with Blackwater USA of Moyock, North Carolina were shot, burned, and mutilated by a mob in the Sunni stronghold of Fallujah. Blackwater had been contracted to the Coalition Provisional Authority to provide personal security for its top leadership. The graphic newspaper photographs and television images of the horrific scenes in Fallujah not only jolted the American public in a manner reminiscent of the images of the bodies of U.S. Army Rangers being dragged through the streets of Mogadishu, Somalia in 1992, but also focused the public's attention on the role of private contractors in the Iraqi war.

It was later revealed that Blackwater had some close connections to the Republican Party and the evangelical right. Blackwa-

---

[31] Center for Public Integrity, op. cit.
[32] Esther Schrader, "US Companies Hired to Train Foreign Armies," op. cit.

ter's founder, Erik Prince, a former Navy SEAL from Holland, Michigan, is the brother-in-law of Dick DeVos, the co-founder of Amway and a major Republican contributor. Prince's sister, Betsy DeVos, was a chairman of the Michigan Republican Party. Prince's father, Edgar Prince, was a founding member of the Family Research Council, the conservative evangelical group led by one-time GOP presidential candidate Gary Bauer.[33]

A number of the Americans working for mercenary companies cited their poor employment situations in the United States as a major reason for their opting for such dangerous, but financially rewarding, work in Iraq. But Americans were not the only mercenaries found to be flocking to Iraq. Veteran mercenaries from a number of past civil wars and rebellions also took advantage of the employment opportunities in lawless Iraq. Former British SAS commandos and South African veterans of the apartheid regime's war against African liberation forces also arrived in force there. Former Chilean dictator Augusto Pinochet's ex-security personnel arrived in Iraq to guard Baghdad airport. Shadowy companies, with names like Janusian, Erinys, Meteoric Tactical Solutions, Armor Group, Global Risk Strategies, Hart Group of Bermuda, Pilgrims Security, Ltd., of the Seychelles, Olive Security, Aegis Defense Services (headed by discredited Sierra Leone and Papua New Guinea soldier of fortune Tim Spicer), ICS (a Panama-registered Israeli-owned firm reportedly provided Israeli interrogators from Israel's "special techniques" interrogation center—Unit 1391), and Grand Lake Trading 46, beat down the doors at the Coalition Provisional Authorities to obtain security work in Iraq.[34]

* * * *

The difficulty in obtaining information about private mercenary firms was highlighted on April 20, 2001, in the skies over Peru. A Cessna airplane carrying an American missionary family was shot down by a Peruvian air force plane. A missionary wife, Veronica

---

[33] Allison Connolly, "Blackwater's Best-Kept Secret: Its founder," *The Virginia Pilot*, May 3, 2004.

[34] Bill Berkowitz, "Mercenaries are U.S.," Dissident Voice, April 5, 2004.< http://www.dissidentvoice.org/April2004/Berkowitz0405.htm

Bowers, and her seven-month old adopted daughter, Charity, were killed in the attack. The Peruvian air force plane had been informed that the Cessna was actually a drug-running plane by another radar-equipped aircraft operated by Aviation Development Corporation of Montgomery, Alabama. Aviation Development was under contract to the CIA to assist the Peruvian air force in shooting down aircraft suspected of running drugs. More than thirty planes had already been shot down over Peru as part of a "no-fly zone" established by the United States. The Pentagon called the attack a "tragic case of friendly fire."[35] The incident over Peru resulted in other U.S. mercenary operations throughout the Andes region being investigated by members of Congress who were concerned about the lack of oversight.

Another proprietary airline came to the forefront in early 2005 when it was discovered that two aircraft, a Gulfstream V executive jet (tail number N379P, later changed to N8068V, originally N581GA) and a Boeing 737 (tail number N313P), owned by Premier Executive Transport Services, were flying captured Al Qaeda suspects between Dulles International Airport; Guantanamo Bay; and Johnson County Airport in Smithfield, North Carolina, and to third countries for special interrogation. The interrogation was called "extraordinary rendition" by the Bush administration, but, in effect, was torture in "ghost prison systems," meaning off-the-books interrogation centers. Other stops for the Boeing 737 included Libya, Majorca, Baghdad, Dubai, Islamabad, Jakarta, Karachi, Riyadh, Tripoli (Libya), Tashkent, Kuwait, Khartoum, Baku, Kabul, Gambia, Cairo, Rabat, Frankfurt, Stockholm, Jamaica, Amman and Larnaca Airport in Cyprus. It was later discovered that the Navy Engineering Logistics Office (NELO) in Arlington, Virginia issued classified contracts for Gulfstreams, a Lear Jet, a Cessna, two Boeing 737s, a DeHavilland DH-8, three Lockheed Hercules cargo aircraft, and a DC-3 to transport renditioned prisoners around the world.[36]

Aero Contractors Ltd., based at Johnson County Airport, leased aircraft to Premier Executive up until 2004, when Premier ceased

---

[35] Wayne Madsen, "Peruvian No-Fly Zone, *The Progressive*, June 2001, p. 35.

[36] Seth Hettena, "Navy Secretly Contracted Jets Used by CIA," Associated Press, September 24, 2005.

operations, but Aero continued to provide unspecified aircraft services to the Pentagon in 2005.[37] Aero Contractors was founded in 1979 by a former CIA pilot for Air America in Southeast Asia. Between its founding and 9-11, Aero provided direct support to Jonas Savimbi's UNITA guerrillas in Angola, King Hussein of Jordan, and U.S. counter-narcotics operations in Colombia. The actual Pentagon customer for the aircraft services is the Joint Special Operations Command (JSOC), based at nearby Fort Bragg, North Carolina.

Premier Executive's principles were identified as Bryan P. Dyess, Steven E. Kent, Timothy R. Sperling and Audrey M. Tailor. Each was associated with five post office boxes maintained in Arlington and Oakton, Virginia; Chevy Chase, Maryland; and Washington, DC, but it appeared that these were false identities outfitted with phony dates of birth and Social Security Numbers. Some of the names were connected to an entity called Executive Support OFC.[38] Another "ghost" executive tied to "Air CIA" is Philip P. Quincannon, who was listed as a Premier officer, as well as an officer of Crowell Aviation Technologies. Both companies were listed at the same Dedham, Massachusetts address. Quincannon was also identified as an officer of Stevens Express Leasing in Tennessee. Other than his rental of post office boxes in Washington, DC and Dunn Loring, Virginia, there are no public records that Mr. Quincannon, like his "ghost colleagues," Messrs. Dyess, Kent, Sperling, and Ms. Tailor, ever existed, except in the minds of the CIA officers who are responsible for developing false identities of individuals and firms.[39]

After Premier ceased operations, the Gulfstream V was purchased by another shadowy carve-out company, Bayard Foreign Marketing LLC of Portland, Oregon. The annual report of the company submitted to the Oregon Secretary of State was signed by Leonard T. Bayard, but no Leonard T. Bayard worked at the firm's offices

[37] Mandy Locke, "Airport Linked to Covert Flights," The News and Observer (Charlotte), March 9, 2005, p. B1; Michael Hersh, Mark Hosenball, and John Barry, "Aboard Air CIA," *Newsweek*, February 28, 2005, p. 32.

[38] Dana Priest, "Jet is an Open Secret in Terror War," *Washington Post*, December 27, 2004, p. A01; Scott Shane, "CIA Expanding Terror Fight Under Guise of Charter Flights," *New York Times*, May 31, 2005.

[39] Shane, op. cit.

in downtown Portland's Pittock Block Building. Other shadowy CIA air charter proprietaries with a new lease on life after 9-11 are ensconced in Florida, the home state of recent CIA Director Porter Goss. They include Pegasus Technologies and Tepper Aviation.[40]

The Gulfstream was the least kept secret in the Pentagon's so-called "Global War on Terrorism." Sighted by plane spotters on airport tarmacs around the world, the plane became known as the Guantanamo Bay Express. After the plane was spotted several times at Prestwick Airport in Glasgow, Scotland, there were demands for assurances by all parties in the Scottish Parliament that Scotland was not participating in America's torture program.[41]

The plane was spotted at least 16 times at Ireland's Shannon Airport,[42] where Celtic tempers against the United States also flared across the Irish Sea. After Sinn Fein Dail members complained about Shannon being used as part of the American global torture network, Sinn Fein and its Northern Ireland leader, Gerry Adams, became persona non grata in Washington, DC, which, in effect, sank the Northern Ireland peace initiatives commenced and overseen by President Bill Clinton. The Bush administration accused Sinn Fein of continuing links with terrorism, the favorite accusation of the Bush administration toward its critics.

The same Gulfstream or another jet bearing tail number N85VM was sighted in Cairo on February 18, 2003, the very day that Abu Omar, an Islamic cleric was delivered to Cairo after he was abducted by the United States in Milan. Gulfstream N85VM had departed Aviano Air Base in Italy the day Abu Omar was snatched by U.S. operatives. The Gulfstream sighted in Cairo was based in Schenectady, New York and chartered from Richmor Aviation of Hudson, New York.

The plane's serial number, 1172, is the same as the serial number on the jet used on occasion by the Boston Red Sox (tail number N227SV). In fact, when the Gulfstream was not sporting the Red Sox logo, it was repainted, assigned a new tail number, and was used to ferry terrorist suspects to torture centers around the world. The

---

[40] Ibid.

[41] Graeme Smith, "'Guantanamo' jet spent night at Prestwick; Airport used more often than first thought," *The Herald* (Glasgow), January 6, 2005, p. 8.

[42] "Is Shannon a Link in a U.S. Chain of Torture?" *The Sunday Independent* (Ireland), January 2, 2005.

plane's owner was listed as Assembly Point Aviation, a company headquartered in Albany, New York with no telephone number. Dun & Bradstreet records identify Assembly Point as a "religious organization" involved with "churches, temples and shrines." Assembly Point's only officer is Philip H. Morse, a multimillionaire who lives in Jupiter, Florida. Morse is a part owner of the Red Sox. The torture jet made stops at Ramstein and Rhein-Main air bases in Germany; Andrews Air Force Base, Maryland; Afghanistan; Morocco; Dubai; Jordan; Italy, Cairo; Aviano, Italy; Osaka, Japan; Switzerland; Azerbaijan; the Czech Republic; and Shannon in Ireland. In addition, the jet made 51 stops at Guantanamo Bay.[43]

* * * *

The creation by Secretary of Defense Donald Rumsfeld of another parallel intelligence agency and covert operations unit within the Pentagon, the Assistant Secretary of Defense for Intelligence and the Office of Special Plans, respectively, is another opportunity for mercenary contractors to engage in clandestine activities. The neoconservative policies of the Pentagon cabal of Deputy Defense Secretary Paul Wolfowitz and other political advisers were often at odds with Federal laws and the wishes of the State Department. Although there was some involvement by the CIA, the torture jets were largely controlled by these Pentagon intelligence entities.

Shortly after the United States launched a pre-emptive attack against Iraq in March 2003, Indonesia's military (TNI) attacked supporters of the Free Acheh Movement and civilians in northwest Sumatra. Wolfowitz, a former U.S. ambassador to Indonesia, favored restoring U.S. military assistance to the country, sanctions having been imposed after the country's brutal repression in East Timor prior to that country's independence. Over the objections from the State Department and Senator Russ Feingold of Wisconsin, the Pentagon released $4 million to Indonesia's military for counter-terrorism training.[44] The provision of such funding violated the Leahy Amendment

---

[43] John Crewdson and Tom Hundley, "Jet's travels cloaked in mystery; Red Sox partner's plane hits spots U.S. sent terror suspects," *Chicago Tribune*, March 20, 2005.

[44] Dana Priest, "A Nightmare, and a Mystery, in the Jungle; Ambush of School Outing Left 3 Dead, 8 Wounded And Suspicion of Involvement by Indonesian Army," *Washington Post*, June 22, 2003, p. A01.

of 1999, which prohibits U.S. military aid to the TNI until it reforms and demonstrates a proper accounting for Indonesia's human rights abuses in East Timor. Not only had the TNI not reformed, but it was implicated in further abuses, including the killing of two American school teachers in West Papua, where another separatist group, the Free Papua Movement, sought independence from Indonesia.

But in both West Papua and Acheh, U.S. companies with significant interests, Freeport McMoran and Exxon Mobil, respectively, were known to support the repression of local separatists by the TNI. In March 2003, Freeport McMoran revealed that it paid $11 million to the TNI during 2001 and 2002 to conduct counter-insurgency operations in West Papua.[45] One such operation by Indonesia's Special Forces Corps, known as KOPASSUS (which had received extensive U.S. military training), may have resulted in the assassination by strangling of a local West Papuan independence leader, Theys Eluay, in November 2001. The American companies operating in Acheh and West Papua received a boost in January 2003, when the U.S. Senate voted 61-36 to reject an amendment by Feingold to prohibit the Pentagon from resuming International Military Education and Training (IMET) for Indonesian military officers.

In February 2003, Ship Analytics, a division of MPRI, received a $53.8 million contract to set up six high technology maritime training schools in Indonesia. The contract, financed through the U.S. Export-Import Bank, was personally backed by Connecticut Senator Joseph Lieberman, a neoconservative ally of Wolfowitz, and Connecticut Representative Rob Simmons, a former CIA operative.[46]

* * * *

In June 2002, Rumsfeld offered to send U.S. Special Forces to India to operate against Islamic terrorist groups in Jammu and Kashmir. With the Pentagon neoconservatives pushing for an Indo-American alliance directed against Islamists and China, India may become a new operating area for mercenary firms, which often fol-

---

[45] Sian Powell, "W Papua mine paid $18.5m to military," *The Weekend Australian*, March 15, 2003, p. 19.

[46] Business Wire, "L-3 Communications Announces $53.8 Million Contract to Upgrade Indonesian Maritime Training," February 10, 2003.

low U.S. Special Operations forces into new theaters of combat. Rumsfeld and his advisers also appear to have interests in India that go beyond operations in Kashmir. In April 2003, Indian and U.S. Special Forces troops participated in a secretive joint exercise code-named BALANCE IROQUOIS 03-1 in a jungle training camp in Vairengte in northern Mizoram near the Myanmar border, where Saddam Hussein's elite anti-terrorist troops trained in the 1980s.[47] Northeast India and neighboring Bhutan are centers for a myriad of ethnic groups seeking independence or autonomy from India.

Bush and Cheney's interest in India and Bangladesh has coincided with concern about a growing Maoist rebellion in nearby Nepal. U.S. military leaders—including Admiral Dennis Blair, commander of U.S. forces in the Pacific—called for increased American military support for Nepal's armed forces in putting down the insurgency. The Sergeant Major of the U.S. Army, Jack L. Tilley revealed the presence of a military training team in Nepal, without elaborating on their mission, at a May 9, 2001 hearing of the House of Representatives Armed Services Committee,[48] just a few weeks before the massacre of Nepal's Royal Family, supposedly by a disgruntled Crown Prince, who also conveniently died in the attack.

American military intervention on the Indian subcontinent was part of Blair's pet project called the Multinational Planning Augmentation Team, or Tempest Express, which seeks to put the U.S. military in charge of "peacekeeping" and "crisis management" exercises in Asia, and is particularly focused on military-to-military links with Nepal and Bangladesh. The Bush administration began holding major exercises with the Indian Navy in the Arabian Sea (EXERCISE MALABAR) and with the Indian Army in Alaska (EXERCISE GERONIMO THRUST).

In February 2002, U.S. Ambassador to India Robert Blackwill showed an unusual interest in Sikkim, a state India occupied by military force in 1975. Blackwill traveled to the Nathu La Pass along the Sikkimese-Chinese border. Blackwill visited the barbed wire fence separating India and China and was videotaped by cu-

---

[47] "Indo-US Training at Vairengte," *The Telegraph* (Calcutta), May 3, 2003. <http://www.telegraphindia.com/1030503/asp/northeast/story_1932193.asp>

[48] Wayne Madsen, "Big Oil Change: What's Really Driving Bush's Foreign Policy," *In These Times*, Aug. 20, 2001, p. 11.

rious Chinese troops on the Chinese side of the border. Blackwill also traveled to other Indian military bases throughout northeast India.[49]

In addition to helping Nepal supress a Maoist rebellion, the U.S. forces there may have also been keeping a close eye on the activities of the Pakistani Inter Service Intelligence (ISI) agency and the Jammu and Kashmir Islamic Front (JKIF). ISI and JKIF activities were increasing throughout India. These activities were particularly concentrating on Delhi, Uttar Pradesh, Bihar, West Bengal, and Sikkim. Sikkim, whose 1975 incorporation into India was not recognized by either China or Pakistan, reported that the ISI had targeted the Sikkimese town of Jorethang, near Darjeeling, as a center for its activities in the area. Sikkim's Chief Minister Pawan Chamling, an ethnic Nepali, feared the ISI was penetrating his state from Nepal through the porous 100-kilometer border. Blackwill, thus, had more reasons to be interested in Sikkim than peering at Chinese troops on its northern border.

Blackwill was Condoleezza Rice's boss in the National Security Council during the first Bush administration and was on good terms with Israeli Prime Minister Ariel Sharon, a relationship that started when Blackwill was the Political Officer at the U.S. Embassy in Tel Aviv. Blackwill is also a close friend of George W. Bush. After his tour in New Delhi, Blackwill returned to the National Security Council to become the Coordinator for Strategic Planning. The neoconservative plan to encircle China thus had an important asset in the national security planning apparatus of the White House.

Christina Rocca, Richard Armitage's old friend at the State Department and the person who huddled with Taliban officials in Pakistan just prior to 9-11, also became the chief champion for the new Nepali regime of King Gyanendra. She repeatedly warned India against harboring any Nepali Maoist leaders. In that, she was supported by Britain's "special envoy" to Nepal, Sir Jeffrey James, who became an adviser to Gyanendra—a sort of position hearkening back to the days of the British Raj when British political officers became the virtual co-rulers for India's numerous princely

---

[49] Praveen Swami, "An Ambassador's Forays," *Frontline*, Vol. 19, No. 7, March 30-April 12, 2002. <http://www.frontlineonnet.com/fl1907/19070410.htm>

states. In fact, Nepali opposition figures referred to James as the "Viceroy of Nepal."

True to form for a U.S.-backed and installed dictator, Gyanendra wasted no time in jailing most of the democratic opposition and journalists. In a February 1, 2005 crackdown, the King declared rule by decree and placed Prime Minister Sher Bahadur Deuba under house arrest. While the Bush administration uttered feints about supporting democracy around the world, the U.S. ambassador played a round of golf with the hated Crown Prince Paras in May 2005. U.S. embassy spokeswoman Constance Coddling Jones (a key disinformation asset at the U.S. embassy in Kathmandu) wrote in an e-mail that Ambassador James F. Moriarty "suggested that the crown prince be invited" to play in the annual U.S. ambassador's golf tournament in early May, because "he saw this as a good opportunity to get a personal impression of Paras since they had not conversed before." The golf tournament took place while former Finance Minister and Nepali Congress Party leader Ram Mahat languished in prison. Later Mahat said, "The ambassador playing golf with the crown prince was a wrong message ... It was in very bad taste. We all commented, 'What is this American ambassador doing?'"[50]

Since the coup, U.S. mercenary forces have been involved in training Nepalese counter-insurgency forces at the Indian Counter-Insurgency Warfare Center at Vairengte in Mizoram, northeast India. Other training is provided by the United States at the Indian High Altitude Warfare School in Kashmir. These training exercises and others held in Nepal and India have been given code names like OPERATION BALANCE IROQUOIS, OPERATION WAR REHEARSAL, OPERATION HOLD FAST, OPERATION BAKER NEPTUNE, and OPERATION TEMPEST EXPRESS.[51]

Why all the sudden interest of the Bush and Blair administrations in Nepal and India? The Bush cabal stated that it was to stem the Al Qaeda threat. They offered up fanciful notions that Nepal's Maoists, India's Marxist Leninists (Naxalites), Al Qaeda, Burma's military government, and some tribal guerrilla movements in In-

---

[50] James Lancaster, "Game of Golf Stirs Up Criticism of U.S. Role in Nepal," *Washington Post*, June 19, 2005, p. A21.

[51] "Les maoïstes s'attendent à une offensive prochaine," September 24, 2003, Geopolitique.com. <http://www.geopolitique.com/voircontenu.php?contenuref=42>

dia's northeast were out to form some sort of "grand coalition"—a mini-"axis of evil."

None of this was true, of course. The real reason for the Bush team's interest in the subcontinent was the same reason for its interest in Iraq, central Asia, and Latin America—oil and natural gas. In a world where desires for ethnic independence and autonomy are viewed by the Bush administration as fronts for terrorism, there is a real possibility that U.S. mercenary firms may soon be engaged in counter-insurgency operations against tribal and nationalist groups in northeast India, Bhutan, Sikkim, Nepal, and Kashmir.

* * * *

Bill Gammell, whom George W. Bush calls "Billy," is a Scottish oil baron who sees India and the subcontinent as a potential huge oil Mecca. Their relationship dates back to 1959, when a teen-age Bush spent the summer at the Gammell family's Scottish estate. That was Bush's first trip to Europe.

The next time Bush traveled to Scotland was in 1982, when he needed Billy to ante up some cash for his fledgling Arbusto Energy Company in Midland, Texas. Billy was one of 50 original investors who sank a total of some $3 million into the enterprise. Arbusto soon fell on hard times (though Bush made millions through a series of bailouts and sweetheart deals). Billy and the other investors, including Osama bin Laden's older brother Salem bin Laden, got back just 20 cents on every dollar of their investment. Not embarrassed, Bush returned to Scotland in 1983 for Billy's wedding. Gammell also has another important friend: his old classmate, Prime Minister Tony Blair.

Unlike Bush, who had the reverse-Midas touch when it came to the oil business, Billy Gammell struck pay dirt in India. After his stint as a Scottish rugby star, Gammell's Cairn Energy discovered oil in 1999 off the west coast of India in the Gulf of Cambay—a lucrative addition to the company's already sizable natural gas interests in Bangladesh and oil wells on the Indian mainland. One of Bush's main political backers, Enron, expanded its operations in

India to include running a privatized electrical distribution system in Bombay.

In January 2004, Cairn Energy struck black gold at the Mangala field in northwest India's Rajasthan state. The estimates on the potential yield ranged up to one billion barrels. Gammell's firm was also reaping huge natural gas yields from its Lakshmi field in northwest India. With Cairn striking huge oil and natural gas deposits in northern India, it turned its attention to exploring for more oil and natural gas in northern India and Nepal.[52]

No wonder Gammell's friends Bush and Blair were pumping military advisers and equipment into India and Nepal to help those countries put down nettlesome guerrilla uprisings. For the first time in its history, the reclusive Kingdom of Bhutan, acting under pressure from India, the U.S., and Britain, was forced to use its army in an aggressive military operation to dislodge three Indian guerrilla groups, the United Liberation Front of Assam (ULFA), the National Democratic Front of Bodoland (NDFB), and the Kamatapur Liberation Organisation, from camps in the southern part of the country. Before launching OPERATION ALL OUT, the Bhutanese troops reportedly received training from U.S. Special Operations personnel at the School of the Americas—like Asia-Pacific Center for Security Studies (APCSS) in Honolulu, Hawaii and at Vareingte in Mizoram.

As energy companies began to seriously deplete the world's supply of fossil fuels, the Shangri Las of the Himalayas and their foothills would become new areas for political, financial, military, and covert intelligence intrigue by the Americans and British. On January 10, 2004, when ULFA guerrillas blew up an oil pipeline near Kunwarpur, Assam, the oil interests in India and the United States decided to ratchet up pressure on the guerrillas and Bangladesh and Bhutan, two states suspected of benignly supporting the insurgents. Big Oil was bringing warfare to the traditionally peaceful Himalayas.

In the 1990s, Cairn Energy and Halliburton, Cheney's firm, were partners in developing Bangladesh's natural gas fields in the Bay of Bengal. Moreover, Cheney had particularly close ties to both Ban-

[52] Terry Macalister, "Shell's loss is Cairn's gain in second Indian oil strike," *The Guardian*, March 10, 2004, p. 19.

gladeshi Prime Minister Sheik Hasina Wazed and former Prime Minister and principal opposition leader Begum Khaleda Zia. In 1998, Cheney went to Bangladesh and met the two women politicians. However, his real interest was in visiting the Sangu offshore natural gas fields, a joint venture between Halliburton (a 25-percent stakeholder), Cairn, Shell Oil, and Bangladesh's state-owned Petrobangla energy company.

But in 2004, Cairn, Petrobangla and Halliburton came in for a rude shock. Shell shut down one of its four gas wells in the offshore Sangu field. In January 2004, Shell drastically cut its natural gas reserve estimates from the Sangu field, resulting in a criminal probe by the U.S. Justice Department.[53] The speculative bookkeeping practices of Shell apparently resembled the "off-balance sheet transactions" pioneered by Enron.

* * * *

The use of private companies in war zones also permits the U.S. government to violate its own and United Nations arms embargoes. In April 1999, MPRI provided Bosnia's military with weapons under a State Department contract to "train and equip." However, it was soon discovered that Bosnia's military had secretly transferred the arms from Bosnian warehouses to members of the Kosovo Liberation Army (KLA), a group designated by the State Department as a terrorist organization, and Yugoslav Muslim militias in the province of Sandzak. An embarrassed State Department was forced to "temporarily suspend" the program. Admiral Carroll said such illegal transfers were not surprising: "The military loses control over the material twice. First, they turn it over to a commercial enterprise, and they turn it over again."[54] However, in a world where the Pentagon increasingly likes to hide its operations from public scrutiny, such embargo busting will undoubtedly become more commonplace.

There is another more dangerous downside to mercenaries acting without proper oversight. According to an adviser for the Bosnia

---

[53] Christine Ferguson, "Shell-shocked Cairn executives head for Bangladesh," *The Herald* (Glasgow), March 24, 2004, p. 21.
[54] Wayne Madsen, "The U.S. Connection to the KLA," op. cit., p. 31.

Defense Fund, a group set up in 1996 to help fund Bosnia with money obtained from a number of Muslim states, including Malaysia, the United Arab Emirates, Saudi Arabia, Brunei, Egypt, and Kuwait, some of the weapons obtained from MPRI also wound up in the hands of mercenaries with the Iranian Revolutionary Guards (Pasdaran) and Al Qaeda, which were then active in Bosnia aiding the Bosnian Muslim government.[55] In fact, several Muslim fighters in Bosnia, some of whom obtained Bosnian passports, were later involved in actual and planned terrorist attacks against the United States. One Somali Bosnian passport holder named Gharib later went to Jakarta, where he worked with an Al Qaeda member to bomb an American Navy ship in Surabaya harbor between May 30 and June 2, 2002.[56]

It is noteworthy that two of the principals in the Bosnia Defense Fund were Richard Perle, the former Reagan Defense Department official who would become chairman of Rumsfeld's Defense Policy Board in the Bush II administration, and Marc Zell, the law partner of Rumsfeld's Assistant Secretary for Policy and Plans, Douglas Feith. According to a former business partner of Perle and Feith in the Bosnia Defense Fund, the fund was supported with large inflows of cash from Islamic countries, notably Malaysia, the United Arab Emirates, Qatar, Kuwait, Egypt, Jordan, Saudi Arabia, Indonesia, and Brunei. The business partner reported that there was a constant problem with the "spillage" of weapons and money, intended for the Bosnian government and military in Bosnia, into less than trusted hands.[57] The following is an excerpt of a secret Mossad report on the funding activities of foundations in the Gulf and the arming of radicals in Bosnia:

> The foundations in the Gulf give considerable aid, of unknown scope, to a broad spectrum of Islamic institutions throughout the world. These are in many cases identified with the activity of fundamentalist Muslim movements, such as the Muslim brotherhood in Egypt, al-Nahdha in Tunisia, FIS in Algeria and others. Some of the foundations are also connected with financing armed activity of Muslim radicals, such as the Mujahidin Afghanistan veterans and

[55] Confidential information obtained in Washington, DC.
[56] Confidential notes from the interrogation of a Jemaah Islamiah prisoner in Indonesia.
[57] Private conversation.

those in Bosnia. Several foundations are also connected with Osama Bin Laden.[58]

Bosnia was not the only location where U.S. mercenary firms, brass plate companies, and terrorist cells crossed paths. Kosovo and Macedonia also provided venues where U.S. mercenaries could interface with terror cells. In Kosovo, MPRI, which had already been involved in training the Croatian Army in its OPERATION STORM and OPERATION STRIKE offensives against the Serbs, trained the KLA, a terrorist group charged with gun running, smuggling, and atrocities. During the summer of 2001, seventeen MPRI "advisers" reportedly assisted Albanian National Liberation Army (NLA) guerrillas, who were supplied by their KLA allies and referred to by then-NATO Secretary General George Robertson as "murderous thugs," in fighting Macedonian security forces in the Battle of Aracinovo. A NATO force subsequently evacuated the MPRI employees and their NLA allies.[59] Typically, MPRI was also under State Department contract to aid the Macedonian armed forces as part of a "train and equip" program.

According to a U.S. State Department source, press reports that there were at least 6000 Al Qaeda cell members and sympathizers in Macedonia were, in fact, correct. Furthermore, the top Al Qaeda leaders in Macedonia were known to U.S. covert operators like MPRI, who were training members of the KLA. The Bush administration was reluctant to go after the Al Qaeda leaders because they were a critical part of the heroin supply chain that originates in Afghanistan and terminates in Macedonia, Albania, and Kosovo, and funds the KLA.

It is the nature of unregulated mercenary activities that governments which fail to closely monitor private military activities can wittingly or unwittingly end up supplying weapons to adversaries in a conflict, as was witnessed in Macedonia. This certainly was also the case in 1997, when MPRI was aiding the Bosnians. In support

---

[58] "Hamas Resources in Saudi Arabia and the Persian Gulf," (undated) SECRET.

[59] Christopher Deliso, "A Connection Between NATO and the NLA?" January 24, 2002, *Reality Macedonia* <http://www.realitymacedonia.org.mk/web/news_page. asp?nid=1355>; Christopher Deliso, "European Intelligence: The US Betrayed Us in Macedonia," June 22, 2002, www.antiwar.com, http://www.antiwar.com/orig/deliso46. html >; Michel Chossudovsky, "Washington Behind Terrorist Attacks in Macedonia," July 23, 2001, www.antiwar.com <http://www.antiwar.com/rep/chuss6.html>

of America's "War on Drugs," the White House Office of Drug Control Policy and the Republican-led House of Representatives pushed through authorizations for "national interest waivers" that permitted the shipment of weapons under the U.S. Foreign Military Sales program to paramilitary forces in both Serbia and Montenegro.[60] In essence, U.S. private military contractors were helping to supply both sides in the Bosnian conflict.

Retired U.S. Army General Richard Griffiths, an MPRI employee, was placed in charge of the operation in Skopje, the Macedonian capital. It was charged that in his role as an adviser to the Macedonian armed forces, Griffiths obtained classified information on the NLA terrorists in Macedonia directly from General Jovan Andrejevski, the chief of staff of the Macedonian Armed Forces. It was also charged that Griffiths directly supplied the classified information to both the NLA and their KLA patrons in neighboring Kosovo.[61]

The Macedonian government of President Boris Trajkovski eventually canceled the MPRI contract in its entirety. On February 26, 2004, Trajkovski was killed in an airplane crash en route to an economic summit conference in Mostar, Bosnia.

* * * *

In Afghanistan, Dyncorp was providing protection for Afghan interim leader Hamid Karzai. However, Karzai was also attempting to negotiate a power-sharing agreement with some members of the former Taliban government, the regime that harbored and gave support to Osama bin Laden and Al Qaeda at a time when they were reportedly planning the September 11 terrorist attacks on the United States.

In Bolivia, Dyncorp and a Bolivian mercenary group called the Expeditionary Task Force (ETF), which is paid, clothed, fed, and trained directly by the U.S. Embassy in La Paz, work hand-in-hand in a program called the "Dignity Plan" to eradicate the coca crop from Bolivia's tropical Chapare region. The ETF has been implicated in a number of human rights violations, including beatings and murders of civilians. Representative Maurice Hinchey of

[60] Madsen, "Mercenaries in Kosovo," pp. 29-30.
[61] Michel Chossudovsky, "Macedonia: Washington's Military-Intelligence Ploy."

New York said, "In the case of Bolivia, I think the war on drugs is being used as an excuse to carry out behavior that we would never otherwise accept.... Our actions in Bolivia represent a gross complacency that borders on complicity. There seems to be purposeful obfuscation about the facts."[62]

On September 11, 2001, attorneys representing 10,000 Quechua Indians in Ecuador filed suit, under the provisions of the U.S. Alien Tort Claims Act and the Torture Victim Protection Act, in Washington, DC, alleging that Dyncorp had endangered their health and poisoned their crops by spraying glyphosate to eradicate marijuana, poppy, and cocaine crops as part of PLAN COLOMBIA. The commercial name for glyphosate, manufactured by Monsanto, is Roundup, and warning labels on the product caution against contact with people or water sources. Emperatriz Cahuache, the president of the Organization of Indigenous Peoples of the Colombian Amazon, said, "These fumigations are contaminating the Amazon and destroying the forest."[63]

In turn, Dyncorp's CEO Paul Lombardi threatened one of the suit's backers, the AFL-CIO-affiliated International Labor Rights Fund. In a letter sent to the board members of the Rights Fund, Lombardi accused them of fronting for the drug cartels. Lombardi also warned the Fund that it was serving the interests of terrorists: "Considering the major international issues with which we are all dealing as a consequence of the events of September 11, none of us need to be sidetracked with frivolous litigation the aim of which is to fulfill a political agenda."

Bishop Jesse DeWitt, one of the board members, responded to Lombardi in a letter, accusing Dyncorp of practicing terrorism:

> We found your reference to September 11 particularly apt, but for a very different reason. Based on what appear to be uncontested facts, a group of at least 10,000 Ecuadorian subsistence farmers have been poisoned from aerial assault by your company. Imagine that scene

---

[62] Anthony Faiola, "U.S. Role in Coca War Draws Fire: Bolivian Anti-Drug Unit Paid by Washington Accused of Abuses," *Washington Post*, June 23, 2002. < http://www.washingtonpost.com/wp-dyn/articles/A29589-2002Jun22.html>

[63] Danielle Knight, "Ecuadorians File U.S. Suit Over Plan Colombia," InterPress Service, September 24, 2001. <http://www.commondreams.org/headlines01/0924-03.htm>

for a moment—you are an Ecuadoran farmer, and suddenly, without notice or warning, a large helicopter approaches, and the frightening noise of the chopper blades invades the quiet. The helicopter comes closer, and sprays a toxic poison on you, your children, your livestock and your food crops. You see your children get sick, your crops die. Mr. Lombardi, we at the International Labor Rights Fund, and most civilized people, consider such an attack on innocent people terrorism. Your effort to hide behind September 11 is shameful, and breathtakingly cynical.[64]

* * * *

In Sri Lanka there are continuing reports about MPRI training of government troops in their battle against Tamil separatist guerrillas. For seven years, the Tamil Tiger guerrillas have claimed that U.S. Special Forces (possibly including MPRI contractors) have been training Sri Lankan counter-insurgency troops at a sophisticated military training camp in the southern Wirawila district. Officials of the US embassy in Colombo, Sri Lanka have refused to comment on MPRI's role in Sri Lanka. However, the embassy did respond to Tamil Tiger charges that the United States had changed its policy of non-involvement in Sri Lanka's civil war and had started to openly support Sri Lankan government troops. The embassy claimed that "any training provided to Sri Lankan forces was of relatively low magnitude and had hardly any bearing on the north-east [Tamil] war." The embassy declined to specify the nature of the training provided by the United States.[65]

However, MPRI's involvement in Sri Lanka was revealed in an interview British journalist Paul Harris gave to Australia's Radio National's program, *Background Briefing*, in 1997. Harris said MPRI's involvement in Sri Lanka was revealed at a going-away party in Colombo:

> MPRI were involved in drawing up I understand, a long-term training strategy for the Sri Lankan army, a program which would vastly

---

[64] Al Giordano, "Dyncorp Charged With Terrorism," *Narconews*, February 23, 2002. <http://www.narconews.com/dyncorpterrorism1.html>
[65] Gaston de Rosayro, "Tricky balancing act on high-wire to peace," *Sunday Times* (Sri Lanka), June 22, 2002. <http://www.dailymirror.lk/2002/06/22/opinion.html>

improve its capability. Well the news of this started to leak out after a drinks party at which the retiring commander of the Sri Lankan army possibly had one over the odds. He revealed that America was coming to the assistance of the Sri Lankans, and he rather let the cat out of the bag. It was very embarrassing to the American Embassy in Colombo, and for those of us who knew how many beans made five, it's quite clear that MPRI was involved, that the U.S. government was involved at a more official level, and the bottom line was that the Americans withdrew from Sri Lanka, announced that withdrawal at the end of August, beginning of September last year in a run-up of course, to Presidential elections [1996]. And the White House was extremely concerned about publicity, which the actions were getting in Washington, and they felt obliged to publicly say that "We're not getting involved in another Asian adventure." They might have added, "In the run-up to an election." People in the U.S. State Department told me, "Nothing to do with us, it must be those MPRI people." And of course MPRI said, "Oh well, we're not involved." And so everybody was using the presence of the other, as you might say, to dodge the column.[66]

Retired General Ed Soyster, MPRI's director of international operations and a former head of the Defense Intelligence Agency, responded to the allegations of his firm's involvement in Sri Lanka's civil war. He confirmed that MPRI had been in Sri Lanka, but said that the company never signed a contract with the Sri Lankan army:

> We were contacted by the Sri Lankan government. In fact I personally went to Sri Lanka with another officer in the company, and discussed the possibility for training there. That contract, like any other business arrangement, was not signed. We did have a license from our State Department because of the nature of the training that we were going to provide, to conduct training. But like any business, I don't know any business contractor that goes out on every opportunity and comes back with a contract. So we've done no work there. Two of us were there for about a week with discussions, and that's our total involvement in Sri Lanka.[67]

---

[66] Stan Corry, "We Don't Do Wars," *Radio National,* June 15, 1997. <http://www.abc.net.au/rn/talks/bbing/stories/s10592.htm>

[67] Ibid.

* * * *

Mercenary firms have also been involved in questionable human rights violations in their covert operations on behalf of totalitarian regimes. Without proper U.S. government or even military oversight, soldiers of fortune are free to engage in all sorts of activities in violation of United Nations treaties. The U.S. military occupation of Iraq has been a virtual license for military brigands and privateers to commit all sorts of abuses against captured combatants and civilians—with a "wink and a nod" from the Pentagon and Bush administration officials. When Amnesty International questioned MPRI's Soyster on what kind of "human rights training" his firm provided to Croatia's military, he said no such specific human rights training was provided to Croatian forces and that as a private organization, MPRI "was not accountable to Amnesty International or to anyone else for the content of their training programs."[68]

In addition to Dyncorp's involvement with child prostitution in the Balkans, another troubling aspect vis-à-vis children and private military companies has arisen in Africa. Firms supplying arms to military and paramilitary forces have often ended up in the hands of child soldiers. For example, Dyncorp supplied assistance to the UN peacekeeping force in Angola and also the Angolan Army,[69] one of the major employers of child soldiers in combat operations. The Namibian human rights group, National Society for Human Rights, has charged the Angolans with "conducting forced recruitment of able-bodied major and minor males on Namibian soil."[70] The fact that companies like Dyncorp were contracted to an army engaged in such practices raises additional concerns about the activities of mercenaries.

In Colombia, Dyncorp has placed itself squarely on the side of the Colombian military and right-wing paramilitaries, both linked

---

[68] Amnesty International, "A Catalogue of Failures: G8 Arms Exports and Human Rights Violations," May 19, 2003. <http://web.amnesty.org/library/Index/ENGIOR3 00032003?open&of=ENG-312>

[69] Wayne Madsen, *Genocide and Covert Operations in Africa 1993-1999*, p.p. 339-341.

[70] National Society for Human Rights, "Child Soldiers and Mercenaries in Cross Border Conflict," January 6, 2000. <http://www.web.net/~iccaf/humanrights/angolainfo/angolanewsjan.htm#CHILD%20SOLDIERS%20AND%20MERCENARIE S%20IN%20CROSS%20BORDER%20CONFLICT>

to horrendous human rights violations in that country's long civil war. Dyncorp operates Vietnam-era OV-10 Broncos that are used for fumigating coca crops there. But in Colombia, the Dyncorp employees operate according to their own rules and are not subject to the Status of Forces agreements the United States signs with sovereign nations governing the activities of U.S. troops on their soil. A soldier in the Colombian anti-drug squad said of the Dyncorp mercenaries he had encountered, "[They] fly in Bermuda shorts, smoke wherever they want, and drink whiskey almost everyday." A Colombian National Guardsman stationed near the Dyncorp base at San Jose del Guaviare air base, said of the Dyncorp mercenaries, "A Vietnam veteran does not subordinate himself to a Colombian police officer, and that's why there have been problems."[71]

* * * *

Dick Cheney's old subsidiary, Kellogg, Brown & Root, received a contract to build up to 2000 detention cells at Camp Delta in Guantanamo Bay, Cuba.[72] The legality of jailing detainees in Guantanamo has been challenged by a number of human rights and civil rights organizations. Brown & Root is also providing logistics support to the U.S. base at Camp Lemonier in Djibouti, a country that sits amid volatile border and internal wars involving Ethiopia, Eritrea, Sudan, Somaliland, Puntland, and rump Somalia. The company also maintained a presence in other trouble spots, including Georgia, Uzbekistan, and Jordan.

Operating from its headquarters at Camp Arijan in Kuwait, Brown & Root established encampments at tent city camps with names like Camp Virginia, Camp Pennsylvania, and Camp New York, prior to the U.S. invasion of Iraq. In a clever bit of psychological warfare operations, the camps were named for states that were affected by the September 11 Al Qaeda terrorist attacks, although

---

[71] Ignacio Gomez, "U.S. Mercenaries in Colombia," totes.com, <http://www.totse.com/en/politics/the_world_beyond_the_usa/latlng.html>

[72] Carol Rosenberg, "Building of Prison at Guantanamo Begins," *Miami Herald*, February 28, 2002. <http://www.miami.com/mld/miamiherald/news/world/cuba/2760497.htm>

there has never been any proof that Saddam Hussein was, in any way, involved with Al Qaeda or the attacks.[73]

Kellogg, Brown & Root also operated dining facilities catering to U.S. forces in Iraq. In addition to overcharging the U.S. military for meals and maintaining filthy kitchens that resulted in U.S. forces getting sick, the company was also implicated in the use of slave labor. Aliyarkunju Faizal, an Indian guest worker in Kuwait, claimed he was forced into slave labor at a military kitchen at Talafar near Baghdad. Three other Indians from Faizal's village in Kerala were also press-ganged into working for the Americans. The operators of the Talafar base claim they "bought" the Indians like slaves. Faizal, a Muslim, claimed he was forced, against his religion, to cook pork during the holy time of Ramadan and was physically abused, prevented from returning home, and underpaid. He was eventually sent to Jordan where he caught a flight back to India.[74]

Jardo Muekalia, who headed UNITA's Washington office until it was forced to close in 1997, said the Angolan military forces who ultimately succeeded in assassinating UNITA leader Jonas Savimbi, a former close ally of the United States, were supported by commercial satellite imagery and other intelligence support provided by Kellogg, Brown & Root.[75]

* * * *

In Croatia, MPRI was accused of assisting that nation's military in the "ethnic cleansing" of Serbs from Krajina and Eastern Slavonia provinces. Although Croatians were accused by the International Criminal Tribunal in The Hague of war crimes, including indiscriminate shelling of civilian targets and summary executions of civilians, no MPRI employee was ever charged. Although it was contracted to the Croatian armed forces at the time, MPRI denies that it played a role in the Croatian ethnic cleansing operations.

When I asked what steps he was taking to ensure that private military companies like MPRI contracted to the Pentagon do not

---

[73] Ashfak Bokhari, "Corporate military makes a killing on Iraq war," *Dawn* (Pakistan), March 31, 2003. <http://www.dawn.com/2003/03/31/ebr3.htm>

[74] "I was tortured for days by American soldiers," *IANS*, Newindpress.com, May 6, 2004.

[75] Wayne Madsen, "Report Alleges US Role in Angola Arms-for-Oil Scandal," *CorpWatch*, May 17, 2002. < http://www.corpwatch.org/issues/PID.jsp?articleid=2576>

hire mercenaries or others with unsavory pasts, EUCOM deputy commander General Charles Wald said, "We don't use mercenaries … that is the most ludicrous thing I've ever heard about the U.S. military," adding, "MPRI is a very professional outfit."[76] In a later conversation with Wald, he assured me that no suspected war criminals were being used as private contractors by the U.S. military.

However, in a raid in southern Iraq by radical Sh'ia supporters in April 2004, a private South African security employee for the Hart Group, who turned out to be a war criminal, was killed and decapitated by his assailants. It was discovered that the dead employee was a former Rhodesian and South African covert special forces agent named Gray Branfield, also known as "Major Brian," "Mhlatini" ("the one of the bush") and "Hound Dog." Branfield worked for a Rhodesian Police Force covert operations group that targeted black African guerrilla groups. Branfield later joined apartheid South Africa's Project Barnacle, a death squad that assassinated African National Congress (ANC) and other opposition political leaders who were in exile in Lesotho, Botswana, Zimbabwe, and Zambia. In 1985, Branfield helped plan a South African raid on Gaborone, Botswana, in which fourteen people, including a five-year-old child, had been killed.[77]

* * * *

Another country where U.S. mercenaries have sought to provide services to a brutal regime is Equatorial Guinea. In 1998, MPRI submitted an application to the U.S. State Department to establish "an effective national security enhancement program" in the oil-rich country. The $10 million program was to have included training the country's military to control the land and sea borders of the country. After objections were raised by the State Department and Congress that the military training program would only benefit the country's brutal dictator, Teodoro Obiang Nguema, the nephew of one of the bloodiest leaders in African history,

---

[76] Comments by General Charles Wald, Center for Strategic and International Studies (CSIS), March 30, 2004.

[77] Julian Rademeyer, "Iraq victim was top-secret apartheid killer," *Sunday Times* (Johannesburg), April 19, 2004.

MPRI received limited approval to help establish a Coast Guard for the country.[78]

However, MPRI's plans for Equatorial Guinea appear to be more far-reaching than establishing a Coast Guard for the nation. MPRI calls its program for the country the "National Security Enhancement Plan" (NSEP). The program states that for NSEP, "MPRI developed an integrated team of defense, security, and Coast Guard experts to provide a detailed set of recommendations to the government of Equatorial Guinea concerning its defense, littoral, and related environmental management requirements, as well as detailed implementation processes."[79]

Equatorial Guinea, which was relegated to a virtual non-entity in 1995 when the U.S. closed its embassy there, became important to U.S. business interests when huge offshore oil reserves were discovered. MPRI's interest followed a typical pattern—oil or other natural resources are discovered in a country plagued by dictatorial regimes and/or civil strife; then to the assistance of the government comes a mercenary firm with close ties to international oil or mineral companies or cartels. This pattern is also seen in the Angolan enclave of Cabinda, where Air Scan provides counter-insurgency support to the Angolan Army in its efforts to protect oil installations from separatist fighters. Air Scan, based in Titusville, Florida, is run by retired Brigadier General Joe Stringham, a veteran of clandestine U.S. Special Forces counter-insurgency operations in El Salvador.[80]

* * * *

In August 2002, in what may portend a financial windfall for U.S. mercenary firms, President Fradique de Menezes, of Sao Tome and Principe, another Gulf of Guinea island state and also sitting atop significant oil reserves, announced that he had agreed to allow the United States to build a naval base on Sao Tome, as "a harbor for

---

[78] Alex Belida, "Background Report/Pentagon / Equatorial Guinea," Voice of America, November 19, 2002. <http://www.globalsecurity.org/military/library/news/2002/11/mil-021119-355e8e4e.htm>

[79] <http://www.mpri.com/subchannels/int_africa.html>

[80] John E. Peck, "Asian Meltdown hits Zimbabwe," *Zmagazine*. <http://zena.secureforum.com/Znet/zmag/articles/pecksept98.htm>

aircraft carriers, patrol boats, and for Marines stationed in the region." In July 2002, General Carlton Fulford, deputy commander of the U.S. European Command, visited Sao Tome to discuss the arrangement.[81]

As discussed before in Chapter Six, in July 2003, a group of Sao Tome army officers, some of whom had been involved in a South African Special Forces group called Battalion 32 and a mercenary firm known as Executive Outcomes, overthrew de Menezes in a coup. The army officers were said to covet the wealth from Sao Tome's newly discovered offshore oil reserves. The Sao Tome coup followed by days the visit of President Bush, Condoleezza Rice and Walter Kansteiner to South Africa and Botswana, where they discussed mounting a rebellion against Zimbabwe's President, Robert Mugabe.

The officers remained as power brokers in the Sao Tome government even after de Menezes was restored to power. One of the companies investing in oil production in waters off Sao Tome is Chevron Texaco. Condoleezza Rice once sat on the corporate board of Chevron.

The very real possibility that conflict may break out between Equatorial Guinea, Cameroon, Gabon, Congo (Brazzaville), and Sao Tome and Principe over competing claims to oil blocks in the Gulf of Guinea also bodes well for mercenary firms, which can be expected to seek maximum profit from all sides of any conflict, as they previously demonstrated in the Balkans.

* * * *

Oil is also what got MPRI involved in training Nigeria's military after years of that country being under the totalitarian grip of dictator Sani Abacha. In August 2000, MPRI received a multi-million dollar Defense Department contract to "professionalize" Nigeria's military. When Nigeria's Army Chief of Staff, General Victor Malu, complained about MPRI's role in the country, he was quickly fired by President Olesegun Obasanjo. Malu complained about MPRI's plan to cut the Nigerian army from 100,000 to 50,000 troops. Based on Nigeria's longtime role in providing the

---

[81] Center for Public Integrity, "The Curious Bonds of Oil Diplomacy," November 6, 2002. <http://allafrica.com/stories/200211210320.html>

lion's share of manpower for Economic Community of West African States (ECOWAS) and United Nations peacekeeping forces throughout the West African region, Malu's criticism seemed justified. MPRI's Soyster criticized the Nigerian army, stating, "From a military point of view, they weren't very effective."[82]

The U.S. military training program with Nigeria collapsed after Nigeria expressed opposition to the Bush administration's war on Iraq. Washington quickly and unilaterally suspended its military assistance programs with Nigeria. Chief Dubem Onyia, Nigeria's Minister of State for Foreign Affairs, told the U.S. ambassador to Nigeria, "If the US has decided to suspend its military assistance to Nigeria, so be it."[83]

* * * *

Under ACOTA (African Contingency Operations Training and Assistance, formerly known as the African Crisis Response Initiative, or ACRI), MPRI is contracted to provide military training, and thus expand its influence, in a number of other African countries. MPRI's Web site states:

> The ACOTA is a U.S. State Department coordinated interagency program that works with African states and other allies to develop and enhance peace operations and humanitarian assistance capabilities among selected African armies. MPRI provides the battalion and brigade task force level command and staff training for the program, in coordination with US military forces that provide initial task oriented training, and provides both training integration and advice to the Interagency Working Group (IWG) utilizing our team of multilingual regional and functional experts. The program focuses on sustainable capabilities and improved interoperability."[84]

ACOTA has been largely unsuccessful in stopping a number of African wars. In actuality, these conflicts benefit the bottom lines of mercenary companies and multinational firms seeking to exploit

---

[82] Ibid.

[83] Tokunbo Olorruntola, "Military reform in troubled waters," Daily Independent (Nigeria), March 28, 2003. <http://www.odili.net/news/source/2003/mar/28/303.html>

[84] <http://www.mpri.com/subchannels/int_africa.html>

Africa's wealth of natural resources. The worst situation where the Bush administration chose to stand on the sidelines is in the Democratic Republic of the Congo. MPRI and other mercenary firms, including Ronco and SAIC, were active in Rwanda before, during, and after that nation's multiple invasions of neighboring Zaire/Congo. Rwanda was the key to U.S. ambitions to control Congo's natural resources by keeping it fractured into separate fiefdoms, and in a state of constant bloody warfare. As I told the Belgian magazine, *Trends*, in an August 2001 interview:

> The United States was interested in the country without mineral wealth [Rwanda] because Kagame's RPF [Rwandan Patriotic Front] was the ideal vehicle to fill up the wish list of its [America's] companies: Barrick, American Mineral Fields (AMF), Banro Resources, Bechtel, Tempelsman & Sons, Halliburton. Microsoft was on the lookout for coltan [columbite-tantalite] ore. Walter Kansteiner, whose father is a trader in tropical raw materials in Chicago, now is Assistant Secretary of State for Africa in the Bush administration. On October 16, 1996, he made a plea for the splitting up of Zaire in [an article for] The Forum for International Policy. At about the same time Laurent-Désiré Kabila started his Blitzkrieg towards Kinshasa—with the active co-operation of American intelligence services. Nowadays that man determines the US Africa policy." [Translated into English from the original Flemish article by the *Trends* staff].[85]

* * * *

In February 2001, the Pentagon declined to renew a $4.3 million contract with MPRI for a "bottom-up review" of Colombia's military. The contract—part of the Andean counter-narcotics program PLAN COLOMBIA—specified that MPRI was to provide "advice and assistance in developing specific plans and programs to assist the Ministry of Defense and the armed forces of Colombia in institution building, long range planning, and interagency cooperation to enhance their counter drug capabilities." The firm sent a team of ten retired military officers to Bogota to conduct the review.

[85] "The U.S. (Under)Mining Job: Interview with Wayne Madsen, *Trends*, August 14, 2001. <http://cryptome.sabotage.org/us-africa-wm.htm>

MPRI's mission immediately raised suspicions in Colombia when it was revealed that the firm's consultants were to "recommend legislation, statutes and decrees to Colombia regarding a military draft, a professional soldier statute, officer entitlements and health law reforms." This was seen as a violation of Colombia's sovereignty. In addition, MPRI staffed its consultants with non-Spanish speaking Pentagon bureaucrats who had little knowledge of Latin America. Colombian officials later said MPRI's work was "largely irrelevant and not tailored for Colombia's needs."[86]

* * * *

Although the mercenary business is highly prized by American firms, there have been times when the Pentagon has given a "nod and a wink" to foreign mercenary firms to engage in clandestine activity. Such was the case in 1997, when a British mercenary firm, Sandline, sought a $36 million contract from the government of Papua New Guinea to help put down a secessionist movement on the island of Bougainville. For a number of years, the island's population had been subjugated by both the Papua New Guinea government and Western-owned mining companies operating on the island. When Sandline attempted to use South African mercenaries to militarily quell the rebellion, Papua New Guinea was rocked in March 1997 with an attempted coup by disgruntled military officers who objected to the presence of mercenaries in the country.

The same year that the Papua New Guinea crisis exploded, Tim Spicer, a retired British commando who worked for Sandline, attended a June 24, 1997 conference at the Pentagon. The conference, organized by the Defense Intelligence Agency, dealt with the "Privatization of National Security Functions in sub-Saharan Africa," though it was clear that sub-Saharan Africa was not the only area of the world where the use of mercenaries was being contemplated by the Pentagon war planners.[87]

The Panguna copper mine on Bougainville was of strategic importance to the United States, and, as with Africa and Indonesia,

[86] Colombia Project, The Center for International Policy, "Military Professional Resources, Inc. in Colombia," December 19, 2001. <http://ciponline.org/colombia/mpri.htm>

[87] Wayne Madsen, *Genocide and Covert Operations in Africa 1993-99*, op. cit. pp. 243-244.

the interests of the Pentagon, mining companies, and mercenary firms coincided. To make matters worse, a U.S. small arms company, Century Arms, was caught in 1998 trying to sell weapons to the nearby civil war-plagued Solomon Islands. The State Department contended the weapons were for the use of the Royal Solomon Islands Police, but a Solomon Island government official believed the weapons were going to one of the warring factions in the civil war.[88]

The United States maintains a myriad of law enforcement and military assistance programs that continue to open doors for outsourcing and for private military firms to engage in privatized foreign policy. And it can be counted upon that the Bush administration, beholden to the interests of oil companies and firms seeking to exploit natural resources, will continue to privatize military, international security, and foreign policy activities.

Peter Singer of the Brookings Institution sees PMCs transforming into three types of support groups for the Pentagon: "This overall industry breaks down into three sectors, and some of them on the first sector are called provider firms. These are what a lot of people refer to as PMCs and they are actually tactical operations. These are sort of the equivalents of corporate mercenaries. The second type is military consultants. They teach clients how to become better at military operations and they advise them. And the third type are military support firms, and these are companies like Brown and Root, that essentially handle the logistics for many western military forces, including the United States, as well as Britain and even Australia in some cases, such as East Timor."[89]

* * * *

Donald Rumsfeld's sweeping plan to transform the U.S. military, particularly the Army, was outlined in his Quadrennial Defense Review, delivered to Congress on September 30, 2001, just a few

---

[88] Raymond F. Bonner, "Business in Booming for Small U.S. Arms Dealers, *New York Times,* June 6, 1998, p. 3. <http://www.mtholyoke.edu/acad/intrel/smallarm.htm>

[89] Stan Correy, "After the War: The US and Iraq," Background Briefing, Radio National, February 23, 2003. <http://www.abc.net.au/rn/talks/bbing/default.htm>

weeks after 9-11. In the review, Rumsfeld emphasized the need for the Pentagon to outsource more support positions as part of the transformation of the Department of Defense. That was a green light for more mercenary and private clandestine operations around the world.

On April 10, 2006, President Bush fielded questions from graduate students at the Paul H. Nitze School of Advanced International Studies at Johns Hopkins University in Washington, DC. One young lady's question in particular pointed out the fact that private military contractors are amassing great fortunes and committing unspeakable war crimes without any interference from the U.S. government.

"Q: My question is in regard to private military contractors. Uniform Code of Military Justice does not apply to these contractors in Iraq. I asked your Secretary of Defense a couple months ago what law governs their actions.

Bush: I was going to ask him. Go ahead. [Laughter.] Help. [Laughter.]

Q: I was hoping your answer might be a little more specific. [Laughter.] Mr. Rumsfeld answered that Iraq has its own domestic laws, which he assumed applied to those private military contractors. However, Iraq is clearly not currently capable of enforcing its laws ... much less against ... over our American military contractors. I would submit to you that in this case, this is one case that privatization is not a solution. And, Mr. President, how do you propose to bring private military contractors under a system of law?

Bush: I appreciate that very much. I wasn't kidding ... [Laughter.] I was going to ... I pick up the phone and say, Mr. Secretary, I've got an interesting question. [Laughter.] This is what delegation ... I don't mean to be dodging the question, although it's kind of convenient in this case, but never ... [Laughter.] I really will ... I'm going to call the Secretary and say you brought up a very valid question, and what are we doing about it? That's how I work. I'm ... thanks. [Laughter.]

Although this laissez-faire and jocular attitude by the Bush administration towards unregulated brigands and mercenaries has been good news for the profit margins of the modern privateers, it is extremely bad news for global human rights, the environment, and the achievement of peace and freedom in the world's most violence-prone trouble spots.

—§—

Afterword

In the shadow world of Big Oil, mercenaries, and carve out brass plate companies, the Bush administration has allowed unscrupulous corporate actors to garner power undreamt of by the likes of Henry Ford and John D. Rockefeller. Modern-day firms act with impunity and disregard for international morés and boundaries.

This book could have delved into many more of the dubious relationships inherent in the Bush administration's entanglement with business interests. But the entanglements are seemingly endless and Byzantine. The reader would likely become literally disoriented in a sea of brass plates, offshores, pass-throughs, and sub-contractors.

There is much more on the Carlyle Group and Barrick Gold, on whose boards George H.W. Bush served—the first company did business with the Bin Laden Group, and had Saudi Ambassador to the United States Prince Bandar bin Sultan (affectionately called "Bandar Bush" by the Bush family) and Saudi Defense Minister Prince Sultan, Bandar's father, as major investors, reportedly financing Carlyle through Cayman Islands bank accounts.[1]

There is Scowcroft Associates, headed by George H.W. Bush's National Security Adviser and George W. Bush's Chairman of the President's Foreign Intelligence Advisory Board, Brent Scowcroft. Scowcroft Associates was involved with shady deals from the privatization of South Africa's state-owned telecommunications company to the CentGas deal with the Taliban.

There is JNB International, an oil firm that, along with Enron, used its influence with Bush to get oil and gas contracts in Argentina. And M&W Pump and its partner Bush-El, two Florida firms that used Jeb Bush to intercede with military-ruled Nigeria in 1989 to get lucrative contracts. Unless there are concrete political and economic reforms in the United States, this list will expand until no public authority will have the power to rein in the unregulated profiteers of war, covert activities, and exploitation.

[1] "Enormous Wealth Spilled Into American Coffers," the *Washington Post*, February 11, 2002, p. A17.

But something can be done. Carlyle, which is a hub of the Bush family business empire, is susceptible to the pressures of its major investors—the largest state employees' pension funds in the United States, most notably the California Public Employees Retirement System (CalPers), which owned more than five percent interest in Carlyle. Other state pension and labor funds investing in Carlyle included those in New York, Michigan, Ohio, and Los Angeles County. A disinvestment or other coordinated stockholder action could rein in Carlyle, eliminate the Bush family's and their friends' interests in the firm, and hold it accountable.

* * * *

A personal note about 9-11. On the evening of September 9, 2001, I was sitting in John F. Kennedy airport waiting for my American Eagle shuttle to Dulles International Airport in Washington after returning from a trip to Finland. If the public had been made more aware of the Al Qaeda terrorist threat to hijack aircraft (found in the President's Daily Briefing of August 6, 2001), the activities of two people also waiting for my flight would have resulted in my contacting the authorities immediately.

One bearded individual, who was wearing the traditional cloth-ing of Pakistan or Afghanistan, had clearly arrived on an earlier flight. He appeared quite nervous, and I made a mental note of that. Another individual, who obviously hailed from the same part of the world, but was wearing western clothes with a black Polo-type shirt and a prominent gold chain necklace, came off a later flight and made it a point to sit next to the south Asian-garbed man. Two men, differently attired and arriving on different flights, struck up an immediate conversation as they waited to fly to Dulles Airport. They obviously knew one another.

After my plane took off, it flew above southern Manhattan, and the last sight I saw was the Twin Towers (they were always an amazing sight either from the ground or from the air). The next time I saw them was on television less than two days later, when one of them was already in flames, workers in both towers unaware of the second fuel bomb jetting toward them.

After the attack, I immediately contacted by email the only FBI agent I knew to be trustworthy, an official of the National Infrastructure Protection Center (NIPC). I sent him the full details on the flight and a description of both individuals. He responded that the information was very helpful and that it was relayed to the Joint Terrorism Task Force in New York City. One big questions remains. What if every American citizen had been warned about the possibility of an Al Qaeda hijacking before 9-11? How many other phone calls and e-mails would the FBI have received about the 19 or more hijackers before they carried out their heinous acts?

There was also the unimpeded access to the gate area at Washington's National Airport a little over a week prior to 911. Upon waiting for several minutes for a screener to approach me after I set off the metal detector, I casually proceeded to catch my shuttle flight to JFK unhindered. At the time, I thought it strange that no screeners were present. Subsequent to 911, it was not so strange considering the fact that the hijackers were casually able to board planes with box cutters. It was clear that there was security laxness and an overall stand down in readiness.

* * * *

In retrospect, 9-11, "as advertised" by the Bush administration, was not what it at first seemed. The Al Qaeda terrorists were intimately tied to American allies in Saudi Arabia, Pakistan, and Israel. Those three countries benefited directly from the aftermath of 9-11, and all three were involved in activities that were linked directly to the terrorist attacks on the United States. 9-11 was a panacea for the three countries. No longer did the United States put pressure on Riyadh and Islamabad to curb human rights abuses and nuclear proliferation—they were at the vanguard of America's so-called Global War on Terrorism. Israel had a virtual carte blanche to carry out, to the applause of both Republican and Democratic leaders in the United States, whatever policies it saw fit.

Almost every U.S. military action during the past thirty years has been stamped with the imprimatur of Bush family deceit. George H.W. Bush's machinations with Manuel Noriega and the mullahs of Iran eventually led to an American invasion of Panama and to the arming of both Saddam Hussein and the Iranian mullahs during the bloody Iran-Iraq War. Father Bush's ambivalence about Saddam's threats against Kuwait led to OPERATION DESERT STORM and the stationing of U.S. troops in Saudi Arabia. That event reportedly triggered a Saudi- and Pakistani-backed Taliban-Al Qaeda "emirate" in Afghanistan deciding to carry out devastating terrorist attacks against the United States, including 9-11, in retaliation for the presence of U.S. troops in the Muslim holy land of Arabia.

The Taliban and Al Qaeda forces that largely comprised the Afghan emirate were originally trained and supplied by U.S. intelligence during the Reagan-Bush administration. The 9-11 attacks presented the George W. Bush administration with an opportunity to attack and occupy Iraq. A series of classified memoranda leaked to the British press provide evidence that 9-11 was used by the Bush II administration as a pretext for the Iraq War. In a March 25, 2002 memorandum written by British Foreign Secretary Jack Straw to Prime Minister Blair, the Foreign Secretary stated, "If 11 September had not happened, it is doubtful that the U.S. would now be considering military action against Iraq.... In addition, there has been no credible evidence to link Iraq with OBL (Osama bin Laden) and al-Qaida." Another memorandum, written by British Foreign Office political director Peter Ricketts states, "U.S. scrambling to establish a link between Iraq and al-Qaida is so far unconvincing.... For Iraq, 'regime change' does not stack up. It sounds like a grudge between Bush and Saddam."[2]

Such grudges have led the United States into wars against Noriega and Saddam (twice). Similar grudges led the George W. Bush administration to joust with Kim Jong Il of North Korea, Jean-Bertrand Aristide of Haiti, Fidel Castro of Cuba, the Iranian government, Venezuela's Hugo Chavez, Bolivia's Evo Morales, and Bashar Assad of Syria.

The Bush administration's covert activities have resulted in the overthrow of one democratically elected government in the Caribbean (Haiti), an attempted overthrow in Latin America (Venezuela), interference in Latin American elections (Nicaragua, Bolivia,

---

[2] Thomas Wagner, "Memos Show British Concern Over Iraq Plans," Associated Press, June 18, 2005.

and El Salvador), the placement of leaders in power with dubious links to Bush administration officials (Karzai in Afghanistan and Chalabi in Iraq), thematic "revolutions" planned and nurtured by U.S. think tanks, non-government organizations, and public relations firms (Georgia, Adjaria, Ukraine, Kyrgyzstan, Palestine, Moldova, and Lebanon), attempted coups in Africa (Equatorial Guinea, Congo, and Sao Tome and Principe), fraudulent elections in Africa (Rwanda, Ethiopia, and the Central African Republic), multinational corporate scandals (Enron, Technip-Halliburton), and the list goes on and on.

It is clear that Big Oil and their allies have injected the United States into Middle East politics to a degree that would have made our Founding Fathers shudder. Big Oil's ties to the Saudis enabled that nation to finance corrupt bankers and terrorists to the detriment of the United States. Reports that Saudi policemen may have been involved in the kidnapping, torture, and beheading of Lockheed-Martin contractor Paul Johnson came as no surprise to those who had for years tracked Saudi Arabia's support for terrorists, including suicide bombers, in Israel, Palestine, Afghanistan, Pakistan, and elsewhere.

America's unbridled support for expansionists in Israel resulted in the United States becoming Target Number Two for every Islamist and Arab radical group around the world. The photographs of U.S. torture of Iraqi prisoners in Abu Ghraib prison were mixed in the minds of every Arab and Muslim with the scenes of Israeli tanks bulldozing down the homes of Palestinians. It is past time for the United States to disengage militarily and politically from the Middle East—the Arab nations and Israel alike. The advice of two of America's presidents, both of whom came from military leadership positions is all the more germane today. President George Washington's Farewell Address in 1796 would apply to the Bush administration's relationship with the neo-conservatives and their allied political partners in Israel:

> Against the insidious wiles of foreign influence (I conjure you to believe me, fellow-citizens) the jealousy of a free people ought to be constantly awake, since history and experience prove that foreign influence is one of the most baneful foes of republican government.

But that jealousy, to be useful, must be impartial, else it becomes the instrument of the very influence to be avoided, instead of a defense against it. Excessive partiality for one foreign nation and excessive dislike of another cause those whom they actuate to see danger only on one side, and serve to veil and even second the arts of influence on the other. Real patriots who may resist the intrigues of the favorite are liable to become suspected and odious, while its tools and dupes usurp the applause and confidence of the people to surrender their interests.

As for America's close relationship with the Saudis and other oil rich potentates that support terrorism and organized criminal activity, Washington's words also have great relevance:

> The great rule of conduct for us in regard to foreign nations is, in extending our commercial relations to have with them as little political connection as possible. So far as we have already formed engagements let them be fulfilled with perfect good faith. Here let us stop.

The fundamentalist zealots who adhere to the three Abrahamic tradition religions—Judaism, Christianity, and Islam—and who have, through their narrow lens on history and reality, brought the world to the brink of perpetual war, should heed the words of Founder Thomas Paine in *The Rights of Man*:

> All national institutions of churches, whether Jewish, Christian or Turkish [Muslim], appear to me no other than human inventions, set up to terrify and enslave mankind, and monopolize power and profit. I do not mean by this declaration to condemn those who believe otherwise; they have the same right to their belief as I have to mine. But it is necessary to the happiness of man that he be mentally faithful to himself. Infidelity does not consist in believing, or in disbelieving; it consists in professing to believe what he does not believe. It is impossible to calculate the moral mischief, if I may so express it, that mental lying has produced in society. When a man has so far corrupted and prostituted the chastity of his mind as to subscribe his professional belief to things he does not believe, he has prepared himself for the commission of every other crime. He takes up the profession of a priest for the sake of gain, and in order to qualify

himself for that trade he begins with a perjury. Can we conceive anything more destructive to morality than this?

Paine's description of corrupted "priests," both clerical and lay, could easily apply to the charlatans of all religious stripes and creeds who today fill our broadcast airwaves with their hate-filled messages and phoniness, and exhort their followers to commit unspeakable acts in the name of their "God."

And, of course, President Dwight Eisenhower's warning in his Farewell Address of 1961 should be viewed as a stark warning against the type of influence Big Oil, defense contractors, and syndicates like the Carlyle Group have over U.S. foreign and domestic policy today:

> This conjunction of an immense military establishment and a large arms industry is new in the American experience. The total influence—economic, political, even spiritual—is felt in every city, every Statehouse, every office of the Federal government. We recognize the imperative need for this development. Yet we must not fail to comprehend its grave implications. Our toil, resources and livelihood are all involved; so is the very structure of our society.
>
> In the councils of government, we must guard against the acquisition of unwarranted influence, whether sought or unsought, by the military-industrial complex. The potential for the disastrous rise of misplaced power exists and will persist.
>
> We must never let the weight of this combination endanger our liberties or democratic processes. We should take nothing for granted. Only an alert and knowledgeable citizenry can compel the proper meshing of the huge industrial and military machinery of defense with our peaceful methods and goals, so that security and liberty may prosper together.

* * * *

The underworld of Brass Plates, Black Ops, and Big Oil has irrevocably altered the psyche of the American people and the fabric of the United States. Their machinations and jaded tasks have made the United States a central battleground for terrorism, and it will take decades for America's democracy to recover from the near fatal blow of 9-11 and its aftermath. Meanwhile, our international and domestic calls are "legally" spied upon, visitors from America's long-time allies are subjected to being photographed and finger-printed upon arrival in the United States, there is talk of random searches of people on trains and buses throughout America, walls have been built around America's most cherished monuments in Washington, and the American President is rarely seen without being surrounded by avid supporters—often wearing uniforms—and menacing armed officers. America has been sold to the high-est and most morally corrupt bidders. James Madison's warning is thus all the more germane:

> The strongest passions and most dangerous weaknesses of the hu-man breast; ambition, avarice, vanity, the honorable or venal love of fame, are all in conspiracy against the desire and duty of peace.

The Bush administration and its global domination fellow trav-elers in the United States and abroad continue to consolidate their power over those international and American institutions that have served to protect this nation and others from totalitarian control: the United Nations, our national legislature, our federal, state, and local courts, the U.S. presidency, our state and local governments, our military, our law enforcers, our educational institutions, and our free press. But hearken to the worlds of Thomas Jefferson, in a letter he wrote in 1798 to John Taylor of Philadelphia:

> A little patience, and we shall see the reign of witches pass over, their spells dissolve, and the people, recovering their true sight, restore their government to its true <u>principles</u>. It is true that in the mean time we are suffering deeply in spirit, and incurring the horrors of a war & long oppressions of enormous public debt.... If the game runs sometimes against us at home we must have patience till luck turns, and then we shall have an opportunity of winning back the prin-ciples we have lost, for this is a game where principles are the stake. Better luck, therefore, to us all; and health, happiness, and friendly salutations to yourself. (underline in original)

—§—

About the Author

Wayne Madsen is a Washington, DC-based investigative journalist and syndicated columnist. His articles and columns have appeared in the *Atlanta Journal Constitution*, the *Miami Herald*, the *Philadelphia Inquirer*, the *Village Voice*, *The Progressive*, *In These Times*, and *Counterpunch*. Madsen is the author of *Genocide and Covert Operations in Africa 1993-1999* (Mellen Press) and *The Handbook of Personal Data Protection* (Macmillan & Stockton Press). Wayne has frequently appeared as a national security analyst on the Fox News Channel. He has also appeared on *60 Minutes*, the PBS *News Hour*, *Nightline*, and *20/20*. In 2003, he spoke at a seminar at Manhattan's famed Riverside Church commemorating the second anniversary of 9-11. He wrote the Foreword for the best-selling book, *Forbidden Truth* (Nation Books, 2002).

A former U.S. Naval officer who worked for the National Security Agency, Madsen has written a screenplay treatment about the ill-fated nuclear submarine, the USS *Scorpion*, which sank in the Atlantic in 1968 after an encounter with a Soviet submarine.

He is a member of the National Press Club, National Writers' Union, American Legion, and was a volunteer in John McCain's 2000 presidential campaign.

Madsen is co-author with John Stanton of *America's Nightmare: The Presidency of George Bush II* (Dandelion Books, 2003).

Index

Symbols

60 Minutes 64, 73, 88
9-11 47, 49, 59, 63, 64, 71, 72, 74,
  101--105, 111, 112, 115–117,
  121–124, 129, 133, 135, 139,
  142, 144, 148-151, 158, 160,
  162, 167, 174, 175, 217, 222,
  227, 236, 246-248, 255, 256,
  260, 281, 284-286, 290

A

Abadi, Haider 55
Abady, Samuel 11
Abashidze, Aslan 89, 225, 226
Abbas, Mahmoud 231
ABC 44, 128, 133-135, 171, 198
ABC World News Tonight 171
Abdelnour, Ziad K. 8
Abraham, Spencer 213
Abraham, Yehuda 140, 141, 147–166,
  170, 173, 178, 179, 213, 217
Abrahamson, James 101
Abramoff, Jack ix, 56, 218
Abramovich, Roman 144, 168
Abrams, Elliot 52, 119, 192, 194,
  199, 200, 230
Abu Ghraib xx, 244, 245, 287
Access Industries, Inc. 104
Adjaria 66, 89, 224, 226, 228, 287
Adleman, Ken 231
Aegis Defense Services 253
Aerocom 176, 177
Aero Contractors Ltd. 254
AeroLink Transportation 104
AES-Telasi 87, 88
Afek, Arik 170
Afghanistan xx, xxii, xxiii, 51,
  56, 79, 89, 100, 105, 108,
  111–115, 121–131, 140, 145,
148, 149, 174, 221, 229, 257,
265, 267, 284, 286, 287
Africa Analysis 216
African National Congress (ANC)
  274
Afridi, Muhammad Abid 163
Ahmed, General 122, 123
Ahmed, Qazi Hussein- 127
Ahtisaari, Martti 54
Air America 242, 255
Air Bas 176
Airbus 176, 177
AirScan 24, 240, 275
AJKMC Lithography Aid Society 177
Akayev, Askar 229
Albanian National Liberation Army
  (NLA) 266, 267
Al Barakaat 43
al Bayoumi, Omar 102
Albright, Madeleine 1–5, 26, 29, 141
al Faisal, Turki 102, 115
al Hazmi, Nawaf 101, 102, 158
al Hazmi, Salem 101, 102
Alibek, Ken xxiv
Al Jazeera ix, 44, 55
al Khersan, Hashim 206
Allbaugh, Joesph 241
Allende, Salvador 1, 196, 212
All the Presidents' Men 24
Al Mada (newspaper) 60
al Maktoum, Shaikh Mohammed bin
  Rashid 112, 113
al Mihdar, Khalid 101, 158
Al Qaeda xxii, 8, 9, 22, 23, 44,
  47, 48, 51, 63, 65, 88, 90,
  99, 112–115, 119, 120, 123,
  124, 128, 139–141, 144–151,
  156–161, 164, 167, 169, 174-
  179, 182, 226, 248, 254, 261,
  265–267, 272, 273, 284–286
al Saud, Sultan bin Abdulaziz 116
al Sharqi, Hamad bin Mohammed 119
al Shehhi, Marwan 113
Ambuy Gem Corp. 152

PUBLISHER'S AFTERWORD

When in the course of human events in America that books are difficult to get published, even stopped, what then becomes necessary? We *do* live in *interesting* times. While some people, hemmed in by their financial and social responsibilities, are seemingly too timid to venture outside the accepted presented discourse. Others have been arrested for simply wearing a T-shirt expressing a controversial political opinion.

The U.S. Constitution's first amendment and two hundred plus years have appeared to produce for us a monopolized corporate press acting as handmaiden to the emerging fascist enterprise. There is "official" history and then there is what really happened. *Jaded Tasks* goes beyond the initial veneer of the news reports into the shadowy netherworld where the rubber hits the road. A world where secrecy is used to hide true history amidst a gaggle of "cover" stories.

To understand this spook sphere, the Internet turns to waynemadsenreport.com, both wondering citizens and mainstream journalists routinely drink up the knowledge Madsen gleans daily from his contacts—high and low, asked and unasked—that then flows from his keyboard. The tens of thousands of daily visits to Madsen's Web site show a population hungrily devouring information, and wanting discussion about vital issues of the day. The fact that it has been left to a small press to help Wayne discuss these concerns is another sign of the times.

TrineDay and other small publishers are a sociological response to a section of our Republic neglecting its job, leaving us with a passel of scoundrels using stealth, secrecy and subterfuges to stupefy us citizens into a new feudal, fascistic world. Wastrels purposefully destroying my country, using America's wallet and blood to bully the world into shape and then … what? … hand it off to themselves in China?

Peace,
Kris Millegan
May 1, 2006

Fixing America
Breaking the Stranglehold of Corporate Rule, Big Media, and the Religious Right
BY JOHN BUCHANAN, FOREWORD BY JOHN MCCONNELL

An explosive analysis of what ails the United States

An award-winning investigative reporter provides a clear, honest diagnosis of corporate rule, big media, and the religious right in this damning analysis. Exposing the darker side of capitalism, this critique raises alarms about the security of democracy in today's society, including the rise of the corporate state, the insidious role of professional lobbyists, the emergence of religion and theocracy as a right-wing political tactic, the failure of the mass media, and the sinister presence of an Orwellian neo-fascism.
Softcover: **$19.95**, (ISBN 0-975290681) 216 Pages, 5.5 x 8.5

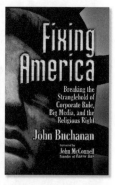

Ambushed
Secrets of the Bush Family, the Stolen Presidency, 9-11, and 2004
BY TOBY ROGERS

A searing examination of the lies and intrigue that brought the Bush family to power

Based on more than a decade of research, this exposé presents troubling information about America's first family and its second member to become president, George W. Bush. Revealed are the Bush administration's deceptions about the September 11 terrorist attacks and the resulting cover-up, the role of long-time Bush family friend Charles W. Kane in tampering with contentious Florida ballots, and the details behind Prescott Bush's stint as the managing director of a Nazi bank. The Bush family's ongoing association with the mysterious Skull and Bones society is also explored. This alternative history sheds light on the darker side of the powerful Bush family that has been ignored by the mainstream media.
Softcover: **$14.95** (ISBN: 0972020772) • 150 pages • Size: 6 x 9

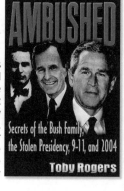

Welcome To Terrorland
Mohammed Atta & the 9-11 Cover-up in Florida
BY DANIEL HOPSICKER

Drug-trafficking, an FBI cover-up, silenced witnesses, and other reasons why the true story has never been told.

This in-depth investigation into the associations of Mohamed Atta and other terrorist pilots in Venice, Florida, as they prepared for the 9/11 attacks discloses that the FBI led a massive postattack cover-up designed to conceal their knowledge of the terrorists' activities. Unreported stories about the rampant drug-trafficking of the financier behind the flight school the terrorist pilots attended are fully discussed, with attention to the stunning evidence that the CIA was aware that hundreds of Arab flight students were pouring into southwest Florida. This examination of the conspiracy behind the 9/11 investigation and the CIA complicity in the illegal activities that allowed the known terrorists' activities to continue offers truth behind the "official" story of the attacks.
Hardcover: **$29.95** (ISBN 0970659164), • 408 pages • Size: 6 x 9

a MadCow Press book

Dr. Mary's Monkey

How the Unsolved Murder of a Doctor, a Secret Laboratory in New Orleans and Cancer-Causing Monkey Viruses are Linked to Lee Harvey Oswald, the JFK Assassination and Emerging Global Epidemics

EDWARD T. HASLAM (AUTHOR), JIM MARRS (FOREWORD BY)

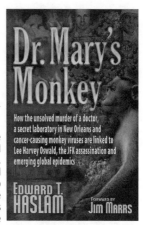

Evidence of top-secret medical experiments and coverups of clinical blunders

The 1964 murder of a nationally known cancer researcher sets the stage for this gripping exposé of medical professionals enmeshed in covert government operations over the course of three decades. Following a trail of police records, FBI files, cancer statistics, and medical journals, this revealing book presents evidence of a web of medical secret-keeping that began with the handling of evidence in the JFK assassination and continued apace, sweeping doctors into coverups of cancer outbreaks, contaminated polio vaccine, the arrival of the AIDS virus, and biological weapon research using infected monkeys.

Softcover: **$19.95** (ISBN: 0977795306) • 320 pages • Size: 5 1/2 x 8 1/2

Expendable Elite

One Soldier's Journey into Covert Warfare

BY DANIEL MARVIN , FOREWORD BY MARTHA RAYE

A special operations perspective on the Vietnam War and the truth about a White House concerned with popular opinion

This true story of a special forces officer in Vietnam in the mid-1960s exposes the unique nature of the elite fighting force and how covert operations are developed and often masked to permit—and even sponsor—assassination, outright purposeful killing of innocents, illegal use of force, and bizarre methods in combat operations. *Expendable Elite* reveals the fear that these warriors share with no other military person: not fear of the enemy they have been trained to fight in battle, but fear of the wrath of the U.S. government should they find themselves classified as "expendable." This book centers on the CIA mission to assassinate Cambodian Crown Prince Nordum Sihanouk, the author's unilateral aborting of the mission, the CIA's dispatch of an ARVN regiment to attack and destroy the camp and kill every person in it as retribution for defying the agency, and the dramatic rescue of eight American Green Berets and hundreds of South Vietnamese.

DANIEL MARVIN is a retired lieutenant colonel in the U.S. Army Special Forces and former Green Beret.

Softcover: **$19.95** (ISBN 0977795314) • 420 pages • 150+ photos & maps • 6 x 9

Without Smoking Gun

Was the Death of Lt. Cmdr. William Pitzer part of the JFK Assassination Conspiracy?

BY KENT HIENER, FOREWORD BY DANIEL MARVIN

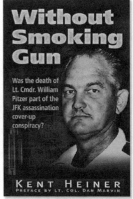

This shocking account of intrigue, lies, and governmental complicity provides inexplicable evidence that suggests a larger conspiracy behind JFK's assassination. Three years after Kennedy's assassination, Lieutenant William Bruce Pitzer, who was reputed to have film that refuted the conclusions of JFK's official autopsy, was found dead in his office at the National Naval Medical Center in Bethesda, Maryland. In 1995, a retired special forces captain claimed that a representative of the CIA recruited him to assassinate Pitzer. Revelations of a possible conspiracy within a conspiracy raise larger questions of the measures taken to suppress the truth and the potential dangers of a government that operates outside the law.

Softcover **$14.95** (ISBN 0972020799) • 156 PAGES • Size: 6 x 9

America's Secret Establishment
An Introduction to the Order of Skull & Bones
BY *ANTONY C. SUTTON*

The book that first exposed the story behind
America's most powerful secret society

For 170 years they have met in secret. From out of their initiates come presidents, senators, judges, cabinet secretaries, and plenty of spooks. They are the titans of finance and industry and have now installed a third member as United States President George W. Bush. This intriguing behind-the-scenes look documents Yale's secretive society, the Order of the Skull and Bones, and its prominent members, numbering among them Tafts, Rockefellers, Pillsburys, and Bushes. Far from being a campus fraternity, the society is more concerned with the success of its members in the post-collegiate world. Included are a verified membership list, rare reprints of original Order materials revealing the interlocking power centers dominated by Bonesmen, and a peek inside the Tomb, their 140-year-old private clubhouse.

ANTONY C. SUTTON was a research fellow at the Hoover Institution at Stanford University and an economics professor at California State University, Los Angeles and is author of 21 books, including *Wall Street and the Rise of Hitler.*

Hardcover: **$24.95** (ISBN 0972020701), Softcover: **$19.95** (ISBN 0972020748) 335 pages • Size: 5 x 8

Fleshing Out Skull & Bones
Investigations into America's Most Powerful Secret Society
EDITED BY KRIS MILLEGAN

An expose of Yale's supersecretive and elite Order of Skull & Bones

This chronicle of espionage, drug smuggling, and elitism in Yale University's Skull & Bones society offers rare glimpses into this secret world with previously unpublished documents, photographs, and articles that delve into issues such as racism, financial ties to the Nazi party, and illegal corporate dealings. Contributors include Antony Sutton, author of *America's Secret Establishment*; Dr. Ralph Bunch, professor emeritus of political science at Portland State University; Webster Griffin Tarpley and Anton Chaitkin, authors and historians; and Howard Altman, editor of the *Philadelphia City Paper.* A complete list of known members, including George Bush and George W. Bush, and reprints of rare magazine articles on the Order of Skull and Bones are included.

Hardcover: **$32.95** (ISBN 0972020721), Softcover: **$24.95** (ISBN 0975290606) 720 pages • Size: 6x9

The Octopus Conspiracy
and Other Vignettes of the Counterculture
from Hippies to High Times to Hip Hop and Beyond ...
BY *STEVEN HAGER*

Insightful essays on the genesis of subcultures from new wave and yuppies to graffiti and rap.

From the birth of hip-hop culture in the South Bronx to the influence of nightclubs in shaping the modern art world in New York, a generation of countercultural events and icons are brought to life in this personal account of the life and experiences of a former investigative reporter and editor of High Times. Evidence from cutting-edge conspiracy research including the real story behind the JFK assassination and the Franklin Savings and Loan cover-up is presented. Quirky personalities and compelling snapshots of life in the 1980s and 1990s emerge in this collection of vignettes from a landmark figure in journalism.

STEVEN HAGER is the author of *Adventures in Counterculture, Art After Midnight,* and *Hip Hop.* He is a former reporter for the New York Daily News and an editor of *High Times.*

Hardcover: **$19.95** (ISBN 0975290614) • 320 pages • Size: 6 x 9

Sinister Forces

A Grimoire of American Political Witchcraft
Book One: The Nine
BY PETER LEVENDA, FOREWORD BY JIM HOUGAN

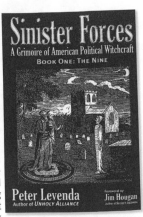

A shocking alternative to the conventional views of American history.

The roots of coincidence and conspiracy in American politics, crime, and culture are examined in this book, exposing new connections between religion, political conspiracy, and occultism. Readers are taken from ancient American civilization and the mysterious mound builder culture to the Salem witch trials, the birth of Mormonism during a ritual of ceremonial magic by Joseph Smith, Jr., and Operations Paperclip and Bluebird. Not a work of speculative history, this exposé is founded on primary source material and historical documents. Fascinating details are revealed, including the bizarre world of "wandering bishops" who appear throughout the Kennedy assassinations; a CIA mind control program run amok in the United States and Canada; a famous American spiritual leader who had ties to Lee Harvey Oswald in the weeks and months leading up to the assassination of President Kennedy; and the "Manson secret."

Hardcover: **$29.95** (ISBN 0975290622) • 396 pages • Size: 6 x 9

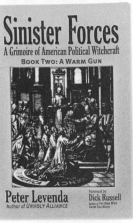

Book Two: A Warm Gun

The roots of coincidence and conspiracy in American politics, crime, and culture are investigated in this analysis that exposes new connections between religion, political conspiracy, terrorism, and occultism. Readers are provided with strange parallels between supernatural forces such as shaminism, ritual magic, and cult practices, and contemporary interrogation techniques such as those used by the CIA under the general rubric of MK-ULTRA. Not a work of speculative history, this exposé is founded on primary source material and historical documents. Fascinating details on Nixon and the "Dark Tower," the Assassin cult and more recent Islamic terrorism, and the bizarre themes that run through American history from its discovery by Columbus to the political assassinations of the 1960s are revealed.

Hardcover: **$29.95** (ISBN 0975290630) • 392 pages • Size: 6 x 9

Book Three: The Manson Secret

The Stanislavski Method as mind control and initiation. Filmmaker Kenneth Anger and Aleister Crowley, Marianne Faithfull, Anita Pallenberg, and the Rolling Stones. Filmmaker Donald Cammell (Performance) and his father, CJ Cammell (the first biographer of Aleister Crowley), and his suicide. Jane Fonda and Bluebird. The assassination of Marilyn Monroe. Fidel Castro's Hollywood career. Jim Morrison and witchcraft. David Lynch and spiritual transformation. The technology of sociopaths. How to create an assassin. The CIA, MK-ULTRA and programmed killers.

Hardcover: **$29.95** (ISBN 0975290649) • 422 pages • Size: 6 x 9